"At a time when the need for independent journalism and for media outlets unaffiliated with and untainted by the government and corporate sponsors is greater than ever, Project Censored has created a context for reporting the complete·truths in all matters that matter. . . . It is therefore left to us to find sources for information we can trust. . . . It is in this task that we are fortunate to have an ally like Project Censored."—Dahr Jamail

"Activist groups like Project Censored . . . are helping to build the media democracy movement. We have to challenge the powers that be and rebuild media from the bottom up."—Amy Goodman

"Project Censored is one of the organizations that we should listen to, to be assured that our newspapers and our broadcasting outlets are practicing thorough and ethical journalism."—Walter Cronkite

"[Censored] should be affixed to the bulletin boards in every newsroom in America. And, perhaps read aloud to a few publishers and television executives."—Ralph Nader

"[Censored] offers devastating evidence of the dumbing-down of mainstream news in America. . . . Required reading for broadcasters, journalists, and well-informed citizens."—Los Angeles Times

"One of the most significant media research projects in the country."—I. F. Stone

"A terrific resource, especially for its directory of alternative media and organizations. . . . Recommended for media collections." —Library Journal

"[Project Censored's] efforts to continue globalizing their reporting network could not be more timely or necessary."—Kristina Borjesson

"A distant early warning system for society's problems."—American Journalism Review

D0205201

CENSORED 2013
DISPATCHES FROM THE MEDIA REVOLUTION

The Top Censored Stories and Media Analysis of 2011–12

Mickey Huff and Andy Lee Roth
with Project Censored

Foreword by
Dr. Nafeez Mosaddeq Ahmed
Cartoons by
Khalil Bendib

Seven Stories Press
New York

Seven Stories Press
140 Watts Street
New York, NY 10013
www.sevenstories.com

ISBN 978-1-60980-422-0 (paperback)
ISBN 978-1-60980-423-7 (electronic)

ISSN 1074-5998

9 8 7 6 5 4 3 2

Book design by Jon Gilbert

Printed in the USA

Contents

SECTION II: TRUTH EMERGENCY: DECONSTRUCTING NARRATIVES OF POWER TO RECLAIM THE COMMON GOOD

SECTION III: PROJECT CENSORED INTERNATIONAL: CASE STUDIES OF "UNHISTORY" IN THE MAKING

PHOTO BY ALAN LIGHT

To Ray Bradbury (1920–2012),
champion of the freedom to think, feel, and express;
and of the responsibility to remember

Foreword

by Dr. Nafeez Mosaddeq Ahmed

At a time when the world faces tipping points in the escalation of multiple crises, the publication of this volume is of momentous significance.

As I write, a sampling of the latest "mainstream" corporate news illustrates the unprecedented nature of our current predicament as a civilization. The bizarre and extreme weather of the early United States summer prompted one leading climate scientist to state boldly that we are "certainly seeing climate change in action,"[1] as a window on a worsening future. Record-shattering heat waves, wildfires, and freak storms are a taste of things to come—"This is just the beginning," said one meteorologist.[2]

Simultaneously, the International Monetary Fund cut its growth forecast for the US economy, warning that the ongoing eurozone crisis, along with the weak housing market, risks triggering a recession by 2013 while the jobless rate morphs into "higher structural unemployment."[3]

As the defunct neoliberal model of casino capitalism wreaks havoc at home, it is doing the same abroad. Global food prices doubled between 2006 and 2008, and despite some fluctuation, remain largely at record levels. One of the key causes has been speculation in derivatives—thirteen trillion dollars was invested in food commodities in 2006, then pulled out in 2008, and then reinvested again by 2011. The rocketing food prices for the global poor have generated an unprecedented global food crisis across the developing world.[4]

But another driver of the food crisis is climate change, which has already led to crop failures in key food basket regions. This is only going to get worse on a business-as-usual model, which could lead to a minimum 4 degrees Celsius rise by mid-century. Even a 2-degree rise would lead to dramatic crop failures and soaring meat prices; at 4 degrees Celsius, rice crops could be reduced by about 30 percent, leading to global food shortages and hunger.[5]

Amid this escalating frenzy of perfect storms, however, over the last year the corporate media has focused on one apparent light at the end of the tunnel: unconventional oil and gas. "Has Oil Peaked?" read one headline in the *Wall Street Journal*.[6] Across the pond, BBC News asked, "Shortages: Is 'Peak Oil' Idea Dead?"[7] Environmentalists have also jumped on the bandwagon. Andrew C. Revkin in the *New York Times* took "A Fresh Look at Oil's Long Goodbye,"[8] while George Monbiot wrote in the *Guardian* that "We Were Wrong On Peak Oil. There's Enough to Fry Us All."[9]

The essence of this uniform message is that new drilling methods—like hydraulic fracturing, i.e. "fracking," among others—have allowed the fossil fuel industry to exploit previously untapped reserves of tar sands, oil shale, and shale gas, bringing them to market at much cheaper prices than hitherto imaginable, and effectively turning the US from net oil importer into a leading exporter.

But it should come as no great surprise to Project Censored readers that, once again, the corporate news media has obfuscated the facts. The latest figures from the US Energy Information Administration (EIA) confirm that the supposedly massive boost in unconventional oil production that is pitched to launch the world into a glorious future of petroleum abundance—capable of sustaining the wonders of capitalist economic growth *ad infinitum*—has had negligible impact on world oil production. On the contrary, despite the US producing a "total oil supply" of ten million barrels per day—up by 2.1 million since January 2005[10]—world crude oil production remains on the largely flat, undulating plateau it has been on since it stopped rising around that very year. As reported by oil markets journalist Gregor Macdonald, who has previously reported for the *Financial Times* and *Harvard Business Review*, among other publications:

> Since 2005, despite a phase transition in prices, global oil production has been trapped below a ceiling of 74 mbpd (million barrels per day). New production from new fields and new discoveries comes on line, but, it has not been at a

rate fast enough to overcome declines from existing fields. Overall, global decline has been estimated at a minimum of 4% per year and as high as 6+% a year. Given that new oil resources are developed and flow at much slower rates, the existing declines present a formidable challenge to the task of increasing supply. I see no set of factors, in combination, that would take global production of crude oil higher in 2012, or next year, or thereafter.[11]

Yet this stark fact has not been reported in any mass media news outlet whatsoever, anywhere in the world. Indeed, Macdonald points out that data from British Petroleum's *Statistical Review of World Energy* shows that oil's heyday is well and truly in decline. In 1973, oil as a percentage of global energy use had peaked at around 48.5 percent. Forty years later, "oil is barely hanging on as the world's primary energy source, with a much reduced role as a supplier of only 33.5% of all world energy consumption."[12]

The disparity in reporting is instructive. In June 2012, the corporate media focus on the unconventional oil boom revolved around one study in particular by oil company executive Leonardo Maugeri—former executive vice president of Italian oil major Eni. The report was not peer-reviewed but was published at Harvard University's Belfer Center for Science and International Affairs by the Geopolitics of Energy Project, "which is supported in part by a general grant from the [same] oil major [i.e. Eni]," conceded the *WSJ*.[13] Hardly an impartial perspective, then.

Meanwhile, a series of peer-reviewed reports by independent scientists published in highly reputable science journals from January through to June 2012—*Science, Nature,* and *Energy*—have been blacked out in corporate news reporting.[14] In *Energy,* Gail E. Tverberg documented that since 2005, "world oil supply has not increased," that this was "a primary cause of the 2008–2009 recession," and that the "expected impact of reduced oil supply" will mean the "financial crisis may eventually worsen." An even more damning analysis was published in *Nature* by James Murray and Sir David King, the latter being the British government's former chief scientific adviser. Murray and King's analysis found that despite reported increases in oil reserves, tar sands production, and hydrofracturing-generated natural gas, depletion of the world's existing fields is still running at 4.5 percent to 6.7 percent per year, and production at shale gas wells could drop by as much as 60 to 90 percent in the first year of operation. Curiously forgotten in the spate of reporting on the opportunities opened up by fracking is a *New York Times* investigation from 2011, which found that "the gas may not be as easy and cheap to extract from shale formations deep underground as the companies are saying, according to hundreds of industry e-mails and internal documents and an analysis of data from thousands of wells." The e-mails revealed industry executives, lawyers, state geologists, and market analysts voicing "skepticism about lofty forecasts" and questioning "whether companies are intentionally, and even illegally, overstating the productivity of their wells and the size of their reserves."[15] A year later, it seems, such revelations were merely destined for the memory hole.

In fact, we now find that the corporate media has trumpeted the declarations of none other than ExxonMobil chief executive officer Rex Tillerson, who in a Council on Foreign Relations speech in late June lauded the future of North American oil production, underpinned by unconventional oil and shale gas production. Tillerson also dismissed climate models predicting devastating impacts for much of the world's population due to rising sea levels and the collapse of agriculture. "We have spent our entire existence adapting. . . . We'll adapt," he prophesized. "It's an engineering problem, and it has engineering solutions." He then blamed an "illiterate public" for the popularity of environmental advocacy groups criticizing the dangers of fracking, before moving on to emphasize that US self-reliance in energy production would not change our foreign policy in the Middle East one iota:

> Now it becomes a question of what's our national security interest in the region, because you have an enormous—as all of you know, enormous national defense footprint in the Middle East because of our interest in the area. . . . It's more a question of the importance of that region to global economic stability. And we're going to still be interested in that.

So if you have a supply—if we're no longer getting any oil from the Middle East because we're secure here, a disruption of oil supplies from that region will have devastating impacts on global economies. Now is that important to us? Probably so.[16]

Tillerson's speech provides a window into the latest strain of elite ideology on how to approach the convergence of crises we are currently facing. It seems fairly simple:

1. Concede some climate change might be happening, but reject repeated scientific warnings that a business-as-usual trajectory will lead to global catastrophe.
2. Insist that technology will save us, while pointing to environmentally devastating methods such as fracking as the solution to our energy woes through obfuscation of data.
3. Reaffirm the rightness of militarization to ensure not just security of energy supplies, but even more importantly, the regional stability necessary to sustain stable global oil prices, and thus, to prevent a massive disruption to "global economic stability"— a euphemism for continued global capital accumulation for the 1 percent at the expense of the 99.

And just what mechanisms has the US been using to ensure its dominance over the Middle East? Terrorism. In Libya, and now in Syria, credible reports confirm that the US, working with its Persian Gulf client regimes like Saudi Arabia, has consciously supported dubious rebel movements with links to al-Qaeda.[17] Such covert operations have neutralized the effect of very real, peaceful, grassroots civil society movements in these countries, with a view to prevent them from metamorphosing into viable national democratic structures that might ultimately undermine US influence.

At first glance, the escalation of these machinations appears overwhelming. But while things are no doubt getting worse, people's movements for progressive social change are getting louder. Popular grassroots movements both east and west—the Arab Spring, Occupy movement—have taken both governments and corporations by complete surprise. And these movements have emerged because Tillerson's "illiterate public" is increasingly unwilling to tolerate lies and propaganda.

The majority of people now hold views about Western governments and the nature of power that would have made them social pariahs ten or twenty years ago. The majority are now skeptical of the Iraq War;[18] the majority want an end to US military involvement in Afghanistan;[19] the majority resent the banks and financial sector, and blame them for the financial crisis;[20] most people are now aware of environmental issues, more than ever before, and despite denialist confusion promulgated by fossil fuel industries, the majority in the US[21] and Britain are deeply concerned about global warming;[22] most people are wary of conventional party politics[23] and disillusioned with the mainstream parliamentary system,[24] due to the continuation of scandal after scandal.

In other words, on a whole range of issues, there has been a massive popular shift in public opinion toward a progressive critique of the current political economic system. It is, of course, largely subliminal, not carefully worked out, and lacks a coherent vision for what needs to be done—but there can be little doubt that this shift has happened, and is deepening. People are increasingly disenchanted, and they are hungry for alternatives.

And it is within this space that the pivotal role of Project Censored comes into play, for the backbone of this transnational industrial juggernaut is the state of "false consciousness" sustained by corporate mass media propaganda.

Project Censored works to uncover and showcase news stories, in the public interest, that have been ignored, misreported, or simply censored by the so-called "mainstream," but more accurately, the corporate media. Each year, its landmark *Censored* publication reviews the Top 25 Censored Stories of the year, and each year the pattern is the same. Stories that challenge, expose, or undermine transnational corporate power are routinely and often systematically suppressed in "mainstream" reporting. By collating and publicizing these stories, Project Censored has been at the front line of resistance against the system for the last few decades.

This volume is no exception. It goes an extra mile by not simply highlighting these suppressed news stories of recent years, but by subjecting them to rigorous political, sociological, historical, and economic analysis in a range of incisive essays that will empower the reader with a deep insight into how the system works, and what can be done. The essays reveal little-known facts about the absurdly unequal structures of resource ownership in the global economy; the continuation of a massive humanitarian crisis in "free" Iraq; lies and propaganda to justify ongoing illegal military actions; the escalation of domestic social control powers to monitor US citizens and curtail dissidence; and especially, ways forward for the Occupy movement.

Censored 2013 is, thus, a rare read of paramount importance, providing a snapshot of the critical transition period in which we find ourselves. It is an essential handbook for activists, students, and scholars, a rallying cry with which we may step further into the New American Century. But most of all, Censored 2013 is a powerful tool, with which to shatter the illusions that comprise the hegemony of the 1 percent. So read this book, and use it to educate your friends, family, and communities, because change, one way or another, is coming.

London
July 4, 2012

DR. NAFEEZ MOSADDEQ AHMED is a best-selling writer and international security analyst. He is Executive Director at the Institute for Policy Research & Development (IPRD) in London. Ahmed has written features, commentary, and analysis for various publications including the *Independent on Sunday*, the *Scotsman*, *Sydney Morning Herald*, the *Age*, *Le Monde diplomatique*, *Foreign Policy*, the *New Statesman*, *Prospect*, the *Gulf Times*, *Daily News Egypt*, *Daily Star* (Beirut), *Pakistan Observer*, *Tehran Times*, *Bangkok Post*, *Prague Post*, the *Georgian Times*, *Open Democracy*, *Raw Story*, and *New Internationalist*, as well as several policy periodicals. Ahmed is coproducer and writer of the critically acclaimed documentary feature film, *The Crisis of Civilization* (2011), adapted by director and producer Dean Puckett from Ahmed's 2010 book, *A User's Guide to the Crisis of Civilization: And How to Save It*. Among other books he has authored, the 2002 book *The War on Freedom: How & Why America was Attacked, September 11, 2001* is archived in the "9/11 Commission" Collection at the US National Archives in Washington, DC; it was among ninety-nine books made available to each 9/11 commissioner of the National Commission on Terrorist Attacks Upon the United States to use during their investigations. Ahmed has taught at the University of Sussex's School of Global Studies and Brunel University's Politics and History Department. He is also a regular media commentator and has appeared frequently, in the US, on C-SPAN, CNN, Fox News, Bloomberg, PBS, National Public Radio, and Progressive Radio Network, and internationally on BBC News, Al Jazeera English, Press TV (Iran), Islam Channel, and more.

Notes

1. Suzanne Goldenberg, "Scientists Say Ongoing Weather Extremes Offer Proof of Climate Change," *Guardian*, July 3, 2012, http://www.guardian.co.uk/environment/2012/jul/03/us-extreme-summer-future-climate-change?newsfeed=true.
2. Ibid.
3. Ian Talley, "IMF Cuts U.S. Growth Outlook, Warns of Potential Recession," *Wall Street Journal*, July 3, 2012, http://online.wsj.com/article/BT-CO-20120703-712016.html.
4. James Goodman, "As Long as the Rich can Speculate on Food, the World's Poor Go Hungry," *Age*, July 1, 2012, http://www.theage.com.au/opinion/politics/as-long-as-the-rich-can-speculate-on-food-the-worlds-poor-go-hungry-20120630-219ja.html.
5. "What's Cooking? The UK's Potential Food Crisis," *Phys.Org*, July 3, 2012, http://phys.org/news/2012-07-cooking-uk-potential-food-crisis.html.
6. Liam Denning, "Has Peak Oil Peaked?," *Wall Street Journal*, June 26, 2012, http://online.wsj.com/article/SB10001424052702304458604577490823345598042.html.
7. Roger Harrabin, "Shortages: Is 'Peak Oil' Idea Dead?," BBC News, June 19, 2012, http://www.bbc.co.uk/news/science-environment-18353962.
8. Andrew C. Revkin, "A Fresh Look at Oil's Long Goodbye," Dot Earth, *New York Times*, June 25, 2012, http://dotearth.blogs.nytimes.com/2012/06/25/a-fresh-look-at-oils-new-boom-time.
9. George Monbiot, "We Were Wrong on Peak Oil. There's Enough to Fry Us All," *Guardian*, July 2, 2012, http://www.guardian.co.uk/commentisfree/2012/jul/02/peak-oil-we-we-wrong.
10. James Hamilton, "Natural Gas Liquids," *Econbrowser* (blog), July 1, 2012, http://www.econbrowser.com/archives/2012/07/natural_gas_liq.html
11. Gregor Macdonald, "Global Oil Production Update: EIA Revises Two Decades of Oil Data," *Gregor.Us* (blog), April 1, 2012, http://gregor.us/oil/global-oil-production-update-eia-revises-two-decades-of-oil-data. Emphasis in quote.
12. Macdonald, "Oil's Bright, Momentary Flash," *Gregor.Us* (blog), April 30, 2012, http://gregor.us/coal/oils-bright-momentary-flash.
13. Denning, "Has Peak Oil Peaked?"
14. Gail E. Tverberg, "Oil Supply Limits and the Continuing Financial Crisis," *Energy* 37, no. 1 (January 2012): 27–34, http://www.sciencedirect.com/science/article/pii/S0360544211003744; James Murray and David King, "Climate Policy: Oil's Tipping Point Has Passed," *Nature* 481 (January 26, 2012): 433–35, http://www.nature.com/nature/journal/v481/n7382/full/481433a.html; and Richard A. Kerr, "Technology Is Turning U.S. Oil Around But Not the World's," *Science* 335, no. 6068 (February 3, 2012): 522–23, http://www.sciencemag.org/content/335/6068/522.summary.
15. Ian Urbina, "Insiders Sound an Alarm Amid a Natural Gas Rush," *New York Times*, June 25, 2011, http://www.nytimes.com/2011/06/26/us/26gas.html?_r=1&pagewanted=all.
16. Rex W. Tillerson, "The New North American Energy Paradigm: Reshaping the Future," Council on Foreign Relations, June 27, 2012, http://www.cfr.org/united-states/new-north-american-energy-paradigm-reshaping-future/p28630.
17. Peter Dale Scott, "Who Are the Libyan Freedom Fighters and Their Patrons?," *Asia-Pacific Journal* 9, no. 13/3 (March 28, 2011), http://www.japanfocus.org/-Peter_Dale-Scott/3504; Karen DeYoung and Liz Sly, "Syrian Rebels Get Influx of Arms with Gulf Neighbors' Money, U.S. Coordination," *Washington Post*, May 16, 2012, http://www.washingtonpost.com/world/national-security/syrian-rebels-get-influx-of-arms-with-gulf-neighbors-money-us-coordination/2012/05/15/gIQAds2TSU_story.html; and Ruth Sherlock, "Leading Libyan Islamist Met Free Syrian Army Opposition Group," *Telegraph*, November 27, 2011, http://www.telegraph.co.uk/news/worldnews/africaandindianocean/libya/8919057/Leading-Libyan-Islamist-met-Free-Syrian-Army-opposition-group.html.

18. Dalia Sussman, "Poll Shows View of Iraq War Is Most Negative Since Start," *New York Times*, May 25, 2007, http://www.nytimes.com/2007/05/25/washington/25view.html?_r=1&oref=slogin.

19. CNN Political Unit, "CNN Poll: Support for Afghanistan War at All Time Low," *Political Ticker* (blog), October 28, 2011, http://politicalticker.blogs.cnn.com/2011/10/28/cnn-poll-support-for-afghanistan-war-at-all-time-low.

20. Dennis Jacobe, "American's Confidence in Banks Remains at Historic Low," *Gallup*, April 6, 2010, http://www.gallup.com/poll/127226/americans-confidence-banks-remains-historiclow.aspx.

21. "Climate Change Poll Finds More Americans Now Believe the Global Is Warming," *Huffington Post*, September 16, 2011, http://www.huffingtonpost.com/2011/09/16/climate-change-poll-american-global-warming_n_966214.html.

22. Damian Carrington, "Public Belief in Climate Change Weathers Storm, Poll Shows," *Guardian*, January 31, 2011, http://www.guardian.co.uk/environment/2011/jan/31/public-belief-climate-change.

23. Michael McDonald, "Multi-Partyism in American Politics?," Pollster.com, May 13, 2010, http://www.pollster.com/blogs/multipartyism_in_american_poli.php?nr=1.

24. Jane Merrick and Brian Brady, "Two in Five Shun Three Main Political Parties," *Independent on Sunday*, May 17, 2009, http://www.independent.co.uk/news/uk/politics/two-in-five-shun-three-main-political-parties-1686268.html.

Introduction

by Dr. Andy Lee Roth and Mickey Huff

In Ray Bradbury's celebrated book *Fahrenheit 451*, the protagonist, the fireman Guy Montag, reaches a turning point after realizing that his actions at work, earlier that day, contradict his inner convictions. In their living room, with multiple entertainment screens bombarding them, Montag confesses this growing unease to his spouse, who refuses to consider his concerns. "Let me alone," she says, "I didn't do anything." Montag responds, "We need not to be let alone. We need to be really bothered once in a while. How long is it since you were *really* bothered? About something important, about something real?"[1]

For anyone paying attention, the past year's real news includes much about which to be bothered. *Censored 2013* holds to account the corporate media who, all too often it seems, would rather be let alone than bothered when it comes to real, important news; and it celebrates the efforts of independent journalists who in 2011–2012 brought forward crucial news stories to stir us from complacency.

Pulitzer Prize–winning sociologist Paul Starr described a "serious long-term crisis" of news media in postindustrial democracies, including the United States: "The digital revolution," Starr wrote, "has weakened the ability of the press to act as an effective agent of public accountability by undermining the economic basis of professional reporting and fragmenting the public."[2] Starr's argument is important to understand for anyone interested in Project Censored's work.

The diffusion of television channels and the development of the Internet mean that the segment of the public interested in politics "sees politics increasingly through the lens of polarized news media," while an increasingly large segment of the population not interested in politics has "effectively dropped out of the public" and is "less likely to encounter news at all."[3]

21

Recent poll data from the Pew Research Center supports Starr's critical assessment. According to a September 2011 Pew report, negative opinions about the performance of news organizations now equal or surpass all-time highs on nine of the twelve core measures that Pew has tracked since 1985.[4] According to one poll, conducted by Pew in July 2011, 66 percent of Americans feel that news stories "often are inaccurate," 77 percent believe that news stories "tend to favor one side," and 80 percent believe that "powerful people and organizations" unduly influence news, to consider just three of Pew's core measures.

Starr argued that, as news organizations lose influence over public opinion, they become "less capable of standing up to powerful interests in both the state and private sector."[5] This ultimately threatens democracy, Starr argued, because studies show that "corruption flourishes where journalism does not." The less news coverage, the more entrenched political leaders become and the more likely they are to abuse power.[6]

Starr's analysis of news media in crisis is sobering for anyone who believes in the importance of a free press to democracy. His argument that the digital revolution has been good for freedom of expression and for freedom of information, but has ultimately weakened freedom of the press, is clear and original. However, by tacitly focusing on a crisis that confronts *corporate* news media most powerfully, Starr may overstate the crisis and risks overlooking the best solution to it.

Unlike their corporate counterparts, independent media have never generated large revenues from advertising; they have never taken for granted the ability to assemble a mass public on a daily basis; and they have, from their inception, treated standing up to powerful state and private interests as their core mission, their *raison d'être*.

Again, data from the Pew Research Center report proves useful to understanding the news crisis and its scope. In a June 2011 survey, Pew asked respondents what came to mind when they thought about "news organizations." The most-named organizations were CNN (43 percent), Fox News Channel (39 percent), and the three TV networks (NBC News, 18 percent; ABC News, 16 percent; CBS News, 12 percent).[7] The data indicate that, when asked about news organizations, most Americans identify *corporate* news media, particularly television.

As *Censored 2013* demonstrates, independent media prove robust, even as corporate media undergo crisis, because independent news workers understand that news is a public good, not a commodity. To borrow a phrase widely attributed to historian Daniel Boorstin, author of *The Image: A Guide to Pseudo-Events in America*,[8] in a democratic society, the value of news "increases by diffusion and grows by dispersion." Project Censored, and the independent journalists and news organizations celebrated in *Censored 2013*, aim to contribute to that diffusion and dispersion on the belief that, through our continuing efforts, we will one day awaken the US public to the realization that independent media—not their corporate counterparts—constitute both the "mainstream" of healthy US journalism and the sturdy foundation of authentic democratic self-government.

INSIDE *CENSORED 2013*

As in previous years, *Censored 2013* consists of three primary sections. Section I features Censored News and Media Analysis, including Project Censored's venerable listing of the top censored news stories. Chapter 1 presents the Top 25 Censored Stories for 2011–12 in the form of five Censored News Clusters. As in *Censored 2012*, this year's clusters draw analytic connections across multiple stories, elaborate on why some topics suffer from chronic underreporting in the corporate media, and address potential forms of engagement for an audience committed to more than just "consuming" the news. This year our chapter 1 team includes Elliot D. Cohen, Rob Williams, Elaine Wellin, James F. Tracy, Susan Rahman and Liliana Valdez-Madera. Of course, the identification, validation, and presentation of the top censored stories and their related Validated Independent News stories would be impossible without the hundreds of students and professors from colleges across the US and around the world, not to mention the courageous independent journalists who first reported these stories.

Chapter 2, Censored Déjà Vu, revisits six selected Top 25 Censored Stories from previous years, focusing on their subsequent corporate coverage and the extent to which they have become part of broader public discourse, or whether they remain "censored" by the corporate media. A team of Project Censored interns, including Jen Eiden,

Nolan Higdon, Aaron Hudson, Mike Kolbe, Michael Lucacher, Ryan Shehee, Juli Tambellini, Andrew O'Connor-Watts, provide updates on five top stories from *Censored 2012*—including soldier suicides, Obama's international assassination campaign, Google spying, the Great Pacific Garbage Patch, and labor abuses in Apple's Chinese factories—and one from *Censored 2008* on the Animal Enterprise Terrorism Act.

In chapter 3, Mickey Huff, Andy Lee Roth and Project Censored interns Nolan Higdon, Mike Kolbe, and Andrew O'Connor-Watts survey Junk Food News and News Abuse, two fields that the corporate media liberally replenish every year. Comical as 2011–12 Junk Food stories may seem—like "Tebow Fever," Kim Kardashian and royal weddings, news commentators arguing with Muppets, Donald Trump's ongoing obsession with President Barack Obama's birth certificate, and the return of the McRib—when analyzed in context they clarify how the infotainment of US corporate news serves serious propaganda functions, offering a diet of McNews no one can use. News Abuse examines coverage of conservative pundit Andrew Breitbart's death, the "threat" of organized labor to the Super Bowl, and the scandal over Mike Daisey's Apple exposé on NPR's *This American Life*, among other stories, showing how the news frames employed by corporate media distort serious stories and spin them into the sensational and trivial while burying the real significance of the subject matter at hand.

By contrast, chapter 4, on Media Democracy in Action, highlights local, national, and international organizations that exemplify independent journalism and activism in service of government transparency. This year, we proudly feature *Yes! Magazine*'s Sarah van Gelder on twelve helpful trends to extend in the coming year; Chris Woods of London's Bureau of Investigative Journalism, which has been a leader in coverage of the US's "covert" drone campaigns; MapLight: Revealing Money's Influence on Politics; Michael Levitin of the *Occupied Wall Street Journal*; Victoria Pacchiana-Rojas on Banned Books Week; Christopher Ponzi of Rebellious Truths; Nora Barrows-Friedman of Electronic Intifada; Andrew Phillips of Pacifica/KPFA Radio; J. R. Valrey of Block Report Radio; and Steve Zeltzer of Work Week Radio. For the reader seeking models of civic action and free press principles, this chapter is for you.

Section II focuses on what Project Censored has called the Truth Emergency, which results from the lack of factual reporting by corporate media over the past decade.[9] This year's Truth Emergency section deconstructs narratives of power to reclaim the common good. Antoon De Baets presents a theoretical framework for analyzing censorship and related issues, including historical propaganda and the abuse of history. Peter Phillips and Kimberly Soeiro provide an organizational "X-ray" of the global ruling class; and Elliot D. Cohen examines the dramatic rise of electronic surveillance, including government programs aimed at Total Information Awareness that lead to social control. Adam Bessie analyzes the attack on public education posed by GERM—the Global Education Reform Movement—and deconstructs the frames of propaganda put forth by GERM's Astroturf funders and political allies in both major political parties which mute the voices of those who should matter most in education: the students and teachers. Laurel Krause and Mickey Huff write to remind us about the importance of getting the past right, as they highlight recent evidence that significantly changes the historical record suggesting that the Kent State Shootings of 1970 were acts of state murder. We conclude this section of understanding conflicts between official and vernacular narratives with the hope to reclaim the common good. Kenn Burrows and Michael Nagler survey the new thinking and nonviolent actions that promise to aid humanity in responding to seven of the prominent challenges we face. They offer positive, proactive solutions to our current crises, solutions the corporate media simply don't address.

The book's third and final section, Project Censored International, provides five case studies in what we call "unhistory" in the making.[10] Elaborating on a concept from George Orwell's 1984, Noam Chomsky has defined an "unperson" as someone "denied personhood because they don't abide by state doctrine"—thus, "we may add the term 'unhistory' to refer to the fate of unpersons, expunged from history on similar grounds."[11] While other chapters in this year's book also address this issue, all of the chapters in the final section of Censored 2013 address the importance of recognizing "unhistory" and countering its withering effects on human rights and dignity. Almerindo E. Ojeda analyzes "Guantánamo Speak" and its role in the manufacture of consent; Andy Lee Roth reports on corporate media coverage of the

United States' targeted killing of US citizen Anwar al-Awlaki; Angel Ryono looks at the ongoing plight of Iraq's refugees; Brian Covert recovers the forgotten history of Japan's nuclear power industry, which prepared the road to disaster at Fukushima; and Tara Dorabji reports on the "occupation of truth" in Indian-administered Kashmir. Each of these news stories goes essentially untold in the corporate media, and the authors encourage us to retrieve them from the memory hole of "unhistory."

"EVERYTHING TO THINK ABOUT, AND MUCH TO REMEMBER"

Censored 2013 represents the accumulated knowledge of Project Censored's thirty-six years and the tireless efforts of scholars, students, activists, and community members from around the world. Like Montag, the protagonist in Bradbury's *Fahrenheit 451*, as individuals, we may find the choice to engage unsettling. Acknowledging the extent of the troubles, crises, and misconduct can be overwhelming. It takes courage. But, just as Bradbury's character eventually comes to know others who share his concerns, the choice to engage connects us with others. The necessity of engagement outpaces the false comfort of complacency.

As *Fahrenheit 451* concludes, Montag has escaped what amounts to a targeted killing (another dimension of our current crisis that Bradbury presciently foresaw), and he has found the companionship of a band of people committed to remembering the past. Outside the burning city, they walk together, for the time in silence. "There was," Bradbury writes, "everything to think about and much to remember."[12]

Welcome to *Censored 2013: Dispatches from the Media Revolution*. Thanks to our courageous independent journalists and our many generous contributors, it too offers much to think about and remember. Read some of what *Censored 2013* has to offer and we believe that you, too, will be energized to address one of the many social problems it identifies, to make our communities and the world a better place to live for all.

Notes

1. Ray Bradbury, *Fahrenheit 451*, 50th anniv. ed. (New York: Ballantine, 1991), 52.
2. Paul Starr, "An Unexpected Crisis: The News Media in Postindustrial Democracies," *Harvard International Journal of Press/Politics* 17, no. 2 (April 2012): 235.
3. Ibid., 238.
4. Pew Research Center, "Views of the News Media, 1985–2011: Press Widely Criticized, But Trusted More than Other Information Sources," September 22, 2011, http://www.people-press.org/2011/09/22/press-widely-criticized-but-trusted-more-than-other-institutions.
5. Starr, "An Unexpected Crisis," 240.
6. Ibid.
7. Pew, "Views." Figures add to more than 100 percent because of multiple responses.
8. For more on Boorstin, see chap. 3 of this volume as we expand upon the thesis of his book *The Image: A Guide to Pseudo-Events in America* (New York: Vintage, 2012 [1961]).
9. On Project Censored's conception of Truth Emergency, see Peter Phillips, Mickey S. Huff, Carmela Rocha, et al., "Truth Emergency Meets Media Reform," chap. 11 in *Censored 2009: The Top 25 Censored Stories of 2007–08*, eds. Peter Phillips and Andrew Roth (New York: Seven Stories Press, 2008), 281–95; and Peter Phillips and Mickey Huff, "Truth Emergency: Inside the Military Industrial Media Empire," chap. 5 in *Censored 2010: The Top 25 Censored Stories of 2008–09*, eds. Peter Phillips and Mickey Huff (New York: Seven Stories Press, 2009), 197–220.
10. For more on the concept of "unhistory," see Noam Chomsky, "Anniversaries from 'Unhistory,'" *In These Times*, February 6, 2012, http://www.inthesetimes.com/article/12679/anniversaries_from_unhistory. Also see the introductions to sections two and three of this volume.
11. Ibid.
12. Bradbury, *Fahrenheit 451*, 164.

CENSORED NEWS AND MEDIA ANALYSIS

Introduction by Mickey Huff and Dr. Andy Lee Roth

All that the sharpest critics of democracy have alleged is true, if there is no steady supply of trustworthy and relevant news. Incompetence and aimlessness, corruption and disloyalty, panic and ultimate disaster, must come to any people which is denied an assured access to the facts. No one can manage anything on pap. Neither can a people.

—Walter Lippmann, "Journalism and the Higher Law," 1920[1]

The first chapter of *Censored 2013* summarizes the twenty-five most important censored news stories for 2011–12. Our annual publication of significant and timely news stories that are absent from the establishment media in the United States raises interesting issues about whether the American public enjoys the "assured access to the facts" that Walter Lippmann identified as necessary to democracy. On the one hand, the corporate media's inadequate coverage of these stories bodes poorly for democracy. By censoring these important stories, the corporate media contribute to the aimlessness, corruption, and disaster about which Lippmann warned. On the other hand, we can celebrate the fact that intrepid independent journalists *do* offer "trustworthy and relevant news" in steady supply. The world would be worse off if the events detailed in their news stories took place and *no one* reported them.

Over the years, skeptics of Project Censored have questioned whether use of the term "censored" is appropriate in the US context. As the representative of the corporate media in Khalil Bendib's insightful cartoon asks, "Project Censored, here, in America? What for?" Put another way, in what sense are this year's Top 25 Censored Stories not only "trustworthy and relevant" but also "censored?"

As Project Censored has argued since its beginning in 1976, a broader definition of censorship is necessary to understand US news media. A narrow definition of censorship focuses on direct government control of news. This definition has contemporary relevance—as the persecutions and prosecutions of WikiLeaks' Julian Assange and Bradley Manning make clear—but it is not sufficient as censorship more often takes on more insidious guises. At Project Censored, we understand censorship as a form of propaganda—deceptive communication used to influence public opinion to benefit a special interest. Thus, we define "modern media censorship" to include the subtle yet constant and sophisticated manipulation of reality by mass media, including the intentional omission of a news story—or an important aspect of a news story—based on anything other than a desire to tell the truth.

Such manipulation can take the form of political pressure (from government officials and powerful individuals), economic pressure (from advertisers and funders), and legal pressure (from the threat of lawsuits from deep-pocket individuals, corporations, and institutions). Censorship includes stories that were never published, but also those that get such restricted distribution that few in the public are likely to know about them. In sum, censorship is not limited to overt, intentional omission, but also includes anything that interferes with the free flow of information in a society that purports to have a free press system.

By this standard, each of the news stories in our listing of the top stories for 2011–12 is a censored story. Some have received no corporate news coverage at all; in other cases, a story has received corporate coverage that is partial—in other words, such stories receive corporate coverage, but reporting is incomplete and/or biased in important ways. In such cases, the story summaries embedded in the Censored

News Clusters compare how the independent coverage differs from, and improves on, the partial corporate coverage.

How do we know that the news stories we bring forward each year are trustworthy and relevant? They have undergone rigorous review, which takes place in multiple stages during each annual cycle. Student researchers initially identify candidate stories in consultation with faculty evaluators. Together they vet the candidate story in terms of its importance, timeliness, strength of its sources, and corporate media coverage. If it fails on any one of these criteria, the story does not go forward. Once Project Censored receives the candidate story, we undertake a second round of judgment, using the same criteria and updating the review of any competing corporate coverage. Stories that pass this round of review get posted on the Media Freedom International website as "Validated Independent News stories" (or VINs).[2]

In early spring, we present all VINs in the current cycle to the faculty and students at all of our affiliate campuses, and to our national and international panel of judges, who cast votes to winnow the candidate stories from nearly 300 down to twenty-five. Once the top twenty-five have been determined, students in Peter Phillip's Media Censorship course at Sonoma State University and Project Censored student interns working with Mickey Huff at Diablo Valley College begin another intensive review of each story using LexisNexis and ProQuest databases. The twenty-five finalists are then sent to our panel of judges, who vote to rank them in numerical order. At the same time, these experts—including communications and media studies professors, professional journalists, and a former commissioner of the Federal Communications Commission, among others—offer their insights on the stories' strengths and weaknesses, if any.[3] Thus, by the time a story appears in *Censored 2013*, it has undergone at least five distinct rounds of review and evaluation. Although the stories that Project Censored brings forward may be socially and politically controversial—and sometimes even psychologically challenging—we are confident that each is the result of serious journalistic effort.

One story that does *not* appear in this year's top twenty-five illuminates our review and evaluation process. In early March 2012, student researcher Sharon Whealy and faculty evaluator Susan Rahman of Santa Rosa Junior College submitted a candidate story on the New York City Police Department's "mosque crawlers," undercover officers engaged in monitoring Islamic congregations by noting their ethnic makeup and cataloging sermons. At that point, only Al Jazeera and a team of reporters from the Associated Press (AP) had reported the story. By late April, as we prepared the ballot for voting by our affiliate campuses and panel of judges, we learned that the AP's Matt Apuzzo, Adam Goldman, Chris Hawley, and Eileen Sullivan had won a Pulitzer Prize for their ongoing investigation of the NYPD's intelligence operations.[4] We decided the NYPD "mosque crawler" story was no longer "censored" in the corporate media, and we deleted it from the ballot. We hope that more of the stories Project Censored brings forward every year will go on to earn this kind of establishment recognition, but we are not going to stand idly by in wait. There are still far more stories—of equal importance, and reported by independent journalists—that not only won't get the Pulitzer, they may not get noticed at all. This is why Project Censored has been Occupying the news media since 1976—to help tell the stories the corporate media miss, ignore, distort, or trivialize into pap. As Lippmann stated, a people cannot manage "if there is no steady supply of trustworthy and relevant news."

For the past two *Censored* books, we changed our format regarding how we present the most censored news stories. We used to merely list the Top 25 Censored Stories in ranked order, as voted on by our judges, give a synopsis of each, and list sources. That didn't call attention to the many topical connections among the top stories, which we think is of even greater importance than simply highlighting the stories themselves. By doing what good journalism should do—connecting the dots, linking the themes among the *types* of stories that are likely to be underreported or censored—we endeavor to better expose the architecture of censorship in a purportedly free press structure. We call these Censored News Clusters, which now house the most censored annual stories with a deeper analysis that leave readers with more of an understanding of the kinds of news reports that are apt to be censored, and why.

This year, the top censored stories are discussed and analyzed within the following topical Censored News Clusters:

- The Police State and Civil Liberties
- From "Bankster Bailout" to "Blessed Unrest": News We Can Use for Creating a US Economy for the 99 Percent
- Environment and Health
- Human Costs of War and Violence
- Women and Gender, Race and Ethnicity

We thank all the courageous independent journalists, their sources and whistleblowers alike, who are on the front lines of the media revolution every day, unveiling the big stories we all need to know about—the ones that the corporate media mangle or miss entirely. We also thank our cluster authors for their expertise, commitment, and acumen in not only highlighting the top censored stories, but for providing a framework, the big picture, required to inform a free people. By assuring access to the facts, we hope the public at large may achieve the wisdom and enlightenment needed for self-governance. With that, we give you the Censored News Clusters and the Top 25 Censored Stories of 2011–12.

Notes

1. Walter Lippmann, *Liberty and the News* (Princeton: Princeton University Press, 2008 [1920]), 6.
2. Validated Independent News stories are archived on the Media Freedom International website: http://www.mediafreedominternational.org/category/validated-independent-news.
3. For a complete listing of the national and international judges and their brief biographies, see the acknowledgments section of this book.
4. "Highlights of AP's Pulitzer Prize–Winning Probe into NYPD Intelligence Operations," Associated Press, http://ap.org/media-center/nypd/investigation.

CHAPTER 1

The Top 25 Censored Stories and Media Analysis of 2011–12

1. Signs of an Emerging Police State

Since the passage of the 2001 PATRIOT Act, the United States has become increasingly monitored and militarized at the expense of civil liberties. The 2012 passage of the National Defense Authorization Act (NDAA) has allowed the military to detain indefinitely without trial any US citizen that the government labels a terrorist or an accessory to terrorism, while President Barack Obama's signing of the National Defense Resources Preparedness Executive Order has authorized widespread federal and military control of the national economy and resources during "emergency and non-emergency conditions." Since 2010, the Department of Homeland Security's If You See Something, Say Something™ campaign has encouraged the public to report all suspicious activity to local authorities, even though actions that the DHS identifies as "suspicious" include the constitutionally protected right to criticize the government or engage in nonviolent protest.

Censored News Cluster: The Police State and Civil Liberties

2. Oceans in Peril

We thought the sea was infinite and inexhaustible. It is not. The overall rise in ocean temperature has led to the largest movement of marine species in two to three million years, according to scientists from the Climate Change and European Marine Ecosystems Research project. A February 2012 study of fourteen protected and eighteen unprotected ecosystems in the Mediterranean Sea demonstrated that this previously healthy sea is now quickly being depleted of resources. An international team of scientists conducted the study over a period of three years and found that in well-enforced marine reserve areas the fish populations were five to ten times greater than the fish populations in unprotected areas. The work of these scientists encourages the establishment and maintenance of marine reserves.

Censored News Cluster: Environment and Health

3. Fukushima Nuclear Disaster Worse than Anticipated

Developing evidence from a number of independent sources suggests that the negative consequences of the 2011 Fukushima Daiichi nuclear disaster are far greater than first acknowledged or understood. An estimated 14,000 excess deaths in the United States are linked to the radioactive fallout in Japan, according to a December 2011 report published in the *International Journal of Health Services.* Meanwhile, the Environmental Protection Agency's radiation-detection network (RadNet) has serious drawbacks, including a lack of maintenance and equipment that is often improperly calibrated.

Censored News Cluster: Environment and Health

4. FBI Agents Responsible for Majority of Terrorist Plots in the United States

The Federal Bureau of Investigation has embarked on an unusual approach to ensure that the United States is secure from future terrorist attacks. The agency has developed a network of nearly 15,000 spies to infiltrate various communities in an attempt to uncover terrorist plots. However, these moles are actually assisting and encouraging people to commit crimes. Many informants receive cash rewards of up to $100,000 per case.

Censored News Cluster: The Police State and Civil Liberties

5. First Federal Reserve Audit Reveals Trillions Loaned to Major Banks

An audit of the First Federal Reserve reveals sixteen trillion dollars in secret bailouts to major American and European banks during the height of the global financial crisis, from 2007 to 2010. Morgan Stanley received up to $107.3 billion, Citigroup took $99.5 billion, and Bank of America $91.4 billion, according to data obtained through

Freedom of Information Act requests, months of litigation, and an act of Congress.

Censored News Cluster: From "Bankster Bailout" to "Blessed Unrest": News We Can Use to Create a US Economy for the 99 Percent

6. Small Network of Corporations Run the Global Economy

A University of Zurich study reported that a small group of companies—mainly banks—wields huge power over the global economy. The study is the first to look at all 43,060 transnational corporations and the web of ownership among them. The researchers' network analysis identified 147 companies that form a "super entity," controlling 40 percent of the global economy's total wealth. The close connections mean that the network could be prone to "systemic risk" and vulnerable to collapse.

Censored News Cluster: From "Bankster Bailout" to "Blessed Unrest": News We Can Use to Create a US Economy for the 99 Percent

7. 2012: The International Year of Cooperatives

The United Nations named 2012 as the International Year of Cooperatives. According to the UN, nearly one billion people worldwide are co-op member-owners, and the co-op is expected to be the world's fastest growing business model by 2025. Worker-owned cooperatives provide for equitable distribution of wealth and genuine connection to the workplace, two key components of a sustainable economy.

Censored News Cluster: From "Bankster Bailout" to "Blessed Unrest": News We Can Use to Create a US Economy for the 99 Percent

8. NATO War Crimes in Libya

Although the rationale of the North Atlantic Treaty Organization (NATO) for entry into Libyan conflict invoked humanitarian principles, the results have proven far from humane. In July 2011, NATO aircraft bombed Libya's main water supply facility, which provided water to approximately 70 percent of the nation's population. And, in a failed attempt to appear unbiased and objective, the BBC has revealed, almost a year after the information was relayed by independent media, that British Special Forces played a key role in steering and supervising Libya's "freedom fighters" to victory.

Censored News Cluster: Human Costs of War and Violence

9. Prison Slavery in Today's USA

The US comprises less than 5 percent of the world's population, yet US prisons hold more than 25 percent of all people imprisoned globally. Many of these prisoners labor at twenty-three cents per hour, or similar wages, in federal prisons contracted by the Bureau of Prisons' UNICOR, a quasi-public, for-profit corporation, which is the US government's thirty-ninth largest contractor. As incarceration rates explode in the US, thousands are placed in solitary confinement, often for having committed minor disciplinary infractions within prison.

Censored News Cluster: The Police State and Civil Liberties

10. HR 347 Would Make Many Forms of Nonviolent Protest Illegal

In March 2012, President Obama signed into law HR 347, the Federal Restricted Buildings and Grounds Improvement Act of 2011. The law specifies as criminal offenses the acts of entering or remaining in areas defined as "restricted." Although pundits have debated to what extent the new law restricts First Amendment rights or criminalizes Occupy protests, it does make it easier for the Secret Service to overuse or misuse existing laws to arrest lawful protesters by lowering the requirement of intent in the prosecution of criminal activity.

Censored News Cluster: The Police State and Civil Liberties

11. Members of Congress Grow Wealthier Despite Recession

The net worth of the members of Congress continues to rise regardless of the economic recession. An analysis of financial disclosure forms by *Roll Call* magazine, using the minimum valuation of assets, showed that members of the House and Senate in 2010 had a collective net worth of $2.04 billion, a $390 million increase from the $1.65 billion held in 2008. Disclosure forms do not include non-income-producing assets.

Censored News Cluster: From "Bankster Bailout" to "Blessed Unrest": News We Can Use to Create a US Economy for the 99 Percent

12. US Joins Forces with al-Qaeda in Syria

The US, Britain, France, and some conservative Arab allies have funded and armed the Syrian rebellion from its start in 2011. In fact, the US has been funding groups against Bashar al-Assad since the mid-1990s. However, the anti-Assad ranks include members of al-Qaeda, Hamas, and other groups that the United States lists as terrorist organizations.

Censored News Cluster: Human Costs of War and Violence

13. Education "Reform" a Trojan Horse for Privatization

Public education is the target of a well-coordinated, well-funded campaign to privatize as many schools as possible, particularly in cities. This campaign claims it wants great teachers in every classroom, but its rhetoric demoralizes teachers, reduces the status of the education profession, and champions standardized tests that perpetuate social inequality. The driving logic for such reform is profits.

Censored News Cluster: From "Bankster Bailout" to "Blessed Unrest": News We Can Use to Create a US Economy for the 99 Percent

14. Who Are the Top 1 Percent and How Do They Earn a Living?

The richest 1 percent of the country now owns more than 40 percent of the wealth and takes home nearly a quarter of national income. Evidence based on tax returns indicates that this superelite 1 percent consists of nonfinancial executives, financial professionals, and members of the legal, real estate, and medical professions. Earnings at this level correlate with deregulation and the other legal changes that brought on the financial crisis. While the 99 percent deal with the direct consequences of that crisis, the 1 percent increasingly have left behind deteriorating neighborhoods in favor of wealthy enclaves, further isolating themselves, according to a 2011 Stanford University study.

Censored News Cluster: From "Bankster Bailout" to "Blessed Unrest": News We Can Use to Create a US Economy for the 99 Percent

15. Dangers of Everyday Technology

Recent research raises compelling concerns about two commonplace technologies, cellular phones and microwave ovens. Heavy, long-term exposure to cell phone radiation increases risks for certain types of cancer, including leukemia, and in males impairs sperm production. Prenatal exposure to cell phone radiation has been shown to produce blood-brain barrier leakage, and brain, liver, and eye damage. The microwave radiation that heats food also creates free radicals that can become carcinogenic, while the consumption of microwaved foods is associated with short-term decreases in white blood cells. The Food and Drug Administration has yet to recognize studies that indicate microwave ovens alter foods' nutritional structure, and, as with the dangers of cell phone use, most studies indicating minimal or no health risks are, in fact, industry-sponsored.

Censored News Cluster: Environment and Health

16. Sexual Violence against Women Soldiers on the Rise and under Wraps

The 2005 death of US Army Private LaVena Johnson, officially ruled suicide by the Department of Defense, in fact exemplifies the sexual violence that female soldiers encounter while serving their country. Johnson's autopsy revealed wounds inconsistent with suicide, including chemical burns that many believe were intended to destroy DNA evidence of rape. The Pentagon has tried to intimidate reporters and editors working on stories about Johnson. Johnson's case is among at least twenty where female soldiers have died under suspicious circumstances. The mysterious deaths coincide with an increase in sexual violence against women in the military. According to the Department of Defense, in 2010, there were 3,158 total reports of sexual assault in the military. The DOD estimates that this number represents only 13.5 percent of the actual assaults, making the total number of military rapes and sexual assaults in excess of 19,000 for the year.

Censored News Cluster: Women and Gender, Race and Ethnicity

17. Students Crushed By One Trillion Dollars in Student Loans

In April 2012, US student loan debt topped one trillion dollars, more than credit card debt. Although corporate media dutifully reported this milestone, they underplayed its significance and ignored one promising solution. Student loan debt is the only form of consumer loan debt that has increased substantially since 2008. The threat of massive student loan defaults requiring another taxpayer bailout is a systemic risk as serious as the bank failures that brought the US economy to the brink of collapse in 2008. The Federal Reserve could introduce a new quantitative easing program to remove student loan debt, giving the economy a boost similar to that created by the GI Bill.

18. Palestinian Women Prisoners Shackled during Childbirth

Female Palestinian prisoners in Israeli prisons are treated inhumanely and often denied medical care, and legal representation, and are forced to live in squalid conditions. The conditions and violations faced by women in Israeli jails need to be addressed from a gender perspective, according to CEDAW, the United Nation's Committee on the Elimination of Discrimination against Women.

Censored News Cluster: Women and Gender, Race and Ethnicity

19. New York Police Plant Drugs on Innocent People to Meet Arrest Quotas

A host of stories document how the New York Police Department operates outside the very laws it is charged with enforcing. In October 2011, a former NYPD narcotics detective testified that he regularly saw police plant drugs on innocent people as a way to meet arrest quotas. The NYPD's controversial "stop and frisk" program has invested seventy-five million dollars to arrest suspects for possessing minimal amounts of marijuana. Each arrest costs approximately $1,000 to $2,000. Although NYPD use of unlawful restraints and disproportionate force to arrest peaceful Occupy protesters has received some news coverage, police brutality directed against people of color continues to go underreported.

Censored News Cluster: The Police State and Civil Liberties

20. Stealing from Public Education to Feed the Prison-Industrial Complex

A systemic recasting of education priorities gives official structure and permanence to a preexisting underclass comprised largely of criminalized, poor people of color. The rise of corporate-backed charter schools and privatized prisons cannot be understood apart from the record closures of public schools across the country.

Censored News Cluster: From "Bankster Bailout" to "Blessed Unrest":
News We Can Use to Create a US Economy for the 99 Percent

21. Conservatives Attack US Post Office to Break the Union and Privatize Postal Services

The US Postal Service has been under constant assault for years from conservative Republicans who aim to eviscerate the strongest union in the country. Under the 2006 Postal Accountability and Enhancement Act, USPS must fully fund retiree health benefits for future retirees—including the retirement packages of employees not even born yet. No other organization, public or private, has to prefund 100 percent of its future health benefits. Thus, the post office's oft-reported nine-billion-dollar deficit is largely a result of government-imposed overpayments.

Censored News Cluster: From "Bankster Bailout" to "Blessed Unrest": News We Can Use to Create a US Economy for the 99 Percent

22. Wachovia Bank Laundered Money for Latin American Drug Cartels

Between 2004 and 2007, Wachovia Bank handled funds totaling $378.4 billion for Mexican currency-exchange houses acting on behalf of drug cartels. The transactions amount to the largest violation of the Bank Secrecy Act, an anti-money-laundering law, in US history. This case is not exceptional; Wachovia is just one of several US and European banks that drug cartels have used to launder money.

Censored News Cluster: From "Bankster Bailout" to "Blessed Unrest": News We Can Use to Create a US Economy for the 99 Percent

23. US Covers up Afghan Massacre

Although the March 2012 massacre of sixteen unarmed Afghan civilians, nine of whom were children, received a great deal of news coverage, independent news sources have focused on whether one US solider acting alone—as US officials have insisted—or multiple US soldiers—as Afghan witnesses and Afghan President Hamid Karzai contend—bear direct responsibility for the killings. These reports highlight the fundamental responsibility of US high military command, including President Obama, for the crimes committed by its troops.

Censored News Cluster: Human Costs of War and Violence

24. Alabama Farmers Look to Replace Migrants with Prisoners

Alabama's expansive anti-immigrant law, HB56, has been so economically devastating that farmers in the state sought legislation to force hard labor on prison inmates eligible for work release programs, to "help farms fill the gap and find sufficient labor." The state's Department of Corrections opposed the legislation, noting that its approximately 2,000 prisoners eligible for work release already have jobs, and that "the prison system isn't the solution to worker shortages caused by the law."

Censored News Cluster: Women and Gender, Race and Ethnicity

25. Evidence Points to Guantánamo Dryboarding

In June 2006, three Guantánamo prisoners were found dead in their cells, hanging from what appeared to be makeshift nooses. Although the Department of Defense declared the deaths suicides, the Naval Criminal Investigative Service (NCIS) inquiry found evidence inconsistent with suicide—including the fact that the prisoners' hands were bound behind their backs. The NCIS evidence suggests that the prisoners died from lethal interrogations that included dryboarding, a technique using controlled suffocation.

Censored News Cluster: Human Costs of War and Violence

The Police State and Civil Liberties

by Dr. Elliot D. Cohen

Censored #1

Signs of an Emerging Police State

Spencer Ackerman and Noah Shachtman, "Read the FBI Memo: Agents Can 'Suspend the Law,'" *Wired*, March 28, 2012, http://www.wired.com/dangerroom/2012/03/fbi-memo-bend-suspend-law.

James Bamford, "The NSA Is Building the Country's Biggest Spy Center (Watch What You Say)," *Wired*, March 15, 2012, http://www.wired.com/threatlevel/2012/03/ff_nsadatacenter.

Chris Hedges, "Why I'm Suing Barack Obama," *Truthdig*, January 16, 2012, http://www.truthdig.com/report/item/why_im_suing_barack_obama_20120116.

White House, *Executive Order: National Defense Resources Preparedness*, Office of the Press Secretary, March 16, 2012, http://www.whitehouse.gov/the-press-office/2012/03/16/executive-order-national-defense-resources-preparedness.

White House, "Statement by the President on H.R. 1540," Office of the Press Secretary, December 31, 2011, http://www.whitehouse.gov/the-press-office/2011/12/31/statement-president-hr-1540.

Student Researcher: Robert Usher (San Francisco State University)

Faculty Evaluator: Kenn Burrows (San Francisco State University)

Censored #4

FBI Agents Responsible for Majority of Terrorist Plots in the United States

Trevor Aronson, "The Informants," *Mother Jones*, September/October 2011, http://www.motherjones.com/politics/2011/08/fbi-terrorist-informants.

"FBI Organizes Almost All Terror Plots in the US," RT.com, August 23, 2011, http://rt.com/usa/news/fbi-terror-report-plot-365-899/print.

Student Researcher: Taylor Falbisaner (Sonoma State University)

Faculty Evaluator: Peter Phillips (Sonoma State University)

Censored #9

Prison Slavery in Today's USA

Sara Flounders, "The Pentagon and Slave Labor in U.S. Prisons," *Workers World*, June 6, 2011, http://www.workers.org/2011/us/pentagon_0609.

James Ridgeway and Jean Casella, "Cruel and Usual: US Solitary Confinement," Al Jazeera English, March 19, 2011, http://www.aljazeera.com/indepth/featur es/2011/03/201137125936219469.html.

Student Researchers: Leta Frolli and Taylor Wright (Sonoma State University)

Faculty Evaluators: Sheila Katz and Patrick Jackson (Sonoma State University)

Censored #10

HR 347 Would Make Many Forms of Nonviolent Protest Illegal

Danny Weil, "Many Forms of Occupy Protests Subjected to New Bill Making Protests Illegal," *The Daily Censored* (blog), March 5, 2012, http://dailycensored.com/2012/03/05/many-forms-of-occupy-protests-subjected-to-new-bill-making-protests-illegal.

Oskar Mosquito, "Enacting the NDAA: Limiting Protesters' Rights," Media Roots, March 5, 2012, http://mediaroots.org/enacting-the-ndaa-limiting-protesters-rights.

Brian Doherty, "Bill Passes House: Protests Near Secret Service Protected Folk Effectively Outlawed," *Reason* (blog), March 1, 2012, http://reason.com/blog/2012/03/01/bill-passes-house-protests-near-secret-s.

Student Researcher: Eric Humphrey (College of Marin)

Faculty Evaluator: Susan Rahman (College of Marin)

Censored #19

New York Police Plant Drugs on Innocent People to Meet Arrest Quotas

John Del Signore, "NYPD Narcotics Detective Admits Cops Regularly Plant Drugs on Perps," *Gothamist*, October 13, 2011, http://gothamist.com/2011/10/13/nypd_narcotics_detective_testifies.php.

Jesse Levine, "New York City Wasting $75 Million a Year on Marijuana Arrests," *AlterNet*, March 15, 2011, http://www.alternet.org/module/printversion/150263.

Student Researcher: Cary Escovedo (Sonoma State University)

Faculty Evaluator: Sheila Katz (Sonoma State University)

RELATED VALIDATED INDEPENDENT NEWS STORY

Joseph Nevins, "Robocop: Drones At Home," *Boston Review*, January/February 2011, http://bostonreview.net/BR36.1/nevins.php.

Student Researcher: Josh Fowler (Santa Rosa Junior College)

Faculty Evaluator: Susan Rahman (Santa Rosa Junior College)

The steady creep toward an increased abridgment of American citizens' constitutional rights by government and its law enforcement agents characterized 2011–12. These abuses of power have, in some cases, been made official law or policy; in other cases, they have involved clandestine perpetration of criminal acts by those whose job it is to enforce the law.

Some of these abuses have involved systematic exploitation of the most vulnerable human beings by government in cooperation with industry. Presently, our prisons have become centers of "recruitment" for slave labor in the service of the military-industrial complex. Within the walls of these prison factories, hidden from the public view, inmates are being subjected to cruel and inhumane treatment without legal recourse. Police have become accessories to this exploitative underworld through violations of due process in order to increase their numbers of arrests. In this intricate web of abuse of authority, citizens on the outside are being entrapped, deceived, and manipulated by law enforcement (including by the Federal Bureau of Investigation [FBI]) for political and self-serving purposes. This includes encouraging and entrapping "would-be" terrorists by FBI agents and informants in order to create an image that the "war on terror" is being won.

At the same time, the Obama administration has encroached on freedom of speech by passing legislation that could prevent peaceful assembly. It has also passed such acts as the National Defense Authorization Act (NDAA), which includes provisions that permit the president to indefinitely detain American citizens without habeas corpus or trial, and even to "rendition" them to nations, such as Syria, that permit torture—and all this without proof of terrorist involvement.

In this brave new world of government power, manipulation, and control, privacy has increasingly become an artifact of the past. Now, the National Security Agency (NSA) has invested in a two-billion-dollar electronic intelligence compound in Utah, which will take to the next level the Total Information Awareness project that was begun during the early years of the Bush administration.

These among other abuses of power discussed below have created the gnawing specter of a burgeoning police state.

Censored #9: Prison Slavery in Today's USA

The military-industrial complex has expanded its tentacles to include a program of forced labor in federal penitentiaries. These prisoners are now being paid twenty-three cents per hour to work on high-tech electronic components for Patriot Advanced Capability-3 missiles, launchers for TOW (Tube-launched, Optically tracked, Wire-guided) antitank missiles, and other guided missile systems. Other products of this slave labor force include night-vision goggles, body armor, camouflage uniforms, radio communication devices, light systems, land mine sweepers, and battleship anti-aircraft guns. This captive community of slave laborers has no organized means of protection. There are no unions to protect them from unfair labor practices. This has resulted in cheap labor at the expense of unsafe working conditions for these inmates, who are exposed to toxic dust without safety equipment, protective gear, air filtration, or masks. These toxic working conditions have led to deadly consequences such as blood clots and cancer.

Labor in federal prisons is contracted out by UNICOR, also known as Federal Prison Industries, Inc. (FPI), a quasi-public, for-profit corporation run by the Federal Bureau of Prisons. UNICOR is now the United States government's thirty-ninth largest contractor, with 110 factories at seventy-nine federal penitentiaries. In fourteen prison factories, more than 3,000 prisoners build electronic equipment for land, sea, and airborne communications.

According to the Federal Bureau of Prisons website,

> FPI is, first and foremost, a correctional program. The whole impetus behind FPI is not about business, but instead, about inmate release preparation . . . helping offenders acquire the skills necessary to successfully make that transition from prison to law-abiding, contributing members of society.[1]

However, this claim is questionable considering the majority of UNICOR's products and services are on contract to orders from the Department of Defense.

Giant multinational corporations purchase parts assembled at some of the lowest labor rates in the world, then resell the finished weapons components at the highest rates of profit. For example, Lockheed Martin and Raytheon Company subcontract components, then assemble and sell advanced weapons systems to the Pentagon. In this light, the exploitation of forced labor in prisons appears to be less about the future welfare of inmates than it is about maximizing profit for the military-industrial complex. Not unlike other giant corporations that outsource and exploit cheap labor abroad, UNICOR exploits inmates held captive in US prisons.

This system of slavery, like that which existed in this country before the Civil War, is also racist, as more than 60 percent of US prisoners are people of color. According to the Federal Bureau of Prisons's own statistics, as of May 2012, 37.4 percent of inmates are black and 34.7 are Hispanic.[2] In addition, tens of thousands of prisoners include undocumented immigrants facing deportation, prisoners awaiting sentencing, and youthful offenders in categories considered reform or detention.

Sadly, this racist, exploitative, corporate system of forced labor has received little to no media attention and has thus been allowed to operate beneath the radar of social and legal scrutiny. For example, in March 2012, the *New York Times* reported that private businesses were losing government contracts to FPI. The story neither broached the Pentagon connection nor disclosed that the prisoners were producing missiles and other military equipment. Instead it said that the prisoners were producing solar panels and other "green" energy goods, quoting a UNICOR spokesperson who stated that the purpose of the program was to "provide inmates with job skills in a new growing market."[3]

With the help of such media whitewashing, the exploitation of forced labor another way inmates in both state and federal prisons are being given cruel and unusual treatment. As incarceration rates explode in the US, thousands are placed in solitary confinement; every day, tens of thousands of prisoners languish in "the hole." Many of these inmates have committed only minor disciplinary infractions, if any, while only a few actually present a threat to others. It has been estimated that about 20,000 inmates are held in "super-max" prisons, which are prisons that isolate their prisoners.[4] Fifty thousand to 80,000 more may be in solitary confinement on any given day in other prisons and local jails. Moreover, the rate at which prisoners have been placed in solitary confinement is continuing to increase every year.[5]

The warden and prison staff often take advantage of their power by playing the prosecutor, judge, and jury in the amount of time a prisoner spends in isolation. Children in adult prisons and jails often end up in solitary because there is simply no place else to prevent them from being victimized, leaving them without physical contact or schooling for years. Even victims of prison rape and whistleblowers are often isolated "for their own protection," or given a choice between solitary confinement and continued sexual assault.[6]

Prisoners who attempt to report on the oppressive conditions on the inside have been silenced and punished for their actions by being placed in solitary confinement. For example, in one case, Timothy Muise, a prisoner at the Massachusetts Correctional Institute at Norfolk, disclosed to prison authorities that guards were operating a sex-for-information racket in which some prisoners were permitted to have sex in exchange for information about others. Muise was placed in solitary confinement for two-and-a-half months, brought up on disciplinary charges for "engaging in or inciting a group demonstration," and sent to another prison.[7]

In another instance, Maine prisoner Deane Brown, serving time for burglary and robbery in the lockdown unit of Maine State Prison, began reporting "Live from the Hole," by sending letters and making phone calls to a community radio station. Accused of disclosing confidential information through the media, Brown ended up at an especially brutal solitary confinement unit in New Jersey. If solitary confinement continues to be used as a means of silencing such protests from the inside, the systematic abuse of inmates, including the exploitation of forced slave labor, will likely continue to flourish within prison walls.

In Europe, solitary confinement has been largely rejected as a form of cruel and inhumane punishment. In contrast, American courts and legislators have been less willing to take a strong stand against solitary confinement.

According to David Fathi of the American Civil Liberties Union (ACLU), legislation and litigation, combined with grassroots activism and investigative journalism, are producing "a breakthrough in public awareness."[8] Nevertheless, solitary confinement is still a fact of prison life in America, and unless there is more public awareness generated through greater media involvement, this is not likely to change.

Censored #19: New York Police Plant Drugs on Innocent People to Meet Arrest Quotas

A number of inmates forced into slave labor and/or placed into solitary confinement may have been innocent persons who were set up by the police. According to former New York Police Department (NYPD) narcotics detective Stephen Anderson, police regularly plant drugs on innocent people as a way to meet arrest quotas.

Testifying under cooperation with prosecutors in the trial of a fellow detective charged with falsifying public documents and business documents, Anderson stated that he frequently witnessed the practice of "flaking," or planting cocaine on innocent people. "The corruption I observed," said Anderson, "was something I was seeing a lot of, whether it was from supervisors or undercovers and even investigators."[9] When asked by Justice Gustin Reichbach how he felt about setting up innocent men, Anderson stated, "It's almost like you have no emotion with it, that they attach the bodies to it, they're going to be out of jail tomorrow anyway; nothing is going to happen to them anyway."[10]

But what happens to someone accused of a drug crime is not always so clear cut. For example, being convicted of transporting illegal drugs across state lines is a federal offense, and there are mandatory minimum sentencing requirements that cannot be commuted by a judge. Thus, planting drugs on someone who crosses a state line could result in an innocent person ending up in a federal penitentiary—and potentially, in turn, working for the Department of Defense under toxic conditions for twenty-three cents per hour.

According to Gabriel Sayegh of the Drug Policy Alliance, an activist organization in favor of alternative drug policies, "One of the consequences of the war on drugs is that police officers are pressured to make large numbers of arrests, and it's easy for some of the less honest cops to plant evidence on innocent people. The drug war inevitably leads to crooked policing—and quotas further incentivize such practices."[11] Insofar as such crooked policing is a result of the "war on drugs," more media attention on the deleterious consequences of the latter may be necessary to address the problem of police corruption.

This so-called war on drugs does not only appear to be generating police corruption and innocent victims of crooked policing; it is also wasting a lot of taxpayers' money. New York City wastes seventy-five million dollars arresting people for having a minimal amount of marijuana (less than an ounce). It costs approximately $1,000 to $2,000 to arrest each person for possession of marijuana. In addition, this "war" appears to be racially biased.

The NYPD arrests more than 1,000 people a week, in large part due to their "stop and frisk" practices—the overwhelming number of these arrests being that of Latinos and blacks. The NYPD also uses illegal, dishonest, and manipulative tactics, such as coercing people to reveal their marijuana by offering a lenient punishment for their cooperation, or searching their pockets without reason or permission.

Hypocritically, NYC Mayor Michael Bloomberg has himself confessed to enjoying smoking marijuana, while having overseen more than 350,000 arrests for marijuana possession since elected in 2002.[12] A study by the Drug Policy Alliance estimates that from 1997-2010 NYPD marijuana arrests cost taxpayers between $500 million to $1 billion,[13] not to mention the serious potential for disrupting citizens' lives and causing them irrevocable harm. While marijuana possession is considered a relatively minor offense, it can dramatically affect people's lives because the offense is permanently entered into criminal databases.

Although corporate media have provided considerable coverage of the NYPD's stop and frisk policy, most of this coverage omits the NYPD's use of manipulation, deception, and entrapment as means of increasing the number of arrests. Even coverage that has discussed racial profiling has fallen short of looking into whether minorities who were stopped were also deceived or entrapped in order to make the arrest.[14]

Corporate media have also tended to dignify the NYPD's defense of its stop and frisk policy, accepting the department's argument that, by concentrating on "quality of life" crimes—small offenses—such as marijuana possession, it can help prevent people from graduating to more serious crimes.[15] This perspective glosses over the fact that, since thousands of those arrested are innocent in the first place, the policy's deterrent effect is exaggerated. In fact, one could argue that when people are arrested for crimes they didn't commit, the experience makes them less apt to respect law enforcement. Further, corporate coverage downplays the repercussions on innocent people who end up with arrest records that affect the quality of their lives.

Censored #4: FBI Agents Responsible for Majority of Terrorist Plots in the United States

The war on drugs is not the only so-called "war" that has been infused with the abuse of policing power and authority. The "war on terror" (or on al-Qaeda) has also involved similar forms of entrapment—this time by the Federal Bureau of Investigation (FBI). According to a report by *Mother Jones* and the Investigative Reporting Program at the University of California–Berkeley, the FBI "maintains a roster of 15,000 spies, some paid as much as $100,000 per case," to "stop" terrorist plots.[16] But the agents themselves are responsible for orchestrating these plots in the first place, so that they can later thwart them.

Trevor Aaronson of *Mother Jones* reports that, in recent years, the FBI has used trained informants and undercover operatives to set up terrorist plots and then "preempt" them by making arrests. Aaronson states that "FBI agents and informants target not just active jihadists, but tens of thousands of law-abiding people, seeking to identify those disgruntled few who might participate in a plot given the means and the opportunity. And then, in case after case, the government provides the plot, the means, and the opportunity."[17]

This approach to counterterrorism orchestrates terrorist plots in order to claim victory in the war on terror. Informants, said Aaronson,

report to their handlers on people who have, say, made statements sympathizing with terrorists. Those names are then cross-referenced with existing intelligence data, such as immigration and criminal records. FBI agents may then assign an undercover operative to approach the target by posing as a radical. Sometimes the operative will propose a plot, provide explosives, even lead the target in a fake oath to Al Qaeda. Once enough incriminating information has been gathered, there's an arrest—and a press conference announcing another foiled plot.[18]

The FBI has used this tactic to stop many of the high-profile would-be terrorist attacks including the Washington DC Metro bombing plot, the New York City subway plot, the attempt to blow up Chicago's Sears Tower, and dozens of other so-called terrorist plots. "The problem with the cases we're talking about is that defendants would not have done anything if not kicked in the ass by government agents" said Martin Stolar, who represented a suspect involved in a New York City bombing plot that was allegedly set up by FBI agents. "They're creating crimes to solve crimes so they can claim a victory in the war on terror."[19]

An essential ingredient of this political strategy to chalk up wins are corporate media that cooperate in reporting what government spokespersons claim, rather than conducting independent investigations. Although there have been some mainstream media reports that have confirmed FBI involvement in encouraging terrorist plots, the mainstream media have generally been complicit in reporting the thwarting of these plots by FBI rather than exposing its role in setting them up. As Naomi Wolf wrote,

The news stories, which quickly surface, long enough to cause scary headlines, then vanish before people can learn how often the cases are thrown out. These are stories about "bumbling fantasists," hapless druggies, the aimless, even the virtually homeless and mentally ill, and other marginal characters with not the strongest grip on reality, who have been lured into discourses about violence against America only after assiduous courting, and in some cases outright payment, by undercover FBI or police informants.[20]

Corporate media coverage has tended to neglect the frequency with which judges throw these cases out of court, while emphasizing those cases that go to trial. This corporate coverage has been careful not to suggest political motivations for the FBI "foiling" terrorist plots of its own creation—namely, to make the administration appear as though it is "winning" the war on terror.

Censored #10: HR 347 Would Make Many Forms of Nonviolent Protest Illegal

Such unchecked power to abuse American citizens for political gain is also enabled and exacerbated by new legislation that gives police more legal ammunition to advance its political interests by silencing its opposition. One such law is HR 347, which could arbitrarily make many nonviolent protests illegal. The Federal Restricted Buildings and Grounds Improvement Act of 2011 would make entering or remaining in areas defined as "restricted areas" a criminal offense, punishable by fining or imprisonment.

The act would place off-limits to peaceful protest any area where an event is taking place that is designated by the Department of Homeland Security as being of "national significance."[21] The vagueness of this language makes it possible to arbitrarily shut down peaceful demonstrations when government deems doing so to its advantage. As such, the act could contravene the First Amendment by targeting groups such as the Occupy movement, which uses public assembly as a primary way of getting its messages out.

This misleadingly titled legislation slipped into law under the guise of being an appropriations bill for money to improve the federal landscaping ("Grounds Improvement"). However, there is nothing in the bill that even remotely pertains to the ordinary understanding of "grounds improvement." Unfortunately, the corporate media helped to foster this false impression of the bill by not covering its far-reaching, dangerous implications for free speech in America.

Censored #1: Signs of an Emerging Police State

Other recent legislation effectively obliterates the balance of powers and legitimizes in its stead a military dictatorship. On December 31, 2011, President Barack Obama signed into law the National Defense Authorization Act (NDAA), which contains provisions that give the president the authority to use military force to indefinitely detain American citizens without trial.

The language of the NDAA vaguely states that this power may be exercised against any person who was a part of or substantially supported al-Qaeda, the Taliban, or associated forces that are engaged in hostilities against the United States or its coalition partners, including any person who has committed a belligerent act or has directly supported such hostilities in aid of such enemy forces.[22]

This act can be applied to American citizens who have not been a part of any terrorist organization but who have been accused of supporting such an organization. And the allegation need not be proven in a court of law in order for the subject to be indefinitely detained.

The NDAA also states that the person in question is subject to "transfer to the custody or control of the person's country of origin, any other foreign country, or any other foreign entity."[23] Thus, the person could even be transferred to a foreign country such as Syria to be tortured.

Effectively, the NDAA gives the president authority to deprive a US citizen of a writ of habeas corpus. This basic constitutional protection guarantees anyone detained by the government the right to be brought before a court to determine whether there is just cause to continue the detainment.

In its capacity as the Fourth Estate, the media's role is to keep a vigilant watch on the government to ensure that it does not abuse its power. Given the magnitude of this alleged breach of constitutionality, corporate media had a responsibility to provide detailed coverage of the NDAA's questionable provisions. Unfortunately, the actual coverage failed to address the dangerous consequences this bill could have on the rule of law in the US. Instead, coverage tended to focus on whether or not President Obama intended to sign the bill.[24]

Further, on March 16, 2012, the Obama administration declared the National Defense Resources Preparedness Executive Order, which authorizes widespread federal and military control of the national economy and resources during "emergency and non-emergency conditions"[25] as well as the right to install "government owned equipment" in private industrial facilities.[26]

In addition to the paucity of coverage of these new laws, additional under-covered developments in the federal government's mass, warrantless surveillance program threaten to move us closer to a full-fledged police state. The National Security Agency (NSA) is building a two-billion-dollar electronic intelligence compound in Utah to be completed in September 2013—a vast complex, shrouded in secrecy. Its purpose is to intercept, decode, analyze, integrate, and store vast amounts of information allegedly for intelligence operations. This information will include the contents of private e-mails, cell phone calls, Google searches, and other personal data such as parking receipts, travel itineraries, bookstore purchases, medical records, and credit card purchases. Because much of this information is encrypted and stored behind passwords, the system is intended to include advanced, state-of-the-art algorithms capable of decoding and gaining access to all such information. As James Bamford has suggested, "It is, in some measure, the realization of the 'total information awareness' program created during the first term of the Bush administration."[27]

But there is more. The Intelligence Advanced Research Projects Activity (IARPA), an intelligence research arm of the US government, is building a software program called Catalyst in order to integrate a vast storehouse of information like that stored in the Utah facility.[28] Beyond linking the data, this software system will also provide sense, meaning, and reference to the strings of language it connects, relating these symbols to real-world people, places, events, and states of affairs, revealing facts about the world that were heretofore unknown. For example, Catalyst will not only relate the name of a person to the name of a terrorist organization, it will also relate these names to categories of people and terrorist organizations, so that data content receives a real-world interpretation (so called "semantic integration"). It will also have the ability to extract patterns—for example that certain groups of people belong to certain terrorist organizations. And it will be able to provide a fully interpreted history or biography of every human being in the world.

Although other semantic integrators exist, what distinguishes Catalyst from the rest is its ability to semantically integrate the vast sea of information from a massive database such as the Utah Data Center, and not just from the databases of individual government agencies. In this way, Bamford's characterization of the Utah Data Center as a realization of Total Information Awareness would be literally true.

But there is even more. The IARPA is also developing an "eye in the sky" system that is intended to predict political instability in the world and threats before they materialize. This would in principle include the ability to predict crimes before they happen and thus carry with it the prospect of arresting individuals before they actually commit these crimes.[29]

Given such a global brain, surveillance tentacles will sprout up to gather data from the general population. This is not conjecture, it is already happening. For example, Manhattan and London feature networks of surveillance cameras with facial recognition software, installed in public places as well as some private places, such as banks. These cameras are also linked to government agency databases and may well in the future link to the Utah Center when it is up and running.[30]

RELATED VALIDATED INDEPENDENT NEWS STORY

Drones at Home

Unmanned Aerial Vehicles (UAVs) are now in operation in cities such as Miami for police surveillance purposes. Although the mainstream media regularly cover the use of such technology for "drone strikes" against terrorists in Afghanistan, there is scarce coverage of the domestic use of UAVs for policing purposes.

Such surveillance technologies may soon add aerial eyes and ears to the network of Total Information Awareness now in progress, thereby converting these devices into police informants that monitor our every move, and adding this information to the global network of data stored in a central data bank. In this brave new world, each of us will be under careful scrutiny by an "all-seeing" global eye with the capacity to draw inferences about our future actions—and "crimes."

When this happens, we will have lost our freedom—not to some foreign nation that "hates our freedom," but to our own devices. As we advance further and further into a police state, these changes may occur subtly, and we may be inclined to accept each successive change on the path to a totalitarian state. Therefore we must, as citizens of the free world, be willing to draw the line while there is freedom enough left to draw it.

ELLIOT D. COHEN is a contributor to *Truthout* and *Truthdig*, editor in chief of the *International Journal of Applied Philosophy*, ethics editor for *Free Inquiry* magazine, and blogger for *Psychology Today*. One of his most recent books is *Mass Surveillance and State Control: The Total Information Awareness Project* (Palgrave Macmillan, 2010).

Notes

1. "UNICOR Federal Prisons Industries, Inc.," Federal Bureau of Prisons, accessed May 21, 2012, http://www.bop.gov/inmate_programs/unicor.jsp.

2. Federal Bureau of Prisons, "Quick Facts About the Bureau of Prisons," May 26, 2012, http://www.bop.gov/about/facts.jsp#2.

3. Diane Cardwell, "Private Businesses Fight Federal Prisons for Contracts," *New York Times*, March 14, 2012, http://www.nytimes.com/2012/03/15/business/private-businesses-fight-federal-prisons-for-contracts.html?_r=2&pagewanted=all.

4. See, for example, Daniel P. Mears and Jamie Watson, "Towards a Fair and Balanced Assessment of Supermax Prisons," *Justice Quarterly* 23 (2006): 232, http://www.supermaxed.com/NewSupermaxMaterials/Mears-Watson-Balanced.pdf.

5. James Ridgeway and Jean Casella, "Cruel and Usual: US Solitary Confinement," Al Jazeera English, March 19, 2011, http://www.aljazeera.com/indepth/features/2011/03/201137125936219469.html.

6. Ibid.

7. Ibid.

8. Ibid.

9. John Del Signore, "NYPD Narcotics Detective Admits Cops Regularly Plant Drugs On Perps," *Gothamist*, October 13, 2011, http://gothamist.com/2011/10/13/nypd_narcotics_detective_testifies.php.

10. Ibid.

11. Ibid.

12. On Bloomberg's confessed marijuana use, see, e.g., Jennifer Steinhauer, "Bloomberg Says He Regrets Marijuana Remarks," *New York Times*, April 10, 2002, http://www.nytimes.com/2002/04/10/nyregion/bloomberg-says-he-regrets-marijuana-remarks.html.

13. Harry G. Levine and Lauren Siegel, "$75 Million a Year: The Cost of New York City's Marijuana Possession Arrests," *Drug Policy Alliance*, March 2011, http://www.drugpolicy.org/docUploads/_75_Million_A_Year.pdf.

14. See John Eligon, "Taking On Police Tactic, Critics Hit Racial Divide," *New York Times*, March 22, 2012, http://www.nytimes.com/2012/03/23/nyregion/fighting-stop-and-frisk-tactic-but-hitting-racial-divide.html.

15. See, for example, Jillian Scharr, "City's Stop-And-Frisks, Marijuana Arrests Raise Controversy," NBC, July 23, 2010, http://www.nbcnewyork.com/news/local/Marijuana-arrests-99108834.html.

16. Trevor Aaronson, "The Informants," *Mother Jones*, September/October 2011, http://www.motherjones.com/politics/2011/08/fbi-terrorist-informants.

17. Ibid.

18. Ibid.

19. Ibid.

20. Naomi Wolf, "The Spectacle of Terror and its Vested Interests," *Guardian*, May 9, 2012, http://www.guardian.co.uk/commentisfree/cifamerica/2012/may/09/spectacle-terror-vested-interests.

21. Federal Restricted Buildings and Grounds Improvement Act of 2011, 8 U.S.C. § 1752 (2011), http://www.gpo.gov/fdsys/pkg/BILLS-112hr347enr/pdf/BILLS-112hr347enr.pdf.

22. National Defense Authorization Act for Fiscal Year 2012, 10 U.S.C. § 1031(b)2 (2011), http://www.gpo.gov/fdsys/pkg/BILLS-112s1867pcs/pdf/BILLS-112s1867pcs.pdf.

23. Ibid., §1031(c)4.

24. See, for example, Charlie Savage, "Obama Drops Veto Threat Over Military Authorization Bill After Revisions," *New York Times*, December 14, 2011, http://www.nytimes.com/2011/12/15/us/politics/obama-wont-veto-military-authorization-bill.html.

25. White House, *Executive Order: National Defense Resources Preparedness*, Part 2, § 201(b), Office of the Press Secretary, March 16, 2012, http://www.whitehouse.gov/the-press-office/2012/03/16/executive-order-national-defense-resources-preparedness.

26. Ibid., Part 3, § 308(a).

27. James Bamford, "The NSA Is Building the Country's Biggest Spy Center (Watch What You Say)," *Wired*, March 15, 2012, http://www.wired.com/threatlevel/2012/03/ff_nsadatacenter.

28. "Meet Catalyst: IARPA's Entity and Relationship Extraction Program," Public Intelligence, April 4, 2012, http://publicintelligence.net/meet-catalyst.

29. Jon Markoff, "Government Aims to Build a 'Data Eye in the Sky,'" *New York Times*, October 10, 2011, http://www.nytimes.com/2011/10/11/science/11predict.html?_r=2&pagewanted=all.

30. Elliot D. Cohen, *Mass Surveillance and State Control: The Total Information Awareness Project* (New York: Palgrave Macmillan, 2010).

From "Bankster Bailout" to "Blessed Unrest"

News We Can Use to Create a US Economy for the 99 Percent

by Dr. Rob Williams

Vice is beneficial, found
When it's by Justice, lop't and bound

—Bernard Mandeville, *The Fable of the Bees: Private Vices, Publick Benefits*

Sometimes the ideas we are certain are true are dead wrong. Rich people don't create jobs.

—Nick Hanauer, Seattle entrepreneur, *Banned TED Talk*

The Daily Prophet *is bound to report the truth occasionally, if only accidentally.*

—Albus Dumbledore, *Harry Potter and the Half-Blood Prince*

Censored #5

First Federal Reserve Audit Reveals Trillions Loaned to Major Banks

Matthew Cardinale, "First Federal Reserve Audit Reveals Trillions in Secret Bailout," Inter Press Service, *Common Dreams*, August 28, 2011, http://www.commondreams.org/headline/2011/08/28-3?.

Student Researcher: Nicole Trupiano (Sonoma State University)

Faculty Evaluator: Peter Phillips (Sonoma State University)

Censored #6

Small Network of Corporations Run the Global Economy

Rob Waugh, "Does One 'Super Corporation' Run the Global Economy? Study Claims it Could be Terrifyingly Unstable," *Daily Mail*, October 20, 2011, http://www.dailymail.co.uk/sciencetech/article-2051008/Does-super-corporation-run-global-economy.html.

Stefania Vitali, James B. Glattfelder, and Stefano Battiston, "The Network of Global Corporate Control," *Public Library of Science*, October 26, 2011, http://www.plosone.org/article/info%3Adoi%2F10.1371%2Fjournal.pone.0025995.

Student Researcher: Sean Lawrence (Sonoma State University)

Faculty Evaluator: Peter Phillips (Sonoma State University)

Censored #7

2012: The International Year of Cooperatives

Jessica Reeder, "The Year of the Cooperative," *Yes! Magazine*, February 1, 2012, http://www.yes-magazine.org/new-economy/2012-the-year-of-the-cooperative.

Monique Hairston, "American Dream 2.0: Can Worker-Owned Coops End Poverty?" *Rebuild the Dream*, March 9, 2012, http://www.rebuildthedream.com/blog/2012/03/09/american-dream-2-0-can-worker-owned-coops-end-poverty.

Student Researcher: Shahin Karimbeik (San Francisco State University)

Faculty Evaluator: Kenn Burrows (San Francisco State University)

Censored #11

Members of Congress Grow Wealthier Despite Recession

Luke Johnson, "Members of Congress Grow Wealthier Despite Recession," *Huffington Post*, November 1, 2011, http://www.huffingtonpost.com/2011/11/01/congress-net-wealth-income-gap_n_1069377.html.

Student Researcher: Ellis Huber (Sonoma State University)

Faculty Evaluator: Peter Phillips (Sonoma State University)

Censored #13

Education "Reform" a Trojan Horse for Privatization

Paul Rosenberg, "Education 'Reform' Vs. the 99%," *Random Lengths News*, February 10–23, 2012, http://www.randomlengthsnews.com/images/IssuePDFs/2012-feb/rl_02-09-12.pdf.

Paul Thomas, "Testing and Poverty in Education," *The Daily Censored* (blog), August 8, 2011, http://www.dailycensored.com/2011/08/08/poverty-and-testing-in-education-the-present-scientifico-legal-complex.

Student Researcher: Samantha George (Sonoma State University)

Faculty Evaluators: Crystal White and Peter Phillips (Sonoma State University)

Censored #14

Who Are the Top 1 Percent and How Do They Earn a Living?

Mike Konczal, "Who Are the 1 Percent and What Do They Do for a Living?," *Rortybomb*, October 17, 2011, http://rortybomb.wordpress.com/2011/10/14/who-are-the-1-and-what-do-they-do-for-a-living.

Student Researcher: Nicole Trupiano (Sonoma State University)

Faculty Evaluator: Peter Phillips (Sonoma State University)

Censored #17

Students Crushed by One Trillion Dollars in Student Loans

Ellen Brown, "A Jubilee for Student Debt?" *Yes! Magazine*, October 20, 2011, http://www.yesmagazine.org/new-economy/a-jubilee-for-student-debt.

Alex Pareene, "The $1 Trillion Student Loan Rip-Off: How an Entire Generation Was Tricked into Taking on Crushing Debt that Just Enriches Banks," *AlterNet*, October 20, 2011, http://www.alternet.org/story/152809/the_$1_trillion_student_loan_rip-off%3A_how_an_entire_generation_was_tricked_into_taking_on_crushing_debt_that_just_enriches_banks/?page=1.

Student Researcher: Joshua Nervis (Sonoma State University)

Faculty Evaluator: David McCuan (Sonoma State University)

Censored #20

Stealing from Public Education to Feed the Prison-Industrial Complex

Adwoa Masozi, "Stealing From The Mouth of Public Education to Feed the Prison Industrial Complex," *Institute for Policy Studies*, February 27, 2012, http://www.ips-dc.org/blog/stealing_from_the_mouth_of_public_education_to_feed_the_prison_industrial_complex.

Student Researcher: Annika Jaeger (Santa Rosa Junior College)

Faculty Evaluator: Susan Rahman (Santa Rosa Junior College)

Censored #21

Conservatives Attack US Post Office to Break the Union and Privatize Postal Services

Allison Kilkenny, "Postal Workers Under Assault in Planned Demolishment Privatization Plan," *Truthout*, September 8, 2011, http://www.truth-out.org/last-union/1315492298.

Matt Taibbi, "Don't Let Business Lobbyists Kill the Post Office," *Rolling Stone*, April 23, 2012, http://www.rollingstone.com/politics/blogs/taibblog/dont-let-business-lobbyists-kill-the-post-office-20120423.

Student Evaluator: Dane Steffy (Sonoma State University)

Faculty Evaluator: Peter Phillips (Sonoma State University)

Censored #22

Wachovia Bank Laundered Money for Latin American Drug Cartels

Clarence Walker, "American Banks 'High' on Drug Money: How a Whistleblower Blew the Lid off Wachovia-Drug Cartel Money Laundering Scheme," *AlterNet*, November 1, 2011, http://www.alternet.org/story/151135/american_banks_'high'_on_drug_money:_how_a_whistleblower_blew_the_lid_off_wachovia-drug_cartel_money_laundering_scheme%3E.

Student Researcher: Alysha Klein (Florida Atlantic University)

Faculty Evaluator: James F. Tracy (Florida Atlantic University)

"OUR ECONOMY?" SAYS WHO?

"Economy." The Greeks had a word for it. *Oikos* (management of the house) is the ancient root of our modern English word that gets bandied about quite a bit during these interesting times, usually possessive, in the singular. You know. "Our economy." Tell me if you've heard this one-sentence story before: More than 300 million Americans "share" an "economy" that, by all accounts, is going through a time of tremendous tumult. Sound familiar? This oft-told story about a mythical "our economy" ignores the ever-deepening socioeconomic divisions in a country more sharply divided along class lines than it has been in decades. Far from shedding light on this situation, our corporate commercial "news" media (air quotes around the word "news," please) too often report on this fabled "our economy" in ways that obfuscate or ignore the most important economic news of our time. What should they be doing? Helping citizens connect the dots to paint a picture of how our collective house is "managed" by federal and state governments, increasingly in the pocket of large transnational corporations whose primary *raison d'etre* is profit maximization over all other social and economic values (think meaningful jobs, safe working environments, clean air and water, affordable education, and accessible health care, for starters). This troubling situation is worth exploring in more depth.

The job of journalists, one wag once noted, channeling the fearless Socialist agitator Mary Harris "Mother" Jones, is "to comfort the afflicted and afflict the comfortable." And a truly democratic news media culture, as media critics have often noted, is one that provides a wide variety of different perspectives on important issues of our time, and continually asks hard questions that challenge the richest and most powerful among us. Alas, our national "news" media too often publish at the behest of their corporate masters, and nowhere is this more true than in how US mainstream news channels report and distort "economic" news.

As the Occupy Wall Street movement has famously proclaimed, Americans live in an economy where the 1 percent of the superrich lord over the other 99 percent—what might be best called a "kleptocracy" ("government by theft") as described by Pulitzer Prize–winning historian Jared Diamond.[1] One spring 2012 estimate of wealth (mal-)distribution in the United States' economy concluded that 400 individuals at the top now own more assets than the bottom 160 million citizens.[2] It is this 1 percent of the US population—CEOs, financial professionals (let's call them "the banksters"), lawyers, real estate, and medical professionals—who have gobbled up the lion's share of the nation's wealth due to excessive deregulation, the decline of unionization, and the off-shoring and outsourcing of real work that has accompanied a complex series of economic trends simplistically dubbed "globalization" by the news media during the past several decades.

Censored #14: Who Are the Top 1 Percent and How Do They Earn a Living?

Mike Konczal charts jobs and income growth of the top 1 percent earners and the causes of changing income inequality. Evidence from tax returns depicts the top occupations as follows: nonfinancial executives first, then financial professionals, followed by lawyers, and then real estate and medical professions. Konczal found that 60 percent of the top percentile of income goes to these top professions. Quoting from J. W. Mason's *Slack Wire* blog, Konczal noted that the way our laws structure corporations, "'a business exists only to enrich its shareholders, including, of course, senior managers themselves,' and this is done by paying out more in dividends that is earned in profits." This reality about "our economy" is what upsets the people of the Occupy Wall Street movement. The top 1 percent are "cashing out wealth during the good times and then leaving workers and the rest of the real economy to deal with the aftermath." There's good reason to focus on the top 1 percent instead of the top 10 or 50 percent. Evidence suggests that financial pay at this elite level is correlated with deregulation and the other legal changes that brought on the crisis. High-ranking senior corporate executives' pay has dwarfed workers' salaries, but is only a reward for engaging in shady financial engineering practices. These problems require legal solutions, a democratic challenge, and a rethinking of how we ought to restructure "our economy."

Who is really in the driver's seat of "our economy"? Let two examples help answer this question, Censored stories #5 and #22.

Censored #5: First Federal Reserve Audit Reveals Trillions Loaned to Major Banks

Matthew Cardinale reported that an audit of the Federal Reserve "revealed 16 trillion dollars in secret bank bailouts." He described how many financial institutions boasted of plenty of cash in their reserves while they were actually receiving loans. Sixteen trillion dollars is a huge figure, and Cardinale explained that "overall, the greatest borrowing was done by a small number of institutions. Over the three years, Citigroup borrowed a total of 2.5 trillion dollars, Morgan Stanley borrowed two trillion," and "the majority of the loans were issued by the Federal Reserve Bank of New York." Cardinale observed that lending and borrowing on this scale illustrates the weakness of the financial sector within "our economy."

Although the banks here at home were taking out massive loans from the Fed, they were not the only ones, as Cardinale concluded. Financial institutions abroad were also taking advantage of the bailout; the United Kingdom, France, and Germany were just a few of the countries that received federal money. "The Federal Reserve has neither explained how they legally justified several of the emergency loans, nor how they decided to provide assistance to certain firms but not others," Cardinale wrote. Without a formal justification from the Fed, Cardinale's sources had some opinions of their own. Some said it was simply a "lack of congressional oversight" while others claimed that it was "a clear case of socialism." The Federal Reserve clearly has some restructuring to do, and according to the audit report, all of the loans are being repaid or have already been repaid.

Censored #22: Wachovia Bank Laundered Money for Latin American Drug Cartels

Writing for *AlterNet*, Clarence Walker provided a second example of who sits in the driver's seat of "our economy." Between 2004 and 2007, Wachovia Bank handled funds totaling $378.4 billion for Mexican currency-exchange houses acting on behalf of drug cartels. Although Wachovia concedes it "didn't do enough to spot illicit funds," the transactions amount to the largest violation of the Bank Secrecy Act, an anti-money-laundering law, in US history. As context, between 2006 and 2010, over 22,000 people have been killed in drug-related battles that have raged mostly along the 2,000-mile (3,200-kilometer) Mexico-US border. Illegal narcotics cost the US economy $215 billion annually. Martin Woods, who directed Wachovia's anti-money-laundering unit in London from 2006 to 2009, left the bank after Wachovia executives disregarded documentation he produced showing

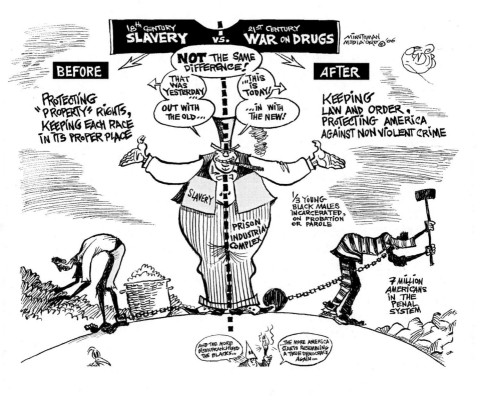

that drug dealers were channeling money through Wachovia's branch network.

What's even more troubling as we consider this example in light of "our economy"? The case of Wachovia is not exceptional. The bank is just one of many US and European banks that the drug cartels have used to launder money. Since the early 1990s, Latin American drug traffickers have gone to US banks to launder their dirty cash, according to Paul Campo, head of the US Drug Enforcement Administration's financial crimes unit. So much for the rules ostensibly governing the "free enterprise" system, financial transparency, and political accountability when it comes to the most wealthy and powerful among us.

In sum, if we look beyond the much-fabled "our economy" jargon as proclaimed by the well-coiffed and well-paid pundits and prognosticators who inhabit the pages and airwaves of corporate commercial "news," it becomes clear that our national economic house is on fire, the arsonists are still in the building, and the US "news" media are too often fanning the flames instead of organizing the bucket brigade. And what of our national government? Are they working on our behalf to create a level playing field to create equality of opportunity for all? Or are they simply high-fiving with Adam Smith's so-called "invisible hand" of the marketplace with one palm, while holding out the other for corporate checks, instead of pushing for "checks and balances" within our economic system?

Start with the Supreme Court. I've got two words for you: Citizens United. What of the executive branch, and President Barack Obama's much-vaunted "hope and change" rhetoric from 2008? Time for a reality check. Congress? Read the much-hyped Dodd-Frank Wall Street Reform and Consumer Protection Act—the most complex, arcane, and toothless legislation devised by the Beltway crowd—and then weep. And what of the Democrats and Republicans in the US Congress? Let's ask the question a different way. Why should members of Congress be too concerned about the real state of the US economy? Story #11 can explain.

Censored #11: Members of Congress Grow Wealthier Despite Recession

While average Americans' net worth declined significantly between 2007 and 2009 (from $125,000 to $96,000) due to declining home equity and investment activity, Luke Johnson reported that the net worth of our congressional representatives continued to rise, from $1.65 billion in 2008, to over $2 billion.

Johnson's analysis of financial disclosure forms did not include non-income-producing assets. Rep. Darrell Issa (R-CA) reported that his assets were worth at least $295 million. House Minority Leader Nancy Pelosi's (D-CA) wealth also increased, from $21.7 million in 2009 to $35.2 million in 2010. Speaker of the House John Boehner (R-OH), Senate Majority Leader Harry Reid (D-NV), and Senate Minority Leader Mitch McConnell (R-KY) all had multimillion-dollar net worths in 2010.

To summarize our two-party system's relationship to "our economy," "there are no longer two political parties in the United States, each offering a constructive if differing view of how to secure the welfare, prosperity, security and liberty of the American people," explained political analyst Mike Krauss. "Instead, there is one party," he concluded, "the party of corporate profit and the status quo, kept in power by the ability to spend vast sums of money no political party can hope to match, and able to so dominate elections as to set up a choice for president that can only be described as one between two sides of the same bent coin."[3]

Censored #6: Small Network of Corporations Run the Global Economy

The consolidation of wealth is not unique to the United States, of course, as is dramatically documented by a 2011 study showing that a small network of corporations exert global influence on the international economy. The study, completed by Stefania Vitali, James B. Glattfelder, Stefano Battiston at the Swiss Federal Institute in Zurich, is the first to look at all 43,060 transnational corporations and the web of ownership among them. They mapped the 1,318 companies at the heart of the global economy and identified 147 companies that form a "super entity" within this web, controlling 40 percent of the world's wealth. Most of the companies comprising this super entity are banks, including, for example, Barclays and Goldman Sachs. The "super" 147 are "at least in the position to exert considerable control, either formally (e.g., voting in shareholder and board meetings) or via informal negotiations." At the same time, their close connections mean that the network is "prone to systemic risk" and vulnerable to collapse.

Economists such as John Driffil of the University of London, a macroeconomics expert, stated that the value of its study wasn't to determine *who* controlled the global economy, but, rather, to illustrate the tight connections among the world's largest companies. Some of the assumptions underlying the study have been under criticism—such as the idea that ownership equates to control. But the Swiss researchers have simply applied mathematical models conventionally used to model natural systems to the world economy, using data from Orbis 2007, a database listing thirty-seven million companies and investors.

So, from both a national and international perspective, "our economy" looks fairly grim, a system run by banksters in collusion with compliant politicians, and an economy marked by bailouts for the superrich (the 1 percent) and shrinking economic opportunities for everyone else (us, the 99 percent). *Censored 2013* offers a number of case studies regarding how the US "news" media cover and cover up our economic life. Here are three dots to connect that help us understand the true scope of our economic challenges.

Censored #13: Education "Reform" a Trojan Horse for Privatization

Begin with news coverage of US public education, one of the oldest and most democratic collective projects in the United States. The history of public education is complex and multifaceted, but the core premise is elegantly simple: to ensure virtuous citizens and a capable work force, the United States must collectively invest time, money, energy, and purpose in preparing its young people for adult life. As Paul Rosenberg of *Random Lengths News*, and Paul Thomas, writing for the *Daily Censored*, made clear, after a decade of local school districts and individual states administering federal testing mandates in the form of the George W. Bush administration's No Child Left Behind (NCLB) policies and the Obama administration's Race to the Top program, national educational progress has actually worsened.

In January 2012, FairTest, the National Center for Fair and Open Testing, reported that a decade of No Child Left Behind (NCLB) policies had actually slowed the rate of education progress. The report, "NCLB's Lost Decade for Education Progress," concluded that the law had "failed badly both in terms of its own goals and more broadly." The FairTest findings are based on data from the National Assessment of Educational Progress (NAEP) and dozens of independent studies. One of NCLB's most outspoken critics, Diane Ravitch, sees current corporate efforts to "reform" public education as a thinly disguised attack on it. "Public education today is the target of a well-coordinated, well-funded campaign to privatize as many schools as possible, particularly in cities. This campaign claims it wants great teachers in every classroom, but its rhetoric demoralizes teachers, and reduces the status of the education profession," Ravitch told a Los Angeles audience in February 2012. "There is no historical comparison to [the] current movement for privatization and de-professionalization."

These reform efforts include President Obama's Race to the Top program, which Ravitch calls "No Child Left Behind 2.0." Race to the Top entails more high-stakes testing, more school privatization, and the closing of schools with large numbers of low-performing students. As Ravitch noted, "A race has one winner and many losers. That's not what we want for our children." Instead, the core rhetoric of "reform" features testing and accountability, the very management principles that have been the status quo in American education for twenty years. The driving logic for such reform is profits. "Wall Street hedge fund managers are heavily invested in this," Ravitch argued. "This is really an issue of the 1 percent vs. the 99 percent. . . . The more privatization, the less people will work together as communities."

As National Education Policy Center managing director Bill Mathis concluded, "This set of reforms has been the dominant educational philosophy for the past 20 years—and has yet to register a single sustained success across any urban district in the nation. . . . A child living in poverty with a single parent, a sketchy neighborhood, rotten teeth and bad nutrition is not going to be saved because the third grade teacher adopted Pearson Corporation's latest national curriculum manual."[4]

What's curious about the "managed" nature of corporate news coverage on this important story is how US "news" purveyors, unlike Mathis, continually fail to ask basic questions about the efficacy of these federal "educational" programs, even as they report on what the "news makers"—Bush, Obama, their secretaries of education, and other important establishment figures—assert about them. What's worse, US news coverage often perpetuates simplistic stereotypes about the alleged failure of the US public education system, helped along by popular documentaries like Davis Guggenheim's 2010 film, *Waiting for Superman*, which functioned as masterful propaganda for the pro-privatization forces interested in co-opting public schools for private gain. The conventional wisdom, Ravitch wrote in a scathing critique of the film, now seems to go something like this:

American public education is a failed enterprise. The problem is not money. Public schools already spend too much. Test scores are low because there are so many bad teachers, whose jobs are protected by powerful unions. Students drop out because the schools fail them, but they could accomplish practically anything if they were saved from bad teachers.

They would get higher test scores if schools could fire more bad teachers and pay more to good ones. The only hope for the future of our society, especially for poor black and Hispanic children, is escape from public schools, especially to charter schools, which are mostly funded by the government but controlled by private organizations, many of them operating to make a profit.[5]

If this *Waiting for Superman* logic sounds familiar, even for *Censored 2013* readers who have not seen the film, it may be because this educational tale is told and retold in our national "news" media *ad nauseum*, to the extent that it is commonly accepted as truth by citizens who lack direct experience with the public schools in their very own communities. What most "news" reports fail to acknowledge is this: as "our economy" continues to defund public schools, de-professionalize educators, and aggressively promote privatization as the solution to the many complexities that bedevil our public education system, it is ultimately our students who end up in a race to the bottom.

Censored #20: Stealing from Public Education to Feed the Prison-Industrial Complex

Even more insidious, as Adwoa Masozi of the Institute for Policy Studies has suggested, is the relationship between the aggressive attacks on our public school system and the rise of the private prison-industrial complex in the United States. What is the big picture behind funding cuts for our public school systems? We do not hear that some of the largest backers of the public school systems also derive lucrative profits from private prisons. "On top of cutting 4 billion dollars from their budget, Texas has also eliminated state funding for pre-K programs that serve around 100,000 mostly at-risk children," Masozi reported. North Carolina also cut half a billion in school programs, resulting in less support for social workers and guidance counselors. Losses in the school programs such as these contribute to dropout rates of approximately 27 percent. Once again, public education is being threatened by for-profit forces operating within "our economy."

"Public education is something more than a right, a liberty, or a privilege," Masozi wrote, "It is a need." At too many schools, metal detectors and police, rather than extracurricular activities, have become the norm. Charter schools offer some creative solutions, but in their current incarnation, they fail to serve all students needing an education. Increasingly, corporate entities such as Wells Fargo, Bank of America, J. P. Morgan, and Wal-Mart back both charter education and private prisons, Masozi reported. The increasing prison population is an indirect result of the school system not supporting students or giving them the proper tools for learning. A majority of the people in prisons do not have high school diplomas.

In sum, a defunded public school system that leaves children behind also promotes a more Hobbesian social milieu marked by greater poverty, misery, and lack of meaningful professional and vocational opportunities. Desperation, despair, and drugs fill the void, and prisons, when they are transformed into privatized for-profit institutions, offer investors more opportunities to maximize their return by increasing the levels of incarceration among US society's most underserved populations. Currently six million citizens are under "correctional supervision," a figure that surpasses Stalin's Gulag Archipelago.[6]

The sinister relationship between attempts to privatize education and the rise of a for-profit prison-industrial complex is one economic story of vital significance that is effectively censored—it never makes the pages or airwaves of the United States' corporate "news" outlets.

Censored #17: Students Crushed by One Trillion Dollars in Student Loans

Turning to higher education, the story of US "news" coverage is a bit different. Remember the Servicemen's Readjustment Act of 1944, commonly called the GI Bill? Passed by Congress in 1944, the visionary education law provided a whole host of benefits for returning World War II veterans, including cash payments to attend college or vocational school. By the time the program ended twelve years later, in 1956, more than two million veterans had gone back to college on the GI Bill, with another more than 6.5 million using the bill to seek some sort of educational training program. Observers from across the political spectrum heralded the legislation, rightly recognizing that a federal government investment in veterans' education would be of tremendous benefit to the United States' economic future. Even today, the GI Bill is remembered as one of the most important pieces of education legislation in US history. How do we judge? Just look at the numbers. The GI Bill produced seven dollars of economic growth for every dollar invested by Congress, making it "one of the best investments Congress ever made," according to independent financial analyst Ellen Brown, author of the must-read history *Web of Debt*.[7]

Fast-forward to today. Talk to US college or university students and you will discover that, most likely, they have borrowed money to help pay for their higher education. What is astonishing is the staggering amount of collective debt burdening college students today. As Alex Pareene reported for *AlterNet* in October 2011, student loan debt was then poised to exceed one trillion dollars, surpassing even US credit card debt.[8] Students have accepted debt loads that sometimes rival those of a home mortgage, before they have graduated and established regular incomes, based on phony promises. Due to a 2005 bankruptcy bill, debtors cannot discharge student loans through bankruptcy; thus, unlike corporations, students cannot declare bankruptcy. Meanwhile, as the government is shielded from the risk, and creditors are licensed to collect by almost any means they deem necessary, the student loan epidemic threatens to lead a generation into wage slavery. If students are lucky enough to find a job during our economic crisis, they will be spending much of their money paying off their student loans, and the banks will continue to see massive profits.

Prompted perhaps by independent media's initial coverage of this story, corporate "news" outlets such as CBS and the *New York Times* began to report on the national student debt crisis during spring 2012. Rarely, however, did their stories highlight the enormous profits made by banksters in particular, or by the system as a whole. One exception? Bloomberg ran a May 2012 story on the piles of cash being raked in by taxpayer-funded student-loan debt collectors like Joshua Mandelman and his boss Richard Boyle of Minnesota-based Educational Credit Management Corporation (ECMC), who together pocketed more than $1.5 million in 2010 for chasing down and recovering student loans in a partnership agreement with the US government.[9]

Instead, the corporate news media's fragmented coverage focused on "human interest" stories of indebted students and their families, and the efforts of higher education to help solve an economic problem spiraling out of control. The titles of the two-part "Degrees of Debt" *New York Times* feature that ran during May 2012 are illustrative—"A Generation Hobbled by the Soaring Cost of College" and "Slowly, as Student Debt Rises, Colleges Confront Costs."[10] *New York Times* journalist Andrew Martin portrayed Wall Street as an interested and helpful observer in the midst of this crisis, a player without any skin in the game, rather than a stakeholder making huge profits from this abysmal situation. Martin quoted an analyst from Moody's Investors Service, saying that "tuition levels are at a tipping point" and that "we anticipate an ongoing bifurcation of student demand favoring the highest quality and most affordable higher education options." This jargon is Wall Street shorthand acknowledging the widening gap between the 1 percent who can afford to pay for an elite college education, and the other 99 percent, who are stuck with deepening levels of debt or a difficult decision not to attend college at all because it is simply unaffordable.[11]

The way that corporate media frame this issue—with an exclusive focus on debt-ridden students, their families, and colleges struggling to rethink "best practices" when it comes to affordable education—ignores the most basic economic issues at the heart of the student debt crisis, including, most significantly, how Wall Street's predatory loaning practices, in collusion with 24/7 corporate commercial marketing, promote usury that enriches banks and lenders at the expense of the hopes and ambitions of our nation's young people. Even more troubling, corporate news seldom reports on potential solutions to the student debt crisis, such as interest-free student loans, for example, or the creation of a student debt jubilee, in which the Federal Reserve would do for students what it has done for the banksters, quantitatively easing one trillion dollars of toxic debt from the backs of students and stimulating the economy as a result.[12]

Censored #21: Conservatives Attack US Post Office to Break the Union and Privatize Postal Services

With the possible exception of the US Constitution and the National Park System (both under siege), the United States Postal Service (USPS) may be one of the most important sociopolitical and economic institutions birthed by the US republic, one of the United States' great gifts to the modern world. Older than the Constitution and currently the nation's largest union and second largest public employer, the USPS employs more than 574,000 workers and has played a central role in stimulating national commerce, promoting ideas, and making possible the low-cost democratic flow of information for all citizens across the country, rich or poor. But these days, "our economy" seems impatient with a national post office that (we are told) may have lost its relevance in the age of Federal Express, UPS, and the Internet. However, Allison Kilkenny, writing for *Truthout*, and Matt Taibbi, of *Rolling Stone*, have provided a different lens through which to view the US Postal Service's "crisis."

The postal service has been under constant assault for years from conservative Republicans, who view the attack on the USPS as an epic battle to take down the strongest union in the country and as a means to roll the United States ever closer toward full privatization. The postal service isn't paid for by taxpayer dollars, but rather fully funded by postage sales. Nonetheless, Congress passed the 2006 Postal Accountability and Enhancement Act (PAEA), mandating that the postal service fully fund retiree health benefits for future retirees. The act requires that USPS pay $5.5 billion to the Treasury every September, to pre-fund future retirees' health benefits. Thus, the USPS must fund the retirement packages of future employees who have not even been born. An audit done by the USPS Office of Inspector General came up with the figure of seventy-five billion dollars in pension overpayments. Revealingly, when the Postal Regulatory Commission, an independent agency that actually received more autonomous power under PAEA, commissioned its own independent audit, they placed the overpayment at fifty billion dollars. Taking these figures into consideration, the projected nine-billion-dollar deficit the USPS now faces seems like small change that could easily be corrected with minor accounting adjustments. This would eliminate the "crisis"— which is driving the proposals to terminate Saturday mail delivery service, close mail processing centers, and lay off 120,000 workers. (Over the last four years, the postal service's work force has shrunk by over 100,000 employees due to attrition).

Let's unwrap this special delivery. The ways that corporate media report on the USPS's current performance is a classic example of mis-framing, drawing narrative lines around a story to emphasize certain elements while completely ignoring other vital contexts that provide a more complete understanding. We are told ad nauseum that the USPS is in crisis because the lightning-fast Internet Age reveals how the Postal Service has become bloated, inefficient, and overly bureaucratic. In this view, competing private carriers deliver packages faster (though more expensively, we might remember). This assertion ignores the fact that 2006 marked the USPS's single biggest mail-carrying volume year in its entire 237-year history, not to mention what a remarkably democratic and accessible national service the USPS provides. "The Postal Service isn't paid for by taxpayer dollars, but rather fully funded by the sale of stamps," noted *Truthout*'s Allison Kilkenny. "It's easy to forget what a marvel this is—that today, in 2011, one can still mail a letter clear across the country for less than 50 cents. And if the impressiveness of that feat still hasn't sunk in, attempt this brain exercise: consider what else you can buy for $0.44."[13]

One of the only US journalists to report on the "crisis" surrounding the USPS in meaningful political terms, Kilkenny went on to interview New York Metro Area Postal Union political director Chuck Zlatkin, who provided a counter to US corporate "news" reporting on the controversy surrounding the USPS. "It's part of the class war and it's against the poor and it's a class war against working people," explained Zlatkin.

> Any time a post office is rumored to be closing, it's devastating to the neighborhood that it's in. . . . What happens when we get involved with elected officials and community people to try and keep a post office open, it's always the same people who turn out: elderly people, disabled people, poor people, and small business owners. They're the people who are the ones that depend on the postal service that they can't really afford or have access to alternatives.

The United States Postal Service "caters primarily to the economically disadvantaged and employs over 574,000 union members," Kilkenny concluded, reframing the issue in new political and economic terms. "No wonder it has become such a mouth-watering target for the GOP," she wrote, whose goal may be "to take out one of the largest unions in the country and simultaneously give the US a nudge in the direction of total privatization by crippling one of the last great public services."[14] Whether or not the USPS will survive in "our economy" remains to be seen, but understanding the larger political context of the USPS "crisis" is one message that our corporate media's "managed" news coverage simply does not deliver (unlike your mail, which arrives faithfully most every day of the week).

THE "BLESSED UNREST": RESTORING GRACE, JUSTICE, AND BEAUTY TO "OUR ECONOMY"

"Poor Americans are urged to hate themselves" and "glorify their betters," wrote Kurt Vonnegut in his masterful dystopian novel *Slaughterhouse-Five*.[15] Vonnegut's fictional observation resonates every day in the pages and on the airwaves of our national corporate "news." In the real world, where infotainment, propaganda, and public relations all substitute for in-depth investigative reporting, we desperately need real news to reclaim "our economy" for everyone, and not just the 1 percent who currently reap its benefits. Indeed, given how high the stakes are for "our economy," the 99 percent best get busy challenging the 1 percent's dominance. The good news, as Project Censored reminds us, is that help is on the way, in the form of the millions of citizens who are doing the hard work of reclaiming "our economy" from the banksters.

In 2007, entrepreneur and *Ecology of Commerce* author Paul Hawken published *Blessed Unrest*, in which he described "how the largest social movement in history is restoring grace, justice, and beauty to the world." He observed, "If you look at the science that describes what is happening on earth today and aren't pessimistic, you don't have the current data." "If you meet the people in this unnamed movement and aren't optimistic, you haven't got a heart."[16] Thus Hawken reminds us of Project Censored's importance, providing global citizens with "current data" to better inform themselves and join the fray over "our economy" and a host of other vital issues. To put it another way, as imprisoned Italian philosopher Antonio

Gramsci famously did, we must all practice "pessimism of the intellect, optimism of the will."[17]

The hopeful news is this: the "blessed unrest" Hawken describes is all around us, even if you won't read much about it in the corporate media. For starters, the Occupy Wall Street movement, which burst onto the international scene in fall 2011, has succeeded in reframing the debate over "our economy" by continually reminding all of us, through street heat, guerrilla action, and a potpourri of new media messaging strategies, that "our economy" is currently managed by and for the rich as a national kleptocracy that robs from the 99 percent to enrich the 1 percent.

While Occupy continues to agitate, US citizens—and people around the world—are moving to reclaim economic and political power and reinvent how economies function at local, state, and regional levels.

Censored #7: 2012: The International Year of Cooperatives

The return of cooperatives is one encouraging example. The United Nations named 2012 the "International Year of the Cooperatives." As Jessica Reeder (*Yes! Magazine*) and Monique Hairston (*Rebuild the Dream*) reported, fully one billion people around the world—one in five adults over the age of fifteen—participate in co-ops as "one person, one vote" member-owners. "Cooperatives, in their various forms, promote the fullest possible participation in the economic and social development of all people, including women, youth, older persons, persons with disabilities and indigenous peoples," explains the UN. They "are becoming a major factor of economic and social development and contribute to the eradication of poverty."[18]

Co-ops are collaboratively owned and operated by their members. The cooperative business model puts money and power back into the hands of people, strengthening communities in the process. Decisions are balanced between pursuit of profit and needs of members and their communities. Co-ops have proven to be just as profitable as their corporate counterparts, yet their profits go back to the community of worker-owners, rather than to investors or high-priced management. Examples include the Evergreen Cooperative Laundry in Cleveland, Ohio, and the Mondragon Corporation founded in the Basque region of Spain, one of the world's largest corporations and a cooperative. Founded in 1965, Mondragon is considered the most successful example of worker-owned enterprise in the world. According to the UN, the co-op is expected to be the world's fastest growing business model by 2025.

Green worker co-ops promise to build strong local economies and to help break the cycle of poverty by keeping community money within the community. Since banks and credit unions typically do not lend money to co-ops, some groups are finding innovative ways to raise money without bank loans. The Alchemy Co-op in Melrose, Massachusetts, raised over $10,000 to start their organic food co-op through online crowd funding. Crowd funding and other forms of collective financing are allowing local co-ops to get off the ground and empower their communities.

At least two other projects within the "blessed unrest" deserve mention here. One is the Move Your Money project, a national grassroots campaign that "aims to empower individuals and institutions to divest from the nation's largest Wall Street banks and move to local financial institutions."[19] The direct language used by Move Your Money cuts to the heart of the national debate about "our economy":

> It has been almost three years since the Wall Street banks, through gross corruption and greed, caused the greatest economic crisis since the Great Depression that caused millions to lose their homes, jobs and livelihoods. And while the Wall Street banks have quickly returned to making record-breaking profits and bonuses, helped in large part by the $700 billion bailout by the American taxpayer, little has changed to prevent the types of abuses that created this mess.

Move Your Money has received corporate commercial news coverage on CNN and CBS, and in the *Wall Street Journal,* in part because their call to action is simple, direct, and powerful; it doesn't directly put Wall Street in the line of legislative or regulatory fire, instead relying on the individual decisions of individual citizens to "move their money." To wit:

We give individuals and institutions the tools and resources they need to divest from "Too Big to Fail" banks and invest in community banks and credit unions. No longer will we stand idle as banks take extraordinary risk with our financial system for their short-term profits; rather we will vote with our dollars and no longer contribute financially to the abusive practices of Wall Street. If Congress is unable to enact meaningful financial reform that will prevent another financial disaster, then we must take action into our own hands and hit the banks where it hurts them the most: their bottom line.[20]

Another national effort taking the long-term view on "our economy" is the Transition Town movement, as reported by Rachel Trachten Fall and Frances Beinecke.[21] First developed in 2005–06 by Rob Hopkins and Naresh Giangrande in Totnes, England, the Transition Town idea has grown into an international network of people committed to socioeconomic re-localization in the face of peak oil, climate change, and international economic instability. Daily news highlights the environmental and health costs citizens are paying, and the unstable future we face. The choice before thoughtful citizens seems clear: stand by old habits and suffer, or find new ways to adapt and thrive. Transition organizations and towns provide such a choice—giving citizens chances to collaborate with others to begin the shift toward a stable, sustainable world. A Transition Town is a place infused with a community-led process that helps the town/village/neighborhood/ organization become independent and sustainable.

This process begins when a small group of motivated individuals within a community comes together with a shared concern: How do we sustain ourselves and thrive as a community in these changing times? How do we significantly increase resilience (in response to peak oil), drastically reduce carbon emissions (in response to climate change), and greatly strengthen our local economy (in response to economic instability)? These core concerns lead to homegrown, citizen-led education, multi-stakeholder planning, and eventually to grassroots community initiatives that seek to mobilize the larger community and build shared resilience in the face of these modern-day concerns. Transition initiatives work to create a fulfilling and inspiring local way of life that can withstand the shocks of rapidly shifting global systems. It's happening in over a thousand highly diverse communities across the world—from towns in Australia to neighborhoods in Portugal, from cities in Brazil to rural communities in Slovenia, from urban locations in Britain to islands off the coast of Canada.

As we consider what's ahead for "our economy," the signs of "blessed unrest" in response to the "bankster bailout" are all around us. Despite corporate media chatter and diversion, an engaged public will not sit idly by, awaiting further victimization by a kleptocratic US national economy that enriches the few at the expense of the many. In May 2012, Gar Alperovitz coined a term called the New Economy Movement to serve as an umbrella phrase for a host of creative and forward-thinking initiatives. Citing a laundry list of meetings, networks, and actions already underway, Alperovitz reported:

> Just beneath the surface of traditional media attention, something vital has been gathering force and is about to explode into public consciousness. The "New Economy Movement" is a far-ranging coming together of organizations, projects, activists, theorists and ordinary citizens committed to rebuilding the American political-economic system from the ground up.[22]

Consider just April to June 2012: The Social Venture Network held its annual gathering in Stevenson, Washington. The Public Banking Institute gathered in Philadelphia. The National Center for Employee Ownership met in Minneapolis, with record-breaking attendance. And the Business Alliance for Local Living Economies (BALLE) held a major conference in Grand Rapids, Michigan. The Consumer Cooperative Management Association met in Philadelphia. The US Federation of Worker Cooperatives gathered in Boston. Other events planned for 2012 include a Farmer Cooperatives conference organized by the University of Wisconsin Center for Cooperatives, and meetings of the National Community Land Trust Network and the Bioneers. The American Sustainable Business Council, a network of 100,000 businesses and 300,000 individuals, has been holding ongoing events and activities throughout 2012.[23]

The rise of the new economy movement, the emergence of a blessed unrest, the call to action embedded in the Move Your Money campaign, the resurgence of member-owned cooperatives, the long-term planning of the Transition Town effort, and the hundreds of other communities carrying out thousands of economic projects with the participation of millions of our fellow citizens ought to serve as a potent reminder that, indeed, another world is not only possible, but emerging full flower before us. Let us not cultivate a false sense of Panglossian optimism about "our economy" based on censored news and information. Instead, let us connect the dots in the midst of these turbulent economic times, and then, like any good gardener, get our hands dirty growing something new. As Martin Luther King Jr. famously observed, "the time is always right to do what is right," and nowhere are his words more important than in the turbulent twenty-first–century life of "our economy."

DR. ROB WILLIAMS is a Vermont-based musician, historian, consultant, journalist, and media educator/maker who founded HigherMind Mediaworks. He teaches media education, communications, history, and business at Champlain College, the University of Vermont, Burlington College, and St. Michael's College. He is web editor and publisher of *Vermont Commons: Voices of Independence*, an independent newspaper, and he co-manages Vermont Yak Company in Vermont's Mad River Valley, where he plays "pholk-phunk" music in the three-piece Phineas Gage Project.

Notes

1. Jared Diamond, *Guns, Germs, and Steel: The Fates of Human Societies* (New York: W. W. Norton, 1997).
2. Gar Alperovitz, "The Rise of the New Economy Movement," *AlterNet*, May 20, 2012, http://www.alternet.org/economy/155452/the_rise_of_the_new_economy_movement.
3. Mike Krauss, "The State Budget Shell Game," May 31, 2012, http://mikekrauss.blogspot.com. Given this dysfunctional symbiotic relationship between our corporate commercial "news" media, our national government, and the transnational corporations that own them both, discriminating citizens are learning to seek out news about the way US economic life truly works, not from corporate sources, but from a variety of independent alternatives: *faux* TeeVee news programs (thanks, Messrs Stewart and Colbert), popular music magazines (gracias, *Rolling Stone*, for publishing Matt "Goldman Sachs = vampire squid" Taibbi), and young adult dystopian fiction which sounds more familiar by the week (read or see Suzanne Collins' "The Hunger Games," in which a pampered oligopolistic elite deploy an annual terrifying teen-warrior media spectacle to live parasitically off of the resources, energy, and work of the economically-deprived masses).
4. William J. Mathis, "Romney's Education Rhetoric More Of The Same," *National Education Policy Center*, May 25, 2012, http://nepc.colorado.edu/blog/romney's-education-speech-more-same.
5. Diane Ravitch, "The Myth of Charter Schools," *New York Review of Books*, November 11, 2010, http://www.nybooks.com/articles/archives/2010/nov/11/myth-charter-schools.

6. See, for example, Adam Gopnik, "The Caging of America," *New Yorker*, January 30, 2012, http://www.newyorker.com/arts/critics/atlarge/2012/01/30/120130crat_atlarge_gopnik.

7. Ellen Brown, "A Jubilee for Student Debt?" *Yes! Magazine*, October 20, 2011, http://www.yesmagazine.org/new-economy/a-jubilee-for-student-debt.

8. Dubbed by advocates of debt forgiveness as "1T Day," the corporate media dutifully covered this milestone in April 2012, though their "news" coverage focused on candidate Mitt Romney's and President Obama's competing reform proposals for student loan interests rates, rather than the possibility of a student loan debt jubilee, as reported by Ellen Brown and others independent journalists. See, for example, Ylan Q. Mui and Felicia Sonmez, "Obama, Romney Focus on Student Debt as Campaign Issue," *Washington Post*, April 23, 2012, http://www.washingtonpost.com/business/economy/obama-romney-focus-on-student-debt-as-campaign-issue/2012/04/23/gIQAnEz6cT_story.html.

9. John Hechinger, "Taxpayers Fund $454,000 Pay for Collector Chasing Student Loans," Bloomberg, May 15, 2012, http://finance.yahoo.com/news/taxpayers-fund-454-000-pay-040100808.html.

10. Andrew Martin and Andrew W. Lehren, "A Generation Hobbled by the Soaring Cost of College," *New York Times*, May 12, 2012, http://www.nytimes.com/2012/05/13/business/student-loans-weighing-down-a-generation-with-heavy-debt.html?_r=2&hp=&adxnnl=1&pagewanted=1&adxnnlx=1336882757-ZNJcHqg5VVwBWw6alouETg.

11. Andrew Martin, "Degrees of Debt," *New York Times*, May 14, 2012, http://www.nytimes.com/2012/05/15/business/colleges-begin-to-confront-higher-costs-and-students-debt.html?pagewanted=all.

12. Brown, "A Jubilee."

13. Allison Kilkenny, "Postal Workers: The Last Union," *Truthout*, September 11, 2011, http://truthout.org/index.php?option=com_k2&view=item&id=3190:postal-workers-the-last-union.

14. Ibid.

15. As quoted in William Deresiewicz, "Capitalists and Other Psychopaths," *New York Times*, May 14, 2012, http://www.nytimes.com/2012/05/13/opinion/sunday/fables-of-wealth.html.

16. Paul Hawken, *Blessed Unrest* (New York: Penguin, 2007), 4.

17. Antonio Gramsci, *Letters from Prison*, ed. Frank Rosengarten (New York: Columbia University Press, 2011 [1929]), 299.

18. Jessica Reeder, "2012: The Year of the Cooperative," *Yes! Magazine*, February 1, 2012, http://www.yesmagazine.org/new-economy/2012-the-year-of-the-cooperative.

19. Find out more at http://moveyourmoneyproject.org.

20. Ibid.

21. Rachel Trachten Fall, "Local Visionaries: Transition Groups Plant the Seeds for a Homegrown Future," *Edible East Bay*, Winter 2012, http://www.ediblecommunities.com/eastbay/harvest-2011/transition-groups.htm and Frances Beinecke, "International Energy Crises Make the Case for Change: Towns Lead Transition," *Shareable*, March 24, 2011, http://www.shareable.net/blog/international-energy-crises-make-the-case-for-change-towns-lead-transition.

22. Alperovitz, "Rise of the New Economy Movement."

23. Ibid.

Environment and Health

by Elaine Wellin

Censored #2

Oceans in Peril

Julia Whitty, "The End of a Myth," *OnEarth*, February 27, 2012, http://www.onearth.org/article/the-end-of-a-myth.

Richard Gray, "Warming Oceans Cause Largest Movement of Marine Species in Two Million Years," *Telegraph* (UK), June 26, 2011, http://www.telegraph.co.uk/earth/earthnews/8598597/Warming-oceans-cause-largest-movement-of-marine-species-in-two-million-years.html.

David A. Gabel, "Overfishing the Mediterranean," Environmental News Network, March 8, 2012, http://www.enn.com/ecosystems/article/44102.

Enric Sala et al., "The Structure of Mediterranean Rocky Reef Ecosystems across Environmental and Human Gradients, and Conservation Implications," *PLoS ONE* 7, no. 2 (February 29, 2012), http://www.plosone.org/article/info%3Adoi%2F10.1371%2Fjournal.pone.0032742.

Student Researchers: Taylor Falbisaner (Sonoma State University); Temple Chemotti (Santa Rosa Junior College)

Faculty Evaluators: Peter Phillips (Sonoma State University); Susan Rahman (Santa Rosa Junior College)

Censored #3

Fukushima Nuclear Disaster Worse than Anticipated

Joseph Mangano and Janette Sherman, "14,000 U.S. Deaths Tied to Fukushima Reactor Disaster Fallout," *International Journal of Health Services*, December 19, 2011, http://www.prnewswire.com/news-releases/medical-journal-article–14000-us-deaths-tied-to-fukushima-reactor-disaster-fallout-135859288.html.

Alex Roslin, "What Are Officials Hiding about Fukushima?" Straight.com (Vancouver), October 20, 2011, http://straight.com/article-491941/vancouver/what-are-officials-hiding-about-fukushima?page=0%2C1.

Danny Schechter, "Beyond Fukushima: A World in Denial about Nuclear Risks," Common Dreams, March 21, 2011, http://www.commondreams.org/view/2011/03/21-0.

"RadNet or SadNet? The EPA's Failed Radiation Detection System," *PSTUPH* (blog), April 4, 2011, http://pstuph.wordpress.com/2011/04/04/radnet-or-sadnet-the-epas-failed-radiation-detection-system.

Lucas W. Hixson, "The EPA Took RadNet Down Because They Were Getting Data From 'Other' Sources," March 23, 2011, Enformable Nuclear News, http://enformable.com/2011/11/march-23rd-2011-the-epa-took-radnet-down-because-they-were-getting-data-from-more-reliable-sources.

James Corbett, "US Radiation Monitoring May Have Been Handed Off to Nuclear Industry Lobbyists," Fukushima Update, November 4, 2011, http://fukushimaupdate.com/us-radiation-monitoring-may-have-been-handed-off-to-nuclear-industry-lobbyists.

Michael Kane, "Fallout," Collapse Network, March 24, 2011, http://www.collapsenet.com/free-resources/collapsenet-public-access/item/723-fallout.

Alexander Higgins, "Confirmed: EPA Rigged RADNET Japan Nuclear Radiation Monitoring Equipment To Report Lower Levels of Fukushima Fallout," Alexander Higgins Blog, May 19, 2011, http://blog.alexanderhiggins.com/2011/05/19/confirmed-epa-rigged-radnet-japan-nuclear-radiation-monitoring-equipment-report-levels-nuclear-fallout-22823.

Student Researchers: Lyndsey Casey, Morgan Womack, and Josh Crockett (Sonoma State University); Alyssa Barbieri (Florida Atlantic University)

Faculty Evaluators: Sheila Katz, Peter Phillips, and Heather Flynn (Sonoma State University); James F. Tracy (Florida Atlantic University)

Censored #15

Dangers of Everyday Technology

Devra Davis, "Cell Phone Radiation: Is It Dangerous?" *Huffington Post*, March 1, 2011, http://www.huffingtonpost.com/devra-davis-phd/cell-phone-radiation-_b_828330.html.

Tamir S. Aldad et al., "Fetal Radiofrequency Radiation Exposure From 800–1900 Mhz-Rated Cellular Telephones Affects Neurodevelopment and Behavior in Mice," *Nature*, March 15, 2012, http://www.nature.com/srep/2012/120315/srep00312/full/srep00312.html.

Carole Bass, "Cell Phones Might Cause ADHD," *Yale Alumni Magazine* (blog), March 15, 2012, http://www.yalealumnimagazine.com/blog/?p=13736.

Markham Heid, "Cell Phones Could Hurt Your Sperm," *Men's Health*, August 16, 2011, http://news.menshealth.com/breaking-cell-phones-could-hurt-your-sperm/2011/08/16.

Markham Heid, "The Worst Place to Keep Your Cell Phone," *Men's Health*, August 4, 2011, http://news.menshealth.com/cell-phone-safeguards/2011/08/04.

Devra Davis, "Beyond Brain Cancer: Other Possible Dangers Of Cell Phones," *Huffington Post*, June 15, 2011, http://www.huffingtonpost.com/devra-davis-phd/cell-phones-cancer_b_874361.html.

Richard Stossel, "Microwaved Water Kills Plant in Home Grown Experiment," NaturalNews, April 2, 2011, http://www.naturalnews.com/031929_microwaved_water_plants.html.

Christopher Gussa, "Microwaves Ovens: The Curse of Convenience," NaturalNews, April 14, 2008, http://www.naturalnews.com/023011_microwave_food_oven.html.

Anthony Lane and Lawrence Newell, "The Hazards of Microwave Ovens," Health & Science, no date, http://www.health-science.com/microwave_hazards.html.

Student Researchers: Aaron Peacock (San Francisco State University); Todd Roller (Florida Atlantic University)

Faculty Evaluators: Kenn Burrows (San Francisco State University); James F. Tracy (Florida Atlantic University)

RELATED VALIDATED INDEPENDENT NEWS STORIES

"Shale Shocked," *The Economist*, November 2, 2011, http://www.economist.com/blogs/blighty/2011/11/gas-extraction?fsrc=nlw%7Cnewe%7CI1-2-2011.

Chris Mooney, "The Truth About Fracking," *Scientific American*, October 19, 2011, http://www.scientificamerican.com/article.cfm?id=the-truth-about-fracking.

Robert Kropp, "Shareowner Pressure on Hydraulic Fracturing Intensifies," Social Funds, May 31, 2011, http://socialfunds.com/news/article.cgi/3231.html.

"Baby's Tub Is Still Toxic," Campaign for Safe Cosmetics, November 1, 2011, http://safecosmetics.org/article.php?id=887.

Jeffrey Smith, "GMOs Linked to Organ Disruption in 19 Studies," Institute for Responsible Technology, April 7, 2011, http://www.responsibletechnology.org/posts/?p=1340.

Mike Adams, "FDA Finally Admits Chicken Meat Contains Cancer-Causing Arsenic (But Keep Eating It, Yo!)," NaturalNews, June 9, 2011, http://www.naturalnews.com/032659_arsenic_chicken.html.

Tom Laskawy, "FDA Admits Supermarket Chickens Test Positive for Arsenic," *Grist*, June 8, 2011, http://www.grist.org/food-safety/2011-06-08-fda-admits-supermarket-chickens-test-positive-for-arsenic.

Brian Shilhavy, "Toxic Fluoride May be More Prevalent in your Food then Your Water," *Health Impact News Daily*, April 9, 2012, http://healthimpactnews.com/2012/toxic-flouride-may-be-more-prevalent-in-your-food-than-in-your-water.

Paul Connett, "50 Reasons to Oppose Fluoridation," Fluoride Action Network, August 2011, http://www.fluoridealert.org/50-reasons.htm.

Paul Beeber, "New Study: Fluoride Can Damage the Brain—Avoid Use in Children," PR Newswire, June 21, 2011, http://www.prnewswire.com/news-releases/new-study-fluoride-can-damage-the-brain---avoid-use-in-children-124299299.html.

Student Researchers: Peter Duke, Elizabeth Marinovich, and Robert Usher (San Francisco State University); Lamise Mansur (Florida Atlantic University); Taylor Falbisaner (Sonoma State University)

Faculty Evaluators: Kenn Burrows (San Francisco State University); James F. Tracy (Florida Atlantic University); Peter Phillips (Sonoma State University)

Censored 2013's Health and Environment cluster encompasses a wide range of issues and threats ignored and/or denied by governments and the corporate press: from threats to Earth's largest environments—our oceans and seas and the atmosphere; to our planet's biggest contemporary problems, including radioactive fallout from Fukushima Daiichi; down to the everyday dangers lurking in our food and water, not to mention on our kitchen countertops.

Censored #2: Oceans in Peril

The good news is that Project Censored participants, and many of the rest of us, are beginning to show a clear concern for the planet's oceans and its myriad inhabitants. This year's top stories include four articles with warnings about water—from the world's oceans down to the safety of our water supplies at the tap.

Only in the last decade have humans begun to recognize that reckless exploitation and utter disregard for the seas is unsustainable. In an article for *OnEarth,* Julia Whitty wrote:

> We thought the sea was infinite and inexhaustible. It is not.
>
> The ocean is our blind spot: a deep, dark, distant, and complex realm covering 70.8 percent of Earth's surface. We have better maps of the surface of Mars than of our own sea floor. Yet under our skin, we're a plasma ocean, so entwined with the outer seas that we can't easily know either ourselves or our water world.[1]

Noting that a single ounce of ocean water can be home to as many as thirty billion microorganisms, Whitty drew attention to the oceans' "silent sirens," which include disappearing horseshoe crabs, missing sea turtles, lost coral debris, and dwindling beach-spawning grunion.

Only in the past decade has science discovered the ocean to be "fragile in the way only really enormous things are fragile: with resilience teetering on the brink of collapse." Two additional stories regarding the health of our water world epitomize Whitty's analysis that "our behavior lags far behind our understanding, and the ocean awaits our enlightened action."

In an article that confirms both global climate change and the startling effects of warming ocean temperatures on the world's marine species, Richard Gray of the *Telegraph* (UK) reported that, according to scientists, the overall rise in ocean temperature has led to the largest movement of marine species in millions of years.[2] Ocean temperatures during recent summers have melted enough ice to create a passage from the Pacific Ocean to the North Atlantic, allowing plankton and fish into unfamiliar territory. The passage has opened multiple times in the last decade, allowing larger species, including the grey whale, to migrate through the newly formed interocean passage.

The discovery has sparked fears that delicate marine food webs could be unbalanced, leading to the extinction of some species as competition for food between native and invasive species stretches resources. Gray reported that researchers on the Climate Change and European Marine Ecosystems Research project found evidence that an invasive plankton species, *Neodenticula seminae*, crossing from the Pacific to the Atlantic by way of the newly developing passage through the Arctic sea, could cause "widespread changes to the Atlantic Ocean's food web." According to Dr. Carlo Heip, one of the project's leaders, "we can expect damaging upheaval as we overturn the workings of a system that's so complex and important. The migrations are an example of how changing climate conditions cause species to move or change their behaviour, leading to shifts in ecosystems that are clearly visible."[3]

While migration between the Pacific and Atlantic threatens species extinction and the collapse of fish stocks, fish and other sea creatures have been under attack by overfishing and depletion worldwide. David Gabel of the Environmental News Network reported on a February 2012 study of fourteen protected and eighteen non-protected ecosystems in the Mediterranean Sea, which demonstrated that this previously healthy sea is now quickly being depleted.[4] Over a period of three years, an international team of scientists conducted the study and found that, in well-enforced marine reserve areas, the fish populations were five to ten times greater than the fish populations in unprotected areas. The work of these scientists encourages the establishment and maintenance of marine reserves.

Enrico Sala, the study's lead scientist, reported, "We found a huge gradient, an enormous contrast. In reserves off Spain and Italy, we found the largest fish biomass in the Mediterranean. Unfortunately, around Turkey and Greece, the waters were bare."[5] Though some in the fishing industry oppose reserves on economic grounds, Sala explained that "the protection of the marine ecosystems is a necessity as well as a 'business' in which everyone wins. The reserves act as savings accounts, with capital that is not yet spent and an interest yield we can live off."[6]

This is an effective, economic way to describe the benefits of ocean sustainability for industry leaders and workers. And there are other economic benefits. Said Sala, "In Spain's Medes Islands Marine Reserve, for example, a reserve of barely one square kilometer can generate jobs and tourism revenue of 10 million Euros, a sum 20 times larger than earnings from fishing." It is clear from these findings that protection and regulation are paths to sustainability—economic sustainability as well as oceanic sustainability.

RELATED VALIDATED INDEPENDENT NEWS STORY

Fracking Our Water Supply

Fracking is the latest technological "fix" in efforts—ultimately doomed to failure—to prolong reliance on fossil fuels. Hydraulic fracturing involves blasting water, chemicals, and sand at high velocity into a shaft to crack rock and extract natural gas from shale beds. A growing international movement against fracking has documented instances of groundwater contamination by industrial fracking operations. In *Scientific American,* Chris Mooney wrote,

> If fracking were defined as a single fracture of deep shale, the process could be benign. However, the standard process, in-

volving multiple "fracks" in adjacent wells, increases the risk for water contamination. If fracking is defined to include the entire industrial operation—not only drilling but also wastewater storage—then contamination has already been found.[7]

Nevertheless, Mooney observed, "regulators are not waiting for better science; they are moving toward allowing fracking on an even wider scale."[8] In addition to concerns over groundwater pollution, critics of fracking also cite evidence that forceful injections, hundreds of feet below the surface, create earthquakes. *The Economist* reported on a November 2011 study suggesting that fifty tiny quakes in northwest England were the result of fracking.[9] In the United States, the Oklahoma Geological Survey has raised similar concerns.[10]

Energy firms in the United States have been able to ignore regulations enforced in other countries, at the expense of environmental damage, partly due to exemptions established in 2005 by Vice President Dick Cheney. Nonetheless, evidence does not support Big Oil's claims that shale gas is the answer to our energy needs.[11]

As Robert Kropp reported, shareholders have begun to confront Chevron, ExxonMobil, and other oil and gas companies in organized opposition to fracking.[12] Resolutions calling for "increased transparency and risk management" of fracking earned 41 percent of the votes of shareowners at Chevron and 28 percent at ExxonMobil, according to Kropp's story. An organizer for As You Sow, which co-filed the resolutions, noted that the Chevron vote was "an exceptionally high level of support for a first-year resolution."[13]

A less obvious impact of fracking is that speculation on carbon-intensive shale gas undermines investment in safer, low-carbon sources of renewable energy, such as solar, wind, and wave technologies.

Censored #3: Fukushima Nuclear Disaster Worse than Anticipated

Once one of the fifteen largest nuclear power stations in the world, Fukushima Daiichi ("Number one" in Japanese) is now disabled, destroyed by the magnitude nine earthquake and subsequent tsunami that hit Japan on March 10, 2011. The earthquake and tsunami disabled the reactor's cooling systems, leading to nuclear radiation leaks, the full effects of which are still unknown though grim evidence continues to surface. The power station is not expected to resume operation.

Despite media and government assurances to the contrary, radioactive fallout from the Daiichi disaster has hit North America. According to a report by Joseph Mangano and Janette Sherman, over 14,000 US deaths, most of them infants under age one in the state of Washington, can be attributed to the disaster.[14] A June 2011 spike in sudden infant deaths in British Columbia, Canada, appears to have a similar explanation. Mangano and Sherman noted that their estimate of excess US deaths in the fourteen weeks after Fukushima is comparable to the 16,500 excess deaths in the seventeen weeks after the 1986 Chernobyl meltdown. Mangano and Sherman reported: "Just six days after the disastrous meltdowns of four reactors at Fukushima, scientists detected toxic fallout over American shores. Subsequent measurements by the US Environmental Protection Agency (EPA) found radiation levels in air, water, and milk to be hundreds of times above normal across the US."[15] A PR Newswire story on the study quoted

Mangano: "Spikes in US and Canadian deaths after Fukushima raise concerns and strongly suggest the need for continuing health studies. This evidence should inform current debates about whether to build new reactors and how long to keep aging ones in operation."[16]

Further independent news coverage has documented that government officials and nuclear power industry spokespersons in both Japan and North America denied the real dangers of Fukushima's radioactive fallout, and in some cases lied about those dangers too. Alex Roslin reported that, in March 2011, a Health Canada monitoring station in Calgary detected radioactive material in rainwater that exceeded Canadian guidelines, but that government officials did not disclose the high radiation readings to the public.[17] Instead, they repeatedly insisted that fallout drifting to Canada was negligible and posed no health concerns. "In fact," Roslin wrote, "rainwater in Calgary in March had an average of 8.18 becquerels (221 picocuries) per liter of radioactive iodine, easily exceeding the Canadian guideline of 6 becquerels (161 picocuries) per liter for drinking water."[18] His report described the unreported rainwater data as "just one example of failings in how Canada monitored radiation from Fukushima" and part of a "pattern of nonchalance and seeming willful ignorance on the part of Canadian health authorities when it comes to the dangers of nuclear power."[19]

Denials of Fukushima's severity form a consistent pattern, as government officials and corporate media fail to inform the public of real dangers.[20] The EPA's radiation-detection network, RadNet, has serious shortcomings, including lack of maintenance and improperly calibrated equipment, as documented by a handful of independent journalists.[21] During the critical weeks after Fukushima, the RadNet monitoring system went down. While radiation from Fukushima spread throughout the northern hemisphere, a nuclear industry lobbying firm operated in place of the EPA's network to monitor fallout in the US.[22] The Nuclear Regulatory Commission (NRC) arranged for the Nuclear Energy Institute (NEI) to provide radiation-monitoring data to the NRC, which in turn provided the data to the EPA. Rigorous testing of food, water, and air throughout the US during the Fukushima crisis period was suspended in favor of industry-provided data.

Well before Fukushima, e-mail communication among EPA officials during the George W. Bush administration suggested plans to obscure radiation reporting in the event of a nuclear disaster.[23] Michael Kane reported that holdovers from the Bush–Cheney administration still in power at the EPA aimed to update the agency's 1992 Protective Action Guide manual to increase "safe" exposure levels for strontium-90, iodine-131, and nickel-63 to levels previously deemed unsafe and unacceptable.[24] Under this logic, public health policy hinges on bureaucratic decisions that appear contrary to scientific evidence and remain mostly shielded from public scrutiny.

Censored #15: Dangers of Everyday Technology

Among the most ubiquitous of consumer technologies, cellular phones and microwave ovens present dangers that the public needs to understand. Government, the media, and the consumer electronics industries often deny people the information necessary to make informed choices about what technologies to bring into their homes, and how to protect themselves and one another when those conveniences prove threatening to health.

Cell phone use is so common that most of us do not consider it risky, except perhaps as a distraction while driving. Yet recent studies suggest otherwise, especially for the most vulnerable among us. Devra Davis reported that studies on rabbits and rats found that "signals from today's smartphones damage sperm, brain, liver, eyes and skin of exposed offspring, and impair their memory and behavior."[25] In a second article, Davis reported on another study showing that just fifty minutes of cell phone radiation affected brain function and metabolism of glucose—the brain's main fuel—in those parts of the brain that receive the most cell phone radiation.[26]

Exposing babies to cell phone radiation *in utero* may contribute to subsequent attention deficit hyperactivity disorder (ADHD), another study reported. Researchers at Yale University positioned a cell phone on an "uninterrupted active call" above a cage containing pregnant mice throughout gestation. Compared to mice that were not exposed to the radiofrequency *in utero*, the offspring showed reduced transmissions in the prefrontal cortex of their brains, which is responsible for screening distractions and maintaining attention in goal-oriented behaviors, and as a result were hyperactive and suffered impaired memory.[27]

And that is not the only reproductive danger from cell phone radiation. Cell phones could be hurting male sperm, according to a *Journal of Andrology* review that examined the links between cell phone radiation and men's reproductive function.[28] According to Markham Heid of *Men's Health*, "Researchers throughout the US and the world have looked at the impact of mobile phones' electromagnetic frequency (EMF) radiation on sperm, and the results—though not yet conclusive—present a compelling case that men who use cell phones have decreased sperm concentration, slower sperm, and damaged sperm, compared to men who do not use cell phones."[29]

In an effort to make consumers more aware of some of the potential dangers of cell phone radiation, San Francisco lawmakers enacted an ordinance requiring cell phone retailers to disclose the amount of radiation emitted, though the city has been battling industry to keep the law in place.[30] Rep. Dennis Kucinich (D-OH) has also attempted to make radiation warnings a requirement on cell phones, so that more knowledge and decision-making power is in the hands of consumers, not just the cell phone manufacturing companies.[31] Phone manufacturers are required by federal law to package every cell phone with information about its specific absorption rate (SAR) values—the higher the SAR value, the more radiation the body absorbs. But there's usually no explanation provided with those numbers, the highest maximum doses of radiation vary, and SARs do not take into account varying levels while in actual use.

Although some scientific studies suggest that these links are inconclusive, these "no-risk" assessments do not always hold up to scrutiny. Many of the studies suggesting cell phones pose no health risks are industry-funded. Despite this bias and serious flaws in risk calculation, these studies are the basis of the US Food and Drug Administration (FDA) position that cell phones are safe. The FDA and most corporate media say that the "weight of scientific evidence has not linked cell phones with any health problems,"[32] including brain tumors from the low-level radiation that phones emit in normal use.[33] Yet if you follow the study-funding trail, you'll find that a key FDA study, "the largest study of its kind," uses data from Interphone, an International Agency for Research on Cancer (IARC) study.[34] Under the auspices of the World Health Organization, the IARC and the Interphone study derive some funding from the Union for International Cancer Control, which in turn receives funding from the Mobile Manufacturers Forum and Groupe Speciale Mobile Association[35]— industry groups with vested interests in keeping mobile and wireless technologies viable.[36] Until more independent studies emerge, it will be difficult to discern the real risks of cell phone radiation and our government's potential failure to better protect us from it.

So, what to do? The most effective ways to minimize risk:

▸ Maintain some distance between the cell phone and your head by using a hands-free headset, or speakerphone, or by sending a text message.
▸ Hold the cell phone away from the head and body (especially when a call is connecting).
▸ Store the phone in some place other than clothes pockets, like in a backpack or purse, to protect organ function and reproductive health.
▸ Limit your use in times of a low signal, as radiation increases when signal strength is weak or blocked.
▸ Reduce use, especially by children.

Radiation danger in everyday life includes that kitchen workhorse, the microwave oven, which is more dangerous than you may realize. Besides diminishing or nearly eliminating the nutrients in your food by changing its chemical structure, microwave ovens can cause burns due to hot spots, leaching of carcinogenic toxins into food, and cataracts.

Microwaves heat food by causing water molecules to resonate at high frequencies, so that the water eventually turns to steam, heating the food. While this process rapidly heats food, it also changes the food's chemical structure. Heating food in any way results in some nutrient loss, but broccoli heated in a microwave loses up to 97 percent of its beneficial antioxidants, microwaved asparagus reduces its vitamin C, while sixty seconds in a microwave inactivates the allinase in garlic, which is its principle active ingredient against cancer. Heating milk reduces the B12 in milk to inert form.

Carcinogenic toxins can leach from plastic or paper containers into microwaved food.[37] Carcinogens from the packaging of common microwavable foods like pizzas, chips, and popcorn include polyethylene terpthalate (PET), benzene, toluene, and xylene. Microwaving fatty foods in plastic containers leads to the release of dioxins (among the most toxic known) and other toxins into your food. Bisphenol A (BPA) is a toxic substance widely in plastic dishes made specifically for microwave ovens.

A 2010 study showed that microwave ovens operating at ordinary household levels caused immediate and dramatic changes in both heart rate and heart-rate variability.[38]

What to do:

- Step away from your microwave while it is in use.
- Plan ahead. Take your dinner out of the freezer in the morning, or the night before, so you don't end up having to scramble to defrost it in time for dinner.
- Heat up foods in alternative warmers like toaster ovens and convection ovens.
- Prepare meals in advance for those days when you're too busy or too tired to cook.
- Eat more organic raw foods: the best way to improve your health over the long run.

RELATED VALIDATED INDEPENDENT NEWS STORIES

Baby's Tub Still Toxic?

In November 2011, the Campaign for Safe Cosmetics reported that Johnson & Johnson is "still using formaldehyde-releasing preservatives in Johnson's Baby Shampoo in some countries (including the U.S.)"[39] In March 2009, the Campaign for Safe Cosmetics had published a report, "No More Toxic Tub," showing that Johnson's Baby Shampoo and other children's bath products contained two known carcinogens—formaldehyde and 1,4-dioxane—that were not listed on product labels. That year the Campaign for Safe Cosmetics joined with organizations representing 1.7 million parents, health care providers, and environmental health advocates to call on Johnson & Johnson to remove both ingredients from the company's bath products.[40]

Formaldehyde is classified as a known human carcinogen by the

US Department of Health and Human Services and the IARC. The National Cancer Institute, the World Health Organization, and the National Toxicology Program have all identified a possible link between formaldehyde exposure and leukemia. The North American Contact Dermatitis Group considers quaternium-15 to be among the most clinically significant contact allergens in children.

In its November 2011 report, "Baby's Tub is Still Toxic," the Campaign for Safe Cosmetics reported that Johnson's Baby Shampoo sold in the US, Australia, Canada, China, and Indonesia continues to contain quaternium-15, while the version of the product sold in Denmark, Finland, Japan, the Netherlands, Norway, South Africa, Sweden, and the UK contains non-formaldehyde preservatives. The Campaign asked, "Why the double standard, especially since it is clear that a non-formaldehyde version can be manufactured?"[41]

The Campaign for Safe Cosmetics study and subsequent media attention worked: after the campaign issued their report, Johnson & Johnson released a statement saying it is phasing out formaldehyde-releasing chemicals from its baby products worldwide.[42] The company says it has reduced its use of the chemical by 60 percent in the US market and 33 percent globally.

What to do? If the statement prompted by campaign pressures is accurate, you still don't know if the product in your hand is safe. You need to check that label before exposing your child to Johnson's Baby Shampoo.

Organ Disruption Linked to Genetically Modified Crops
A study published in March 2011 by French researchers suggested that genetically modified (GM) crops could pose more of a threat to our health than originally thought, Jeffrey Smith of the Institute for Responsible Technology reported.[43] In a study published in *Environmental Sciences Europe*, the researchers reviewed nineteen cases of mammals fed a GM soybean and maize diet and found significant changes to the animals' organs, especially their livers. The study's authors pointed out that livers and kidneys are "the major reactive organs" in cases of chronic food toxicity, though other organs may be affected too, such as the heart and spleen, or blood cells. In fact, some of the animals given GM feed had altered body weights in at least one gender, which is "a very good predictor of side effects in various organs."[44]

The GM soybean and corn varieties used in the feeding trials "constitute 83% of the commercialized GMOs"[45] currently consumed by billions of people. While the findings may have serious ramifications for the human population, the authors demonstrated how a multitude of GMO-related health problems could easily pass undetected through the superficial and largely incompetent safety assessments that are used around the world. "New experiments," the study concluded, "should be systematically performed to protect the health of billions of people who consume directly or indirectly these transformed products."[46]

Food and Drug Administration Comes Clean on Arsenic-Laced Chickens

For the past sixty years, American consumers of chicken have been ingesting small amounts of a known cancer-causing agent. As Mike Adams of Natural News and Tom Laskawy of *Grist* reported, the FDA now admits that chicken meat sold in the United States contains arsenic, that the arsenic is *intentionally added* to chicken feed, and that arsenic present in chicken meat is, in fact, consumed by humans.[47]

Prior to this, both the poultry industry and the FDA denied that arsenic given to chickens ended up in the meat, arguing that the arsenic in feed was excreted as chicken feces. However, no evidence existed for making this claim. Pfizer, the manufacturer of Roxarsone, the drug that was added to chicken feed, is now pulling the product. Roxarsone is one of several such drugs used in chicken feed that have been banned in the European Union, but remain on the market in the US. Despite these dramatic findings, the FDA maintains that arsenic levels found in chicken meat are low and that such chicken meat is safe to eat.

What to do? Do not count on the Environmental Protection Agency to protect you. Choose safe, free-range, organic chickens and eggs.

Toxic Fluoride: In Your Water *and* Your Food

Most of us know that fluoride is added to drinking water in order to protect teeth from decay. But you may not know that it also causes fluorosis, which can damage children's teeth.[48] Worse yet, prolonged *ingestion* of fluoride may cause significant health damage, particularly to the nervous system.

The FDA classifies fluoride as a drug when used to prevent or mitigate disease.[49] However, as Brian Shilhavy reported, the hidden doses of fluoride we absorb from food coated with residues from fluoride pesticides comes in much greater amounts than what we get from water fluoridation.[50]

Fluoride can be toxic when ingesting a dose of one part per million (ppm)—exactly the amount added to most drinking water systems. Deleterious effects are not immediate but can take twenty years or more to become evident. Although we can actually see how fluoride has damaged children's teeth with dental fluorosis, we cannot see the harm it is doing to their brains and other organs.

Paul Beeber summarized recent research on fluoride, including a 2011 study showing that fluoride induces changes in the brain's physical structure and biochemistry, and affects the neurological and mental development of cognitive processes such as learning and memory.[51] Animal studies have shown that fluoride's toxic effects include classic brain abnormalities found in patients with Alzheimer's disease. Fluorides also increase the production of free radicals in the brain, which may increase the risk of developing Alzheimer's disease.[52] Beeber also described the 2008 findings of Tang, et al., who declared, "A qualitative review of the studies found a consistent and strong association between the exposure to fluoride and low IQ."[53]

Nonorganic food could account for as much as one-third of the average person's fluoride exposure. Indeed, the most common source of exposure is conventionally farmed, nonorganic food because fluoride-based pesticides like Cryolite, or sodium aluminum fluoride, is sprayed on food crops.[54] Cryolite leaves a resistant residue that is difficult to rinse off, especially on greens, citrus fruits, and grapes.

None of this is new, but corporate media have marginalized the issue for years.[55] In light of growing public and scientific concern, the EPA has begun to examine its own guidelines for fluoridation. It recently proposed setting the level of fluoride in drinking water at the lowest end of the standard range of water treatment, while it initiates a further review of adding fluoride to drinking water.[56]

What to do?

▸ If your city has not looked at this problem, you might reduce fluoride consumption by becoming active in supporting a local initiative to do so.

▸ Buy more organic foods.

▸ See a dentist who understands the issues.

▸ Get a reverse osmosis filter to remove fluoride from drinking water.

ELAINE WELLIN teaches environmental sociology, social inequalities, and social gerontology at Sonoma State University; works with environmental and social action organizations mostly in Sonoma County, California; and serves on the Media Freedom Foundation/Project Censored board.

Notes

1. Julia Whitty, "The End of a Myth," *OnEarth*, February 27, 2012, http://www.onearth.org/article/the-end-of-a-myth.
2. Richard Gray, "Warming Oceans Cause Largest Movement of Marine Species in Two Million Years," *Telegraph* (UK), June 26, 2011, http://www.telegraph.co.uk/earth/earthnews/8598597/Warming-oceans-cause-largest-movement-of-marine-species-in-two-million-years.html.
3. Ibid.
4. David A. Gabel, "Overfishing the Mediterranean," Environmental News Network, March 8, 2012, http://www.enn.com/ecosystems/article/44102. Gabel's report summarizes the findings of Enrico Sala et al., "The Structure of Mediterranean Rocky Reef Ecosystems across Environmental and Human Gradients, and Conservation Implications," *PLoS ONE* 7, no. 2 (February 29, 2012), http://www.plosone.org/article/info%3Adoi%2F10.1371%2Fjournal.pone.0032742.
5. Gabel, "Overfishing the Mediterranean."
6. Ibid.
7. Chris Mooney, "The Truth about Fracking," *Scientific American*, October 19, 2011, http://www.scientificamerican.com/article.cfm?id=the-truth-about-fracking.
8. Ibid.
9. "Shale Shocked," *Economist*, November 2, 2011, http://www.economist.com/blogs/blighty/2011/11/gas-extraction?fsrc=nlw%7Cnewe%7C7C11-2-2011.
10. See, for example, Paul Voosen, "Oklahoma Quakes Associated with Fracking," E&ENews PM, November, 2, 2011, http://www.eenews.net/public/eenewspm/2011/11/02/1.
11. See, for example, "Corporate Greenwashing and Other Questionable 'Green' Ads (VIDEOS)," *Huffington Post*, October 3, 2011, http://www.huffingtonpost.com/2011/10/03/corporate-green-washing-ads_n_989274.html#s377966&title=Exxon_Fracking.
12. Robert Kropp, "Shareowner Pressure on Hydraulic Fracturing Intensifies," Social Funds, May 31, 2011, http://socialfunds.com/news/article.cgi/3231.html.
13. Ibid.
14. Joseph Mangano and Janette Sherman, "14,000 U.S. Deaths Tied to Fukushima Reactor Disaster Fallout," *International Journal of Health Services*, December 19, 2011, http://www.prnewswire.com/news-releases/medical-journal-article–14000-us-deaths-tied-to-fukushima-reactor-disaster-fallout-135859288.html.
15. Ibid.
16. "Medical Journal Article: 14,000 U.S. Deaths Tied to Fukushima Reactor Disaster Fallout," PR Newswire, December 19, 2011, http://www.prnewswire.com/news-releases/medical-journal-article--14000-us-deaths-tied-to-fukushima-reactor-disaster-fallout-135859288.html.

17. Alex Roslin, "What Are Officials Hiding about Fukushima?" *Georgia Straight* (Vancouver), October 20, 2011, http://straight.com/article-491941/vancouver/what-are-officials-hiding-about-fukushima?page=0%2C1.

18. Ibid.

19. Ibid.

20. See, for example, Danny Schechter, "Beyond Fukushima: A World in Denial about Nuclear Risks," Common Dreams, March 21, 2011, http://www.commondreams.org/view/2011/03/21-0.

21. Lucas W. Hixson, "The EPA Took RadNet Down Because They Were Getting Data From 'Other' Sources," Enformable Nuclear News, March 23, 2011, http://enformable.com/2011/11/march-23rd-2011-the-epa-took-radnet-down-because-they-were-getting-data-from-more-reliable-sources; James Corbett, "US Radiation Monitoring May Have Been Handed Off to Nuclear Industry Lobbyists," Fukushima Update, November 4, 2011, http://fukushimaupdate.com/us-radiation-monitoring-may-have-been-handed-off-to-nuclear-industry-lobbyists; Alexander Higgins, "Confirmed: EPA Rigged RADNET Japan Nuclear Radiation Monitoring Equipment To Report Lower Levels of Fukushima Fallout," *Alexander Higgins Blog*, May 19, 2011, http://blog.alexanderhiggins.com/2011/05/19/confirmed-epa-rigged-radnet-japan-nuclear-radiation-monitoring-equipment-report-levels-nuclear-fallout-22823; and "RadNet or SadNet? The EPA's Failed Radiation Detection System," *PSTUPH* (blog), April 4, 2011, http://pstuph.wordpress.com/2011/04/04/radnet-or-sadnet-the-epas-failed-radiation-detection-system.

22. Hixson, "EPA Took RadNet Down"; Corbett, "US Radiation Monitoring May Have Been Handed Off"; Higgins, "Confirmed: EPA Rigged RADNET."

23. Michael Kane, "Fallout," Collapse Network, March 24, 2011, http://www.collapsenet.com/free-resources/collapsenet-public-access/item/723-fallout.

24. Ibid.

25. Devra Davis, "Beyond Brain Cancer: Other Possible Dangers of Cell Phones," *Huffington Post*, June 15, 2011, http://www.huffingtonpost.com/devra-davis-phd/cell-phones-cancer_b_874361.html.

26. Devra Davis, "Cell Phone Radiation: Is It Dangerous?" *Huffington Post*, March 1, 2011, http://www.huffingtonpost.com/devra-davis-phd/cell-phone-radiation-_b_828330.html.

27. Carole Bass, "Cell Phones Might Cause ADHD," *Yale Alumni Magazine* (blog), March 15, 2012, http://www.yalealumnimagazine.com/blog/?p=13736; Bass's story summarizes the findings of Tamir S. Aldad et al., "Fetal Radiofrequency Radiation Exposure From 800-1900 Mhz-Rated Cellular Telephones Affects Neurodevelopment and Behavior in Mice," *Nature*, March 15, 2012, http://www.nature.com/srep/2012/120315/srep00312/full/srep00312.html.

28. For a summary of the study's findings, see Markham Heid, "Cell Phones Could Hurt Your Sperm," *Men's Health*, August 16, 2011, http://news.menshealth.com/breaking-cell-phones-could-hurt-your-sperm/2011/08/16; and Markham Heid, "The Worst Place to Keep Your Cell Phone," *Men's Health*, August 4, 2011, http://news.menshealth.com/cell-phone-safeguards/2011/08/04.

29. Heid, "Cell Phones Could Hurt Your Sperm."

30. Eric Bangeman, "San Francisco Cell Phone Warning Law Fails Science, Judge Says," CNN, October 28, 2011, http://www.cnn.com/2011/10/28/tech/mobile/cell-phone-law-fails/index.html.

31. "Kucinich Introduces Cell Phone Research, Warning Label Bill," Congressman Dennis J. Kucinich website, press release, June 30, 2010, http://kucinich.house.gov/news/documentsingle.aspx?DocumentID=192995.

32. "Health Issues: Do Cell Phones Pose a Health Hazard?," US Food and Drug Administration, May 18, 2010, http://www.fda.gov/Radiation-EmittingProducts/RadiationEmittingProductsandProcedures/HomeBusinessandEntertainment/CellPhones/ucm116282.htm.

33. "No Evidence Linking Cell Phone Use to Risk of Brain Tumors," US Food and Drug Administration, May 17, 2010, http://www.fda.gov/downloads/ForConsumers/ConsumerUpdates/UCM212306.pdf.

34. Ibid.

35. "The Interphone Study: Funding," International Agency for Research on Cancer, http://interphone.iarc.fr/interphone_funding.php.
36. See "About the MMF," Mobile Manufacturers Forum website, http://www.mmfai.org/public; and "Brief History of GSM & the GSMA," Groupe Speciale Mobile Association website, http://www.gsma.com/aboutus/history.
37. Joseph Mercola, "Why did Russia Ban an Appliance Found in 90% of American Homes?" Mercola.com, May 18, 2010, http://articles.mercola.com/sites/articles/archive/2010/05/18/microwave-hazards.aspx.
38. Magda Havas et al., "Provocation Study Using Heart Rate Variability Shows Microwave Radiation from DECT Phone Affects Autonomic Nervous System," in *Non-Thermal Effects and Mechanisms of Interaction between Electromagnetic Fields and Living Matter*, ed. Livio Guiliani and Morando Soffritti, monograph, *European Journal of Oncology* 5 (2010):273–300.
39. "Baby's Tub is Still Toxic," Campaign for Safe Cosmetics, November 1, 2011, http://safecosmetics.org/article.php?id=887.
40. Ibid.
41. Ibid.
42. See "Johnson & Johnson Promises to Remove Carcinogens from Baby Products," Campaign for Safe Cosmetics, November 16, 2011, http://safecosmetics.org/article.php?id=903.
43. Jeffrey Smith, "GMOs Linked to Organ Disruption in 19 Studies," Institute for Responsible Technology, April 7, 2011, http://www.responsibletechnology.org/posts/?p=1340.
44. Gilles-Eric Séralini et al., "Genetically Modified Crops Safety Assessments: Present Limits and Possible Improvements," *Environmental Sciences Europe* 23, no. 10 (2011), http://www.enveurope.com/content/23/1/10.
45. Ibid.
46. Ibid.
47. Mike Adams, "FDA Finally Admits Chicken Meat Contains Cancer-Causing Arsenic (But Keep Eating It, Yo!)," NaturalNews, June 9, 2011, http://www.naturalnews.com/032659_arsenic_chicken.html; Tom Laskawy, "FDA Admits Supermarket Chickens Test Positive for Arsenic," *Grist*, June 8, 2011, http://www.grist.org/food-safety/2011-06-08-fda-admits-supermarket-chickens-test-positive-for-arsenic.
48. Paul Connett, "50 Reasons to Oppose Fluoridation," Fluoride Action Network, August 2011, http://www.fluoridealert.org/50-reasons.htm.
49. Ibid.
50. Brian Shilhavy, "Toxic Fluoride May be More Prevalent in your Food than Your Water," *Health Impact News Daily*, April 9, 2012, http://healthimpactnews.com/2012/toxic-flouride-may-be-more-prevalent-in-your-food-than-in-your-water.
51. Paul Beeber, "New Study: Fluoride Can Damage the Brain—Avoid Use in Children," PR Newswire, June 21, 2011, http://www.prnewswire.com/news-releases/new-study-fluoride-can-damage-the-brain---avoid-use-in-children-124299299.html.
52. Valdez-Jimenez et al., "Effects of the Fluoride on the Central Nervous System," *Neurologia* 26, no. 5 (June 2011):297–300.
53. Tang et al., "Fluoride and Children's Intelligence: A Meta-Analysis," *Biological Trace Element Research* 126, no. 1–3 (Winter 2008):115–20. Also see Connett, "50 Reasons to Oppose Fluoridation."
54. Shilhavy, "Toxic Fluoride May be More Prevalent in your Food than Your Water," 2012.
55. For one notable exception, see Alice Park, "The Hazards Lurking at Home," *Time*, April 1, 2010, which identified fluoride as one of the "Top Ten Common Household Toxins," describing it as both "neurotoxic and potentially tumorigenic if swallowed," http://www.time.com/time/specials/packages/article/0,28804,1976909_1976895_1976914,00.html.
56. Environmental Protection Agency, "Fluoride Risk Assessment and Relative Source Contribution," January 7, 2011, http://water.epa.gov/action/advisories/drinking/fluoride_index.cfm.

Human Costs of War and Violence

by Dr. James F. Tracy

Censored #8

NATO War Crimes in Libya

Michael Collins, "NATO War Crimes: The Wanton Destruction of Sirte," Global Research, October 15, 2011, http://www.globalresearch.ca/index.php?context=va&aid=27092.

Michael Collins, "Smoking Guns: War Crimes in Libya," The Daily Censored (blog), November 2, 2011, http://dailycensored.com/2011/11/02/smoking-guns-war-crimes-in-libya.

Timothy Bancroft-Hinchey, "NATO's Ultimate War Crime: Destroying Libya's Water Supply," Global Research, August 1, 2011, http://globalresearch.ca/index.php?context=va&aid=25861.

Timothy Bancroft-Hinchey, "NATO War Crime: Libya Water Supply," Pravda, July 23, 2011, http://english.pravda.ru/news/world/23-07-2011/118577-nato_war_crimes-0.

Franklin Lamb, "Where Have Libya's Children Gone?" Counterpunch, August 8, 2011, http://www.counterpunch.org/2011/08/08/where-have-libyas-children-gone.

Gerald A. Perreira, "British Intelligence Worked with Al Qaeda to Kill Qaddafi," Global Research, March 25, 2011, http://www.globalresearch.ca/index.php?context=va&aid=23957.

Patrick Martin, "A CIA Commander for the Libyan Rebels," World Socialist Web Site, March 28, 2011, http://www.wsws.org/articles/2011/mar2011/pers-m28.shtml.

Global Research, "BBC 'Reveals' After the Facts how British Special Forces Supervised and Spearheaded Libya Rebels to Victory," Global Research, February 1, 2012, http://globalresearch.ca/index.php?context=va&aid=29001.

Student Researchers: Beatriz Alcazar, Andrea Perez, Robert Block, and Harmen Sidhu (Sonoma State University); Paloma Tur (Universidad Complutense de Madrid)

Faculty and Community Evaluators: Alfredo V. Moran, Bryan Polkey, Luis Luján, and Miguel Álvarez-Peralta (Universidad Complutense de Madrid); Peter Phillips and Gregg Adams (Sonoma State University)

Censored #12

US Joins Forces with al-Qaeda in Syria

Michel Chossudovsky and Finian Cunningham, "Syria: Clinton Admits US on Same Side as Al-Qaeda to Destabilize Assad Government," Global Research, February 27, 2012, http://www.globalresearch.ca/index.php?context=va&aid=29524

Eric Margolis, "The Dangerous Mess in Syria Grows Murkier," Information Clearing House, March 25, 2012, http://www.informationclearinghouse.info/article30908.htm.

Alex Lantier, "U.S. Violates Syrian Air Space: Drones Over Syria As Fighting Spreads," Global Research, February 20, 2012, http://www.globalresearch.ca/index.php?context=va&aid=29395.

Student Researchers: Rachel Miller-Hee, Dane Steffy, and Lisa Pollack (Sonoma State University)

Faculty Evaluators: Noel Byrne, Peter Phillips, Robert Switky, and Glenn Wallace (Sonoma State University)

Censored #23

US Covers up Afghan Massacre

Al-Akhbar, "More than One US Soldier Involved in Massacre: Afghan President," *Al-Akhbar English*, March 16, 2012, http://english.al-akhbar.com/content/multiple-soldiers-involved-killing-afghan-civilians-afghan-president.

James Petras, "The Massacre of the Afghan 17 and the Obama Cover-Up," Information Clearing House, March 27, 2012, http://www.informationclearinghouse.info/article30922.htm.

Student Researchers: Annie Keating (College of Marin); Dane Steffy (Sonoma State University)

Faculty Evaluators: Susan Rahman (College of Marin); Peter Phillips (Sonoma State University)

Censored #25

Evidence Points to Guantánamo Dryboarding

Almerindo Ojeda, "Death in Guantánamo: Suicide or Dry Boarding?" *Truthout*, November 3, 2011, http://www.truth-out.org/death-guantanamo-suicide-or-dryboarding/1320182714.

Jeffrey Kaye, "Citing Truthout Report, UN Special Rapporteur 'Looking Into' Guantanamo 'Suicides,'" *Truthout*, March 27, 2012, http://truth-out.org/news/item/8112-citing-truthout-report-un-special-rapporteur-looking-into-guantanamo-suicides.

Student Researcher: Dane Steffy (Sonoma State University)

Faculty Evaluator: Peter Phillips (Sonoma State University)

RELATED VALIDATED INDEPENDENT NEWS STORY

Mike Ludwig, "US Military Paid $1.1 Trillion to Contractors That Defrauded the Government," *Truthout*, October 20, 2011, http://truth-out.org/index.php?option=com_k2&view=item&id=4141:us-military-paid-11-trillion-to-contractors-that-defrauded-the-government.

Persuading a population to go to war is a struggle that involves the employment of varied and ubiquitous messages to gain the unquestioning allegiance of hearts and minds. "So great are the psychological resistances to war in modern nations," World War I propagandist Harold Lasswell famously remarked, "that every war must appear to be a war of defense against a menacing, murderous aggressor. There must be no ambiguity about whom the public is to hate."[1]

Over the past century the process by which societies are sold wars has remained remarkably consistent. Citizens are told a great evil force seeks to do them harm and must therefore be triumphed over. Yet since the 1920s the promotion of war has also become more-and-more finely tuned. Today, public relations techniques and cutting-edge technologies combine to infuse wartime huckstering and disinformation that deceptively masquerades as news. Further, portions of the population have arguably become more receptive as war and

violence are routinely valorized and celebrated in a wide array of clever and persuasive American culture, from cinematic and televisual narratives to disturbingly true-to-life video games.

Such "advances" in information and cultural management are increasingly necessary for thought control, for since September 11, 2001, the United States has entered what its leaders have deemed an endless war. A foremost technique for suppressing news and controlling minds in the perpetual warfare state is myth. As Herbert Schiller observes, "By using myths which explain, justify, and sometimes even glamorize the prevailing conditions of existence, manipulators secure popular support for a social order that is not in the majority's long term real interest."[2] The corporate media's mythic narratives seek to persuade the public to mistake a war utilizing terror and violence carried out in its name for a war *against* "terrorism" and sinister antiheros.

Told often and forcefully enough, myth is a countervailing force to facts, for myth acts as a structural narrative that obscures or appropriates facts to fit the purposes of the myth creators. For example, the heavily promoted and widely shared myth that al-Qaeda is the arch enemy of Western powers acts to dismantle factual assertions that al-Qaeda has been and remains a mercenary grouping and Western intelligence asset, most recently employed in the destabilizations of Libya and Syria.

In this manner, the prevalent notion that US soldiers are, with the exception of a few bad apples, noble and benevolent peacekeepers out to battle al-Qaeda tends to mitigate the impact of reports on how the overall dehumanizing process of modern warfare potentially transforms GIs into ruthless murderers of women and children, as the story of the Afghanistan massacre revealed in March 2012.

As America enters its second decade at war, myth remains an underlying element in the war of ideas. Those who witness world events through the corporate media prism accept the continued Middle East occupation apart from its everyday horrors. With few exceptions, corporate media dutifully repeat the "struggle with al-Qaeda" narrative linking the Islamic world to the attacks on September 11, 2001. In this way the "9/11 myth" becomes an essential opinion-shaping component of twenty-first-century Western expansionism.[3]

On May 1, 2011, the story culminated in Hollywood style with President Barack Obama announcing the extrajudicial killing of Osama bin Laden at his alleged safe house in Pakistan. As alternative news media provided an array of information and analysis questioning the official story, corporate outlets upheld the Obama administration's line while initiating a rearguard action against detractors by labeling calls for actual proof of bin Laden's demise "conspiracy theories." In Orwellian fashion, the terrorist mastermind's date of death is officially May 1, 2011, by combined government and corporate media diktat; alternative accounts of bin Laden's demise have been dispatched to the memory hole.[4]

The extremely limited understanding of and desensitization to the human and fiscal costs of war fostered by corporate media has allowed the Obama administration to carry out and even publicly admit to policies that contradict the long-running "war on terror" narrative. After it became public knowledge that the US and North Atlantic Treaty Organization (NATO) were using al-Qaeda personnel in Libya—the same terrorist group such forces were apparently combatting throughout the Middle East and whose leader US Special Forces allegedly corralled on May 1, 2011—Secretary of State Hillary Clinton admitted in a BBC television interview that the US was allied with al-Qaeda in Syria. Yet US corporate media further perpetuated the dominant 9/11 storyline by failing to clarify or expand on this admission in subsequent reportage.

The mass-mediated spectacle of bin Laden's assassination is one of many examples highlighting the commercial news media's continued fealty to US-led imperialism. The Censored stories here provide an explanatory cross section of how such media act to cleanse the routine barbarity of war from the public mind. Indeed, as war outlays are predicted to escalate to as much as $4 trillion and counting,[5] a persistent function of the military-industrial complex and its myth-making apparatus is to keep serious analysis of monetary and human war costs sufficiently distanced from public consciousness.

Censored #8: NATO War Crimes in Libya

Under President Obama, the US and its NATO allies continue to actively expand the international war on terror begun by George W. Bush. While US troops remain mired in Iraq and Afghanistan purportedly fighting al-Qaeda and its allies, a rag-tag mercenary army with al-Qaeda elements joined forces with NATO to topple Libya's Muammar Qaddafi regime. In the name of protecting Libyan civilians from what Western government sources and corporate media reported as an alleged Qaddafi crackdown, the declaration of a "no-fly zone" precipitated US and NATO military aircraft and insurgent forces' attacks on civilian targets, causing untold numbers of injuries and deaths of innocent Libyans, while leaving many more homeless.[6]

Independent media provided a historical context for understanding the links between the US and NATO-backed Libyan and Syrian destabilizations and their relationship to al-Qaeda that mainstream outlets routinely obfuscated through fragmented and under-contextualized news pieces. As French author Thierry Meyssan reported, back in the 1990s Libya was the first state to initiate a hunt for bin Laden, which eventually prompted America's future arch enemy to relocate to Afghanistan in 2001.

In the early 1980s, Abdel Hakim Belhadj, now the NATO-installed military governor of Tripoli and commander of Libya's new army, fought against the Soviets in Afghanistan alongside bin Laden, becoming leader of bin Laden's Libyan Islamic Fighting Group (LIFG) in 1992. Belhadj went into hiding following the US invasion of Afghanistan in 2001, then was taken into custody by Western intelligence in 2004 and held in Libya. The al-Qaeda operative moved to Qatar after his release from custody in 2010.[7]

Seymour Hersh reported that a US policy to align with Sunni Arab states dates to the latter years of the George W. Bush administration, when the US committed to a substantial "redirection" in Middle Eastern foreign policy. The shift was intended to undermine influence of the Shiite Hezbollah organization and its backer, the predominantly Shiite Iran, by allying with Israel, Sunni Gulf states, including Saudi Arabia and Qatar, and Sunni extremist groups, the most well-known being al-Qaeda and the Muslim Brotherhood.[8] Pointing to Hersh's perceptive work, journalist Tony Cartalucci commented, "As the West feigns shock and horror over the rise of their Sunni front, from Egypt to Syria, and beyond, along with the resurrection of the Muslim Brotherhood . . . it is clear that in reality this is the fruition of a complex premeditated plan, years in the making."[9]

The strategic relationship with Sunni states remains intact through the Obama administration. In early 2011, Saudi Prince Bandar Bin Sultan and the Central Intelligence Agency (CIA) headed up an ambitious program to broaden recruitment of al-Qaeda mercenaries to carry out jihad in Libya, Syria, and Yemen. A 10,000-man army was eventually gathered and unleashed as "Libyan rebels," beginning with the "day of anger" in Benghazi on February 17, 2011. When Qaddafi's forces attempted to quell what was essentially a small-scale foreign invasion, Western leaders and media pounced on the action as evidence of the regime's oppression of its citizens. This provided the pretext for the extensive NATO bombing, the al-Qaeda army's continued looting of the country, and Qaddafi's eventual ouster.

On May 1, 2011, Barack Obama announced the extrajudicial killing of Osama bin Laden. As Meyssan observed, "The announcement padlocked the al-Qaeda file and enabled the revamping of the jihadists into the renewed allies of the United States as in the good old days of the Afghanistan, Bosnia, Chechnya, and Kosovo wars."[10] Months later, Belhadj returned to Libya in a Qatar military aircraft under NATO auspices to preside over the new Libyan army.[11] The lack of a sufficient historical backdrop combined with the myth of America's humanitarian largesse renders much of the corporate media's coverage of the Libyan incursion ambiguous. For example, in "Smoking Guns: War Crimes in Libya," Michael Collins argued that NATO's actions in Libya had nothing to do with protecting Libyan civilians:

> There was no mention of assisting the military operations of the Libyan rebels fighting the Gaddafi regime. There was no authorization to attack and destroy civilian targets. Most importantly, there was no authorization whatsoever, no matter how tortured the logic, that enabled the coordination of land and air forces to win a military victory.

Along these lines, Professor Michel Chossudovsky, editor of the website Global Research, republished a flattering photographic essay from a prominent UK paper of al-Qaeda insurgents destroying the Libyan city of Sirte. Chossudovsky's prefatory statement simultaneously spoke to the importance of context while nullifying the article's propagandistic potential.

> The following report by the *Daily Mail* confirms that NATO by targeting civilians is responsible for extensive war crimes in Libya. The pictures . . . confirm what the *Daily Mail* fails to mention: the extensive criminal bombing of a country of 6 million people under an alleged humanitarian mandate.[12]

The photos depicted a city that has been devastated by what is admitted to be a small band of Libyan nationalists. The so-called rebels are depicted in a positive, almost heroic light. "These photographs show the rebel fighters taking some time out from battle," one caption read, "some carrying a guitar [sic] while others ride their bicycles." Elsewhere, anti-Qaddafi insurgents are shown "having a little nap" or "flash[ing] the victory sign at photographers during the Battle of Sirte." The article is revealing in its graphic representations that succeed precisely as propaganda under the auspices of the US and NATO's larger narrative: the intervention is necessary to protect Libyan civilians from Qaddafi's alleged crackdown.

Libya's destruction is a tragedy of historic proportions, especially given the country's modern features and formerly bright future. Indeed, Qaddafi's plans for the inhabitants of Libya and the broader African continent included the creation of a vast irrigation program designed to prevent the desertification of Africa, an independent financial system for Libyans, a potential United States of Africa, and a wealth redistribution process financed through oil revenues.[13]

Background knowledge and historical context confirming al-Qaeda and Western involvement in the destabilization of the Qaddafi regime are also essential for making sense of corporate news narratives depicting the Libyan operation as a popular "uprising." The ground war and NATO air bombardment are one chapter in the West's alleged humanitarian war that has proven anything but humanitarian. Significant reportage that did appear frequently surfaced following Qaddafi's overthrow. For example, after the smoke cleared in Libya, the BBC revealed how British Special Forces played a key role in overseeing Libya's so-called "freedom fighters" that were equipped with state-of-the-art weapons and communications equipment.

Lamb Franklin documented in *Counterpunch* how Human Rights Watch and Amnesty International further revealed that Libyan rebels abducted 105 children from a Libyan government orphanage, with testimonies suggesting that the children were last seen being taken to a Turkish, Italian, or French vessel, and more than one witness claiming they saw some of the children being sold in Tunisia.

NATO forces were also responsible for bombing Libya's main water source, the Nubian Sandstone Aquifer System, on July 22, 2011. Reports for Global Research and Pravda by Timothy Bancroft-Hinchey explained how the apparatus provides water for close to three-quarters of the Libyan population. On April 3, Libya warned that NATO air strikes could cause a "human and environmental disaster" if the plant were hit. Not only did NATO attack the aquifer structure, but also the Brega pipe production plant necessary to repair the system.

Corporate news coverage was slow to acknowledge NATO's war

crimes against the Libyan people. For example, in a posthumous on-the-ground investigation of the seven-month air campaign, the *New York Times* "found credible accounts of dozens of civilians killed by NATO in many distinct attacks," yet admits its deficiencies given the new Libyan leadership's limited interest in a detailed investigation, especially since the new regime's "survival and climb to power were made possible largely by the airstrike campaign." No mention is made of NATO's destruction of Libya's major aquifer system.[14]

In November 2011, Tripoli's military governor Belhadj was busy coordinating with leaders of the "Free Syrian Army" to aid in destabilization of Syria's Bashar al-Assad regime by committing weapons, money, and LIFG soldiers to train and accompany the Syrian insurgents. "Having ousted one dictator," the UK *Telegraph* reported, "triumphant young men, still filled with revolutionary fervor, are keen to topple the next. The commanders of armed gangs still roaming Tripoli's streets said yesterday that 'hundreds' of fighters wanted to wage war against the Assad regime."[15] Despite abundant information to the contrary, these forces remain obscure in corporate media accounts of Syria's destabilization. As was the scenario for Libya, the event is framed as an internecine people's rebellion that the Assad regime is seeking to ruthlessly crush.

Censored #12: US Joins Forces with al-Qaeda in Syria

Secretary of State Hillary Clinton's recognition that the US and al-Qaeda are on the same page in supporting clandestine activities to weaken the Assad government appears bizarre only if taken out of the above context and specifically viewed through the corporate media lens.[16] "Since the middle of March 2011," Chossudovsky and Cunningham noted,

> Islamist armed groups—covertly supported by Western and Israeli intelligence—have conducted terrorist attacks directed against government buildings, including acts of arson. Amply documented, trained gunmen and snipers, including mercenaries, have targeted police, armed forces as well as innocent civilians.[17]

In November 2011, independent journalist Webster Tarpley traveled to the Syrian towns of Damascus, Homs, and Baniyas. After interviewing dozens of Syrian officials and frightened citizens, he further confirmed that the violence was attributable to CIA- and NATO-backed death squads and snipers operating within the country.[18]

In light of such research and analysis, corporate US coverage relying heavily on US government sources appears to be not only ill-informed but intentionally confusing. For example, quoting US Director of National Intelligence James R. Clapper, a *Washington Post* report highlighted the Obama administration's claim, days before Clinton's admission on the BBC, that recent bombings "'had all the earmarks of an al-Qaeda–like attack'" and that "the network's affiliate in Iraq 'is extending its reach into Syria.'" Neglecting al-Qaeda's resurgence under Saudi, Israeli, and US intelligence aegis in Libya and Syria, the report amazingly asserted,

> Al-Qaeda has largely been relegated to the sidelines in a series of uprisings across the Arab world over the past year, and its affiliate in Iraq has struggled to regroup after being hunted to near extinction by Shiite militias aligned with the American military "surge."[19]

In the cases of Libya and Syria, the US government and corporate media have used the guise of humanitarian intervention to perpetuate the myth of Western altruism and good intent. These techniques obscure what are in reality altogether brutal and ruinous policies. Yet when US soldiers are directly implicated in carrying out atrocities against innocent civilians, the media's damage control and propagandistic function on behalf of military and government entities are in many ways even more deliberately repressive.

Censored #23: US Covers Up Afghanistan Massacre

Some wartime coverage has the potential to strongly stir public sentiment against a given conflict. As the US–NATO destabilizations in Libya and Syria suggest, the victims of war's physical and emotional violence involve not only soldiers in the battlefield, but far too often defenseless civilians. In Afghanistan and Iraq, there have been frequent reports of civilians murdered, execution-style, in their homes during nighttime raids by US soldiers—a practice Afghan President Hamid Karzai says is commonplace. The corporate media's framing of the March 2012 massacre of Afghans in their homes by US forces eerily resembled an incident that took place forty-four years earlier. Just before 8:00 a.m. on March 16, 1968, the US Army's C Company, First Battalion, Twentieth Infantry, Eleventh Brigade, American Division entered the My Lai hamlet in Vietnam on one of many common "search and destroy" missions that typically inflicted a high civilian toll. By noon as many as 500 women, children, and elderly Vietnamese were slaughtered. A young Seymour Hersh interviewed several dozen members of "Charlie Company" and broke the story for the small Dispatch News Service. When *Newsweek* picked up the piece, it was pitched to the American public as "An American Tragedy"—simply a severe yet uncommon glitch in the largely humane US war machine. "This set the tone for the coverage of My Lai," John Pilger observed, "as an aberration that called for sympathy for Americans, not the Vietnamese—even though other atrocities were being revealed."[20]

On March 11, 2012, in rural Kandahar Province, Afghanistan, at least sixteen Afghan civilians were executed in their homes by what Afghans claimed was a US Special Forces team. Performing something akin to what *Newsweek* had done with reporting on My Lai, the Obama administration and Pentagon directly intervened to shape the unfolding story. President Obama asserted that the massacre was the work of a single soldier—Staff Sargent Robert Bales—who had buckled under the strains of war.

The United Nations reported that in 2011 alone, pro-government forces, which include NATO troops and the Afghan Army, killed 410 Afghans. Of these, 187 died due to botched NATO air strikes of homes occupied by suspected insurgents. Overall, 3,021 Afghans died in 2011 due to the US–NATO occupation.[21] The brutal March 2012 event appeared to be the last straw for Afghan President Hamid Karzai, who announced that eyewitness testimonies of the massacre differed markedly from the US military's account. An Afghan parliamentary investigation and an inquiry by Afghan Army General Sher Mohammed Karimi revealed how the occasion was in fact one of many carefully coordinated nighttime raids by US Special Forces.

Survivors and onlookers pointed out how it was not possible for one soldier to kill nine children, four men, and three women in two villages three miles apart.

On March 16, Karzai requested that US forces leave rural areas of the country. In an article appearing in *Al Akhbar*, a rare exchange between Karzai and Obama is explained through the Afghan president's recounting. "This morning, Obama called regarding this issue," Karzai remarked. "He asked, 'Did you announce this?' I said, 'Yes, I announced it.'"[22] News of Karzai's announcement in international and alternative media contrasted sharply with the US version of events. As James Petras observed,

> Whatever triggered the mass murder of mothers and children in their nightclothes in those villages in Kandahar, one thing is clear: the President of the United States conspired with the US military command to obstruct justice in the cover-up of a heinous war crime, a felony punishable with impeachment.[23]

Then, a report from Yalda Hakim for World News Australia's SBS Dateline program further brought the Afghan government's investigations and survivors' accounts to an international audience. The story involved poignant testimonies of survivors, including an eight-year-old girl, Noorbinak, who was one of many witnesses to note that more than one soldier was involved. "My mother was screaming and he held a gun to her and my father said, 'Leave her alone' and then he shot him right there." The soldier then shot Noorbinak in the leg. "One entered the room and the others were standing in the yard, holding lights."

The reference to numerous US soldiers and even helicopters looming overhead was a consistent claim made by other adult eyewitnesses and village elders interviewed by General Karimi. "The noise of the helicopters were there [sic] from the very beginning, when the shooting started," Karimi said. "That means there were many Americans that were supporting this issue, that were doing this deliberately—it's not one individual. That's the claim of the people."[24]

Yet in the US corporate mediascape, the Afghan government and military's investigations were heavily suppressed and Hakim's account unfairly represented. The handful of outlets that touched on Hakim's exposé gave the impression that her interviews were all with young children, and hence unreliable. Overlooking the Afghan inquiries, MSNBC wrote of the "two versions of what happened the night of March 11 . . . the Army version" and "the account that child witnesses provided Yalda Hakim."[25] Hakim even confirmed this misleading frame in an interview with CNN where, again, the Afghan government findings were completely overlooked. "I spoke mainly to children and it is always difficult to assess whether a child is actually aware of what they saw. . . . They were open and I felt they were heartfelt but there were disparities between the stories certainly."[26]

US journalism's approach to this story—parroting the government propaganda—is emblematic of its overall treatment of US involvement in the Middle East. Even if Obama's storyline were true, the event might have sparked a broad and enduring national discussion in the US over the high cost of the war in terms of its carnage and the systematic terror and killing visited upon the civilians vis-à-vis the frayed emotional and psychological conditions of the soldiers.

Yet in typical fashion, media tightly focused on Sargent Bales's plight, personalizing the story around the likeable soldier and devoted family man who had some tough luck, suffered a Traumatic Brain Injury (TBI), and went astray after too many tours of duty. After three weeks of profuse coverage that included Bales's flamboyant defense attorney, the story faded from view and the Obama administration's lone soldier account carried the day.

Further absent from the corporate media's frame is consideration of corporate media's largest cash cows[27]—psychotropic drugs and their well-documented record of causing suicidal and homicidal behavior. Shortly after the story broke, Mike Adams of NaturalNews.com raised this very concern, reporting how, since the 2007 surge, over 20,000 US troops were prescribed antidepressants by army physicians for Post-Traumatic Stress Disorder and TBI, and how their heavy use in stressful situations could have disastrous results.[28] "Many of the drugs prescribed by military doctors, like Paxil and Zoloft, are also accompanied by warnings about an increased risk of suicide," Adams noted.[29] While mainstream accounts gave considerable attention to Bales's probable emotional and mental problems, the important question of the role such drugs played in his alleged actions was never broached.

Censored #25: Evidence Points to Guantánamo Dryboarding

Framing, selective sourcing, or omission also aid in the cover-up of violence and cruelty inflicted on those held in captivity by US forces. In 2006, three Muslim detainees at the Guantánamo Bay detention camp allegedly committed suicide by hanging. The US camp commander claimed the deaths were a form of "asymmetrical warfare" to advance al-Qaeda's larger cause. However, subsequent research and evidence unearthed by *Truthout* strongly suggested how the prisoners were tortured, killed, then returned to their cells by prison guards and arranged to appear as suicides. As with the Afghan massacre, where President Obama's explanation of the single deranged soldier was accepted almost unquestioningly by major media, so too is the media's unquestioning acceptance of the Guantánamo "suicides," even though the military's own investigation indicated otherwise.

A close analysis of the Naval Criminal Investigation Service's (NCIS) report by Almerindo Ojeda reveals that the three prisoners' bodies all shared similar features and abnormalities that could not have been self-inflicted. Had mainstream journalists looked past the Department of Defense's press release calling the deaths suicides, a far more disturbing picture comes into focus.

The NCIS inquiry also classified the deaths as suicides, even though the report's severely redacted pages could not warrant such a conclusion. For example, the prisoners were found hanging with their hands tied, their mouths stuffed with rags, and mask-like devices on their faces. The unusual measures taken to kill themselves are identical to those necessary for "dryboarding"—a method of torture where the victim's mouth is stuffed with cloth and bound in duct tape for controlled suffocation.

Other circumstances also call the military's explanation into question. Guards on duty the night of the deaths came forth to point out that three unidentified prisoners were taken from their cells and driven in a white van to a secret facility on the Guantánamo Naval Base. A colonel at the base then held a meeting to inform personnel that three prisoners had committed suicide by having rags stuffed down their throats. The colonel then informed the servicemen that the news media would report how the prisoners hanged themselves, and that it was essential that no one say anything contradicting the official report.

The military's use of dryboarding as torture came to light as a result of Ali Saleh Kahlah al-Marri's case. Al-Marri was a Qatar citizen visiting the US in 2001 to pursue graduate studies. He was detained by US authorities, held in solitary confinement for almost a year and a half, then declared an enemy combatant by President George W. Bush in 2003, transferred to a US Naval brig, and mercilessly tortured. The significance of al-Marri's case for explaining the 2006 deaths of the Guantánamo detainees' fate is that the account of al-Marri's dryboarding, described by his attorney at the sentencing trial, was undisputed by the US government's legal representative.

The most unfortunate upshot of the unresolved deaths of the three Guantánamo prisoners is the blatant subterfuge and unaccountability of the US military in fully coming to terms with the crime. As Ojeda concludes,

There is a need for a thorough, independent, and transparent investigation into the June 10, 2006, deaths at Guantánamo and, more broadly, for a thorough, independent and transparent inquiry into all the practices and policies of detention enacted since the terrorist attacks of September 11, 2001.

RELATED VALIDATED NEWS STORY

US Military Pays $1.1 Trillion to Contractors that Defrauded Government

In previous *Censored* yearbooks, reports on the costs of war have been highlighted as especially important yet overlooked news items. As the above stories suggest, the costs extend beyond quantifiable markers. The moral lopsidedness of war's consequences involves the forfeiture of an immense number of unimaginably shattered lives and dreams for the economic gains of a select few. In the end, inequitable power relations are only strengthened. "Nations acquire territory," World War I Brigadier General Smedley Butler wrote. "This newly acquired territory promptly is exploited by the few—the same few who wrung dollars out of blood in the war. The general public shoulders the bill."[30] After more than ten years of war, at the dawn of the new millennium, little has changed. With the war on terror myths laid bare, the US public is left with an immense bill and nothing to show for it but a severely tarnished national reputation and far greater social and economic inequality.

A study on the costs of the "post-9/11 wars" in Afghanistan, Iraq, and Pakistan conducted by over twenty academics with the Eisenhower Research Project at Brown University's Watson Institute for International Studies estimates the overall price to US taxpayers of $3.2 to $4 trillion.[31] The report received considerable coverage in mainstream media in the lead-up to the tenth anniversary of 9/11.

Along these lines, however, a story with similar significance was afforded far less attention. In "US Military Paid $1.1 Trillion to Contractors that Defrauded the Government," Mike Ludwig reports on the findings of an investigation by US Senator Bernie Sanders. Since

2001, the defense department paid $1.1 trillion to military contractors that had been found guilty of defrauding the government.[32] A tentative conclusion may be drawn that discussion of war costs is at least partially acceptable in major media if there is no express notice that many of the multinationals owning the corporate news outlets benefit handsomely from the public war subsidy. Drawing attention to and interrogating the massive profits and unaccountable behavior of their corporate parents is another matter entirely.

JAMES F. TRACY is associate professor of media studies at Florida Atlantic University where he teaches courses on media history and the role of journalism in the public sphere. Tracy's work on media history has appeared in numerous journal articles and book chapters. He is editor of *Democratic Communiqué*, journal of the Union for Democratic Communications, and a contributor to GlobalResearch.ca.

Notes

1. Harold Lasswell, *Propaganda Technique in the World War* (London: Kegan Paul, Trench, Trubner, 1938 [1927]), 47.
2. Herbert I. Schiller, *The Mind Managers* (Boston: Beacon Press, 1973), 1.
3. Mickey S. Huff and Paul W. Rea, "Deconstructing Deceit: 9/11, the Media, and Myth Information," in *Censored 2009: The Top 25 Censored Stories of 2007-08*, eds. Peter Phillips and Andrew Roth, 341–364 (New York: Seven Stories Press, 2008).
4. James F. Tracy, "The 9/11 Myth: State Propaganda, Historical Revisionism, and the Perpetuation of the 9/11 Myth," Global Research, May 6, 2012, http://globalresearch.ca/index.php?context=va&aid=30721.
5. Daniel Trotta, "Cost of War At Least $3.7 Trillion and Counting," Reuters, June 29, 2011, http://www.reuters.com/article/2011/06/29/us-usa-war-idUSTRE75S25320110629.
6. A formal framework for the Obama administration's 'humanitarian" intervention was established in August 2011 with the creation of an Atrocities Prevention Board. The governmental APB facilitates more direct US involvement in "leading international efforts to bring pressure to bear on the abusive Qadhafi and Assad regimes through the formation of Groups of Friends, the imposition of extensive sanctions, support for the opposition, and support for efforts to bring perpetrators of atrocities to justice." Fact Sheet: A Comprehensive Strategy and New Tools to Prevent and Respond to Atrocities, The White House, August 4, 2011, http://www.whitehouse.gov/the-press-office/2012/04/23/fact-sheet-comprehensive-strategy-and-new-tools-prevent-and-respond-atro.
7. Thierry Meyssan, "How Al Qaeda Men Came to Power in Libya," *Voltaire Network*, September 7, 2011, http://www.voltairenet.org/How-Al-Qaeda-men-came-to-power-in. See also, Azhar Masood, "CIA Recruits 1,500 From Masar-e-Sharif to Fight in Libya," *The Nation* (Pakistan), August 31, 2011, http://www.nation.com.pk/pakistan-news-newspaper-daily-english-online/Politics/31-Aug-2011/CIA-recruits-1500-from-MazareSharif-to-fight-in-Libya.
8. Seymour M. Hersh, "The Redirection: Is the Administration's New Policy Benefitting Our Enemies in the War on Terrorism?" *New Yorker*, March 5, 2007, http://www.newyorker.com/reporting/2007/03/05/070305fa_fact_hersh.
9. Tony Cartalucci, "Extremists Ravaging Syria Created by US in 2007," *Land Destroyer Report*, May 11, 2012, http://landdestroyer.blogspot.com/2012/05/sunni-extremists-ravaging-syria-created.html.

10. Meyssan, "How Al Qaeda Men Came to Power in Libya."
11. Labib Nasir and Alastair Macdonald, "Libyan Islamist Commander Swaps Combat Rig for Suit," Reuters, November 11, 2011, http://www.reuters.com/article/2011/11/11/us-libya-islamist-belhaj-idUSTRE7AA52320111111.
12. Michel Chossudovsky, "NATO War Crimes: The Wanton Destruction of Sirte. Extraordinary Pictures Show Libyan City Shelled to Smithereens," Global Research, October 15, 2011, http://www.globalresearch.ca/index.php?context=va&aid=27092.
13. Mahdi Darius Nazemroaya, "Who Was Muammar Qaddafi? Libya's Wealth Redistribution Project," Global Research, October 27, 2011, http://www.globalresearch.ca/index.php?context=va&aid=27327.
14. C. J. Chivers and Eric Schmitt, "In Strikes on Libya by NATO, An Unspoken Civilian Toll," New York Times, December 17, 2011, http://www.nytimes.com/2011/12/18/world/africa/scores-of-unintended-casualties-in-nato-war-in-libya.html?_r=1&pagewanted=all.
15. Ruth Sherlock, "Leading Libyan Islamist Met Free Syrian Army Opposition Group," Telegraph, November 27, 2011, http://www.telegraph.co.uk/news/worldnews/africaandindianocean/libya/8919057/Leading-Libyan-Islamist-met-Free-Syrian-Army-opposition-group.html.
16. Cartalucci, "Extremists Ravaging Syria Created by US in 2007."
17. Chossudovsky and Finian Cunningham, "Syria: Clinton Admits US on Same Side As Al Qaeda to Destabilise Assad Government," Global Research, February 27, 2012, http://globalresearch.ca/index.php?context=va&aid=29524.
18. Webster G. Tarpley, "No Civil War in Syria, but a Killing Spree by CIA-NATO Death Squads Including the Al Qaeda Mass Murderer Belhadj of Libya," Kevin Barrett Show, November 28, 2011, http://tarpley.net/2011/11/28/no-civil-war-in-syria-but-a-killing-spree-by-cia-nato/. See also, "NATO-Backed Death Squads Basic Cause of Syria Unrest," PressTV, May 10, 2012, http://www.presstv.com/detail/240482.html.
19. Greg Miller, "Al Qaeda Infiltrating Syrian Opposition, U.S. Officials Say," Washington Post, February 16, 2012, http://www.washingtonpost.com/world/national-security/al Qaeda-infiltrating-syrian-opposition-us-officials-say/2012/02/16/gIQA9LDJIR_story.html.
20. John Pilger, ed., Tell Me No Lies: Investigative Journalism that Changed the World (New York: Thunder's Mouth Press, 2005), 86.
21. Allissa J. Rubin, "Record Number of Afghan Civilians Died in 2011, Mostly in Insurgent Attacks, U.N. Says," New York Times, February 4, 2012, http://www.nytimes.com/2012/02/04/world/asia/afghanistan-civilian-deaths-hit-record-un-says.html.
22. "More Than One US Soldier Involved in Massacre: Afghan President," Al Akhbar English, March 16, 2012, http://english.al-akhbar.com/content/multiple-soldiers-involved-killing-afghan-civilians-afghan-president.
23. James Petras, "The Massacre of the Afghan 17 and the Obama Cover-Up," Veterans Today, March 27, 2012, http://www.veteranstoday.com/2012/03/27/the-massacre-of-the-afghan-17-and-the-obama-cover-up.
24. Yalda Hakim, "Anatomy of a Massacre," SBS Dateline, March 27, 2012, http://www.sbs.com.au/dateline/story/about/id/601431/n/Anatomy-of-a-Massacre.
25. "Child Witnesses to Afghan Massacre Say Robert Bales Was Not Alone," MSNBC March 29, 2012, http://worldnews.msnbc.msn.com/_news/2012/03/29/10927844-child-witnesses-to-afghan-massacre-say-robert-bales-was-not-alone?lite.
26. Peter Shadbolt, "Afghan Massacre: Truth of Events Remains Elusive," CNN, March 30, 2012, http://www.cnn.com/2012/03/30/world/asia/afghanistan-massacre.
27. In 2009 the pharmaceutical industry spent $4.5 billion on direct-to-consumer advertising. David Rosen, "How Does the Drug Industry Get Away with Broadcasting Those Deceptive Ads?" AlterNet, March 12, 2011, http://www.alternet.org/media/149909/how_does_the_drug_industry_get_away_with_broadcasting_those_deceptive_ads/?page=entire.
28. Mike Adams, "Afghanistan Massacre by U.S. Sergeant Reveals Epidemic of Psychiatric Drugging of Soldiers," NaturalNews.com, March 13, 2012, http://www.naturalnews.com/035232_US_troops_psychiatric_drugs_Afghanistan.html.
29. Ibid.

30. Smedley D. Butler, *War is a Racket* (Port Townsend, WA: Feral House, 2003), 23–24.
31. "Estimated Cost of Post-9/11 Wars: 225,000 Lives, Up to $4 Trillion," Brown University, press release, June 29, 2011, http://news.brown.edu/pressreleases/2011/06/warcosts.
32. Mike Ludwig, "US Military Paid $1.1 Trillion to Contractors that Defrauded the Government," *Truthout*, October 20, 2011, http://truth-out.org/index.php?option=com_k2&view=item&id=4141:us-military-paid-11-trillion-to-contractors-that-defrauded-the-government.

Women and Gender, Race and Ethnicity

by Susan Rahman and Liliana Valdez-Madera

Censored #16

Sexual Violence against Women Soldiers on the Rise and under Wraps

John Lasker, "Sexual Violence Against Women in the US Military: The Search for Truth and Justice," *Toward Freedom*, July 14, 2011, http://www.towardfreedom.com/women/2474-sexual-violence-against-women-in-the-us-military-the-search-for-truth-and-justice.

Student Researcher: Taylor Falbisaner (Sonoma State University)

Faculty Evaluator: Peter Phillips (Sonoma State University)

Censored #18

Palestinian Women Prisoners Shackled during Childbirth

Fabrizia Falcione, interview by Mehru Jaffer, "Interview: Palestinian Women Prisoners Shackled During Childbirth," Electronic Intifada, March 11, 2011, http://electronicintifada.net/v2/article11852.shtml.

Student Researcher: Kaitlyn Vargas (Sonoma State University)

Faculty Advisor: Diana Grant (Sonoma State University)

Censored #24

Alabama Farmers Look to Replace Migrants with Prisoners

Agence France-Presse, "Alabama Farmers Look to Replace Migrants with Prisoners," *Raw Story*, December 6, 2011, http://www.rawstory.com/rs/2011/12/06/alabama-farmers-look-to-replace-migrants-with-prisoners.

CanyonWren, "Of Course! Inmate Labor in Place of Migrants in Alabama," *Daily Kos* (blog), December 8, 2011, http://www.dailykos.com/story/2011/12/08/1043143/-Of-Course!-Inmate-Labor-in-Place-of-Migrants-in-Alabama.

Mike Elk and Bob Sloan, "The Hidden History of ALEC and Prison Labor," *Nation*, August 1, 2011, http://www.thenation.com/article/162478/hidden-history-alec-and-prison-labor.

Student Researcher: Liliana Valdez-Madera (Santa Rosa Junior College)

Faculty Evaluator: Susan Rahman (Santa Rosa Junior College)

RELATED VALIDATED INDEPENDENT NEWS STORIES

Susan Williams, "The Color of an Unequal Recession," *Freedom Socialist*, October 2011, http://www.socialism.com/drupal-6.8/?q=node/1730.

Jodi Jacobson, "Honduran Supreme Court Upholds Most Sweeping Ban on Emergency Contraception Anywhere," *RH Reality Check*, February 14, 2012, http://www.rhrealitycheck.org/article/2012/02/14/honduran-supreme-court-upholds-complete-ban-on-emergency-contraception-o.

Human Rights Watch, "US: Protect Detainees in Immigration Facilities from Rape; Don't Exempt These Facilities from Protection Measures," Human Rights Watch, February 15, 2011, http://www.hrw.org/en/news/2011/02/15/us-protect-detainees-immigration-facilities-rape.

Human Rights Watch, "Detained and at Risk," Human Rights Watch, August 25, 2010, http://www.hrw.org/reports/2010/08/25/detained-and-risk.

Student Researchers: Taylor Falbisaner (Sonoma State University); Eileen Harlin (Santa Rosa Junior College); Mayra Garces and Natalie Hill (DePauw University)

Faculty Evaluators: Peter Phillips (Sonoma State University); Susan Rahman (Santa Rosa Junior College); Kevin Howley and Glen David Kuecker (DePauw University)

Women and racialized minorities have unequal access to power both in the United States and around the world: statistically, they earn less money and hold fewer high-profile or powerful positions, and they have fewer decision-making opportunities and allowances than white males. Furthermore, racialized minorities, particularly African American and Latino men, make up a disproportionately high number of people who are incarcerated—which in essence leaves them permanently marginalized from mainstream society.[1] Because media are one of many institutions that shape society, the larger problem of disenfranchisement of women and racialized minorities is exacerbated by how media discuss these groups.

The media have failed to adequately represent women and people of color throughout history. Although women and people of color make up over half the total US population, they are disproportionately left out of the stories that we consume and not given a voice as the storytellers, directors, writers, and owners of corporate media. It seems clear that corporate media speak for the interests of the dominant culture, and so what is deemed important to communicate fails to address a growing segment of the population. Vast numbers of people are left out of the story. With the consolidation of media ownership over the last thirty years, the few have been speaking for and about the many. Women and racialized minorities become invisible or only partially represented as a result of the lack of diversity in media ownership. And when women and racialized minorities *are* represented, there is inevitable bias as a result of the economic interests that maintain corporate media. Jason Smith wrote, "As the American Society of Newspaper Editors has reported, racial and ethnic minorities make up less than 13 percent of newsroom employees. Minority ownership of television stations hovers around 3 percent, while radio station ownership is at 7 percent, despite the fact that the minority population of the US is roughly 28 percent."[2]

In recent years, the faces featured on local news stations, especially in metropolitan areas, have been increasingly diverse, but we have to remember that anchors are often not the people who write the stories, but rather those acting the role of storyteller. This shift in who is in front of the camera is a positive one, but it needs to be accompanied by more diversity at all stages of the news production process. Stories involving women are starkly underreported. In 2002, Fairness & Accuracy in Reporting (FAIR) found that women made up only 15 percent of all story sources and were rarely featured as experts on *ABC World News Tonight, CBS Evening News,* and *NBC Nightly News.*[3] Ten years later, in March 2012, Media Report to Women found that employment of women and racialized minorities in media has remained disproportionately low.[4]

The media's current power structure does not favor improvement on these numbers. Women own just 6 percent of the commercial broadcast TV stations in the US, and people of color own just 3 percent. At local television stations that air news, about half of their anchor positions are filled by women, but only 28 percent of news director positions and 16 percent of general manager positions. People of color hold just 16 percent of local news director positions and 10 percent of general manager positions.[5]

These figures exemplify how women and people of color are left out of the stories told by corporate media. When corporate media do include women and people of color, they often tell just one type of story without complexities, and therefore distort our perceptions and create a narrow view of the subjects. For example, African American males and Latinos typically feature in the news as criminals, white women usually play in ancillary roles, and women of color are often simply ignored.

Undocumented women of color fare especially poorly in corporate media coverage. They are invisible and unimportant in our culture to the extent that laws protecting everyone else do not apply to them. For example, in February 2011, Attorney General Eric Holder proposed revisions to the 2003 Prison Rape Elimination Act to detect, prevent, reduce, and punish sexual abuse of people in government custody. Although the proposal extended new protections to women prisoners, it excluded immigrant women in detention centers. Thus, immigrant women of color are not entitled to the same protections against sexual assault.[6] Actions speak louder than words, and these actions clearly say that immigrants are not entitled to human rights. Are they not human? If we know that the incidence of sexual assault is higher in the US than in any other industrialized nation, and we seek, as an ideal cultural value, to eliminate it, then we have to wonder why immigrant detainees are not worthy of full protection under this law.

So why do the media report news primarily for and by white men? One answer could be that those in power are well served by media that broadcast narratives that suit their purposes. The media become an important tool in shaping perceptions and values, and also play a large role in teaching about "the other"—people or groups who are "not like us." This serves to give us the impression that we do understand groups we may otherwise not know personally, thus increasing in-group solidarity, a useful tool in gearing up for war, military spending, and general fear-mongering. If we make the argument that corporate media serve as a tool of those in power, to tell the stories that help maintain that power both in the US and globally, then we wonder: What are the important stories that have not been reported? When it comes to issues of gender and ethnicity, here are some of the themes we see left out of the stories.

Censored #18: Palestinian Women Prisoners Shackled during Childbirth

Female Palestinian prisoners in Israeli prisons are treated inhumanely. They are often denied medical care, legal representation, and are forced to live in squalid conditions, including sharing cells with cockroaches, rodents, and overflowing sewage. Fabrizia Falcione, a women's human rights officer for the United Nations Entity for Gender Equality and the Empowerment of Women (UN Women) stated that it is critical to reveal the human face behind this breach of international law and international humanitarian law.

Since 1967, more than 700,000 Palestinians have been arrested or detained in Israeli prisons and detention centers. Approximately 10,000 of these prisoners have been women. Falcione stated that "the plight of female prisoners is worse than the men. The situation, condition and violations faced by women in jails in Israel needs to be addressed from a gender perspective." Women require medical attention regularly, which is their right during confinement as recognized by the United Nation's Committee on the Elimination of Discrimination against Women (CEDAW). Imprisoned Palestinian women receive little or no medical attention during childbirth. The women are shackled and often disregarded during the birthing process.

Throughout the jails, many other laws and regulations are broken. Women's religious customs and beliefs are disregarded, and untried women are housed with convicted prisoners, which is a violation of rule 85 of the United Nations standard minimum rules for the treatment of prisoners: "Untried prisoners shall be kept separate from convicted prisoners."

In the United States, unless a woman of color has achieved fame in some arena, her story is not likely to be told. Similarly, it is not deemed important for mainstream America to hear that incarcerated Palestinian women are being shackled as they give birth. If we know that approximately 50 percent of Americans hold negative attitudes toward Arabs in general, and may not have very much compassion toward any prisoner, this is a story that is just not very compelling.[7]

This story is not just about Israel's mistreatment of incarcerated Palestinian women; more broadly, it reveals the inhumane treatment of women inmates. In a 2011 *Color Lines* article about the shackling of women prisoners during labor in the United States, which is legal in thirty-six states, Miriam Zoila Pérez reported:

> The arguments in favor of shackling prisoners usually come down to two points: flight risk and safety of the surrounding officers and medical professionals. For people who've been in labor or worked with women in labor, these arguments usually get no more than a laugh, as they find it hard to imagine a woman in labor getting very far, or posing a danger to anyone else. "I'm sure you can create your own

visual about a woman eight centimeters dilated and in labor. The chances of her getting up and running away are pretty slim," said Jeanne Conry, a district chair of American Congress of Obstetricians and Gynecologists in a recent article in the *Daily Beast*. These arguments also ignore the fact that the majority of women in prison are there for non-violent crimes.[8]

We see multiple underreported stories of women being mistreated in prison. Why is this subject not newsworthy? Could it be that this is a shameful practice, and that if more people knew about it, they would be outraged? Human rights atrocities like this happen all the time to women and people of color, and because they are not made public, they continue to occur.

Censored #16: Sexual Violence against Women Soldiers on the Rise and under Wraps

It is not just jailed women who find themselves stripped of their power and victims of abuse, harassment, and sexual assault. The US has the highest rate of rape in all of the industrialized nations.[9] This story details the alleged suicide of nineteen-year-old US Army Private LaVena Johnson, whose body showed evidence of brutal sexual assault, but whose death was called a suicide despite the evidence to the contrary. The mainstream media has neglected LaVena Johnson's story, as well as the incredible rise in suicides that have resulted from violence against women serving in the US military.

According John Lasker, every year the Cold Case Investigative Research Institute (CCIRI) takes on high-profile cold cases. So far, CCIRI has had its own ballistic and forensic experts and a psychologist, who is an expert on suicides, take a good look at the military's investigative file and autopsy photos; all raise serious doubts that Private Johnson killed herself. Her own father, Dr. John Johnson, has expressed strong skepticism regarding the Pentagon's version of the story. He also believes the Pentagon has a choking grip on any media coverage that might damage the military financially. Thus, if *60 Minutes* or ABC News were to air stories such as Johnson's, the military would pull advertising from those channels, he said.

The military sure as heck don't want to admit black female soldiers are being raped and murdered because they're having a hard time recruiting and retaining black females. Major media stories of brutally raped black female soldiers would devastate recruiting.

The US military's first autopsy of Johnson revealed broken teeth and scratch marks on her neck, but no serious injuries. Yet after being disinterred for a second autopsy, new X-rays revealed a broken neck. Even stranger, the second autopsy also showed that the military had removed parts of Johnson's tongue, vagina, and anus—about which they did not inform the Johnsons or document in the first autopsy.

Private Johnson's story is strange and twisted, but stories like hers are sadly becoming more and more common in Afghanistan and other war zones occupied by US troops. The mysterious deaths of female soldiers coincide with an increase in reported sexual violence against women in the military, during a time when women are joining like never before. In 1970, female soldiers made up 1 percent of the entire armed forces; today, that number has jumped to roughly 15 percent, nearly 200,000 in all. According to the Department of Defense (DOD), in 2010, there were 3,158 total reports of sexual assault in the military. The DOD estimates that this number represents only 13.5 percent of the actual assaults, making the total number of military rapes and sexual assaults in excess of 19,000 for the year.

We are experiencing a strange time in our societal evolution. Even as power in family structures has become more egalitarian, we've also seen a rise in sexual assaults, as well as policy shifts that seek to subordinate women by restricting their abilities to control their own reproduction. The February 2012 decision by the Honduran Supreme Court to uphold the "most sweeping ban on emergency contraception" in the world serves as one such cautionary tale.[10]

The Honduran ban criminalizes the sale, distribution, and use of emergency contraception known as the "morning-after pill." If a woman is caught in possession of an emergency contraception pill, the act is treated as severely as an abortion attempt, and the woman can be sentenced to three to six years in prison. Abortion is completely restricted in Honduras.

Many organizations, including the Inter-American Commission on Human Rights, contend that extreme bans on emergency contraception constitute a violation of women's ability to exercise their fundamental rights. By contrast, the Catholic Church has actively promoted these bans. Many members of Honduras's government are also members of the ultra-conservative Catholic Opus Dei movement.

Honduras's poverty and adolescent birth rates add to the concerns. In a country where 70 percent of the population lives in poverty and half of all women give birth before the age of twenty,[11] the Supreme Court's sweeping ban on emergency contraception further tilts the scales of justice against women by compromising their reproductive rights.

Though implemented in Honduras, not in the US, this policy is something we here must note carefully. Many among the power elite in the US would like to see our policy shift in this direction. To connect the dots, just pay attention to the vaginal ultrasound requirements, waiting periods on abortions, and other restrictive policies now being proposed in some states, as well as Mississippi's new abortion bill, which could lead to the closure of the state's only clinic that offers abortions.[12] Policies of this type are proposed under the guise of "protecting" women, in line with the white patriarchal ideology that has enacted oppressive policies and violated women and people of color since the country's inception. During a full-scale backlash against women, which takes the form of legislating what we can do with our bodies, the message that women in the military kill themselves is much more effective than the message that women are being sexually assaulted and killed by their fellow soldiers. We accept the idea that perhaps women are just not suited for military life due to something inherent in their makeup, rather than the alternative explanation: that men—supposedly on "the same team"—victimize them.

Private Johnson's story is another example of a non-famous woman of color being disregarded and left out of the cultural narrative—and in her case dismembered and literally thrown away. To add insult to injury, her story is then changed to suit those who would be harmed if the truth were to surface. It seems that truth-telling is not the main goal of our media system.

CENSORED 2013

Time and time again, we end up seeing the media as a tool to shape ideologies of the masses, in order to pursue what the American government wants to pursue. None of this is new, but when stories go unreported or are blatantly altered to serve an agenda, we have to ask: Does the media have an obligation to be truth seekers or not? And if not, can they at least be honest about their goal to serve at the will of the power elite and to create a narrative that keeps people calm and in check?

Censored #24: Alabama Farmers Look to Replace Migrants with Prisoners

The lack of media coverage of the continuing inequality experienced by communities of color is telling. As a country, we don't want to be reminded of an unequal or unfair past, much less present-day economic and wealth inequalities.[13]

One of the harshest anti-immigra nt laws in the nation, Alabama's expansive HB 56 requires local police to verify the immigration status of anyone they have a "reasonable suspicion" of being in the country illegally. The law spurred an exodus of mainly Hispanic workers who moved to other states for fear of being deported. The Obama administration has challenged HB 56's constitutionality, arguing that it infringes on federal powers.

HB 56 has been so economically devastating that Alabama farmers are seeking legislation to force hard labor on prison inmates eligible for work release programs, to "help farms fill the gap and find sufficient labor." In December 2011, Alabama Department of Agriculture and Industries officials met with farmers to discuss their proposal to use prisoners in place of migrant workers. The state's Department of Corrections opposes the proposed legislation, noting that its approximately 2,000 prisoners eligible for work release already have jobs, and that "the prison system isn't the solution to worker shortages caused by the law."[14]

Prison labor-for-profit is possible due to passage of the Prison Industries Act, which the American Legislative Exchange Council (ALEC) championed, and which expanded the existing Prison Industry Enhancement Certification Program (PIECP).

The proposal to employ prison labor for private farming operations is not new. Idaho has used prison labor on potato farms for nearly a decade. Corporate media, such as the *Wall Street Journal*, have praised the prison-farm business model, noting that inmates are "enthusiastic" about their jobs.[15] In reality, corporate prison labor exploits prisoners by forcing them to work or else face longer prison terms or the loss of otherwise earned "good time."

The Alabama farmers' story is inconsistent with the narrative that oppressed people are happy. This idea goes back to early on in US culture, when there became a need for a moral justification for oppression, enslavement, abuse, and murder of indigenous people and African slaves. Did slaves enjoy their work? It is clear they did not, and with the exploitation of prison inmates, it is as if we are going back in time. We may think that slavery has ended, but we rarely think about our prison system. As documented in Censored story #9, "Prison Slavery in Today's USA," the prison system has become a source of cheap labor comparable to overseas labor markets.[16] This story has not been adequately reported; it is an example of the manipulation the media employs simply by remaining silent. When the story is left out of media, the problems of the incarcerated—many of whom are minority men and women—become invisible to the public at large. In a country where freedom is a right stated in the Constitution, this forced labor should be shocking.

By contrast, corporate media omit this part of the prisoner narrative, instead demonizing prisoners and creating a sense of fear about them. This portrayal of prisoners gives the public moral justification for why they should be made to do hard labor. The public deserves to know the whole story, but, more importantly, the incarcerated deserve a voice. In her book *The New Jim Crow*, Michelle Alexander points out that society is quick to blame the incarcerated for their crimes, while we fail to look at how our current legal system makes it more likely for racialized minorities to be profiled, arrested, and convicted.[17] The American Civil Liberties Union has urged the Senate to pass legislation that would forbid local, state, and federal law enforcement agencies from racially profiling criminal suspects.[18] The End Racial Profiling Act of 2011 (S 1670) is in the first steps of the legislative process, awaiting consideration by the Senate Judiciary Committee. If the bill were to become law, it would define racial profiling and prohibit law enforcement agents from stopping, investigating, arresting, or detaining any individual based on his or her race, ethnicity, religion, or national origin. The End Racial Profiling Act of 2011 addresses an issue of extreme importance that has not been given the priority it deserves, with the consequence that, up to now, many racialized minorities have been unjustly criminalized by this profiling.

THE COLOR OF AN UNEQUAL RECESSION

For many Americans, these past several years have been economically devastating, and unfair laws have made it harder, particularly for minorities, to support families. Many of the statistics we see in the media tell the story of a global economic crisis but they do not tell the whole truth. What they fail to highlight are the disproportionate unemployment rates:

> It's been roughly four years since the economic recession first hit the United States, leaving a majority of the population with economic hardship and financial insecurity. Unbeknownst to most, people of color as well as other racial minorities have been hit the hardest during this four year recession, creating depression-like circumstances for most Blacks, Latinos, Latinas, and Native Americans.[19]

The job gap widens as time passes. We have reached disparity in employment over the past ten years: ten years ago, employment was at 64.9 percent for white men compared to 60.5 percent for black men, while now it is 68.8 percent for white men and 57 percent for black men. Latino unemployment has also increased. Latinos and Latinas have lost over 600,000 jobs,[20] leaving those who are undocumented in an even more dangerous situation.

With the corporate elite twisting the typical role of Robin Hood, the rich seem to be taking from the poor as they themselves continue to get richer, all while the most impoverished seem to get poorer. Thus, few were likely surprised when the Institute for Policy Studies revealed that the twenty-five highest-paid chief executive officers were paid more in salary than their entire companies paid in taxes.[21] Similarly, members of Congress seem not to have been harmed by the recession. *Roll Call* magazine's analysis of financial disclosure forms showed that members of the House and Senate have a collective net worth of $2.04 billion, up from the $1.65 billion held in 2008.[22] They have the money, and they also have the power. The United States' (predominantly white) political and economic elites are far removed from minorities' real-life problems.

By choosing which stories to tell, the corporate media support the power elites' perspective. It is up to us, the public, to remain skeptical and vigilant. We must see the whole picture. The media have been framing all these issues as separate problems, when they address them at all. But we can see the connecting threads, and we must require that stories be told in their totality and complexity, so that an informed public can effectively address serious social issues. As George Orwell wrote, "During times of universal deceit, telling the truth becomes a revolutionary act."

SUSAN RAHMAN is a sociology instructor who currently teaches at two Northern California community colleges. Her area of interest is identifying power, privilege, and inequalities, with the goal of social transformation to create a more balanced society. She is also a mom; motherhood has increased her sense of urgency to achieve this goal.

LILIANA VALDEZ-MADERA, a native of Jalisco, Mexico, came to the United States seven years ago at the age of fourteen. She is an aspiring poet and psychology major currently attending Santa Rosa Junior College, but she plans to transfer to Sonoma State University and continue her involvement in Project Censored.

Thanks to NOLAN HIGDON, MICHAEL KOLBE, MIKE LUCACHER, RYAN SHEHEE, JULI TAMBELLINI, ANDREW O'CONNOR-WATTS for additional media research on the Top 25 stories.

Notes

1. Michelle Alexander, *The New Jim Crow: Mass Incarceration in the Age of Colorblindness* (New York: The New Press, 2010).
2. Jason Smith, "Media is Growing More White. What's the FCC doing about it?" *Color Lines*, August 11, 2011, http://colorlines.com/archives/2011/08/lack_of_diversity_in_newsrooms_reaches_critical_point.html.
3. Ina Howard, "Power Sources: On Party, Gender, Race and Class, TV News Looks to the Most Powerful Groups," *Extra!*, May/June 2002, http://www.fair.org/index.php?page=1109.

4. Sheila Gibbons, comp., "Industry Statistics," *Media Report to Women*, March 2012, http://www.mediareporttowomen.com/statistics.htm. See also Janine Jackson, "New Media—But Familiar Lack of Diversity," *FAIR Extra!*, June 2012, http://www.fair.org/index.php?page=4551.

5. National Organization For Women, "Women in Media Fact Sheet," no date, http://www.now.org/issues/media/women_in_media_facts.html.

6. Human Rights Watch, "US: Protect Detainees in Immigration Facilities from Rape; Don't Exempt These Facilities from Protection Measures," Human Rights Watch, February 15, 2011, http://www.hrw.org/en/news/2011/02/15/us-protect-detainees-immigration-facilities-rape. See also, Human Rights Watch, "Detained and at Risk," Human Rights Watch, August 25, 2010, http://www.hrw.org/reports/2010/08/25/detained-and-risk.

7. On American Islamophobia, see, for example, Dhaya Ramarajan and Marcella Runell, "Confronting Islamophobia in Education," *Intercultural Education* 18, no. 2 (May 2007): 87–97; and Emad Rahim, "The Growing Epidemic of 'Islamophobia' in America: Social Change through Appreciative Inquiry," *The International Journal of Diversity in Organizations, Communities and Nations* 10, no. 1 (2010): 239–246.

8. Miriam Zoila Pérez, "The Movement to Stop Prisons From Shackling Women in Labor Builds," *Color Lines*, October 4, 2011, http://colorlines.com/archives/2011/10/shackling_women_in_prison_during_childbirth.html. See also Alex Berg, "Stop Shackling Pregnant Prisoners!" *The Daily Beast*, September 4, 2011, http://www.thedailybeast.com/articles/2011/09/04/stop-shackling-pregnant-prisoners-new-push-to-ban-controversial-practice.html.

9. For example, see Bruce M. King, *Human Sexuality Today*, 7th ed. (New Jersey: Prentice Hall, 2011), 376. See also, United Nations Office on Drugs and Crime, Division for Policy Analysis and Public Affairs, *Eighth United Nations Survey of Crime Trends and Operations of Criminal Justice Systems, Covering the Period 2001–2002*, (2005): Table 2.8, 41, http://www.unodc.org/pdf/crime/eighthsurvey/8sv.pdf.

10. Jodi Jacobson, "Honduran Supreme Court Upholds Most Sweeping Ban on Emergency Contraception Anywhere," *RH Reality Check*, February 14, 2012, http://www.rhrealitycheck.org/article/2012/02/14/honduran-supreme-court-upholds-complete-ban-on-emergency-contraception-0.

11. Latino Politics Blog, "Women's Rights & Reproductive Freedoms Under Attack with Honduran Coup," *Latino Politics Blog*, November 16, 2009, http://latinopoliticsblog.com/2009/11/16/women%E2%80%99s-rights-reproductive-freedoms-under-attack-with-honduran-coup.

12. Laura Bassett, "Mississippi Abortion Bill May Force State's Only Clinic to Close," *Huffington Post*, April 5, 2012, http://www.huffingtonpost.com/2012/04/05/mississippi-abortion-bill_n_1404705.html.

13. Meizhu Lui, Bárbara Robles, Besty Leondar-Wright, Rose Brewer, and Rebecca Adamson, *The Color of Wealth: The Story Behind the U.S. Racial Wealth Divide*, with United for a Fair Economy (New York: The New Press, 2006).

14. Associated Press, "Alabama May Turn to Prison Inmates to Replace Lost Immigrant Farm Workers," *Al.com*, December 6, 2011, http://blog.al.com/wire/2011/12/alabama_may_turn_to_prison_inm.html.

15. Joel Millman, "Captive Labor on the Farm," *Wall Street Journal*, October 18, 2011, http://online.wsj.com/article/SB10001424052970204774604576630972860034248.html.

16. See Sara Flounders, "The Pentagon & Slave Labor in U.S. prisons," *Workers World*, June 6, 2011, http://www.workers.org/2011/us/pentagon_0609/ covered in the Censored News Cluster on "The Police State and Civil Liberties."

17. Alexander, *New Jim Crow*.

18. Eric W. Dolan, "ACLU Urges Senate to Support Ban on Racial Profiling," *Raw Story*, February 2, 2012, http://www.rawstory.com/rs/2012/02/02/aclu-urges-senate-to-support-ban-on-racial-profiling.

19. Peter Phillips and Taylor Falbisaner, "Minorities Facing Full-Blown Depression in the United States," Media Freedom International, October 24, 2011, http://www.mediafreedominternational.org/2011/10/24/minorities-facing-full-blown-depression-in-the-united-states/ summa-

rizing Susan Williams, "The Color of an Unequal Recession," *Freedom Socialist*, October 2011, http://www.socialism.com/drupal-6.8/?q=node/1730.

20. Williams, "Unequal Recession."

21. Sarah Anderson, Chuck Collins, Scott Klinger, and Sam Pizzigati, "Executive Excess 2011: The Massive CEO Rewards for Tax Dodging," Institute for Policy Studies, August 31, 2011, http://www.ips-dc.org/reports/executive_excess_2011_the_massive_ceo_rewards_for_tax_dodging.

22. Paul Singer and Jennifer Yachnin, "And Congress' Rich Get Richer," *Roll Call*, November 1, 2011, http://www.rollcall.com/issues/57_51/And-Congress-Rich-Get-Richer-209907-1.html.

CHAPTER 2

Déjà Vu

What Happened to Previous Censored Stories?

by Mickey Huff and Dr. Andy Lee Roth, with Project Censored
interns Jen Eiden, Nolan Higdon, Aaron Hudson, Mike Kolbe,
Michael Lucacher, Ryan Shehee, and Andrew O'Connor-Watts

*It is not the simple statement of facts that ushers in free-
dom; it is the constant repetition of them that has this
liberating effect.*

—Quentin Crisp, *The Naked Civil Servant*

By definition, news is information about events that are important
and recent. The advent of a nonstop 24/7 news cycle adds emphasis
to recency as the hallmark of newsworthiness. For both news professionals and audiences, most of today's headline stories rapidly depre-
ciate in value, pushed to peripheral status as soon as the next, newer
story breaks.

Some news stories deserve sustained attention, nonetheless. The
annual Déjà Vu feature is our attempt to maintain focus on past stories of continued significance. We update selected Top 25 Censored
Stories from previous years, focusing on whether they have subsequently received corporate coverage, to what extent they have become
part of broader public discourse, or whether they remain "censored"
outside of independent journalism.

Of course, we believe that every *Censored* story from the previous
year's Top 25 list is important. In this chapter, Project Censored interns update six stories characterized by a combination of continued

significance and noteworthy developments. Specifically, from *Censored 2012*, we review story #1 on soldier suicides, story #3 covering Obama's "international assassination campaign," story #6 about Google spying, story #12 regarding plastic garbage and the Great Pacific Garbage Patch, story #16 on labor abuses in Chinese factories that contract with Apple, and, from *Censored 2008*, story #20 on the Animal Enterprise Terrorism Act.

As the following updates indicate, a number of past *Censored* stories either directly relate to, or resonate powerfully with, stories from this year's Top 25. We hope that Project Censored's continued attention on these past stories contributes to their potentially liberating effects.

Censored 2012 #1

More US Soldiers Committed Suicide than Died in Combat
Update by Andrew O'Connor-Watts and Aaron Hudson

SUMMARY: For the second year in a row, the year ending 2010, more US soldiers killed themselves (468) than died in combat (462).

ORIGINAL SOURCES:

Chris Hedges, "Death and After in Iraq," *Truthdig*, March 21, 2011, http://www.truthdig.com/report/item/the_body_baggers_of_iraq_20110321.
Cord Jefferson, "More US Soldiers Killed Themselves Than Died in Combat in 2010," *GOOD*, January 27, 2011, http://www.good.is/post/more-us-soldiers-killed-themselves-than-died-in-combat-in-2010.
Medea Benjamin and Charles Davis, "Ten Reasons the Iraq War Was No Cakewalk," *AlterNet*, March 18, 2011, http://www.alternet.org/world/150297/ten_reasons_the_iraq_war_was_no_cakewalk.

UPDATE: Since publication of *Censored 2012*, corporate media provided partial coverage of the challenges facing veterans, including their disproportionate suicide rates. More often, however, this coverage has focused on other aspects of veterans' experiences, including violent crimes committed by veterans who have returned home. CNN, the *New York Times*, the *Los Angeles Times*, and the *Washington Post* covered the story, but few addressed the magnitude of the epidemic. The *Washington Post* was the only major news publication to mention the monthly suicide statistics, which the US Army has maintained since 2009.

In April 2011, the *New York Times*' Nicholas Kristof wrote in an editorial that, for every combat death, there are twenty-five veteran suicides. According to Kristof, "An American soldier dies every day and a half, on average, in Iraq or Afghanistan. Veterans kill themselves at a rate of one every eighty minutes. More than 6,500 veteran suicides are logged every year—more than the total number of soldiers killed in Afghanistan and Iraq combined since those wars began." In September 2011, CNN reported Army Lt. Gen. Thomas Bostick's theory of a link between the number of deployments and soldier suicides, but CNN's report also noted that other officials contested this link. A November 2011 CNN story compared suicide rates for that year with those of 2009, the second-highest year for soldier suicides, but it framed soldiers' self-inflicted deaths as an unfortunate inevitability of a decade-long war.

In March 2012, the *Los Angeles Times* addressed military suicides but focused only on the years 2004 to 2008, a time period prior to the highest suicide rates. The article did not address the July 2011 spike in suicides.

CORPORATE SOURCES:

Greg Jaffe, "Army Suicides Set Record in July," *Washington Post*, August 8, 2011, http://www.washingtonpost.com/world/national-security/army-suicides-set-record-in-july/2011/08/12/gIQAfbGlBJ_story.html.
Nicholas D. Kristof, "A Veteran's Death, the Nation's Shame," *New York Times*, April 15, 2011, http://www.nytimes.com/2012/04/15/opinion/sunday/kristof-a-veterans-death-the-nations-shame.html.
Larry Shaughnessy, "For Two Lawmakers, Military Suicides Hit Too Close to Home," CNN, September 9, 2011, http://articles.cnn.com/2011-09-09/us/congress.military.suicides_1_military-suicides-suicide-rate-multiple-deployments.
Charlie Keyes, "Army Still Grappling with Soldier Suicides," CNN, November 18, 2011, http://articles.cnn.com/2011-11-18/us/us_soldier-suicides_1_suicides-multiple-deployments-reserve-soldiers.
Shari Roan, "Suicides among Army Personnel up 80% in Four Years," *Los Angeles Times*, March 8, 2011, http://www.latimes.com/health/boostershots/la-heb-army-suicide-20120308,0,7002109.story.

Censored 2012 #3

Obama Authorizes International Assassination Campaign
Update by Mike Kolbe

SUMMARY: The Obama administration has adopted practices inherited from George W. Bush's presidency, continuing and expanding an executive "international assassination program" in its fight against global terrorism.

ORIGINAL SOURCES:

William Fisher, "Judge Declines to Rule on Targeted Killings of U.S. Citizens," Inter Press Service, December 8, 2010, http://www.ipsnews.net/2010/12/judge-declines-to-rule-on-targeted-killings-of-us-citizens.

"Letter to President Obama on Targeted Killings and Drones," Human Rights Watch, December 7, 2010, http://www.hrw.org/news/2010/12/07/letter-obama-targeted-killings.

Glenn Greenwald, "Confirmed: Obama Authorizes Assassination of U.S. Citizen," Salon, April 7, 2010, http://www.salon.com/2010/04/07/assassinations_2.

Philip Alston, Project on Extrajudicial Executions, UN Special Rapporteur on Extrajudicial Executions Handbook, March 30, 2010, http://www.extrajudicialexecutions.org/application/media/Handbook%20Chapter%201%20Use%20of%20Force%20During%20Armed%20Conflicts5.pdf.

Francis A. Boyle, "Extrajudicial Killings: U.S. Government 'Death List' for American Citizens," Global Research, February 10, 2010, http://www.globalresearch.ca/index.php?context=va&aid=17527.

"Obama Administration Claims Unchecked Authority to Kill Americans Outside Combat Zones," Common Dreams, November 8, 2010, http://www.commondreams.org/headline/2010/11/08-4.

UPDATE: Just as *Censored 2012* was going to press, President Barack Obama authorized the May 2011 killing of Osama bin Laden, as widely reported in both corporate and independent media. Since then, the Central Intelligence Agency (CIA) and the military's Joint Special Operations Command (JSOC) collaborated on the targeted killing, without trial, of a citizen of the United States. On September 30, 2011, a US drone strike targeted and killed Anwar al-Awlaki, a defining moment that corporate media have failed to adequately cover. The strike killed a second US citizen, Samir Khan, although he was not officially targeted. These high-profile deaths occurred against the backdrop of the Obama administration's massive, but still officially "covert" drone campaigns in Pakistan, Yemen, and Somalia, which corporate media have only begun to document with any seriousness.

In October 2011, the *New York Times'* Charlie Savage stated that the legal basis for al-Awlaki's targeted killing came from an Office of Legal Counsel (OLC) memorandum drafted by lawyers David Barron and Martin Lederman. They based their legal opinion on the classification of al-Awlaki as a "cobelligerent" with al-Qaeda. Consequently, OLC lawyers concluded that, as an al-Qaeda operative, al-Awlaki could be legally killed. The document allegedly permitted the Obama administration to circumvent laws prohibiting assassinations by the executive branch and the murder of US citizens abroad, constitutional rights granted by the Fourth Amendment, and international laws regarding warfare.

On news of al-Awlaki's death, President Obama argued that al-Awlaki "repeatedly called on individuals in the United States and around the globe to kill innocent men, women and children"—though evidence for these claims has never been made public—and he characterized the US citizen's death as "another significant milestone in the broader effort to defeat al-Qaeda and its affiliates." Though Obama was careful not to claim US responsibility for al-Awlaki's death, on subsequent occasions he has claimed that the US drone program is "on a very tight leash." These assertions have gone largely unchallenged in the corporate media, though a mounting record of evidence, documented by independent organizations such as the Bureau of Investigative Journalism and New America Foundation, contradicts the administration's claims. For more on this aspect of the story, see the contribution by senior Bureau reporter Chris Woods to chapter 4 of this volume, "Media Democracy in Action."

In May 2012, the *New York Times* broke a lengthy investigative report on Obama's drone "kill list," including the most specific details published to date about the selection of targets for CIA and Pentagon strikes outside of conventional battlefields. The report also detailed President Obama's personal endorsement of a controversial policy to redefine the term "civilian" in ways that have helped limit public controversy over "noncombatant" deaths due to the drone campaign. Despite the vital significance of these findings for an understanding of the drone war and media coverage of it, corporate media beyond the *New York Times* ignored the report—prompting Fairness and Accuracy in Reporting (FAIR) to issue a "Media Advisory" on the story, which asked, "What was more newsworthy than the president personally approving drone strikes on specific individuals?" For one answer to FAIR's question, see "From Birthers to Death: Obama's Citizenship Matters More than Civilian Deaths," in chapter 3.

See Andy Lee Roth's chapter, "Framing Al-Awlaki: How Government Officials and Corporate Media Legitimized a Targeted Killing," later in this volume for additional analysis of corporate media coverage of al-Awlaki's targeted killing.

CORPORATE SOURCES:

Charlie Savage, "Secret U.S. Memo Made Legal Case to Kill a Citizen," *New York Times*, October 8, 2011, http://www.nytimes.com/2011/10/09/world/middleeast/secret-us-memo-made-legal-case-to-kill-a-citizen.html.

Greg Miller, "Under Obama, a Deadly Drone Network Grows," *Washington Post*, December 28, 2011, http://www.washingtonpost.com/national/national-security/under-obama-an-emerging-global-apparatus-for-drone-killing/2011/12/13/gIQANPdILP_story.html.

Peter Finn and Sari Horwitz, "Holder says U.S. Has Right to Kill Terrorist Citizens Abroad," *Washington Post*, March 6, 2012, http://www.washingtonpost.com/world/national-security/holder-us-can-lawfully-target-american-citizens/2012/03/05/gIQANknFtR_story.html.

Jo Becker and Scott Shane, "Secret 'Kill List' Proves a Test of Obama's Principle and Will," *New York Times*, May 29, 2012, http://www.nytimes.com/2012/05/29/world/obamas-leadership-in-war-on-al-qaeda.html?_r=1&hp#.

SOURCES:

"Drone Kill List Not News?," *Extra!*, June 6, 2012, http://www.fair.org/index.php?page=4561.

Chris Woods, interview by Amy Goodman, "U.S. Accused of Using Drones to Target Rescue Workers and Funerals in Pakistan," *Democracy Now!*, February 6, 2012, http://www.democracynow.org/2012/2/6/us_accused_of_using_drones_to.

New America Foundation, "Year of the Drone," June 13, 2012, http://counterterrorism.newamerica.net/drones.

Censored 2012 #6

Google Spying?

Update by Michael Lucacher

SUMMARY: In 2010, the Federal Trade Commission (FTC) investigated Google for illegally collecting personal data such as passwords, e-mails, and other information from online activities from unsecured Wi-Fi networks in homes and businesses across the United States and around the rest of the world. Google claimed the data was accidentally obtained by its Street View cars. In October 2010, the director of FTC's Bureau of Consumer Protection informed Google that the FTC had ended its inquiry, based on Google's assurance that it would make "improvements to its internal processes" and "continue its dialogue with the FTC."

ORIGINAL SOURCES:

Eric Sommer, "Google's Deep CIA Connections," *Pravda Online*, January 14, 2010, http://english.pravda.ru/world/asia/14-01-2010/111657-google_china-0/.

David C. Vladeck to Albert Gidari, Office of the Director, Bureau of Consumer Protection, United States Federal Trade Commission, October 27, 2010, http://www.ftc.gov/os/closings/101027googleletter.pdf.

Nicholas Carlson, "Google's Marissa Mayer Hosting Obama At $30,000-A-Head Fundraiser Tonight (GOOG)," *San Francisco Chronicle*, October 21, 2010, http://www.sfgate.com/business/article/Google-s-Marissa-Mayer-Hosting-Obama-At-2530676.php.

UPDATE: In March 2012, Google implemented a single privacy policy for all of its services (including Gmail, Google Maps, YouTube, and

Google+). The new policy allows Google to collect information on its customers and sell it to third parties (such as advertising agencies).

On March 16, 2012, France's data-protection watchdog, the Commission nationale de l'informatique et des libertés (CNIL), gave Google three weeks to address basic questions about the new privacy policy. In a letter to Google chief executive officer Larry Page, CNIL asked Google to explain what it will do with the user data it collects, how long it will store the data, whether the data will be linked to the person's real identity, and the legal justification for its approach. Privacy laws are more stringent in Europe than in the United States.

In July 2011, a US federal judge ruled against the Electronic Privacy Information Center (EPIC) in its suit seeking disclosure of information by the National Security Agency (NSA) regarding its possible relationship with Google. The District of Columbia District Court ruling made it impossible for citizens to know if the NSA was making use of private information obtained by Google. EPIC had sought documents under the Freedom of Information Act because "such an agreement between Google and the NSA could reveal that the NSA is developing technical standards that would enable greater surveillance of Internet users," the organization explained. After Chinese hackers accessed Google's mainframe in January 2010, Google and the NSA allegedly partnered to analyze the attack. To date, the NSA, CIA, and Federal Bureau of Investigation (FBI) all appear to be working with Google.

On the broader topic of electronic surveillance, including government programs aimed at Total Information Awareness, see Elliot D. Cohen's chapter later in this volume, "The Information War: How Government Is Seeking Total Information Awareness and What This Portends for Freedom and Democracy."

CORPORATE SOURCES:

Hayley Tsukayama, "FAQ: Google's New Privacy Policy," *Washington Post*, January 25, 2012, http://www.washingtonpost.com/business/technology/faq-googles-new-privacy-policy/2012/01/24/gIQArw8GOQ_story.html?tid=pm_business_pop.
Leila Abboud and Claire Davenport, "Google Defends Privacy Policy to European Watchdog," Reuters, April 5, 2012, http://www.reuters.com/article/2012/04/05/net-us-google-privacy-idUSBRE8340ZC20120405.

SOURCES:

Bob Unruh, "Google Spying on You for NSA? Judge: 'None of Your Business,'" *WorldNetDaily*, July 15 2011, http://www.wnd.com/2011/07/322113.

Lauren Kelley, "Internet Users Up in Arms Over Google's Orwellian New Privacy Policy That It's Forcing on All of Us," *AlterNet*, January 26, 2012, http://www.alternet.org/newsandviews/article/767020/internet_users_up_in_arms_over_google%27s_orwellian_new_privacy_policy_that_it%27s_forcing_on_all_of_us.

Censored 2012 #12

Pacific Garbage Dump: Did You Really Think Your Plastic Was Being Recycled?
Update by Aaron Hudson and Andrew O'Connor-Watts

SUMMARY: In July 2010, the 5 Gyres Institute estimated that there were 315 billion pounds of plastic garbage in the ocean. This plastic has dire effects on marine life. Much of the world's trash has accumulated in one part of the Pacific Ocean, known as the Great Pacific Garbage Patch.

ORIGINAL SOURCES:

Fabien Cousteau, "TEDxGreatPacificGarbagePatch: Fabien Cousteau: Ocean Animals and Plastic Pollution," YouTube video, 10:10, from a TEDx talk for GreatPacificGarbagePatch given on November 6, 2010, posted by TEDxTalks, December 17, 2010, http://www.youtube.com/watch?v=BXv4Xc_6oC8.
David de Rothschild, "Message on a Bottle," United Nations Environmental Program, UNEP: Our Planet, April 2011, http://www.unep.org/pdf/op_april/EN/OP-2011-04-EN-ARTICLE7.pdf.
Jaymi Heimbuch, "The Great Pacific Garbage Patch Is Bigger than the Continental US: Here's What We Can Do About It," *AlterNet*, July 13, 2010, http://www.alternet.org/water/147528/the_great_pacific_garbage_patch_is_bigger_than_the_continental_us%3A_here's_what_we_can_do_about_it/?page=entire.
Jocelyn Kaiser, "The Dirt on Ocean Garbage Patches," *Science* 328, no. 5985 (June 18, 2010).
Stiv Wilson, "The Fallacy of Gyre Cleanup: Part One, Scale," 5 Gyres, July 5, 2010, http://5gyres.org/posts/2010/07/05/the_fallacy_of_gyre_cleanup_part_one_scale.

UPDATE: Few corporate media outlets have covered the story, despite the Great Pacific Garbage Patch's continuing growth. Among those that reported on this important issue were MSNBC, Fox, and ABC.

Debris from the March 2011 Tohoku earthquake and tsunami spread from the Japanese coast to the North Pacific Subtropical Gyre and eventually to the Great Pacific Garbage Patch, magnifying the hazardous gyre. In March 2012, the *New York Times* reported that a team of scientists at the University of Hawaii's International Pacific Research Center was using computer models to predict the tsunami debris' path. According to their model, tsunami debris would make its first landfall at Midway Island in winter 2011, before progressing to Hawaii (2012) and the West Coast (2013). The scientists reported that most of the debris will end up in the Great Pacific Garbage Patch.

For competing accounts of the spread of debris from the Japanese disaster, as reported by independent media, see chapter 1 in this volume, Censored story #3, "Fukushima Nuclear Disaster Worse than Anticipated."

In May 2012, CNN ran an in-depth report on a marine expedition, organized by the Algalita Marine Research Foundation and the 5 Gyres Institute. Led by Dr. Marcus Eriksen, a former US Marine, the expedition set out to take water samples and conduct research on the state of our planet's oceans. According to Eriksen, "We've been finding lots of micro plastics, all the size of a grain of rice or a small marble. We drag our nets and come up with a small handful, like confetti." The CNN story reported the expedition's finding that the world's oceans are "plasticized." "Everywhere you go in the ocean," Eriksen says, "you're going to find this plastic waste."

For more on the state of the world's oceans, as reported in independent media, see chapter 1 of this volume, Censored story #2, "Oceans in Peril."

CORPORATE SOURCES:

Malia Wollan, "On West Coast, Looking for Flotsam of a Disaster," *New York Times*, March 13, 2012, http://www.nytimes.com/2012/03/13/us/looking-for-tsunami-debris-on-west-coast-beaches.html.

Rose Hoare, "Research Ship Finds the World's Oceans Are 'Plasticized,'" CNN, May 22, 2012, http://www.cnn.com/2012/05/21/world/asia/algalita-eco-solutions/index.html.

Ian Johnston, "Study: Plastic in 'Great Pacific Garbage Patch' Increases 100-fold," MSNBC, May 9, 2012, http://worldnews.msnbc.msn.com/_news/2012/05/09/11612593-study-plastic-in-great-pacific-garbage-patch-increases-100-fold?lite.

Bliss Davis, "Researchers Say 'Plastic Pollution' Destroying Earth's Oceans," Fox8-Cleveland, May 21, 2012, http://fox8.com/2012/05/21/researchers-say-plastic-pollution-destoying-earths-oceans.

Censored 2012 #16

Sweatshops in China Are Making Your iPods While Workers Suffer
Update by Mike Kolbe

SUMMARY: Although Apple claims to be a socially responsible company, some of its suspected Chinese suppliers, including Foxconn, Dafu, and Lian Jian Technology, routinely violate Chinese labor laws. A report from China's Institute of Public and Environmental Affairs, *The Other Side of Apple*, criticized the company for harmful environmental and health practices in suppliers' plants.

UPDATE: The story of working conditions in Chinese factories that contract with Apple has drawn significant corporate media coverage since publication of *Censored 2012*. However, much of this coverage has focused on controversy over a National Public Radio (NPR) broadcast of *This American Life*, often in ways that have diverted attention from abusive labor practices, problematic environmental consequences, and, ultimately, Apple's corporate responsibility for these.

In January 2012, NPR's *This American Life* featured an appearance by Mike Daisey, an actor best known for his monologues about controversial individuals and issues. Daisey presented parts of his monologue, "The Agony and the Ecstasy of Steve Jobs," in which he charges Apple with a multitude of worker abuses. Listeners downloaded the broadcast 888,000 times, making it NPR's most popular podcast. In March 2012, *This American Life* host Ira Glass retracted the Apple story, explaining that NPR had failed to inspect Daisey's claims, several of which had not held up to subsequent fact checking. Corporate media pounced on the story, and some, like Charles Isherwood of the *New York Times*, took the opportunity to chide Daisey for lack of fidelity to the truth. Tim Worstall of *Forbes* magazine took advantage of the situation to effectively pardon Apple and Foxconn, acknowledging less-than-ideal conditions in Apple-supported factories, but urging the American public to accept that working conditions in Chinese factories are uniformly inferior to those in the US.

For more on the controversy over the *This American Life* broadcast, see "Who's the Rotten Apple? *This American Life* Goes Daisey Crazy," in chapter 3 of this volume.

In response to increasing public awareness of worker abuses in its contractor factories, Apple released a list of its main suppliers. In a practice common to multinational corporations, Apple implemented a self-auditing campaign, which allegedly identifies and addresses suspected abuses. An investigation performed by the Fair Labor Association (FLA) was funded by Apple, leading many critics to question its findings' credibility. "The FLA does not have a great track record of conducting effective investigations," Taren Stinebrickner-Kauffman, executive director of SumOfUs.org, told *Wired*. According to FLA Watch, members of the apparel industry created and control the FLA. Critics expressed concern that the FLA "investigation" of Foxconn facilities in China was little more than a guided tour by the owners. In February 2012, the *New York Times* reported that the 229 audits conducted the previous year by Apple yielded some improvements, but at least half of the workers exceeded the sixty-hours-a-week work limit at ninety-three of its facilities.

The October 2011 death of Apple CEO Steve Jobs also diverted corporate media attention from ongoing abuses in Chinese factories that contract with Apple. In their tributes to Apple's "visionary in a black turtleneck," corporate media skirted human rights issues.

CORPORATE SOURCES:

Ira Glass, "Retraction," *This American Life*, NPR, March 16, 2012, http://podcast.thisamericanlife. org/special/TAL_460_Retraction_Transcript.pdf.
Becky Bratu et al., "'This American Life' Retracts Damning Report on Apple Manufacturer Foxconn," MSNBC, March 16, 2012, http://worldnews.msnbc.msn.com/_ news/2012/03/16/10720955-this-american-life-retracts-damning-report-on-apple-manufacturer-foxconn.
Charles Duhigg and David Barboza, "In China, Human Costs Are Built Into an iPad," *New York Times*, January 25, 2012, http://www.nytimes.com/2012/01/26/business/ieconomy-apples-ipad-and-the-human-costs-for-workers-in-china.html.
Charles Isherwood, "Speaking Less than Truth to Power," *New York Times*, March 18 2012, http:// www.nytimes.com/2012/03/19/theater/defending-this-american-life-and-its-mike-daisey-retraction.html.
Julianne Pepitone, "Apple Supplier Audit Finds Major Wage and Overtime Violations," CNNMoney, March 29, 2012, http://money.cnn.com/2012/03/29/technology/apple-foxconn-report/ index.htm.
Steven Greenhouse, "Early Praise in Inspection at Foxconn Brings Doubt," *New York Times*, February 16, 2012, http://www.nytimes.com/2012/02/17/business/early-praise-in-foxconn-inspection-brings-doubt.html.
Tim Worstall, "Finally: The Truth About Conditions Inside Apple's Foxconn Factories," *Forbes*, April 13, 2012, http://www.forbes.com/sites/timworstall/2012/04/13/finally-the-truth-about-conditions-inside-apples-foxconn-factories.

SOURCES:

Christina Bonnington, "Apple's Foxconn Auditing Group 'Surrounded With Controversy,' Critics Say," *Wired*, February 13, 2012, http://www.wired.com/gadgetlab/2012/02/apple-foxconn-investigations.
Courteney Palis, "Apple Publishes Data on Foxconn Working Conditions," *Huffington Post*, March 22, 2012, http://www.huffingtonpost.com/2012/03/21/apple-foxconn-working-conditions_n_1369878.html.
"What's Wrong with the FLA?," FLA Watch, May 20, 2012, http://flawatch.usas.org/about/events.

Terror Act Against Animal Activists

Update by Jen Eiden

SUMMARY: In November 2006, President George W. Bush signed the Animal Enterprise Terrorism Act (AETA) into law. AETA expands an existing law, the Animal Enterprise Protection Act (AEPA) of 1992, by broadening the definition of "animal enterprise terrorism." Under AETA, any person who interferes with, has a connection to interfering with, or conspires to interfere with an "animal enterprise" can be prosecuted for "animal enterprise terrorism." AETA threatens First Amendment rights and attempts to criminalize dissent as terrorism.

ORIGINAL SOURCES:

David Hoch and Odette Wilkens, "The AETA is Invidiously Detrimental to the Animal Rights Movement (and Unconstitutional as Well)," *Vermont Journal of Environmental Law*, March 9, 2007, www.vjel.org/editorials/ED10060.html.

Will Potter, "US House Passes Animal Enterprise Terrorism Act With Little Discussion or Dissent," *Green Is the New Red*, November 14, 2006, http://www.greenisthenewred.com/blog/aeta-passes-house-recap/142.

Budgerigar, "22 Years for Free-Speech Advocates," *Earth First! Journal*, November, 2006, http://www.earthfirstjournal.org/article.php?id=6.

UPDATE: Since publication of "Terror Act Against Animal Activists" in *Censored 2008*, the Animal Enterprise Terrorism Act (AETA) has met fierce resistance, including an ongoing lawsuit, *Blum v. Holder*, in the US District Court in the District of Massachusetts. On December 15, 2011, the Center for Constitutional Rights filed a federal lawsuit challenging AETA as an unconstitutional infringement on free speech. The case received coverage in a *Los Angeles Times* article, which claimed that AETA "has not been used as much as initially expected," as well as more in-depth coverage from independent media sources, including Will Potter's *Green Is the New Red* blog. As *Censored 2013* went to press, the government had moved to dismiss the case, and the Center for Constitutional Rights had opposed the motion. *Blum v. Holder* is a crucial step for activists working to repeal AETA.

Previous corporate coverage has marginalized these efforts. For example, an October 2009 CNN report acknowledged that AETA demonizes animal rights activists, but went on to quote extensively from an article in the *Journal of Neuroscience* that described activists as "misguided animal-rights militants" and "terrorists," whose "attacks" and "domestic terrorism" were unaffected by AETA. A September 2011 *Wall Street Journal* article provided more balanced coverage, describing AETA as an "overly broad law" that "clashed with First Amendment free-speech protections."

In *Censored 2008*, David Hoch and Odette Wilkins stated that AETA would "serve as a template for the further limitations on the free speech of all activists." Recent legislation has proven this statement to be accurate. Both the National Defense Authorization Act of 2012 (NDAA) and the Federal Restricted Buildings and Grounds Improvement Act of 2011 (HR 347) bear resemblances to AETA: they infringe on First Amendment rights to speech, press, and assembly, and they threaten citizens who act on these rights with legal sanctions and the possibility of being deemed "terrorists."

The NDAA and HR 347 receive additional coverage in chapter 1 of this volume. See Censored story #1, "Signs of an Emerging Police State," and Censored story #10, "HR 347 Would Make Many Forms of Nonviolent Protest Illegal."

CORPORATE SOURCES:

Dean Kupers, "Lawsuit Challenges Animal Enterprise Terror Law as Unconstitutional," *Los Angeles Times*, December 15, 2011, http://articles.latimes.com/2011/dec/15/local/la-me-gs-lawsuit-challenges-animal-enterprise-terror-law-as-unconstitutional-20111215.
Thomas G. Watkins, "Researchers to Animal Rights Activists: We're Not Afraid," CNN, October 8, 2009, http://www.cnn.com/2009/CRIME/10/08/animal.rights.threats/index.html?iref=allsearch.
Gary Fields and John R. Emshwiller, "The Animal Enterprise Terrorism Act Sets an Unusual Standard for Crime," *Wall Street Journal*, September 27, 2011, http://online.wsj.com/article/SB10001424053111903791504576586790205241376.html.

SOURCES:

Will Potter, "New Lawsuit Challenges the Animal Enterprise Terrorism Act as Unconstitutional," *Green Is the New Red*, December 15, 2011, http://www.greenisthenewred.com/blog/animal-enterprise-terrorism-act-lawsuit-ccr/5397.
Center for Constitutional Rights, "Blum v. Holder," http://www.ccrjustice.org/ourcases/Blum.

MICKEY HUFF is director of Project Censored and professor of social science and history at Diablo Valley College.

ANDY LEE ROTH is Project Censored's associate director.

JEN EIDEN, NOLAN HIGDON, AARON HUDSON, MIKE KOLBE, MICHAEL LUCACHER, ANDREW O'CONNOR-WATTS, and RYAN SHEHEE are current or past interns with Project Censored. JULI TAMBELLINI helped with additional research for this chapter.

CHAPTER 3

American Idle
Junk Food News, News Abuse, and the Voice of Freedumb

by Mickey Huff and Dr. Andy Lee Roth, with Nolan Higdon, Michael Kolbe, and Andrew O'Connor-Watts

We expect anything and everything. We expect the contradictory and the impossible. We expect compact cars that are spacious; luxurious cars that are economical. We expect to be rich and charitable, powerful and merciful, active and reflective, kind and competitive. . . . We are ruled by extravagant expectations. . . . By harboring, nourishing, and ever enlarging our extravagant expectations we create the demand for the illusions with which we deceive ourselves. And which we pay others to make to deceive us.

—Daniel J. Boorstin, *The Image*, 1962[1]

Project Censored's founder, Dr. Carl Jensen, coined the term Junk Food News almost thirty years ago. Responding to Jensen's criticism that news in the United States suffered from censorship, members of the press claimed that they lacked sufficient space in print or time on air to cover everything important. They called it news judgment, not censorship. Unsatisfied with this explanation, Jensen decided to expand Project Censored's scope of inquiry to include not only "the news that didn't make the news," but also what establishment media actually *did* cover.

Jensen and his Sonoma State University students found that the major corporate media outlets reported titillating, nonsensical, tabloid-type stories as if they were *real* news. Jensen cataloged these frivolous stories, identified the recurrent themes that unified them, and contrasted them with serious news that the media could have covered instead, like the stories Project Censored has researched each year. Junk Food News was born.[2]

Across three decades, the problem of Junk Food News—or "Twinkies for the brain," as Jensen called it—has worsened. So much so that Jensen's successor as Project Censored director, Dr. Peter Phillips, created an expanded category, News Abuse. This category consists of otherwise newsworthy stories about powerful people or important political issues that the corporate media render trivial and inconsequential through sensationalism and spin. Like Junk Food News, News Abuse epitomizes the failure of corporate media to inform the public in ways that promote democratic self-government.

Our annual chapter on Junk Food News and News Abuse does more than catalog inane news coverage. It looks beneath the surface to examine the cultural values and frames that give rise to faulty news coverage.

ANTECEDENTS TO JUNK FOOD NEWS AND NEWS ABUSE: PSEUDO-EVENTS IN AMERICA

The year 2012 is the fiftieth anniversary of Daniel Boorstin's *The Image: A Guide to Pseudo-Events in America.*[3] Among the most prescient critics of twentieth-century American culture, Boorstin not only documented the rise of manufactured events in an increasingly media saturated culture, he also anticipated the hyperreal mediascape of the twenty-first century: "The story of the making of our illusions—'the news behind the news'—has become the most appealing news of the world."[4]

Boorstin analyzed pseudo-events at a time when the mass media were undergoing rapid growth and change in a cultural context of rising consumerism and an intensifying Cold War. Pseudo-events, such as press conferences and political candidate debates, were the products of public relations gurus like Edward Bernays, who wrote that "the engineer of consent must create news."[5] In a world increasingly made for television, ever more scripted pseudo-events became principal ingredients of news.

Pseudo-events are now the norm. From faux "reality" television shows to the canned happenings of American Idol, millions of viewers turn eagerly to their screens for a vicarious fix as the day's celebrities chase after the perfect job, the perfect house, the perfect car, the best performance, and, of course, the perfect partner. As Boorstin observed, "We are ruled by extravagant expectations."[6]

These desires not only drive consumer demand for the faux world of reality TV but also for "news" media, which consequently display many of the same sensational features. Corporate American news culture increasingly favors dramatic myopia of the personal over sober analysis of public policy and the social distribution of power and wealth. Titillating images and interpersonal dramas distract us from the real issues facing our local communities, our nation, and our place in the world as a whole. Thus, Boorstin observed, "We have become so accustomed to our illusions that we mistake them for reality. We demand them. And we demand that there be always more of them, bigger and better and more vivid."[7]

The Voice of Freedumb: The Rise of Anti-Intellectualism and Junk Food News

The television show The Voice proclaims to herald America's new hot talent, its new "voice." But if this reality program's stars are the voice of Americans, they aren't singing, or saying, much. From shows about shark hunting or house hunting, to rags-to-riches programs about hoarder finds or pawnshop culture, America is amusing itself to death in ways that media theorist Neil Postman might not have anticipated.[8] The lines between entertainment and news blurred long ago, and now it seems life imitates reality TV and pseudo-event news.

If one tunes into the corporate media, it's apparent the culture has suffered a civic disconnect and is permeated with anti-intellectualism, from insipid forms of infotainment to carnival-like political debates. If that's not enough, in Texas the Republican Party's platform includes the aim of halting the teaching of critical thinking skills in public schools altogether, as they are a threat to "the student's fixed beliefs" and lead to "undermining parental authority."[9] It doesn't get much more anti-intellectual than that. Sadly, these developments are hardly out of sync with what many scholarly works are revealing about the decline of critical thinking and general knowledge among Americans, about the triumph of partisanship and belief over reasoned argument, and about how mass media contribute to these problems.[10]

Morris Berman, author of a trilogy of books on America's decline over the past eleven years, summed up what's wrong in a string of stinging statistics.[11] In his review of Berman's work, George Scialabba asked, "How Bad Is It?" He concluded, "Pretty bad," recapping some of the lowlights that Berman's books identify:

> Here is a sample of factlets from surveys and studies conducted in the past twenty years. Seventy percent of Americans believe in the existence of angels. Fifty percent believe that the earth has been visited by UFOs; in another poll, 70 percent believed that the U.S. government is covering up the presence of space aliens on earth. Forty percent did not know whom the U.S. fought in World War II. Forty percent could not locate Japan on a world map. Fifteen percent could not locate the United States on a world map. Sixty percent of Americans have not read a book since leaving school. Only 6 percent now read even one book a year. . . .
>
> Among high-school seniors surveyed in the late 1990s, 50 percent had not heard of the Cold War. Sixty percent could not say how the United States came into existence. Fifty percent did not know in which century the Civil War occurred. Sixty percent could name each of the Three Stooges but not the three branches of the U.S. government.
>
> . . . Of the 20 advanced democracies in the Organization for Economic Cooperation and Development (OECD), the U.S. has the highest poverty rate, for both adults and children; the lowest rate of social mobility; the lowest score on UN indexes of child welfare and gender inequality; the highest ratio of health care expenditure to GDP, combined with the lowest life expectancy and the highest rates of infant mortality, mental illness, obesity, inability to afford health

care, and personal bankruptcy resulting from medical expenses; the highest homicide rate; and the highest incarceration rate. . . .

Contemplating these dreary statistics, one might well conclude that the United States is—to a distressing extent—a nation of violent, intolerant, ignorant, superstitious, passive, shallow, boorish, selfish, unhealthy, unhappy people, addicted to flickering screens, incurious about other societies and cultures, unwilling or unable to assert or even comprehend their nominal political sovereignty.[12]

The corporate media contribute to American anti-intellectualism when they invest precious journalistic resources in the production and distribution of Junk Food News and News Abuse, rather than real news. In this chapter we critically assess the celebrity takeovers of the news media, whether through sports drama, Donald Trump's ongoing obsession with President Barack Obama's birthplace, America's infatuation with royalty, the Muppets' "attack" on Fox News, and more McNews® than anyone should have to stomach. Reach for the antacids as mental engines idle and the images in Plato's cave flicker on flat screens, all while Americans fiddle as Rome burns in a reality series that may not be renewed for a another season. Here is this year's Junk Food News media menu and what the corporate media could have and should have been covering instead if they had practiced sound journalism.

JUNK FOOD NEWS FOR 2011–12

The celebrity is a person who is known for his well-knownness.

—Daniel J. Boorstin

SOPA Gets "Tebowed"

Traditionally, sex scandals, violence, and celebrity exploits have been mainstays of Junk Food News; however, in fall 2011, the corporate media temporarily abstained from these worldly delights in favor of a "higher path" by focusing on National Football League (NFL) quarterback Tim Tebow, whose public behavior had the media dub him "God's quarterback."[13]

Tebow is a devout Christian with a history of displaying his faith during games by painting biblical verses under his eyes and kneeling in prayer with head bowed. In 2010, when the NFL (and its collegiate counterpart, the National Collegiate Athletic Association [NCAA]) forbade messages inscribed in players' eye paint, Tebow found another way to demonstrate his faith during games: kneeling in prayer. The media christened this stance "Tebowing," inspiring an Internet meme, with celebrities and fans imitating Tebow's pose, and spinoffs including holiday cards with the quarterback "Tebowing" to baby Jesus, T-shirts, and *Saturday Night Live* skits.

With Tebow fever rising, the media found religious significance in Tebow's statistics in a game during which he completed ten passes for 316 yards, an average of 31.6 yards per completion.[14] For some, the figure invoked the biblical passage John 3:16, which led to "John 3:16" becoming the most searched term on Google for January 9, 2012, the day after the game.[15] Religious organizations capitalized on Tebow hype. John Cass, of the Billy Graham Evangelistic Association website, reported to the *Christian Post* that after the "316" game, 170 people accepted Jesus Christ.[16] The fervor continued through April 2012, when Pastor Joe Champion, at Celebration Church in Texas, announced at an Easter service featuring Tebow that when it comes to "Christianity, it's the Pope and Tebow right now."[17]

Although Tebow is not the first to use sport as a platform to proselytize, the media's uptake is unprecedented.[18] Thus, some news outlets equated criticism of Tebow with criticism of Christianity. Fox News in particular has interpreted *Saturday Night Live* skits and comments by former player and sports commentator "Boomer" Esiason—which both mock Tebow—as attacks on Christianity itself by secular media sources with a pro-Muslim/anti-Christian bias. Fox sports reporter Jen Floyd Engel asserted that "all hell would break loose" if a Muslim player made similar displays of faith, because "you cannot mock Muslim faith, not in this country, not anywhere really."[19]

While Tebow preoccupied pundits and public alike, more pressing stories went underreported. Media Matters for America noted that little or no attention was paid to the Stop Internet Piracy Act (SOPA), which Congress was developing and debating at the same time. From October 26, 2011, through January 12, 2012, television news and "opinion broadcasts" aired forty-one segments about Tim Tebow while devoting only two to SOPA coverage.[20] It is likely that corporate media ignored SOPA due to their interest in the passage of the bill. Fortunately, it was reported by independent media sources, including *Wired, AlterNet,* and the *Daily Censored.*

Proponents of SOPA argued that it offered owners of copyrighted material greater protection against piracy, especially by foreign infringing sites. The bill also would have afforded the government greater ability to monitor Internet content, including the authority to shut down offending sites. These mandates entailed a level of unprecedented governmental supervision of the Internet. SOPA's reach apparently triggered concern, as several online media outlets protested SOPA's potential censorship of the Internet by calling an online blackout.[21]

The driving champion of SOPA legislation was Texas Representative Lamar Smith, who garnered support from business interests including the Recording Industry Association of America, the Motion Picture Association of America, and the US Chamber of Commerce. As Ben Dimiero of Media Matters for America reported, Comcast (NBC and MSNBC), News Corp. (Fox News), CBS Corporation (CBS), Time Warner (CNN), Disney (ABC), and the National Cable & Telecommunications Association hired twenty-eight different lobbying firms to lobby Congress on SOPA.[22]

While corporations were buying congressmen in hopes of controlling the Internet, America debated divine intervention on the football field.

Military Spending Can't Keep Up with the Kardashians

Quickie marriages and quicker divorces are nothing new to Hollywood culture. However, few received the media coverage that socialite Kim Kardashian and National Basketball Association star Chris Humphries enjoyed. Their wedding, which cost an estimated ten million dollars, was celebrated in a two-night, four-hour television special titled *Kim's Fairytale Wedding: A Kardashian Event,* broadcast to coincide with the finale of season six of *Keeping Up with the Kardashi-*

ans. The wedding broadcasts had a combined audience of 8.4 million viewers, and *E! Entertainment* ultimately aired thirty-two hours of coverage. Just seventy-two days later, news of the subsequent divorce drew the ire of reporters and fans, who charged that the whole affair was a publicity stunt, prompting Kardashian to issue this public explanation: "I had hoped this marriage was forever, but sometimes things don't work out as planned. We remain friends and wish each other the best."[23] The statement seems insincere, particularly when one takes into consideration that the couple signed a prenuptial agreement and gained a reported eighteen million dollars from magazine deals, TV coverage, and endorsements.

The celebrity gossip site TMZ initially reported the divorce, and the news spread virally to other corporate outlets. According to the Pew Research Center's Project for Excellence in Journalism, the Kardashian–Humphries divorce was the number one blogging topic and the fifth most discussed topic on Twitter for the week of October 31 to November 4, 2011.[24]

While the corporate media had no trouble keeping up with American demand for celebrity gossip, they have been reluctant to cover lobbying efforts to oppose military spending cuts. According to a report by the Stockholm International Peace Research Institute (SIPRI), US military spending has nearly doubled since 2001, and is six times greater than China's, the world's second largest military spender.[25] Globally, nations spent $1.6 trillion on defense, with the United States accounting for 42.8 percent of total military expenditures. At the time of the Kardashian divorce, the Center for International Policy and Common Cause issued a report showing that, for 2010, the defense industry spent $144 million on lobbying and employed over 1,000 lobbyists. The report also found that the defense industry contributed $22.6 million to political candidates during the 2009–10 election cycle. That amount included $1.1 million that went to members of the "super committee" charged with a deficit reduction plan, in an effort to avoid military cuts.[26]

While entertainment media encouraged Americans to feel cheated by the short run of the Kardashian–Humphries union, they did little or nothing to educate the public about the long-term *ménage à trois* among defense contractors, their lobbyists, and Congress—even though the American public foots the impressive bill for *that* ongoing revel.

Royal Escape from Guantánamo Bay

After a ten-year relationship, England's Prince William and Catherine Middleton married. US corporate media settled in London, investing millions of dollars to cover the media event. ABC pledged twenty hours of coverage. Highly sought-after "royal experts" signed contracts worth over $100,000, some with multiple outlets. Based on Neilson Report data, the *Huffington Post* reported that US media offered more coverage than even the UK press.[27] A Pew Research Center study found that, during the run-up to the royal wedding, two-thirds of Americans felt it was getting too much coverage,[28] though lack of interest did little to dissuade the corporate media from investing heavily in the event.

While the mainstream media force-fed Americans' undesired royal wedding coverage, prisoners confined without charge or trial at Guantánamo Bay in Cuba challenged the human rights abuses of their US captors. Jason Leopold reported in *Truthout* that fifteen "high-value" Guantánamo detainees were staging a hunger strike to protest the conditions of their confinement, which included an indefinite detention order signed by President Obama in March 2011.[29] The executive order called for their relocation to another camp at the facility with worse conditions and greater restrictions.

The hunger strike lasted about a month and may have been a last-ditch effort to expose conditions at Guantánamo. "The men know that this is just the latest sign that the Obama administration has no intention of closing Guantánamo," said Candace Gorman, an attorney for one of the hunger-striking prisoners, Algerian detainee Abdal Razak Ali.[30]

Royal wedding coverage also preempted coverage of the Stop Internet Piracy Act (SOPA). A report issued by Media Matters for America found that during October 26 through January 12, 2012, corporate and television media outlets aired forty-seven segments about the royal wedding.

From Birthers to Death: Obama's Citizenship Matters More than Civilian Deaths

In late May 2012, real estate mogul Donald Trump drew media attention by renewing his doubts about whether President Obama was born in the United States. "A lot of people are questioning his birth certificate," Trump told CNBC. ". . . There are some major questions here and the press doesn't want to cover it."[31] As if contestants on Trump's *Celebrity Apprentice*, the press got to work and covered the story. Again.[32] This time reporters hung the tired story on a new hook, speculating how Trump's fixation on Obama's birth certificate might impact Republican candidate Mitt Romney's presidential campaign. Trump has been one of Romney's high-profile backers, and the two were scheduled to appear together at a Las Vegas fundraiser for Romney.

Coverage of Trump's remarks focused on Romney's damage control and the Obama campaign's efforts to capitalize on it. Romney told CNBC that, although he disagreed with Trump about Obama being born in the United States, he would not condemn Trump for claiming so. "I don't go around telling all my supporters what they should think or what they should say," Romney replied.[33] The press also covered the Obama campaign's efforts to contrast Romney with 2008 candidate John McCain, who corrected his supporters when they made spurious claims about Obama's citizenship during his campaign. A widely quoted Obama campaign video said, "As the Republican nominee, John McCain stood up to the voices of extremism in his party. Why won't Mitt Romney do the same?"[34]

While broadcast media and other factions of the establishment press dutifully covered another round of electoral spectacle, a far more serious story involving legality and the Obama administration went all but unnoticed. On May 29, 2012, the *New York Times* published a key investigation on the Obama administration's escalating drone campaign in Pakistan, Yemen, and Somalia.[35] Based on interviews with three dozen current and former Obama advisors, the report documented how President Obama has personally approved drone strikes on specific individuals, and how his administration has embraced a disputed method for counting civilian casualties: by treating all military-aged males in a strike zone as "combatants," unless posthumous intelligence could prove otherwise.

Since June 2011, when US chief counterterrorism advisor John Brennan claimed that the Central Intelligence Agency (CIA) had not killed "a single non-combatant in almost a year," critics of the CIA drone strikes, including some journalists, have questioned official accounts of civilian deaths caused by those attacks.[36] The *Times* report documented concerns of "false accounting" regarding civilian casualties within Obama's administration. Given that news outlets often rely on government-supplied information about those killed or injured in a strike, the *Times* story suggested that headlines announcing the death of a certain number of "militants" really only indicate that a number of men were killed, and it gives further reason to be skeptical when officials deny that drone strikes cause civilian deaths.[37]

Despite findings of vital importance to understanding US drone programs, corporate media essentially ignored the *New York Times* report and its implications. Fairness and Accuracy in Reporting (FAIR) issued a media advisory noting that among the three major broadcast networks, only CBS mentioned the report, while one of the authors of the *Times* report, Scott Shane, appeared on PBS and NPR. "What was more newsworthy than the president personally approving drone strikes on specific individuals?" FAIR's media advisory asked.[38]

The contrast between the establishment media's fixation on the electoral spectacle of Trump's "birther" concerns and the unaddressed questions about the Obama administration's escalating campaign of drone strikes could not be more profound. While corporate media fan the embers of a burnt-out debate over Obama's citizenship, they largely ignore smoking gun evidence of his administration's willingness to embrace a redefinition of "civilian" that excludes hundreds of innocent victims of US drone strikes around the globe.

Next on the McNews: The Return of the McRib

The corporate news outlets were abuzz with reportage of *actual* junk food, including "fried butter on a stick" at the Iowa Straw Poll, and the much-heralded return of the McRib in 2011–12.[39] The "rib-like" sandwich (actually pork shoulder) has had six farewells since 2004. The Associated Press, CNN, *USA Today*, and Fox News offered a plethora of coverage, which Tommy Christopher of Mediaite termed "McNews," leaving legitimate news stories starving for attention.[40]

Corporate media intensely reported on the mystery-less mystery of the McRib disappearance, on how an unofficial McRib Locator showed how loved the McRib was among fans on Facebook and Twitter,[41] and on the video game titled *The Quest for the Golden McRib*.[42] Willy Staley of TheAwl.com reported that the McRib's reappearance is no mystery, as it coincided with downturns in the price of pork.[43] McDonald's continues to perpetuate the attraction and mystery online by maintaining a full-time staff that measures the response and effects of social media upon its products. It maintains lists of bloggers and encourages them to write about the company, even providing them with coupons for free items (pseudo-events know no bounds).[44]

A comedian was the only voice who noted that the media's infatuation with the McRib was leaving more important stories uncovered. Jon Stewart of *The Daily Show* mocked media outlets for covering the "rib-like sandwich" instead of covering the independent investigation that cleared the scientists who were accused of falsifying data to prove global warming. Right-wing pundits ignored the findings and sided with studies funded by oil magnates the Koch brothers, who concluded that climate change was a hoax. When Climategate was a scandal at the expense of the believers it garnered mass attention, but when it proved the naysayers wrong, the media gobbled the McRib.[45]

The McRib story also diverted attention from the court decision in the case *NDLON v. ICE*. The case compelled Immigration Customs Enforcement (ICE) to disclose an internal memorandum that claimed that racial profiling and deportation policies were in fact legal. The court's decision to force the document's release was regarded as a rebuke on the government agencies that had attempted to resist and ignore Freedom of Information Act requests.[46] Corporate media in the US were more interested in the return of the McRib than informing Americans about their rights to knowing what the government is doing behind closed doors.

Faux News: Murdoch's Puppets vs. Henson's Muppets

Fox News knows that controversy builds ratings, and since 2009 has been creating one out of thin air, when the network began an ideological feud with the Muppets. It began with a Muppet skit conservatives considered to be a thinly veiled jab at Fox: In one *Sesame Street* episode, Oscar the Grouch runs a television network entitled Grouch News Network (GNN). A caller phones the show to complain that the content is not grouchy enough, then proclaims: "I am changing the channel. From now on, I am watching 'Pox' News. Now there is a trashy news show."[47] Larry O'Conner, a conservative blogger, argued: "I can't even sit my kids in front of *Sesame Street* without having to worry about the Left attempting to undermine my authority."[48] Fox has resorted to calling the Muppets "felt-covered socialists." On *Follow the Money*, right-wing guests charged that a Muppet character, a fictional oil magnate named "Tex Richman," threatened to undermine capitalism, conveying an anticorporate, anti-wealth agenda to children.[49] Dan Gainor, a Fox News contributor and the vice president of business and culture for the conservative Media Research Center, bemoaned that Hollywood has repeatedly affronted the petroleum industry. He claimed that Hollywood's films fail to remind "people what oil means for most people which is fuel to light a hospital or heat your home."[50] The Muppet writers threw fuel on the fire by writing a joint statement from Kermit the Frog and Miss Piggy: "It's almost as laughable as accusing Fox News of, you know, being news."[51] *The Huffington Post*, CBS News, ABC, the *Los Angeles Times*, and the *New York Daily News* dedicated hours of coverage to the story. One is hard-pressed to put it better than the Muppets themselves in the lyrics to the original *The Muppet Show* from the 1970s, as they sang, "Why do we always come here? I guess we'll never know. It's like a kind of torture, to have to watch the show." This would be more fitting as the soundtrack to the corporate media's nightly broadcasts.

The fabricated Muppet War received coverage in place of the *AlterNet* story, "Radiation From Cell Phones and WiFi Are Making People Sick—Are We All at Risk?" The article by Christopher Ketcham used findings from multinational scientific organizations indicating numerous safety concerns with electromagnetic radio waves.[52] Previous studies minimizing these risks were largely industry funded, which raises questions about those studies' objectivity.[53] However, Ketcham's findings were no match for the Muppet War.

The Muppet War also distracted attention from the dangers of nuclear power, which were documented in Justin McCurry's *Guardian* story, "Fukushima Fuel Rods May Have Completely Melted."[54] Karl

Grossman of FAIR noted that, for years, the nuclear industry has taken advantage of a compliant corporate media to enable deception, obfuscation, and denial about the risks of nuclear power.[55] The lack of coverage may be due to extensive financial links between corporate media and the nuclear power industry; prominent nuclear energy titans General Electric and Westinghouse own or have owned major media outlets, including NBC and CBS, among others. NPR has received hundreds of thousands of dollars in contributions from Sempra Energy and Constellation Energy, leading to "pro-nuclear" stories.[56] Rupert Murdoch and Fox News have championed the deregulation of nuclear power.[57] Shying away from the Muppet War, independent media sources have reported that radiation from the Fukushima reactor has already caused deaths in the United States.

NEWS ABUSE AS PROPAGANDA AND DISTRACTION

We must first awake before we can walk in the right direction. We must discover our illusions before we can even realize we have been sleepwalking.

—Daniel J. Boorstin[58]

News Abuse became part of Project Censored's scope when Dr. Peter Phillips expanded Junk Food News to include news stories that treated serious societal matters but suffered from distortion. News Abuse occurs when corporate media transform a partially factual news story into propaganda through spin, obfuscation, and omission. As such, News Abuse is subtler than Junk Food News. The term draws attention to how corporate media report important news stories in partial ways that make the story distracting, titillating, and even confusing, often at the expense of the story's fundamental facts and overall significance. The following stories from 2011–12 give evidence of the wide range of News Abuse.

Conservative Pundit and Pop Diva Reach #1 on Grief Porn Charts

There is little that corporate news media love more than a good cry. In the past year, they have eulogized the deaths of radio and television personality Dick Clark, kitsch artist Thomas Kinkaid, author and illustrator Maurice Sendak, singer Etta James, former Monkee

Davy Jones, Beastie Boy Adam "MCA" Yauch, Bee Gee Robin Gibb, singer Donna Summer, pop diva Whitney Houston, and conservative blogger Andrew Breitbart, among others. Though news media have a clear responsibility to report the deaths of important public figures, they have no legitimate license to peddle what British journalist Mick Hume called "mourning sickness," or what Robert Yates, assistant editor of the *Observer*, has aptly described as "grief porn." As with Michael Jackson's death in 2009, the media frenzies over the deaths of conservative blogger Andrew Breitbart and pop singer Whitney Houston crossed the line from responsible reporting to grief porn.[59]

Breitbart died March 1, 2012, of an enlarged heart and heart disease.[60] Not since Reagan's death has there been such a public outpouring of right-wing grief. Fox News described the blogger as a courageous "happy warrior" fearlessly seeking the truth.[61] *Forbes* cast Breitbart as one of the "most prominent critics of liberal elitism," with condolences from those across the political spectrum.[62] Conservative media hailed Breitbart's lies and propaganda as exemplary journalism, citing among his notable "achievements" the editing of a video to portray statements made by Shirley Sherrod as racist, which destroyed her career; exposing private photos of Rep. Anthony Weiner, leading to his resignation; and posting spurious video footage that discredited the Association of Community Organizations for Reform Now (ACORN).[63] *Rolling Stone*'s Matt Taibbi, who had previously been harassed by Breitbart supporters, was among the few journalists who bravely attacked Breitbart's inflated record.[64]

"True believers" refused to accept that a heart condition, and not foul play, caused his death.[65] Prior to his death, Breitbart had promised to release a damning video of Barack Obama before the election.[66] Breitbart supporters flooded the Internet with allegations of the Obama administration's involvement in Breitbart's death. These turned out to be false, according to the final coroner's report.[67]

Breitbart's death was no match for the tidal wave of attention paid to the death of pop singer Whitney Houston, who topped the grief porn charts in February 2012. The diva's life was rife with quintessential elements of the grief porn narrative: talent and stardom eroded by drug addiction, an abusive marriage resulting in erratic behavior, a hysterical orphaned daughter, and allegations that foul play led to her demise. News media coverage of the pop icon was extensive. ABC-News.com devoted an entire section to Houston, featuring speculative articles such as "Was Whitney Houston in Financial Trouble?" and "Was Whitney Up for 'X Factor' Judge?" Within a month, Reuters.com had provided 118 articles on Houston's death, while FoxNews.com and CBSNews.com had posted 135 and 128 articles, respectively. CNN ran a whopping 380 articles on Houston's death. With that obscene number, we hope outlets have finally reached their climax on grief porn coverage, as mourning sickness has likely already kicked in among the viewing public.

Corporate Media Profit from Tragedy (Again)

The trial of twenty-two-year-old Casey Anthony, who stood accused of murdering her two-year-old daughter Caylee in 2008, became a media sensation in 2011. Extensive pretrial media coverage created problems in seating an untainted jury. The trial itself lasted six weeks and was covered by all the major outlets. In the words of one publication, "As perverse as it may sound, the Casey Anthony trial is the kind of news event that TV executives dream of."[68]

Though Anthony was ultimately acquitted of murder but found guilty of aggravated child abuse and four misdemeanor counts of providing false information, her lawyer J. Cheney Mason lambasted the press for coverage that amounted to "media assassination."[69]

Anthony almost instantly became the focal point of the corporate press. The audience for HLN's *Nancy Grace* rose 150 percent during the trial, while *Dr. Drew* ratings tripled after devoting its show to the trial. The Pew Research Center said it was the most followed story from July 7 to July 10, 2011.[70] Bing, the Microsoft search engine, identified the Casey Anthony trial as the most searched story of 2011—even topping the death of Osama bin Laden.[71]

The corporate media obsession with Anthony overlooked the American Civil Liberties Union (ACLU) federal court case in opposition to electronic devices being searched at border checkpoints. Under the current law, authorities may search all electronic items without suspicion. Government documents revealed that thousands of Americans had been searched. Catherine Crump, staff attorney with the ACLU's Speech, Privacy and Technology Project, argued that searching materials "without reasonable suspicion is unconstitutional, inconsistent with American values and a waste of limited resources." However, Anthony's trial by media garnered the attention from the case with Bill of Rights implications.[72]

Indiana Workers' Rights "Threaten" America's Super Bowl

In February 2012, after more than a month of pitched battle, Indiana lawmakers passed a right-to-work bill, making Indiana the first Rust Belt state and the nation's twenty-third overall with such a law. But the real story, as far as corporate media were concerned, was whether union protests would disrupt the NFL's Super Bowl. Not only did corporate coverage obfuscate public understanding about the consequences of right-to-work laws, it pitted the Super Bowl against the preservation of workers' rights. Fear of the game's interruption, rather than the bill's effects, became the focal story.

There can be little doubt that right-to-work laws have hastened US labor unions' decline. Roger Bybee wrote that elites in the old Confederacy first instituted right-to-work policies, which have historically reduced wages and weakened unions by forcing them to provide services and protections to laborers who pay no dues, and by providing incentives to employers to screen out union sympathizers.[73] "'Right to work,'" Bybee observed, "is a brilliant piece of corporate marketing, as such laws provide absolutely no rights to workers and have nothing to do with guaranteeing full employment."[74]

The track record of right-to-work states is poor at best: such states lack constraints against corporate power, low wages, and reductions in spending on health care, education, and other public goods. The Bureau of Labor Statistics has reported that 11.8 percent of American wage and salary earners belonged to a union, representing 14.8 million workers. In 1983, union members accounted for 20.1 percent of the total workforce and represented 17.7 million workers. These numbers are considerably lower in the southern states.[75]

But Indiana's lawmakers were not concerned with statistics like these. Spurred by the state's corporate interests and enabled by corporate news coverage that amounted to cheerleading on behalf of right-to-work, they did a Super Bowl hustle of their own and passed the law.

Who's the Rotten Apple? *This American Life* Goes Daisey Crazy

On January 6, 2012, author and actor Mike Daisey appeared on NPR's *This American Life* to discuss his monologue, "The Agony and Ecstasy of Steve Jobs."[76] The monologue referenced Apple's largest supplier, Foxconn in China, and their alleged immoral business practices and unsafe working conditions. In his monologue, Daisey, who is not a journalist, describes a trip to China to investigate Foxconn's working conditions, which he found horrible. For example, Daisey told *This American Life* about a man working at a Foxconn factory who was poisoned by n-hexane, a "potent neurotoxin."[77] Daisey claimed that many Foxconn workers were similarly exposed. "Their hands shake uncontrollably. Most of them can't even pick up glass."[78]

On March 16, 2012, Ira Glass, host of *This American Life* (*TAL*), dramatically retracted the story, alleging that Daisey had "fabricated" aspects of it.[79] The retraction countered Daisey's version of Foxconn conditions with accounts by two other people: Rob Schmitz, a reporter for NPR's *Marketplace*, and Cathy Lee, Daisey's interpreter in China.[80] Though many interpreted this retraction as a wholesale refutation of Daisey's claims against Foxconn and Apple, Glass did acknowledge that much of what Daisey had reported regarding working conditions had been confirmed independently. Instead, the decision to retract hinged on more subtle aspects of Daisey's story: he had not witnessed all the events he described firsthand, and he had compiled some of his story from observations made by others. While the *TAL* retraction portrayed Daisey as a rotten reporter, Tim Worstall of *Forbes* magazine took advantage of the situation to effectively pardon Apple and Foxconn, acknowledging less-than-ideal conditions in Apple-supported factories but urging the American public to accept that working conditions in Chinese factories are uniformly inferior to those in the US.[81]

Both *TAL*'s retraction and *Forbes*' absolution sought to shift the frame in ways that simultaneously blamed Daisey and soft-pedaled the investigative work of professional journalists who, independent of Daisey, had documented the same dangerous and exploitative conditions for workers. For example, *Censored 2012* honored Dan Margolis for his story—filed in January 2011, an entire year before Daisey's *TAL* appearance—documenting systemic conditions that threaten workers' health in factories contracted with Apple, as well as Apple's efforts to hide those conditions behind "a secretive supply chain."[82] Conditions had certainly not improved by the time of the original *TAL* story featuring Daisey, as Malcolm Moore's January 2012 report for the *Telegraph* (UK) indicated: Moore reported that 150 Foxconn factory workers threatened to kill themselves by jumping from the factory's roof, prompting management to install safety nets to prevent them. In 2010, eighteen Foxconn workers did jump in protest and fourteen died as a result.[83] If Apple's corporate mantra is "Think Different," they'll likely have to reboot pretty soon if they are to escape the slave labor culture they've emulated, one that has been a mainstay of capitalist and imperialist countries' practices for a very long time.

Fox News: Occupy Occupy's Agenda

Since the Occupy Wall Street protests began in fall 2011, corporate media have lashed out at protesters despite their overwhelmingly peaceful, nonviolent methods. Of course, less-than-flattering corporate coverage is no surprise when the Occupy movement emerged to question corporate greed and big business dominance.[84] Hyperbolic, right-wing Fox News—the champion of past Tea Party protests—has provided the most egregious examples of anti-Occupy reporting, though rarely with sound logic and often with fallacious reasoning. Bill O'Reilly has made numerous attacks on the Occupy movement, calling protesters "anti-capitalist" and dismissing them as apologists for President Obama, who O'Reilly named as actually responsible for the destruction of the nation's economy.[85] In his attempt to portray Occupy as a partisan movement along traditional (i.e., Democrat vs. Republican) lines, O'Reilly has ignored the reality that many in the Occupy movement are also critical of Obama and the Democrats.

Corporate coverage of Occupy protests across the country has downplayed—or entirely ignored—acts of violence committed by police forces against Occupy participants. For example, Scott Olsen, a twenty-four-year-old marine who served two tours of duty in Iraq, was hit in the head with a tear gas canister while standing peacefully across from police in Oakland; and Dorli Rainey, an eighty-four-year-old Occupy protester, was pepper sprayed alongside a pregnant woman in Seattle.[86] These were hardly isolated incidents. Stephen Rosenfeld of *AlterNet* reported that local police departments, supported by a decade of Homeland Security funds, now show "no reluctance to put on riot gear, conduct mass arrests and use pepper spray, teargas and concussion grenades . . . just as they have shown no reluctance to spy on protesters and preemptively arrest people they suspect, often erroneously, of being leaders."[87]

Despite evidence from a number of sources that the US is becoming a police state (see "Signs of an Emerging Police State," *Censored 2013*'s top story, as reported in chapter 1), Fox commentators and other reactionary pundits continue to attack Occupy as the catalyst of violence and oppression.

EPILOGUE

America today is not the country it once was—nor is it the nation it could be. We need a free and aggressive press more now than ever before, a press that will stand up to those who would control it and assume once again the independence it once celebrated.

—Project Censored founder Carl Jensen, 1993[88]

Carl Jensen's call for a free and aggressive press is as necessary today as it was twenty years ago. By examining the corporate media's Junk Food News and News Abuse, we call readers to recognize the importance of a free press—one that informs the public about important issues of the day—in service of democratic self-government. That recognition entails both critique and affirmation, as delicately captured in one of the concluding metaphors from Boorstin's *The Image*:

> The least and the most we can hope for is that each of us may penetrate the unknown jungle of images in which we live our daily lives. That we may discover anew where dreams end and where illusions begin. This is enough. Then we may know where we are, and each of us may decide for himself where he wants to go.[89]

Identifying and tracking Junk Food News and News Abuse allows us to penetrate deeper into the "unknown jungle of images"—without becoming lost in it. Once we recognize Junk Food News and News Abuse as recurrent species in that jungle, we are less likely to be enthralled by sensational celebrityhood or entwined by the distractions of pseudo-events. Only then will we find ourselves, as individuals and communities, in a clearing where we can see, and act, lucidly.

MICKEY HUFF is the director of Project Censored and a professor of social science and history at Diablo Valley College.

ANDY LEE ROTH, PHD, is the associate director of Project Censored.

NOLAN HIGDON is an adjunct instructor of history at Diablo Valley College and a former intern and research assistant for Project Censored.

MICHAEL KOLBE and ANDREW O'CONNOR-WATTS are Project Censored interns and students at Diablo Valley College.

Special thanks to Diablo Valley College's Critical Reasoning in History classes, fall 2011 and spring 2012, and to Ryan Shehee for editing of early drafts.

Notes

1. Daniel J. Boorstin, *The Image: A Guide to Pseudo-Events in America* (New York: Atheneum, 1962), 4–5; see also the 50th ann. ed., with afterword by Douglas Rushkoff (New York: Vintage Books, 2012), which is a reissue from 1987 and 1992. The book was originally alternately titled *The Image, or What Happened to the American Dream?*
2. A recounting of the development of Junk Food News is published in Mickey Huff and Peter Phillips, eds., *Censored 2011: The Top Censored Stories of 2009–10* (New York: Seven Stories Press, 2010), chap. 3; and Mickey Huff, ed., *Censored 2012: The Top Censored Stories and Media Analysis of 2010–11* (New York: Seven Stories Press, 2011), chap. 3. Also see Carl Jensen and Project Censored, *Censored 1994* (New York: Four Walls Eight Windows, 1994), 142–43; Jensen further added to this sentiment in "Junk Food News 1877–2000," as chap. 5 of Peter Phillips, ed., *Censored 2001* (New York: Seven Stories Press, 2001), 251–64.
3. Boorstin, *The Image*.
4. Ibid., 4–5.
5. Edward L. Bernays, "The Engineering of Consent," *Annals of the American Academy of Political Science* 250 (March 1947), 113–20. See also Stuart Ewen, *PR! A Social History of Spin* (New York: Basic Books, 1996).
6. Boorstin, *The Image*, 4–5.
7. Ibid., 5–6.
8. Neil Postman, *Amusing Ourselves to Death: Public Discourse in the Age of Show Business* (New York: Penguin, 1985).
9. Danny Weil, "Texas GOP Declares: No More Teaching of Critical Thinking Skills in Texas Public Schools," *Truthout*, July 7, 2012, http://truth-out.org/news/item/10144-texas-gop-declare. States Weil, "Reactionaries have long known that enshrining ignorance and hierarchy in both thought and practice within the school curriculum is essential if the control of young minds is to be accomplished softly and quietly yet profoundly through propaganda and perception management."

10. See Thomas H. Benton, "On Stupidity," *Chronicle of Higher Education*, August 1, 2008, http://chronicle.com/article/On-Stupidity/45764; Bruce D. Olsen, "The Causes of Anti-Intellectualism," November 20, 2011, http://diogenesii.wordpress.com/2011/11/20/anti-intellectualism-revisited; Bruce D. Olsen, "A Nation at Risk," http://diogenesii.wordpress.com/a-nation-at-risk-this-time-for-real; Rick Shenkman, *Just How Stupid Are We: The Truth about the American Voter* (New York: Basic Books, 2008); Richard Hofstadter, *Anti-Intellectualism in American Life* (New York: Knopf, 1963); Susan Jacoby, *The Age of American Unreason* (New York: Pantheon, 2008); and Chris Hedges, "How to Think," *Truthdig*, July 9, 2012, http://www.truthdig.com/report/page2/how_to_think_20120709.

11. Morris Berman, *Why America Failed: The Roots of Imperial Decline* (Hoboken: John Wiley and Sons, 2012); *Dark Ages America: The Final Stages of Empire* (New York: W. W. Norton, 2006); and *The Twilight of American Culture* (New York: W. W. Norton, 2000).

12. George Scialabba, "How Bad Is It?," *New Inquiry*, May 26, 2012, http://thenewinquiry.com/essays/how-bad-is-it.

13. See, for example, Patton Dodd, "Tim Tebow: God's Quarterback," *Wall Street Journal*, December 10, 2011, http://online.wsj.com/article/SB10001424052970203413304577084770973155282.html.

14. For example, "Tebow's Biblical Game: 316 Yards Invokes Key Verse," Fox News, January 9, 2012, http://www.foxnews.com/us/2012/01/09/tebows-biblical-game-316-yards-invokes-key-verse.

15. Alex Murashko, "Did Tim Tebow's 316 Yards Passing Lead 170 to Jesus?" *Christian Post*, January 14, 2012, http://www.christianpost.com/news/did-tim-tebows-316-yards-passing-lead-170-to-jesus-67178/

16. Ibid.

17. "Tim Tebow Draws Big Crowd to Texas Easter Service," CBS News, April 8, 2012, http://www.cbsnews.com/8301-400_162-57411052/tim-tebow-draws-big-crowd-to-texas-easter-service.

18. For example, as early as 1977, Rollin Stewart, a born-again Christian, appeared at major sporting events including NFL playoff games, the Olympics, the Indy 500, and the NBA Finals, wearing a rainbow wig, a shirt stamped with the word "repent," and holding a sign that read "John 3:16."

19. Jen Floyd Engel, "What if Tim Tebow Were a Muslim?," Fox News, December 2, 2011, http://nation.foxnews.com/tim-tebow/2011/12/02/what-if-tim-tebow-were-muslim.

20. Ben Dimiero, "Study: SOPA Coverage No Match for Kim Kardashian and Tim Tebow," Media Matters for America, January 13, 2012, http://mediamatters.org/blog/201201130015.

21. "SOPA Blackout Aims to Block Internet Censorship Bill," *Huffington Post*, January 18, 2012, http://www.huffingtonpost.com/2012/01/18/sopa-blackout-internet-censorship_n_1211905.html.

22. Ben Dimiero, "How Much Did Media Companies Spend Lobbying On SOPA And PIPA?," Media Matters for America, February 3, 2012, http://mediamatters.org/blog/2012/02/03/how-much-did-media-companies-spend-lobbying-on/184807.

23. Ann Oldenburg, "Kim Kardashian: Sometimes Things Don't Work Out as Planned," *USA Today*, October 31, 2011, http://content.usatoday.com/communities/entertainment/post/2011/10/kim-kardashian-filing-for-divorce-from-kris-humphries/1#.UAXUvjEsAWU.

24. Paul Hitlin and Sovini Tan, "Bloggers Debate the Cain and Kardashian Stories," Pew Research Center's Project for Excellence in Journalism, October 31–November 4, 2011, http://www.journalism.org/node/27320.

25. "Background Paper on SIPRI Military Expenditure Data, 2010," Stockholm International Peace Research Insitute, April 11, 2011, http://www.sipri.org/research/armaments/milex/factsheet2010.

26. William D. Hartung, "Tools of Influence: The Arms Lobby and the Super Committee," Common Cause, October 2011, http://www.commoncause.org/atf/cf/%7Bfb3c17e2-cdd1-4df6-92be-bd4429893665%7D/CIP%20DEFENSE%20AND%20SUPER%20COMMITTEE.PDF.

27. "Royal Wedding Getting More News Coverage in U.S. than in U.K.: Nielsen Study," *Huffington Post*, April 25, 2011, http://www.huffingtonpost.com/2011/04/25/royal-wedding-coverage-us-uk_n_853420.html.

28. "Modest American Interest in Royal Wedding," Pew Research Center, April 27, 2011, http://pewresearch.org/pubs/1975/public-interest-royal-wedding-prince-william-kate-middleton-economy-storms.

29. Jason Leopold, "Guantánamo Detainees Stage Hunger Strike to Protest Confinement Conditions," *Truthout*, April 29, 2011, http://truth-out.org/index.php?option=com_k2&view=item&id=827:guantanamo-detainees-stage-hunger-strike-to-protest-confinement-conditions.

30. Ibid.

31. Sam Youngman, "Trump Birther Remarks Overshadow Romney Appearance," Reuters, May 29, 2012, http://www.reuters.com/article/2012/05/29/us-usa-campaign-idUSBRE-84S19O20120529.

32. In part because of Trump's prior claims, Obama's campaign released his Hawaiian birth certificate during the 2008 presidential race; when this failed to quell suspicions, the Obama administration released his long-form birth certificate in April 2011, http://www.whitehouse.gov/blog/2011/04/27/president-obamas-long-form-birth-certificate.

33. Emily Friedman, "Romney Won't Tell Trump to Stop Birther Comments," ABC News, June 1, 2012, http://abcnews.go.com/blogs/politics/2012/06/romney-wont-tell-trump-to-stop-birther-comments.

34. See, for example, David Jackson, "Obama Team Bashes Romney Over Trump Support," *USA Today*, May 29, 2012, http://content.usatoday.com/communities/theoval/post/2012/05/obama-team-bashes-romney-over-trump-support/1#.T9EDOI7gCXs.

35. Jo Becker and Scott Shane, "Secret 'Kill List' Proves a Test of Obama's Principles and Will," *New York Times*, May 29, 2012, http://www.nytimes.com/2012/05/29/world/obamas-leadership-in-war-on-al-qaeda.html?_r=1.

36. ABC's George Stephanopoulos pressed Brennan on his remarkable claim. For one example of independent press scrutiny, see Chris Woods, "Analysis: Why We Must Name All Drone Attack Victims," Bureau of Investigative Journalism, May 10, 2012, http://www.thebureauinvestigates.com/2012/05/10/analysis-why-we-must-name-all-drone-attack-victims. As Woods notes, the CIA and other elements of the US intelligence community have aggressively attacked the bureau for its reporting.

37. Glenn Greenwald, "Obama the Warrior," *Salon*, May 29, 2012, http://www.salon.com/2012/05/29/obama_the_warrior/singleton.

38. "Drone Kill List: Not News?," Fairness and Accuracy in Reporting, June 6, 2012, http://www.fair.org/index.php?page=4561.

39. Christina Rexrode, "The McRib Makes a McComeback," Associated Press, October 24, 2011, http://www.usatoday.com/money/industries/food/story/2011-10-24/mcdonalds-mcrib-sandwich/50888872/1.

40. Tommy Christopher, "Great Moments in McJournalism: McDonald's McRib McMakes Mc-News," Mediaite, October 25, 2011, http://www.mediaite.com/tv/great-moments-in-mcjournalism-mcdonalds-mcrib-mcmakes-mcnews.

41. Raphael Brion, "McDonald's McRib Returns Nationwide November 2nd," Eater.com, October 11, 2010, http://eater.com/archives/2010/10/11/the-a-returns-nationwide-november-2nd.php.

42. Laurent Belsie, "McRib is Back . . . Along with Unicorns, Viking Accountants," *Christian Science Monitor*, October 25, 2012, http://alice.dvc.edu/docview/900462658?accountid=38376.

43. Daniel Hamermesh, "The Marginal Cost of the McRib," Freakonomics.com, December 1, 2011, http://www.freakonomics.com/2011/12/01/the-marginal-cost-of-the-mcrib.

44. Nicole Carter, "The McRib's Magic Marketing Sauce," Inc.com, October 25, 2011, http://www.inc.com/articles/201110/marketing-lessons-from-the-mcdonalds-mcrib.html; and Kevin McKeough, "Who's Doing Social Media Right? McDonalds Corp," *Crain's Chicago Business*, January 2, 2012, http://alice.dvc.edu/docview/915478161?accountid=38376.

45. "Jon Stewart Rips Media for Ignoring 'Climategate' Debunking, Covering McRib Instead," *Huffington Post*, October 27, 2011, http://www.huffingtonpost.com/2011/10/27/jon-stewart-climategate-debunkin-media-mcrib_n_1034792.html.

46. "Court Criticizes ICE's Efforts to Avoid Disclosure as "Offensive" to Freedom of Information Act District Court Orders Release of Key ICE Memorandum," Center for Constitutional Rights, October 25, 2011, http://www.commondreams.org/newswire/2011/10/25-5.

47. "'Sesame Street' Ombudsman Says Fox News Parody 'Should Have Been Resisted,'" Fox News, November 6, 2009, http://www.foxnews.com/entertainment/2009/11/06/sesame-street-ombudsman-says-producers-crossed-line-fox-news-stab/#ixzz1sGnDQTsh.

48. "Bolling's Muppet-Bashing Just the Latest Right-Wing Attack on Kids' Programs," Media Matters for America, December 6, 2011, http://mediamatters.org/research/201112060018.

49. Ibid.

50. Gael Fashingbauer Cooper, "Fox Says 'Muppets' Are Brainwashing Kids," MSNBC, December 5, 2011, http://entertainment.msnbc.msn.com/_news/2011/12/05/9229560-fox-says-muppets-are-brainwashing-kids?lite.

51. Ethan Sacks, "Miss Piggy & Kermit Fire Back at Fox Business," *New York Daily News*, January 30, 2012, http://articles.nydailynews.com/2012-01-30/news/31007492_1_oil-companies-steve-whitmire-liberal-agenda.

52. Christopher Ketcham, "Radiation from Cell Phones and WiFi Are Making People Sick—Are We All at Risk?," *AlterNet*, December 2, 2012, http://www.alternet.org/environment/153299/radiation_from_cell_phones_and_wifi_are_making_people_sick_—_are_we_all_at_risk.

53. Project Censored, "Research Clarifies Cell Phone Danger," Media Freedom International, April 9, 2011, http://www.mediafreedominternational.org/2012/04/09/research-clarifies-cell-phone-danger.

54. Justin McCurry, "Fukushima Fuel Rods May Have Completely Melted," *Guardian*, December 2, 2011, http://www.guardian.co.uk/world/2011/dec/02/fukushima-fuel-rods-completely-melted.

55. Karl Grossman, "Money Is the Real Green Power: The Hoax of Eco-Friendly Nuclear Energy," Fairness and Accuracy in Reporting, January/February 2008, http://www.fair.org/index.php?page=3258.

56. Ibid.

57. "Right-Wing Media Push for Removal of 'Obstacles' to Nuclear Power in Wake of Japan's Nuclear Crisis," Media Matters for America, March 14 2011, http://mediamatters.org/research/201103140032.

58. Boorstin, *The Image*, 261.

59. For more on the concepts of "mourning sickness" and "grief porn" as mentioned here, see the Junk Food News and News Abuse sections in Mickey Huff and Peter Phillips, eds., *Censored 2011: The Top Censored Stories of 2009–10* (New York: Seven Stories Press, 2010), chap. 3; and Mickey Huff, ed., *Censored 2012: The Top Censored Stories and Media Analysis of 2010–11* (New York: Seven Stories Press, 2011), chap. 3.

60. "Conservative Blogger Andrew Breitbart Died of Heart Failure," CNN, April 20, 2012, http://articles.cnn.com/2012-04-20/politics/politics_breitbart-autopsy_1_andrew-breitbart-conservative-activist-social-media-conservative-blogger?_s=PM:POLITICS.

61. "Conservative Commentator Andrew Breitbart Is Dead at 43," Fox News, March 1, 2012, http://www.foxnews.com/politics/2012/03/01/andrew-breitbart-dies-natural-causes-website-reports/#ixzz1vlWEOr8W.

62. Jeff Bercovinci, "Huffington, Drudge and Beck on Andrew Breitbart's Death," *Forbes*, March 1, 2012, http://www.forbes.com/sites/jeffbercovici/2012/03/01/huffington-drudge-and-beck-on-andrew-breitbarts-death.

63. "Conservative Commentator Andrew Breitbart Is Dead at 43."

64. Matt Taibbi, "Andrew Breitbart: Death of a Douche," *Rolling Stone*, March 1, 2012, http://www.rollingstone.com/politics/blogs/taibblog/andrew-breitbart-death-of-a-douche-20120301.

65. Maer Roshan and Hunter R. Slayton, "What Really Killed Andrew Breitbart? The Likely Cause of Death the Mainstream Media Ignored," *AlterNet*, March 8, 2012, http://www.alternet.org/

drugs/154463/what_really_killed_andrew_breitbart_the_likely_cause_of_death_the_main-stream_media_ignored?page=entire.

66. Dylan Stableford, "Andrew Breitbart Death Sparks Conspiracy Theories," Yahoo! News, March 2, 2012, http://news.yahoo.com/blogs/cutline/andrew-breitbart-death-sparks-conspiracy-theo-ries-galore-175523779.html.

67. Ibid. See also Paul Joseph Watson, "Only Eyewitness to Breitbart's Death Disappears," InfoWars.com, May 8, 2012, http://www.infowars.com/only-eyewitness-to-breitbarts-death-dis-appears; and "Andrew Breitbart Died of Heart Failure, Narrowing of Artery, Coroner Finds," Los Angeles Times, May, 16, 2012, http://latimesblogs.latimes.com/lanow/2012/05/commentator-and-editor-andrew-breitbart-died-of-heart-failure-and-hard-up-to-a-60-narrowing-of-a-major-artery-and-was-unde.html. The article read in part, "Conservative commentator and website editor Andrew Breitbart died of heart failure and had up to a 60% narrowing of a major artery, a Los Angeles County coroner's office report released Wednesday said. The office ruled that the cause of Breitbart's death was heart failure and hypertrophic cardiomyopathy with focal coronary atherosclerosis, or hardening of the arteries. Coroner's officials deemed the death 'natural.'" Some conspiracies really are a figment of imagination, as the facts here show.

68. Maxine Shen, "TV's Hottest Ticket," New York Post, June 20, 2011, http://www.nypost.com/p/entertainment/tv/tv_hottest_ticket_581uQbnfbbFSixnPFbfzAP.

69. See, for example, Jose Baez, "Anthony Lawyers Decry Media Coverage," CNN, July 5, 2011, http://articles.cnn.com/2011-07-05/justice/florida.casey.anthony.lawyers_1_casey-anthony-case-anthony-lawyers-defense-team?_s=PM:CRIME.

70. "Casey Anthony Verdict Top Story for Public and Social Networkers," Pew Research Center, July 13, 2011, http://pewresearch.org/pubs/2057/-casey-anthony-economy-debt-limit-deficit-facebook-twitter.

71. "Casey Anthony Trial: Bing's Most Searched News Story of 2011," Huffington Post, November 29, 2011, http://www.huffingtonpost.com/2011/11/29/casey-anthony-trial-bing-most-searched-news-story-2011_n_1118756.html; and "The Top 2011 Searches from Bing: A Year of Breakthroughs and Heartbreaks," Bing, November 28, 2011, http://www.bing.com/commu-nity/site_blogs/b/search/archive/2011/11/28/2011trends.aspx#News%20Stories.

72. "ACLU in Federal Court Today Challenging Government's Searches of Laptops at Border," American Civil Liberties Union, July 8, 2011, http://www.aclu.org/technology-and-liberty/aclu-federal-court-today-challenging-governments-searches-laptops-border.

73. Roger Bybee, "Super Bowl-Level Stakes for Indiana Labor in Battle vs. 'Right-to-Work,'" In These Times, January 6, 2011, http://www.inthesetimes.com/working/entry/12494/supedr-bowl-vel_staes_for_labor_in_indiana_battle_vs_right-to-work.

74. Ibid.

75. Bureau of Labor Statistics, "Union Members Summary," January 27, 2012, http://www.bls.gov/news.release/union2.nr0.htm.

76. "Mr. Daisey and the Apple Factory," This American Life, NPR, January 6, 2012, http://www.thisamericanlife.org/radio-archives/episode/454/transcript.

77. Ibid.

78. Ibid.

79. "Retraction," This American Life, NPR, March 16, 2012, http://podcast.thisamericanlife.org/special/TAL_460_Retraction_Transcript.pdf.

80. Ibid.

81. Tim Worstall, "Finally: The Truth About Conditions Inside Apple's Foxconn Factories," Forbes, April 13, 2012, http://www.forbes.com/sites/timworstall/2012/04/13/finally-the-truth-about-conditions-inside-apples-foxconn-factories.

82. Dan Margolis, "Rotten Apple: iPod Sweatshops Hidden in China," People's World, January 25, 2011, http://www.peoplesworld.org/rotten-apple-ipod-sweatshops-hidden-in-china. See also Andy Lee Roth, "Power, Abuse and Accountability," Censored 2012: The Top Censored Stories and Media Analysis of 2010–11, ed. Mickey Huff (New York: Seven Stories, 2011), 91–92.

83. Malcolm Moore, "'Mass Suicide' Protest at Apple Manufacturer Foxconn Factory," *Telegraph* (UK), January 11, 2012, http://www.telegraph.co.uk/news/worldnews/asia/china/9006988/Mass-suicide-protest-at-Apple-manufacturer-Foxconn-factory.html.

84. For one such example, see "Occupy Movement (Occupy Wall Street)," *New York Times*, May 2, 2012, http://topics.nytimes.com/top/reference/timestopics/organizations/o/occupy_wall_street/index.html.

85. See, for example, Bill O'Reilly, "Real Reason 'Occupy Wall Street' Protest Is Taking Place," Fox News, October 11, 2011, http://www.foxnews.com/on-air/oreilly/2011/10/12/bill-oreilly-real-reason-occupy-wall-street-protest-taking-place.

86. Justin Berton and Will Kane, "Hurt Protester Scott Olsen Was 'Provoking No One,'" *San Francisco Chronicle*, October 28, 2011, http://www.sfgate.com/cgi-bin/article.cgi?f=/c/a/2011/10/27/BAD61LN3LM.DTL#ixzz1x8WWphEd; and Dean Praetorius, "Dorli Rainey, 84-Year-Old Occupy Seattle Protester, Pepper Sprayed in the Face," *Huffington Post*, November 16, 2011, http://www.huffingtonpost.com/2011/11/16/dorli-rainey-pepper-spray-occupy-seattle_n_1097836.html.

87. Steven Rosenfeld, "Will a Militarized Police Force Facing Occupy Wall Street Lead to Another Kent State Massacre?," *AlterNet*, May 3, 2012, http://www.alternet.org/rights/155270/will_a_militarized_police_force_facing_occupy_wall_street_lead_to_another_kent_state_massacre. For more on the unreported history of the 1970 Kent State massacre, see chap. 9 in this volume.

88. Carl Jensen, *Censored: The News that Didn't Make the News—And Why* (Chapel Hill: Shelburne Press, 1993), 96.

89. Boorstin, *The Image*, 261.

CHAPTER 4

Media Democracy in Action

Compiled by Mickey Huff, with contributions by Sarah van Gelder
and *Yes! Magazine*; Chris Woods of the Bureau of Investigative
Journalism; Jay Costa and Darby Beck of MapLight; Michael
Levitin of the *Occupied Wall Street Journal*; Victoria Pacchiana-
Rojas on Banned Books Week; Christopher Ponzi of Rebellious
Truths; Nora Barrows-Friedman of Electronic Intifada; Andrew
Phillips of Pacifica/KPFA Radio; J. R. Valrey of Block Report Radio;
Steve Zeltzer of Work Week Radio

ON MEDIA FREEDOM:

*The only security of all is in a free press. The force of
public opinion cannot be resisted when permitted freely
to be expressed. The agitation it produces must be submitted to. It is necessary, to keep the waters pure.*

—Thomas Jefferson, 1823

ON THE RIGHT TO KNOW:

*Freedom of the press, or, to be more precise, the benefit of
freedom of the press, belongs to everyone—to the citizen
as well as the publisher. . . . The crux is not the publisher's "freedom to print"; it is, rather, the citizen's "right
to know."*

—Arthur Sulzberger, 1990, American newspaper publisher

ON JUSTICE:

*When our days become dreary with low-hovering clouds
of despair, and when our nights become darker than a*

thousand midnights, let us remember that there is a creative force in this universe, working to pull down the gigantic mountains of evil, a power that is able to make a way out of no way and transform dark yesterdays into bright tomorrows. Let us realize the arc of the moral universe is long but it bends toward justice.

—Dr. Martin Luther King Jr., 1967, in an address to the Southern Christian Leadership Conference, "Where Do We Go from Here?"

In the past, critics of Project Censored have complained that we point out problems in our society that go underreported but do not offer solutions. Over the past several years, we've been addressing this concern through our research of so-called good news, news of real change and community building, and through our efforts to reclaim the fair share of the common heritage.[1]

Addressing censorship in news media is certainly a major issue, but in doing so, Project Censored also works to provide tangible information that empowers people to be active agents in their own information gathering and to be more willing to share knowledge in meaningful ways. This sharing comes through the many social circles we inhabit, not merely in the increasingly virtual world of social media, but in the *real* world, face-to-face, on the ground, in local communities that can be connected globally via vast communications technologies. It is important to note that merely having an active presence on the World Wide Web cannot be the only means by which we share knowledge and information, by which we organize and act to achieve social and political change.

In this spirit, Project Censored not only works to *un*censor major news stories that the corporate media ignore or distort, it also works to maintain a vibrant free press system through education, media literacy, and civic activism. Over the years, we've partnered with individuals and groups that dedicate their lives to media freedom, transparency, access to information, and a solid democratic communications principle—the right to be heard, and the commitment to ensuring that others are heard too.

Project Censored hopes to continue building solidarity with those who, like us, believe that our world is on the verge of a paradigm shift in information availability and dissemination. This shift could revitalize our democratic institutions and restore hope to hundreds of millions, reinforcing the ideal that self government can work, but only if we, the people, have access to highly accurate, trustworthy, relevant information. This is paramount if we are to develop intelligent, compassionate actions for social change. We encourage more networking and community building in maintenance of a free press.

Again this year we highlight a mix of exciting newcomers in the realm of media democracy and we celebrate veteran media freedom advocates. We must all work to keep the waters of information pure, as we have a right to know what those in power are doing and what many have done in the past that has led to our current state.

In 1786, Thomas Jefferson wrote to fellow founder John Jay—who believed that the people who owned the country ought to run it—and stated, "Our liberty cannot be guarded but by the freedom of the press, nor that be limited without danger of losing it." We must be liberty's protectors, we must be the media, and we must support others in the quest to report about what is really going on in our society. In short, we guard against today's John Jays—the 1 percent. We are the *vox populi*.

There has been much excitement this past year, from the uprisings in the Middle East, to Occupy, and beyond. The following people and organizations represent media democracy in action. They all embody the right of citizens to truly know what is happening in the real world, past to present. They all work to ensure that the arc of the moral universe bends toward justice. We proudly highlight their work and stories. These are dispatches from the front lines of our media revolution.

YES! MAGAZINE: THE TWELVE MOST HOPEFUL TRENDS TO BUILD ON IN 2011–12
by Sarah van Gelder

An earlier version of this piece originally appeared in *Yes! Magazine* on December 31, 2011. *Yes! Magazine* is a national, nonprofit media organization that fuses powerful ideas with practical actions.

Who would have thought that some young people camped out in Lower Manhattan with cardboard signs, a few Sharpies, some donated pizza, and a bunch of smartphones could change so much?

The viral spread of the Occupy movement[2] took everyone by surprise. With politicians and the media fixated on the debt ceiling, everyone seemed to forget that we were in the midst of an economic meltdown—everyone except the 99 percent who were experiencing it.

But by the end of 2011, people ranging from Ben Bernanke, chair of the Federal Reserve, to filmmaker Michael Moore were expressing sympathy for the Occupy movement and concern for those losing homes, retirement savings, access to health care, and hope of ever finding a job.

This uprising was the biggest reason for hope in the months that followed. The following are twelve ways the Occupy movement and other major trends have offered a foundation for a transformative future.

1. Americans rediscover their political self-respect.

In 2011, members of the 99 percent began camping out in New York's Zuccotti Park, launching a movement that quickly spread across the country. Students at the University of California–Davis sat nonviolently through a pepper spray assault, Oaklanders shut down the city with a general strike, and Clevelanders saved a family from eviction. Occupiers opened their encampments to all and fed all who showed up, including many homeless people. Thousands moved their accounts from corporate banks to community banks and credit unions, and people everywhere created their own media with smartphones and laptops.

The Occupy movement[3] built on the Arab Spring, occupations in Europe, and on the early 2011 uprising in Wisconsin, where people occupied the state capitol in an attempt to block major cuts in public workers' rights and compensation. Police crackdowns couldn't crush the surge of political self-respect experienced by millions of Americans.

2. Economic myths get debunked.

Americans now understand that working hard and playing by the rules doesn't mean you'll get ahead. They know that Wall Street financiers are not working for their interests. Global capitalism is not lifting all boats. As this mythology crumbled, the reality became inescapable: the

CENSORED 2013

United States is not broke. The 1 percent have rigged the system to capture a larger and larger share of the world's wealth and power, while the middle class and poor face unemployment, soaring student debt burdens, homelessness, exclusion from the medical system, and the disappearance of retirement savings. Austerity budgets only sharpen the pain, as the safety net frays and public benefits, from schools to safe bridges, fail. The European debt crisis is front and center today, but other crises will likely follow. Just as the legitimacy of apartheid began to fall apart long before the system actually fell, today the legitimacy of corporate power and Wall Street dominance[4] is disintegrating. The newfound clarity about the damage that results from a system dominated by Wall Street will further energize calls for regulation and the rule of law, and fuel the search for economic alternatives.

3. Divisions among people are coming down.

Middle-class college students camped out alongside homeless occupiers. People of color and white people created new ways to work together. Unions joined with occupiers. In some places, Tea Partiers and occupiers discovered common purposes. Nationwide, anti-immigrant rhetoric backfired.[5] Tremendous energy is released when isolated people discover one another; look for more unexpected alliances.

4. Alternatives are blossoming.

As it becomes clear that neither corporate chief executive officers nor national political leaders have solutions to today's deep crises, thousands of grassroots-led innovations are taking hold. Community land trusts,[6] farmers' markets, local currencies,[7] time banking,[8] micro-energy installations,[9] shared cars and bicycles,[10] and cooperatively owned businesses[11] are among the innovations that give people the means to live well on less and build community. And the Occupy movement, which is often called "leaderless," grew many emerging leaders who are building the skills and connections to shake things up for decades to come. This widespread leadership, coupled with the growing repertoire of grassroots innovations, has set the stage for a renaissance of creative rebuilding.

5. Popular pressure halted the Keystone XL Pipeline—for the moment.

Thousands of people stood up to efforts by some of the world's most powerful energy companies and convinced the Obama administration to postpone approval of the Keystone XL Pipeline,[12] which would have sped up the extraction and export of dirty tar sands oil. Environmental science scholar James Hansen says, "If the tar sands are thrown into the mix, it is essentially game over" for the planet. Just a year ago, few had heard of this project, much less considered risking arrest to stop it, as thousands did outside the White House in 2011.[13] As a result, President Barack Obama initially rejected the permit for the pipeline in January 2012, much to the chagrin of Big Oil.

Unfortunately, Obama bowed to pressure in March 2012 and ordered an expedited review of a portion of the pipeline, after which the pipeline company TransCanada submitted a new permit application. If the protests that forced the initial permit rejection can be revived and appropriately harnessed, we can avoid an environmental disaster yet.[14]

6. Climate responses move forward despite federal inaction.

Throughout the United States, state and local governments are taking action where the federal government has failed. California's new climate cap-and-trade law took effect in 2012. College students are pressing campus administrators to quit using coal-fired sources of electricity.[15] Elsewhere, Europe is limiting climate pollution from air travel, Australia has enacted a national carbon tax, and there is a global initiative[16] underway to recognize the rights of Mother Nature. Talks at the November 2011 United Nations' Climate Change Conference in Durban,[17] South Africa, arrived at a conclusion that, while far short of what is needed, at least keeps the process alive.

7. There's a new focus on cleaning up elections.

The Supreme Court's *Citizens United* decision,[18] which lifted limits on corporate campaign contributions, is opposed by a large majority of Americans. The year 2011 saw a growing national movement to get money out of politics;[19] cities from Pittsburgh to Los Angeles past resolutions calling for an end to corporate personhood.[20] Constitutional amendments have been introduced. And efforts are in the works to push back against voter suppression policies that target people of color, low-income people, and students, all of whom tend to vote Democratic.

8. Local government is taking action.

City and state governments are moving forward, even as Washington DC remains gridlocked, even as budgets are stretched thin. Towns in Pennsylvania, New York, and elsewhere are seeking to prohibit hydraulic fracturing, or "fracking,"[21] to extract natural gas, and while they're at it, declaring that corporations do not have the constitutional rights of people. Cities are banning plastic bags,[22] linking up local food systems,[23] encouraging bicycling and walking, cleaning up brown fields, and turning garbage[24] and wasted energy into opportunity. In part because of the housing market disaster, people are less able to pick up and move.

9. Dams are coming down.

Two dams[25] that block passage of salmon up the Elwha River into the pristine Olympic National Park in Washington State are coming down. After decades of campaigning by Native tribes and environmentalists, the removal of the dams began in 2011. The assumption that progress is built on "taming" and controlling nature is giving way to an understanding that human and ecological well-being are linked.

10. The United States ended the combat mission in Iraq.

US troops are home from Iraq at last.[26] What remains is a US embassy compound the size of the Vatican City, along with thousands of private contractors. Iraq and the region remain unstable.

11. Progress toward single-payer health care.

The state of Vermont[27] took action to respond to the continuing health care crises, adopting, but not yet funding, a single-payer health care system similar to Canada's.[28]

In June 2012, the Supreme Court upheld the Affordable Care Act by a vote of five to four. Although President Obama's overhaul of health care law is far from a single-payer system, it will sharply reduce the number of Americans without coverage.[29] Responding to the Supreme Court decision, Sen. Bernie Sanders of Vermont stated, "While the Affordable Care Act is an important step in the right direction and I am glad that the Supreme Court upheld it, we ultimately need to do better."[30] Michael Moore characterized the decision as a "victory" and "momentum" toward "true universal health care in this country."[31]

12. Gay couples can get married.

In 2011, New York State and the Suquamish Tribe in Washington State (home of the author of this piece) adopted gay marriage laws. Navy Petty Officer Second Class Marissa Gaeta won a raffle allowing her to be the first to kiss her partner upon return from eighty days at sea, the first such public display of gay affection since Don't Ask Don't Tell was expunged. The video and photos went viral.

This momentum built in 2012. In February, Washington became the seventh state to legalize gay marriage,[32] and, in March, Maryland became the eighth to do so.[33] In May 2012, President Obama affirmed his support of same-sex marriage, making him the first US president to take this position while holding office.[34] In July 2012, Rep. Barney Frank (D-MA) married his partner, Jim Ready, making Frank the first member of Congress to enter a same-sex marriage.[35]

2011–12 may be remembered as the time when opposition to gay marriage lost its power as a rallying cry for social conservatives. The tide has turned, and gay people will likely continue to win the same rights as straight people to marry.

With so much in play, as the worldviews and institutions based on the dominance of the 1 percent are challenged, as the global economy frays, and as we run headlong into climate change and other ecological limits, one era is giving way to another. There are too many variables to predict what direction things will take. But our best hopes can be found in the rise of broad grassroots leadership, through the Occupy movement, the Wisconsin uprising, the climate justice movement, and others, along with individual but interlinked efforts to build local solutions everywhere. In many ways, 2011–12 have been years of transformation and rebuilding—this time, with the well-being of all life front and center.

SARAH VAN GELDER is *Yes! Magazine*'s cofounder and executive editor, and editor of the new book *This Changes Everything: Occupy Wall Street and the 99%*.

THE BUREAU OF INVESTIGATIVE JOURNALISM
by Chris Woods

The London-based Bureau of Investigative Journalism, while only in its third year, has had a powerful impact on national and international journalism. The not-for-profit news organization, funded by the David and Elaine Potter Foundation, focuses on producing complex high-end investigations, often in collaboration with major media partners such as the BBC, Al Jazeera, the *Guardian* and many others.

Its core team of reporters has exposed the cozy relationships between some of Britain's top lobbying firms and the world's worst dictators.[36] Working with WikiLeaks, the Bureau's award-winning Iraq War Logs series and website also helped to put a very human context to hundreds of thousands of secret US military documents.[37] And the bureau continues to scrutinize a global surveillance industry that increasingly spies on the world's citizens.[38] Other major investigations have examined UK deaths in police custody; have exposed the abuse of international aid money in Ethiopia; and have explored the alleged secret riches of Russia's ruler Vladimir Putin.

One ongoing investigation led by senior reporter Chris Woods— "The Covert War on Terror"—continues to engage the Obama administration, the Pentagon, and the Central Intelligence Agency (CIA) over their "secret" wars in Pakistan, Yemen, and Somalia.[39]

In summer 2011, the bureau comprehensively refuted claims by the CIA that it had not killed any civilians in Pakistan with its drone strikes since May 2010.[40] Yet, an extensive field investigation in Waziristan identified by name at least forty-five civilians killed by US drones in that time frame. The CIA's false claims had gone unchallenged by the US media for almost six months prior to the investigation.

Shortly afterward, the bureau published a complete, dynamic database of all known US drone strikes inside Pakistan since 2004.[41] For the first time, credible reports of civilian casualties were mapped, concluding that CIA attacks have led to more deaths than previously understood. Some 174 children were identified among at least 2,400 people reported killed. There were credible reports of at least 479 civilians among the dead.[42]

The intended targets—militants in the tribal areas—appear to make up the majority of those killed. To date, the bureau has identified 167 named militants among the dead since 2004, from groups such as al-Qaeda, the Pakistan Taliban, and the Haqqani Network. Hundreds more are unknown, low-ranking fighters. Yet the bureau has also identified 317 named civilians killed over the same period, raising legitimate concerns about the strategic success of the campaign, at a time of rising protest in Pakistan.[43]

A further major investigation in February 2012, with the London *Sunday Times*, provided shocking evidence that the CIA had repeatedly attacked Pakistani rescuers seeking to aid victims of previous drone strikes, or those attending funerals.[44] More than seventy civilians were identified by the investigation team as being killed in such attacks, along with many Taliban. The US did not refute the findings.

This year the drones team has significantly expanded its coverage of the covert war, focusing on US secret operations in East Africa and the Gulf. Its report on Somalia showed for the first time the extent of clandestine US military engagement there since 2007—with up to twenty attacks killing as many as 169 people.[45] In 2011, US armed drones also began stalking the troubled country's skies. As part of that same investigation, the bureau also refuted false claims by an

Iranian broadcaster of more than sixty "US drone strikes" in Somalia, which supposedly had killed more than 1,300 people.[46] The bureau's ongoing and internationally respected work on Yemen shows the growing scale of Obama's secret war there. Until December 2009, only one US covert military action had been recorded in the Gulf nation. Since then, as many as 140 individual US strikes, mostly with drones, appear to have taken place.[47] While casualty figures remain difficult to obtain, the bureau estimates that between 300 and 800 people have so far been killed in this counterterrorism campaign, which some fear will backfire.

Unfortunately, the US intelligence community has gone to some lengths to attack the bureau's work on the covert war on terror. An anonymous US official claimed for example that the Pakistan rescuers story was "helping al-Qaeda." Pressure has been applied to the bureau's media partners. The CIA has also claimed that the bureau was getting its information from a "Pakistani spy" (in fact a respected lawyer representing drone strike victims.)[48]

Nevertheless, the drones team continues diligently to map strikes by the CIA and Pentagon in Pakistan, Yemen, and Somalia and to identify, where possible, those killed.[49]

CHRIS WOODS is a senior reporter at the Bureau of Investigative Journalism. He is an award-winning, London-based investigative journalist and documentary filmmaker. He specializes in world affairs, notably the global war on terror. For many years he was based at the BBC, working as a senior producer on flagship programs *Newsnight* and *Panorama*. More recently, he has written and directed major documentaries for Channel 4's *Dispatches* and for Al Jazeera. He leads the bureau's covert war investigation team, and was recently shortlisted for a Foreign Press Association award.

MAPLIGHT: REVEALING MONEY'S INFLUENCE ON POLITICS
by Jay Costa and Darby Beck

Whether you're interested in protecting the environment, changing immigration law, cutting the deficit, or influencing just about any policy issue in the United States, you're bound to hit a common obstacle: the people who make our laws are more focused on fundraising than serving the public interest. As political scientist David Mayhew put it, members of Congress are "single-minded seekers of re-election."[50] To run a competitive campaign for Congress, one must raise literally *millions* of dollars, and that money has to come from somewhere. In the United States, the vast majority of it comes from relatively few special interests that have a vested stake in having legislators owe them a favor. MapLight (MapLight.org), a Berkeley, California–based nonprofit, nonpartisan money tracker, provides tools that allow citizens to see just where this money comes from and how it influences the kind of policies that get passed.

Often when people think about money influencing politics, they imagine smoke-filled backrooms where promises are made, money is exchanged, and everyone leaves in separate cars. The reality is much more mundane, insidious, and perfectly legal. Rarely do candidates and contributors engage in a *quid pro quo* exchange of money for votes. But a feature deeply ingrained in our political system is that candidates who take stances favorable to wealthy interests receive more money to run their campaigns than those who do not, making them more competitive. Once legislators are in office, those who funded their campaigns naturally have more influence on and access to them than do others; the interests of funders are reflected in what issues get considered, what regulations are put into place, how resources are allocated, and so many other decisions that our elected officials make each day.

Wealthy interests wouldn't spend millions of dollars unless they believed they'd get something in return. Although a single example of legislators voting with their funders is not proof of corruption, over time a pattern emerges that shows how moneyed interests often get their way. MapLight shows the effects of this influence by combining three data sets: campaign contributions, legislative votes, and the positions that special interests take on particular issues for Congress and the California and Wisconsin state legislatures. At a glance, visitors to the site can see which interest groups and companies support or oppose a particular bill, how campaign contributions correlate with legislators' votes, the timing of contributions and votes, the biggest contributors to a legislator's campaign, the biggest recipients of a particular interest's contributions, and more.

Just as important, the site translates abstract issues of "influence" into concrete and tangible examples of how campaign finance affects voters' everyday lives. In 2005, the year MapLight was established, California legislators passed California Fresh Start, an eighteen-million-dollar pilot program intended to help schools pay for fresh fruit in students' breakfasts. The only problem was that fresh fruit doesn't generate income for the food-processing industry, which from 2001 to 2006 contributed $2.3 million to various California candidates according to data from FollowTheMoney.org.[51] At the industry's behest, a Central Valley lawmaker changed the word *fresh* in the bill to the word *nutritious*. The bill was signed into law. Schools used millions of dollars, originally intended for fresh fruit, to serve canned fruit served in sugar syrup.

Flash forward to 2012 and the Stop Online Piracy Act (SOPA). Proponents of the bill claimed it would help enhance copyright protection of online material. Opponents claimed it would jeopardize free speech protections and stifle innovation. MapLight revealed that legislators sponsoring SOPA received nearly four times as much money from the entertainment industry,[52] which supported the bill, as from the software and Internet industries, which opposed it. In addition to being featured in over 150 news stories, MapLight's data was used by the online advocacy tool Sopatrack to alert users to the pro-SOPA and anti-SOPA funding received by their lawmakers and to encourage them to take action. Amid this flurry of media attention and massive protest, consideration of SOPA has been postponed indefinitely.

As the examples above illustrate, campaign money has a tangible influence on our legislative process, and there are countless more examples not listed here. Fortunately, as the latter example shows, there are ways we can counter this undue influence. MapLight makes it possible to draw back the curtain on what's really going on in our government, arming voters with facts as they head to the polls, and giving citizens the tools they need to hold elected officials accountable. To have a healthy democracy, the public must be informed about its operations. Is your elected official representing your interests or moneyed interests? Visit MapLight.org today and find out.

JAY COSTA is the program director and DARBY BECK the program coordinator at MapLight.org

OCCUPY: REPORTING THE REBELLION
by Michael Levitin

Producing a newspaper in a revolution is dirty work. It may also be the most gratifying work some of us, as journalists, ever get to do.

On the night before the first edition of the *Occupied Wall Street Journal* went to press in late September 2011, a handful of people in a tiny office in New York's West Village neighborhood attempted to transcend activism and journalism, working through dawn to finish what we hoped would be a clean, clear, professional publication that fairly represented the two-week-old Occupy Wall Street movement.

There was nothing naïve about it. We were after legitimacy, and we didn't exactly think as much as we reacted to circumstances around us. By the first of October, 50,000 copies of the four-page broadsheet were circulating through New York City's streets and subways, at cafés, in bookstores and parks—especially The Park, Zuccotti, which had become the apparent center of the world. We had occupied the media with our dirty, beautiful print. Then it was on to issue two.

Now, a year later, it's a good time to ask: where is the Occupied Media that sprang from the Occupy movement, and where is the Occupy movement itself? The response sounds almost like a Zen koan: Occupy is everywhere and it is nowhere. It is visible as it is invisible. In early June 2012, as this piece was written, the Occupy message of economic justice was once again far removed from most Americans' radar. Encampment closures and police crackdowns from Oakland to Boise to Little Rock had soured moods and displaced people's energy within Occupy. And the corporate mainstream media treated the movement already like a footnote, something that was a part of history, that had flared up, died, and was now roundly forgotten due to some "failure" to capitalize properly through the usual political channels.

The problem with that assessment, of course, is that the functional political channels died long ago, swallowed up by a corporate-owned state that sees no merit in a genuine democratic process, fairness under the law or the constitutional freedom of its citizens . . . while the spirit that ignited the Occupy movement has only just been born.

In response to the waiting and wondering, some of us decided to try something new: to help those who sympathized with Occupy find their place in the nascent national movement by bringing the message of economic justice out onto the open American roads, through cities and countrysides, realizing the power of the 99 percent in places that had scarcely heard about the autumn uprising in Manhattan and across the nation—and if they had, they knew little of what the movement was about and what its goals were.

We called the trip the Occupy Caravan, and we mapped out a course with multiple routes traveling across the country for three weeks, starting on the West Coast and ending on the East in a stream of vehicles and color and collective noise that would carry our voices through the heartland to the seats of power, ending at the first-ever Occupy National Gathering in Philadelphia, which took place from June 30 to July 4, 2012.

The Occupy Caravan found its theme in the 100th anniversary of the birth of Woody Guthrie, who rode west with the Oklahomans during the Depression and sang about economic injustice and inequality in his own time. In our journey three quarters of a century later, entitled "This Land is Our Land" after Guthrie's seminal song, the same core issues and values remained at stake: fairness, justice, equality, accountability. Occupy never set out to be a political movement. It ignited spontaneously as a social movement and ignored the trap of traditional politics altogether. As we liked to say: It was never about a park. It was about ideas—about power and the rights of free people to decide their own fate, not someplace overseas where we generally see our battles taking shape, but right here at home.

In the process of reaching out to Occupies across the country, we discovered just how badly the communities had fractured and divided and withered into near nonexistence in the six months since the camps had closed. Partly because of the state's federally coordinated assault, which succeeded as a tactic of brute intimidation, and partly due to the movement's own lack of leadership or an articulated, long-term strategy, the caravan was an opportunity to revive that spirit of Occupy and push our message out more favorably, not least during an absurd election season in which the question nagged: how bad do you want your democracy—enough to take it back?

One of the signs at a Blockupy Frankfurt march, which drew tens of thousands into the streets of Germany's financial capital in May

2012, read: "When unfairness becomes the rule, resistance becomes a duty." In our case, nine months into the movement, resistance would come not in the form of encampments but of roving occupations. Pop-up occupations. Flash occupations that are here today and gone tomorrow, almost too quick to notice but not quick enough that the force of presence isn't felt. We coordinated welcoming events and media coverage in dozens of cities, which included marches and take-the-streets protests; car parades and demonstrations outside of corporate offices; potlucks and discussions and theatrical entertainment. We hoped to create a sense of the folky America that many of us scarcely know is missing, though we can feel its loss somewhere deep in our culture; the America that celebrated vaudeville and Mark Twain and travelers who brought with them a message, often an important one, from the world that lay beyond the next hill.

On this journey, while Americans by the millions were living without jobs and homes and any hopes of a prosperous future, we knew our cause was just. But justice, as Guthrie sang many decades ago, can take a while for some people to get used to.

In thinking about where Occupy Wall Street once was and where it appears to be going, I can't help but wonder if we made a mistake early on by calling ourselves—or rather, by allowing ourselves to be called—a movement. It happened instantly, in the second week of Occupy, which was perhaps far too soon for any "movement" to merit by proven actions, too soon for plans that had yet to be devised and lived up to.

By calling ourselves a movement—by revealing an eagerness to be affirmed, to be acknowledged and already celebrated as an historic body, simply for standing up—is it possible we that put ourselves into a box and created our own, almost inevitable endpoint? Movements die if they do not transform—if they do not stay one step out in front of the historic moment they presume to be leading. But is it possible, by thinking of ourselves as a movement, that we precluded becoming something much more, whether more lasting or with an impact that is greater and more real? To say yes to a social movement finally means to join it, and not all of us can say yes. We are not all ready—in fact, most of us are not ready—to commit ourselves to something about which we know too little. We want evidence and clarity; we want definition, purpose, some secure knowledge about where we are going before we say yes, I will march with you because I know what I am marching for.

What if we looked at the past year not as a movement, although we chose to be one, but as something else? Something global, moving through us but not necessarily inside us, much as we're witness to the tsunamis and torrential waves of energy now sweeping across our Earth—as fires and storms, as heat and melting and drying, as disappearance—waves of energy we are unable to stop, but which we must find a way to join if we are to survive. This energy—which we sense is moving through us and around and inside us, which we don't understand though it must be in our psyche to follow as autonomous Beings able to decide Right from Wrong, Justice from Injustice, Fairness from Abuse, Humility from Hubris, Necessity from Greed—is this energy enough reason to believe that we must Occupy? Or do we have any other choice?

MICHAEL LEVITIN is cofounder and coeditor of the *Occupied Wall Street Journal*. His work has been published in *Newsweek*, the *Los Angeles Times*, and the *Times Literary Supplement*, among others. Levitin holds a degree from the Columbia Graduate School of Journalism.

BANNED BOOKS WEEK IN 2012: DOES LITERATURE NEED LIBERATING?

by Victoria Pacchiana-Rojas

In September 2011, the five-day event Banned by the Bay brought San Francisco its first festival devoted to celebrating Banned Books Week. People met in bookstores to discuss the state of the First Amendment with lawyers and activists, crammed into bars to sing and dance to performances inspired by banned books, filled library auditoriums to hear local authors read from and discuss their favorite banned books, and gathered in cafés to swap banned classics. The books and authors featured were the usual set—Judy Blume and J. K. Rowling, *To Kill a Mockingbird* and *Tropic of Cancer*, *Ulysses* and *Fahrenheit 451*—yet one title appeared that many were unfamiliar with: Paulo Freire's *Pedagogy of the Oppressed*.[53]

Freire's theory on education and the power relations that teachers and students inhabit has seen renewed interest since the state of Arizona's 2011 decision to remove the book, among many others—and along with the Mexican-American Studies program in which it was taught—from its curriculum. Though the entire text itself warrants attention, the crux of Freire's theory is that education should break down the barrier between student and teacher, between an empty vessel to be filled and one with the power to fill it, through an equal exchange of ideas. Such a dialogue allows the components of education—textbooks, historical narratives, literary texts—to become not something produced by an Other with authority, inscribing the reader as its object, but as something produced by its readers who give it meaning. In this way, the reader is able to see him or herself as the subject of a collective text that constitutes our history, and through this recognition, one gains not only the ability to comprehend one's position in history, but as Freire suggests, the ability to understand how one fits into that history and—intrinsic in the responsibility that comes with education—to transform its future. Thus, through education one can write one's own future. But in order to write, one must read.

Which brings us to the theme of this year's Banned Books Week: "Thirty Years of Liberating Literature." Since its founding in 1982, Banned Books Week has sought to draw attention to instances of censorship that happen every day in small ways. Through heightened visibility, books deemed immoral, obscene, or blasphemous by censors of all shapes and sizes are cast into the spotlight and, for one week, put on display as a reminder of our professed belief in free expression and of the rich literary history which, through its very existence, serves to reinforce that belief. And yet that the books are put on display at all speaks to the charge put forth by critics of Banned Books Week, who point out that the idea of a banned book in a twenty-first-century United States is misleading.

Indeed, much of the data comprising the American Library Association's list of challenged texts is taken from reports about school libraries and classrooms where books are routinely challenged and removed based on their usefulness in imparting a particular worldview to young minds. And while it's true that anyone with the desire—and a library card or Internet access—could obtain any book on the ALA's list, for fifty-one weeks out of the year the majority of the books are a little less visible.

The reasons for this are many, and a comprehensive analysis is beyond the scope of this essay, though suffice it to say that a mix of a changing literacy rate, an industry saturated with franchise titles, and a marketplace driven to promote for profit over other measures of value drives the promotion of some titles and not others. And as our theme of "Liberating Literature" reminds us, visibility is important. We in the United States have the freedom to choose what we consume, but how we exercise that freedom is a result of the decisions we make based on the information available to us.

Which is why the phrase Liberating Literature is a misnomer, for the literary texts are, for the present, available to anyone who goes searching for them. What is at risk is not the texts themselves, but the *reading* of them, for it's in the process of reading that we are able to see ourselves in the motivations and actions of the character, or Other, before us. What we do with that recognition is the great unknown that compels the censor to act. That historically banned or challenged literature often shows viewpoints that fall outside of the mainstream, or that challenge dominant institutions and ideologies, is a testament to this threat that reading poses. Such a threat is what Freire embraced and found essential to an education that encourages a reader to find in the text a likeness, and through that recognition be empowered to enact change. Thus, year after year, when we see books like *The Catcher in the Rye* and *Slaughterhouse-Five* on display in our bookstores or libraries, we're reminded not of the texts' inherent subversiveness, but of what gets excluded from our acculturating media and institutions—how *not* to act and who *not* to be. In 2012, the banned book is certainly available. It is the allowance and capability to think critically, and to develop a unique sense of self from the ideas one encounters through reading, that is under fire.

VICTORIA PACCHIANA-ROJAS is founder of Banned by the Bay, San Francisco's celebration of Banned Books Week, and a graduate student in the literature program at San Francisco State University.

REBELLIOUS TRUTHS (AND THE RESPONSIBLE REVOLUTION)
by Christopher Ponzi

If you're reading this book, you must be a rebel. Does that mean you throttle-twist torque-drenched pistons while hurling Molotov cocktails at crooked cops? Maybe, but probably not. Yet the "truth" has been branded an outlaw. Through corruption and greed, the status quo has fine-tuned itself into a well-oiled manipulation machine, making all those who value the pursuit of truth rebels by default. This is the origin behind the name of our organization, Rebellious Truths (rebellioustruths.org).

So what are we?

Rebellious Truths is an *antipartisan* nonprofit dedicated to exposing the fact-led truth and igniting a responsible revolution here in America. A "responsible" revolution would be nonviolent and focused on unification regardless of partisan labels, with revolutionaries well-educated on pertinent subjects. We aim to creatively expose and educate youth about corporate media's propaganda and manipulation, those often buried economic truths, and the rampant political corruption on *all* sides. We wish to bridge ideological divides, foster mutual understanding and respect, inspire people to question polemical labels, and engage in nonviolent direct action against corrupt forces.

While we are undoubtedly a media-focused organization, it would be misleading to label Rebellious Truths as simply a distributor of media, for media revolutionaries today must go beyond simply being purveyors of accurate information. We are developing an ecosystem for intellectual exploration through robust online and local community networks, combining educational, fact-based material; cutting-edge visual and digital activism; concert rallies; and on-the-ground action. We are seeking a complete shift of mentality within the American sociopolitical framework of left/right, liberal/conservative, Democrat/Republican—all of which perpetuate false divisions, preventing Americans from uniting under common goals and reaching sustainable solutions. We are also attempting to eject Americans from a political savior mentality that rears its well-coiffed head every election cycle. This is a people's revolution. To replace all this, we are constructing a freethinking framework of exchange that more eloquently reflects the fundamental human values of truth, integrity, justice, community, and empathetic compassion. We believe that without this fundamental cultural value shift, no amount of well-intentioned legislation will suffice, and therefore we focus on being agents of that shift.

Through new media, we focus on illuminating the narratives of American youth particularly, because they—or, more to the point, we—have contributed least to the deep problems facing us today yet bear the brunt of the burden. Despite the fact that youth are systematically demonized, commodified, disenfranchised, and immobilized, we will and must help lead this revolution. Our creativity, entrepreneurship, innovation, tolerance, and understanding are what will move humanity toward a better world.

In a culture of deceit, the ideal of authenticity is crucial. The youth at Rebellious Truths are facing the same problems as our peers, thus can connect authentically. Our narratives are not traditional or dry, but artistic and passionate, mirroring the organic journey of intellectual evolution that is at times abstract and fictional, but is always a reflection of what is really going on. We must be upfront, humble, and painfully honest. While "questioning" is a major theme of organizations worth their salt, "*question us too*" is usually not, but it must be so.

Style and artistry have been traditionally confined to the realms of entertainment or advertising, and are often neglected by information entities and activist organizations. This can no longer be. Fearless creativity must become an integral aspect of the media revolution, and it will be up to us pioneers to make sure it is both gorgeous *and* ethical.

Rebellious Truths is about inviting youth into the dialogue. We need to be role models for the changes we seek, not control-freak guardians of information. We must establish solid frameworks for others to feel empowered to engage in a constructive conversation. We must also change the conversation regarding ethics in our society, and part of that change is not to lecture, but to inspire. The youth perspective is not to be dismissed as simply an unrefined product yet to complete filtration through the maturity machine, but is a valid and necessary perspective on its own merits.

We are young, fresh to the scene, and incorrigibly idealistic. Will we survive? That's hard to say. Yet we believe wholeheartedly in our approach and mission that we are doing our part in the media revolution. We are honored to share our message with Project Censored readers. Thanks for listening.

CHRISTOPHER PONZI is cofounder of Rebellious Truths.

ELECTRONIC INTIFADA
by Nora Barrows-Friedman

The Jaber family land is rapidly diminishing. Over time it has been reduced from an expansive, fruitful mountainside to a scarred and struggling enclave, eaten up slowly by the neighboring Israeli settlement, a miniature model of Israel's land grab in the shrinking territories of Palestine.

"There are peace negotiations, but all the time there are demolitions, they are building the settlements, they are arresting people," said Atta Jaber. "All the world is looking but their eyes are blinded. We are alone, without power, without any kind of defense to continue to live in this land."

. . . Atta and [his family] were born from this hillside, and their roots run deep in their land.

"Even with the occupation, we continue our lives here," Atta said. "We still have Jerusalem and Palestine inside our hearts. We are not beggars, we have education. We can rebuild."[54]

A quick scan of the human rights section on the website Electronic Intifada reveals a reality censored by the Western establishment media and elected officials, the cheerleaders and apologists of Israeli policy. Without the international spotlight and effective condemnation of Israeli policies, Palestinians, many of whom are refugees in their own land, are left alone to face further land confiscation and displacement. Rampant home demolitions. Extreme settler violence. Aerial bombing attacks. Resource theft. Apartheid policies. And further dehumanization by Israel's propaganda ministry and the government's global lobbies.

This year, like all years in Palestine, those stark injustices are ubiquitous—but the "mainstream" corporate media continue to cheerlead for the Israeli government and its policies, and feign ignorance at the ongoing Palestinian struggle. Despite this, grassroots resistance—and international solidarity—remains at the heart of the Palestinian struggle, a movement that continues to grow on the ground and expand across the globe.

In April 2012, for example, thousands of Palestinians shut away inside Israeli jails and detention centers began a mass hunger strike—reminiscent of unarmed, historical resistance tactics in Ireland, India, and Guantánamo Bay—to draw attention to Israel's draconian and frequent practice of administrative detention (indefinite imprisonment without charge or trial) and to demand basic humanitarian conditions, health care, and other rights (such as family and lawyer visits) inside the prisons.

Looking at the global solidarity movement, the Palestinian-led campaign for boycott, divestment, and sanctions (BDS) against Israel is continuing to gain momentum. Since the BDS call was initiated in 2005, dozens of international artists, performers, musicians, academics, scholars, writers, and cultural icons have refused to cross what is now one of the world's biggest picket lines.

Communities across the planet, from students on college campuses to activists in major cities, continue to organize campaigns within their local BDS groups in order to send a message to Israel and its corporate and political benefactors: until Israel complies with international law and affords Palestinians equal human rights and lasting justice, there will be no business as usual.

The international BDS campaign against companies that sell equipment to the Israeli military, financial institutions that hold Israeli bonds, and corporations that sign contracts with the Israeli government—is not only one of the most effective ways to hold Israel accountable, it's also been instrumental in educating the general public about the situation in Palestine and expanding the global solidarity movement. The Electronic Intifada was at the forefront of reporting on the hunger strikes, working alongside human rights advocates and prisoner support organizations to send pertinent information and analysis out to readers and activists across the world. As we say in our mission statement, the Electronic Intifada exists simply to provide a forum where commonly excluded perspectives and challenging viewpoints are presented, and our editorial choices are informed by a commitment to universal principles of human rights, international law, antiracism, and equal justice.

In 2012, we have continued our groundbreaking reporting as Israeli policies tighten around the necks of Palestinians inside the occupied West Bank and Gaza Strip, inside the state of Israel itself, and in the global diaspora. We've curated a world-class cadre of independent reporters and correspondents who regularly highlight news, analysis, and action items on our new blog and through the powerful social media avenues Twitter and Facebook, and since April 2012 have produced a weekly news podcast culled from the top stories of the week, featuring interviews with reporters, human rights advocates, and analysts who can further contextualize the headlines. These continuous efforts help to break the media censorship barriers that are already beginning to slowly crumble with the rise of independent, grassroots media.

NORA BARROWS-FRIEDMAN is an associate editor and reporter for the Electronic Intifada and a board member of the Media Freedom Foundation/Project Censored.

RIDING THE WAVES AT PACIFICA RADIO
by Andrew Leslie Phillips

The Pacifica Foundation was founded in 1946 by poet and journalist Lewis Hill and a small group of pacifists, intellectuals, and experienced radio people. They did not have the same political or economic philosophy, but they shared a vision that supported a peaceful world, social justice, and creativity. At 3:00 p.m., April 15, 1949, Lew Hill sat behind the microphone and announced: "This is KPFA, listener-sponsored radio in Berkeley, the first such radio station in the world."[55]

At the time, less than 9 percent of the Bay Area radio audience owned the new FM receivers, so Pacifica gave potential listeners special KPFA radios with 94.1 on the FM dial to get people tuned in. Frequency modulation (FM) broadcasting was a new technology, thus Pacifica was backing the future, along the way inventing an entirely new funding mechanism: the theory of listener-sponsored radio. It was daring, audacious, and brilliant. And it caught on. Today there are Pacifica radio stations in five of the top ten radio markets.[56]

The concept of listener sponsorship appealed to the politically savvy and zealously left-leaning progressive community in the Bay Area. They were happy to support a radical alternative to commercial pabulum, incipient McCarthyism, and the atomic bomb/Cold War politics of the 1950s. The social, political, and cultural leadership eagerly sought the free access offered by KPFA, as they do to this day. Now the audience is more diverse, reflecting the current milieu.

Access to airtime has always been at the center of controversies at Pacifica and community radio everywhere. Most on-air people at Pacifica were unpaid volunteers until the mid-1990s, though they made money to support the foundation by pitching their programming on free-speech Pacifica Radio. That was the deal. It was a tacit agreement—Pacifica provided opportunity and access while producers agreed to pitch on-air pledges. By far, the largest percentage of financial support for Pacifica still comes from listener donations.[57]

This model changed when the National Federation of Community Broadcasters, under Lynn Chadwick and David LePage, adopted the so-called Healthy Station Project. (Chadwick later moved to Pacifica as executive director during a disastrous 1999 shutdown and police raid at KPFA.) The Healthy Station Project called for reducing the power of volunteers, professionalizing on-air sound, and adopting more paid on-air producers. A model more like National Pubic Radio (NPR) than community radio, it was designed to increase listenership and revenue, and to increase the amount of money the Corporation for Public Broadcasting (CPB) might potentially give the stations. And it was a tacit control strategy designed to moderate Pacifica's radical message.

CPB has had close connections with known US mechanisms of propaganda including Voice of America, Radio Free Europe, Radio Liberty, and Radio and TV Martí. Personnel move through a revolving door among these agencies. After almost destroying Pacifica, Lynn Chadwick landed a job at CPB.[58]

At the time the Healthy Station Project was being foisted on community radio, the CPB was headed by Bob Coonrod, deputy managing director of Voice of America. And at the helm of National Public Radio was Kevin Klose, formerly director of the International Broadcasting Bureau, which oversees Voice of America, Radio Free Europe, Radio Liberty, and Radio and TV Martí. The revolving door goes round and round.

The Public Broadcasting Act of 1967 requires that the CPB operates with a "strict adherence to objectivity and balance" in all programs of a controversial nature, and so the CPB regularly reviews national programming for objectivity and balance. When Pacifica agreed to take money from the CPB, it engaged in self-censorship for dollars. Of course, concern for objectivity and balance is extremely subjective, and when it came to the Gulf Wars, such sentiments counted for nothing at NPR and "mainstream" corporate media. Community radio was one of the few places one could hear an opposing point of view—one that turned out to be presciently accurate.

As a result of the CPB's relationship to Pacifica, programming was "professionalized" and moderated. The presentations were less abrasive, the music more homogeneous and consistent—ideas derived from NPR programming consultants—with the mission to smooth the rough radical edges. The same consultants would go on to advise Pacifica when, in November 1996, Pacifica—led by former KPFA manager and then executive director Pat Scott—rolled out *Vision for Pacifica Radio Creating a Network for the 21st Century—A Strategic 5 Year Plan*.

The strategic plan was impractical and showed little understanding of the realpolitik of the five stations. It led to more expenses and more need to raise money to feed the beast and make the payroll. And the more money the station garnered from listener support, the more it received from the CPB. It also created a two-tiered system of paid and unpaid staff, encouraging a them-and-us culture in which volunteers subsidized paid staff; volunteers paid their own expenses as they pitched during fundraising periods, while paid staff received salaries and health benefits. It was and continues to be unfair. The old hippie paradigm of diverse programming and volunteer-based management has disappeared. Today at Pacifica, paid staff call the shots and the community is less a part of community radio than it used to be. The Healthy Station Project didn't go over well with community radio volunteers. In 1996, the Grassroots Radio Coalition emerged as a reaction against the increasing commercialization of public radio and the lack of support for volunteer-based stations. The coalition is now stronger than ever, and grassroots community radio presses on, while Healthy Station Project stations like the Pacifica network are floundering.

Today, the five Pacifica stations revolve in a loose, sometimes wobbly orbit around the Pacifica mothership. The Pacifica Foundation owns the Federal Communications Commission (FCC) licenses for all five stations, whose local boards elect the foundation's board of directors.[59] This current unwieldy and expensive governance structure that emerged in the new millennium, following the removal of Pacifica board chair Mary Frances Berry and executive director Lynn Chadwick, has created slates and factions within Pacifica. Pacifica boards of directors comprise truculent political diehards with little radio experience who have not done much to improve programming, revenue, or audience numbers.

Yet, Pacifica retains a most valuable asset: its intellectual capital, past, present, and future. It is the seed germ and should be protected. Pacifica continues to be an incubator for many important broadcasters and programs like *Democracy Now!, Counter Spin, Flashpoints, Explorations with Michio Kaku,* and now the *Project Censored Radio Show.* Radio crosses over to the Internet to become a transmedia system with opportunities for international distribution, video streaming, interactivity, and e-commerce. Creating and being a part of these transmedia systems is the future.

I fear that the more things change, the more they remain the same. A popular KPFA general manager, Nicole Sawaya, whose controversial firing by Lynn Chadwick precipitated the crisis at KPFA in 1999, was subsequently twice selected as Pacifica executive director in 2007 and 2008. In her September 24, 2008, departure letter in the form of a letter to late Pacifica founder Lewis Hill, Sawaya wrote:

. . . Sadly, it [Pacifica] is no longer focused on service to the listeners but absorbed with itself and the inhabitants therein. I call it Planet Pacifica, a term I coined during my hiring process. There is an underlying culture of grievance coupled with entitlement, and its governance structure is dysfunctional. The bylaws of the organization have opened it up to tremendous abuse, creating the opportunity for cronyism, factionalism, and faux democracy, with the result of challenging all yet helping nothing. Pacifica has been made so flat, that it is concave—no leadership is possible without an enormous struggle through the inertia that committees and collectives . . . can engender.

Pacifica calls itself a movement, yet currently it behaves like a jobs program, a cult, or a social service agency. And oftentimes, the loudest and most obstreperous have the privilege of the microphone. There are endless meetings of committees and "task forces"—mostly on the phone—where people just like to hear themselves talk. . . .[60]

Can Pacifica change, or is it too late? Has Lew Hill's experiment been supplanted by the Internet and smartphones? At a time when the need for community radio and citizen journalism seems more important than ever, can Pacifica adapt and change? Unfortunately, the prognosis is not good. Ironically, should Pacifica finally collapse, it will be in large part due to the Healthy Station Project, which ripped the heart out of community radio. Let's hope for a revitalized Pacifica, for true free speech radio in the years to come.

A native of Australia, ANDREW LESLIE PHILLIPS spent seven years in Papua New Guinea as a government patrol officer, radio journalist, and filmmaker before coming to New York in 1975. He produced award-winning investigative radio documentaries on a wide range of environmental and political issues for the Australian Broadcasting Corporation and WBAI community radio in New York City. He taught journalism, radio, and "sound image" as an adjunct professor at New York University for ten years. He is a permaculture teacher and interim general manager at KPFA, Pacifica Radio, in Berkeley.

THE HISTORY AND POLITICS OF BLOCK REPORT RADIO
by The Minister of Information JR

One of my earliest recollections of my hometown of Oakland, California, is of police beating up young, unarmed Black men in the streets and stripping them of everything in their pockets, including their dignity, in what people are now calling nationally "stop and frisk," and what people in other countries call "occupation." This rather common experience of police and government terror in the Black community is the root of what Block Report Radio (BlockReportRadio.com) was created to combat.

In 2003, I created Block Report Radio to be the fighting-back voice of an international group of people who were being oppressed all over the planet—low-/no-income Black people. The name of the show comes from a rap recording called "the Block Report." That name spoke to exactly what I was trying to do: truly educate Black people, who have been discarded by capitalist society on the neighborhood blocks and in the cellblocks.

I think that a true education about the society in which we live, and our position in it, is almost as important as food, clothes, and shelter. A tree without roots is dead. If we can't understand where we've been, it is impossible to chart where we are and where we need to go.

Although the idea for the radio show came from the streets of East Oakland, the people of Los Angeles, Philadelphia, New Orleans, London, Port-au-Prince, Rio de Janeiro, Harare, Tripoli, and Kinshasa are also in need of unfiltered broadcasted voices that speak to the politics and cultures governing our lives. We believe that having access to the creation of media should be a human right because otherwise, in such a highly technocratic society, to many people we wouldn't exist, we'd be literally dispensable.

The mission of Block Report Radio is two-pronged: to be the frontline voice of an international community that is under the rifle's scope, and to teach people outside of our community about the campaigns, ideas, art, media, and community voices that are important to us. In a society born out of white supremacy, the Bryant Gumbels, Al Sharptons, Michael Eric Dysons, Van Joneses, and Cornel Wests are given the nod from society's puppet masters, including mainstream and "alternative" media, to misrepresent us. But this doesn't need to be the case.

Some of the unique voices that we have featured on the Block Report recently have included people like Danika Chatham, the mother of unarmed nineteen-year-old Kenneth Harding, who was murdered by San Francisco Police Department in July 2011 because he failed to pay for a two-dollar Muni (municipal transit) ticket; Mac Gaskins, a former prisoner of Red Onion State Prison in Virginia, where a hunger strike is now taking place to combat the torture by guards on a regular basis; as well as former US congresswoman Cynthia McKinney, who has been around the world investigating and talking about the evils of imperialism in Libya, the Congo, Haiti, and Palestine, to name a few of the places that she concentrates on. We have also featured linguist Dr. Ernie Smith to talk about the history of Ebonics; musician Seun Kuti, son of the legendary Fela Kuti; political prisoner and journalist Mumia Abu-Jamal; and Leo Sullivan, one of Bill Cosby's partners in creating the 1970s cartoon *Fat Albert*.

The most obvious hardship in maintaining a media platform of this caliber is an economic one. Most people in today's society have not been conditioned to pay for the type of media that they support and that supports them. I often meet people who give two thumbs up to the work of the Block Report, talk on and on about what they have learned from it, but who never offer any financial help, as if they assume that someone else will foot the bill. These same people don't think twice about forking over seventy dollars a month for cable that mostly entertains without offering any substantive resonating content.

The first lesson in high school economics is "there is no such thing as a free lunch." If we fail to financially support the innovative, cutting-edge work of Block Report Radio, it may one day soon cease to exist, be it that there are costs involved with survival, and with getting to and from places to cover stories.

Anyone can become a part of the Block Report Radio listening family by tuning in online at BlockReportRadio.com. People could also become supporters by donating online, buying our debut literary work, *Block Reportin'*, or purchasing one of our many documentaries, including *Block Reportin' 101*, which is about the journalistic politics of Block Report Radio, and *Haiti Rising from the Ashes*, which is our look at the island one month after the catastrophic 2010 earthquake. I would like to also extend a special thanks to Project Censored for allowing me this space to voice my views on media and the world.

J. R. VALREY is cohost of the *Morning Mix* and is the minister of information for Block Report Radio.

WORK WEEK RADIO COVERS STORIES ON THE ATTACK ON WORKERS, WHISTLEBLOWERS, AND THE COMMUNITY
by Steve Zeltzer

Work Week Radio (WorkWeekRadio.org) reports and publicizes news and analysis relevant to Labor and the working class. In 2011–12, Work Week Radio (WWR) covered life and death issues facing working people in the US and abroad, including biotech contamination, attacks on public education, and nuclear energy whistleblowers. Here is some of what WWR covered in 2012.

In March, WWR focused on the contamination of US biotech workers who have been injured due to improper protections in US biological laboratories. As part of its coverage of an international conference on the Bay Area Bio Lab and synthetic biology, WWR interviewed biotech workers who talked about their own injuries and the deaths of fellow workers.

When Becky McClain, a top-flight scientist and molecular biologist for Pfizer, noticed fumes from a biological cabinet at the company's Groton, Connecticut lab, she complained, only to be told by Pfizer that it would do no more than required by law to protect the employees at its 6,000-scientist facility. After officially filing Occupational Safety and Health Administration (OSHA) and health and safety complaints, McClain was harassed and ultimately fired by Pfizer. In April 2010, a federal jury awarded $1.3 million in damages to McClain, based on her case against Pfizer, but she has not yet received any of this money, or justice, from her former employer.

We also interviewed AgraQuest biotech worker David Bell who worked at a Davis, California, firm owned by former Monsanto pesticide director Pam Marrone. Work conditions sickened Bell, but the company, which produces genetically engineered pesticides, denies responsibility, even though examinations have identified seventeen patented materials in Bell's body.

Finally, we interviewed former University of Chicago virologist Joany Chou. Her husband, the professor Malcolm Casadaban, was killed by a strain of plague used in research at the university, a fact that came to light after Chou demanded an autopsy. The university refused to pay for Professor Casadaban's funeral, although this is required by Illinois workers' compensation law.

These cases show systemic health and safety problems in the biotech industry, and lack of proper oversight. They also show that OSHA and the National Institute of Health, along with the Obama administration, have refused to properly protect the American people.

In May, WWR investigated the case of California Commission on Teacher Credentialing lawyer Kathy Carroll. At the commission, which is run by Governor Jerry Brown's office, Carroll began to see evidence of a campaign of intimidation against public educators. Carroll discovered systemic corruption and conflicts of interests not only by members of the state commission, who were also running or representing charters, but also at dozens of school boards and in other government positions, where officials illegally voted on funding for charters in which they had financial interests. She began to connect the dots, linking this conduct to the Gates Foundation, the Broad Foundation, the Kaplan Foundation, WestEd, and the publisher Pearson, each of whom push testing, online education, and other programs that produce profits for them.

First dozens, and eventually hundreds, of teachers contacted Carroll to share their experiences of being denied credentials and harassed on the job for similar reasons. (For more on the scapegoating of public education, see Censored story #13, "Education 'Reform' a Trojan Horse for Privatization," in chapter 1.)

WWR uncovered the harassment of nuclear plant whistleblowers, including former General Electric (GE) inspector Kei Sugaoka. Prior to the March 2011 disaster at Fukushima, Sugaoka inspected their facilities and found health and safety problems. After filming a cracked dryer, he was forced to edit his videotape, even though this is illegal. When he went public, he was never hired again by GE. Dozens of GE-designed plants have similar designs.

WWR reported on efforts by Japanese government officials and the managers of Tokyo Electric Power Company to deny that there were serious health problems. We also covered the story of Japanese railway workers who refused to be sent out to a contaminated area and went on strike with the support of the community. On similar cases of discrimination at the San Onofre Nuclear Generating Station in California, WWR was there to report, while the corporate media were apparently elsewhere. Southern California Edison's plant has the worst record of health and safety among US nuclear plants. Whether in Japan or the US, the protection of health and safety nuclear plant whistleblowers is of critical importance to the workers and the communities. (For more on official cover-ups of the Fukushima disaster, see Censored story #3, "Fukushima Nuclear Disaster Worse than Expected," in chapter 1.)

Though corporate news regularly reports on the economy from the perspective of big business, this coverage typically excludes the standpoint of Labor or the working class. Work Week Radio plays a crucial role in breaking this information blockade, reporting real news and perspectives that champion workers' interests and challenge corporate rule.

STEVE ZELTZER is a longtime labor activist and producer of Work Week Radio.

Notes

1. For more on the Fair Share of the Common Heritage see http://fairsharecommonheritage.org.
2. See "Occupy Wall Street," *Yes! Magazine*, October 5, 2011, http://www.magazine.org/people-power/occupywallstreet.
3. Sarah van Gelder, "This Changes Everything: How the 99% Woke Up," *Yes! Magazine*, November 18, 2011, http://www.magazine.org/people-power/this-changes-everything-how-the-99-woke-up.
4. Sarah van Gelder, ed., "Stand Up to Corporate Power," *Yes! Magazine*, July 29, 2007, http://www.magazine.org/issues/stand-up-to-corporate-power/table-of-contents.
5. Suman Raghunathan, "Rejecting Arizona: States Say No to Anti-Immigrant Bills," *Yes! Magazine*, August 11, 2010, http://www.magazine.org/people-power/rejecting-arizona-the-failure-of-the-anti-immigrant-movement.
6. Susan Witt and Merrian Fuller, "Community Land Trusts," *Yes! Magazine*, May 9, 2005, http://www.magazine.org/issues/what-makes-a-great-place/community-land-trusts.
7. Judith Schwartz, "Dollars with Good Sense: DIY Cash," *Yes! Magazine*, June 5, 2009, http://www.magazine.org/issues/the-new-economy/dollars-with-good-sense-diy-cash.
8. Edgar Cahn, "Time Banking: An Idea Whose Time Has Come?" *Yes! Magazine*, November 17, 2011, http://www.magazine.org/new-economy/time-banking-an-idea-whose-time-has-come.

9. Talli Nauman, "Henry Red Cloud: Solar Warrior for Native America," *Yes! Magazine*, December 19, 2011, http://www.magazine.org/issues/the--breakthrough-15/henry-red-cloud-solar-warrior-for-native-america.

10. Jay Walljasper, "Lessons from a Surprise Bike Town," *Yes! Magazine*, September 28, 2011, http://www.magazine.org/planet/lessons-from-a-surprise-bike-town.

11. Gar Alperovitz, Ted Howard, and Steve Dubb, "Cleveland's Worker-Owned Boom," *Yes! Magazine*, June 5, 2009, http://www.magazine.org/issues/the-new-economy/clevelands-worker-owned-boom.

12. "Red State Ranchers Vs. the Pipeline," *Yes! Magazine*, October 7, 2011, http://www.magazine.org/planet/nebraskans-speak-out-against-the-pipeline.

13. Brooke Jarvis, "Protesters Win Pipeline Delay," *Yes! Magazine*, November 10, 2011, http://www.magazine.org/blogs/brooke-jarvis/protesters-win-pipeline-delay.

14. For more background on the Keystone XL Pipeline, see the Friends of Earth website at http://www.foe.org/projects/climate-and-energy/tar-sands/keystone-xl-pipeline.

15. Jen Horton, "The Coming of the Coal-Free Campus," *Yes! Magazine*, September 1, 2011, http://www.magazine.org/issues/new-livelihoods/students-push-coal-off-campus.

16. *Vancouver Sun*, "UN Document Would Give 'Mother Earth' Same Rights as Humans," Common Dreams, April 13, 2011, http://www.commondreams.org/headline/2011/04/13-2.

17. Madeline Ostrander, "After Durban: Climate Activists Target Corporate Power," *Yes! Magazine*, December 13, 2011, http://www.magazine.org/blogs/madeline-ostrander/after-durban-climate-activists-target-corporate-power.

18. Doug Pibel, "Real People v. Corporate 'People': The Fight Is On," *Yes! Magazine*, May 27, 2010, http://www.magazine.org/issues/water-solutions/real-people-v.-corporate-people-the-fight-is-on.

19. Brooke Jarvis, "Can't Buy My Vote: Maine's Fight for Fair Elections," *Yes! Magazine*, October 27, 20111, http://www.magazine.org/people-power/keeping-it-clean-maines-fight-for-fair-elections.

20. Thomas Linzey and Jeff Reifman, "Turning Occupation into Lasting Change," *Yes! Magazine*, October 14, 2011, http://www.magazine.org/people-power/turning-occupation-into-lasting-change.

21. "How to Fight Fracking and Win," *Yes! Magazine*, April 26, 2011, http://www.magazine.org/planet/how-to-fight-fracking-and-win.

22. Rebecca Leisher, "Cities Take Up 'Ban the Bag' Fight," *Yes! Magazine*, December 19, 2011, http://www.magazine.org/issues/the--breakthrough-15/cities-take-up-the-ban-the-bag-fight.

23. Richard Conlin, "Reflections on a Growing Local Food Movement," *Yes! Magazine*, May 27, 2010, http://www.magazine.org/blogs/richard-conlin/reflections-on-a-growing-local-food-movement.

24. Richard Conlin, "Sustainability in Seattle: Disposable Bag Fee," *Yes! Magazine*, October 20, 2008, http://www.magazine.org/multimedia/-video/2994.

25. Jennifer Kaye, "Hope for Salmon as Dams Come Down," *Yes! Magazine*, December 26, 2011, http://www.magazine.org/issues/the--breakthrough-15/hope-for-salmon-as-dams-come-down.

26. David Smith-Ferri, "Building Peace in Iraq," *Yes! Magazine*, October 3, 2008, http://www.magazine.org/issues/columns/building-peace-in-iraq.

27. Wendell Potter, "'The Single-Payer Train Has Left the Station,'" *Yes! Magazine*, May 25, 2011, http://www.magazine.org/people-power/wendell-potter-on-vermonts-health-care-plan.

28. Holly Dressel, "Has Canada Got the Cure?" *Yes! Magazine*, August 4, 2006, http://www.magazine.org/issues/health-care-for-all/has-canada-got-the-cure.

29. Robert Weissman, "Medicare for All: A Single Solution to the Health Care Fracas," *Yes! Magazine*, June 29, 2012, http://www.yesmagazine.org/people-power/medicare-for-all-a-single-solution-to-the-health-care-fracas

30. Bernie Sanders, "Sen. Bernie Sanders on Health Care Ruling: A Good Day for Americans, but We Can Do More," BuzzFlash, June 28, 2012, http://blog.buzzflash.com/node/13573.

31. Michael Moore, "More Than a Victory: Health Care Ruling Was a Mandate For Us to Act," *Truthout*, July 2, 2012, http://truth-out.org/opinion/item/10114-more-than-a-victory-health-care-ruling-was-a-mandate-for-us-to-act.

32. Tracy Simmons, "Washington Becomes Seventh State to Legalize Gay Marriage," *Washington Post*, February 13, 2012, http://www.washingtonpost.com/national/on-faith/washington-becomes-seventh-state-to-legalize-gay-marriage/2012/02/13/gIQAnm9ZBR_story.html.

33. Aaron C. Davis, "Md. becomes eighth state to legalize gay marriage," *Washington Post*, March 1, 2012, http://www.washingtonpost.com/blogs/maryland-politics/post/md-to-become-eighth-state-to-legalize-gay-marriage/2012/03/01/gIQAJKxmkR_blog.html.

34. Peter Wallsten and Scott Wilson, "Obama Endorses Gay Marriage, Says Same-Sex Couples Should Have Right to Wed," *Washington Post*, May 9, 2012, http://www.washingtonpost.com/politics/obama-endorses-same-sex-marriage/2012/05/09/gIQAivsWDU_story.html.

35. Tim McLaughlin, "Rep. Barney Frank Weds in Same-Sex Marriage," Reuters, July 13, 2012, http://www.reuters.com/article/2012/07/13/us-usa-barneyfrank-wedding-idUS-BRE86CoTH20120713.

36. "Lobbying's Hidden Influence," Bureau of Investigative Journalism, December 5, 2011, http://www.thebureauinvestigates.com/category/projects/lobbying-projects.

37. "Iraq War Logs," Bureau of Investigative Journalism, http://www.iraqwarlogs.com.

38. "State of Surveillance," Bureau of Investigative Journalism, November 30, 2011, http://www.thebureauinvestigates.com/category/projects/surveillance-2.

39. "Drones," Bureau of Investigative Journalism, http://www.thebureauinvestigates.com/category/projects/drones/.

40. Chris Woods, "US Claims of 'No Civilian Deaths' Are Untrue," Bureau of Investigative Journalism, July 18, 2011, http://www.thebureauinvestigates.com/2011/07/18/washingtons-untrue-claims-no-civilian-deaths-in-pakistan-drone-strikes.

41. "Covert War on Terror: the Data," Bureau of Investigative Journalism, http://www.thebureauinvestigates.com/category/projects/drone-data.

42. May 2012 figures.

43. Chris Woods, "Analysis: We Must Name All Drone Attack Victims," Bureau of Investigative Journalism, May 12, 2012, http://www.thebureauinvestigates.com/2012/05/10/analysis-why-we-must-name-all-drone-attack-victims.

44. Chris Woods and Christina Lamb, "Obama Terror Drones: CIA Tactics in Pakistan Include Targeting Rescuers and Funerals," Bureau of Investigative Journalism, February 4, 2012, http://www.thebureauinvestigates.com/2012/02/04/obama-terror-drones-cia-tactics-in-pakistan-include-targeting-rescuers-and-funerals.

45. Chris Woods, "Militants and Civilians Killed in Multiple US Somalia Strikes," Bureau of Investigative Journalism, February 22, 2012, http://www.thebureauinvestigates.com/2012/02/22/militants-and-civilians-killed-in-up-to-20-us-somalia-strikes-new-study-shows.

46. Emma Slater and Chris Woods, "Iranian TV Station Accused of Faking Reports of Somalia Drone Strikes," *Guardian*, December 2, 2011, http://www.guardian.co.uk/world/2011/dec/02/iranian-tv-fake-drone-somalia.

47. "Yemen: Reported US Covert Action 2012," Bureau of Investigative Journalism, May 8, 2012, http://www.thebureauinvestigates.com/2012/05/08/yemen-reported-us-covert-action-2012.

48. Chris Woods, "Attacking the Messenger: How the CIA Tried to Undermine Drone Study," Bureau of Investigative Journalism, August 12, 2011, http://www.thebureauinvestigates.com/2011/08/12/attacking-the-messenger-how-the-cia-tried-to-undermine-drone-study.

49. "Drones," Bureau of Investigative Journalism.

50. David R. Mayhew, *Congress: The Electoral Connection*, (New Haven: Yale Univeristy Press, 2004, 5), originally published in 1974.

51. See the data, searchable online at http://www.followthemoney.org, and see the MapLight study by Dan Newman, "What is the Price of Our Children's Health?" March 20, 2006, http://maplight.org/fresh-fruit.

52. Pamela Heisey, "SOPA Act (Anti-Piracy) Sponsors Received 4 Times As Much Money in Campaign Contributions From Hollywood Than Silicon Valley," December 19, 2011, http://

maplight.org/data-release/sopa-act-anti-piracy-sponsors-received-4-times-as-much-money-in-candaign-contributions-.

53. For Paulo Freire, language was inextricably tied to power, and reading and writing were thus essential tools in his project: "To exist, humanly, is to *name* the world, to change it. Once named, the world in its turn reappears to the namers as a problem and requires of them a new naming." Freire, *Pedagogy of the Oppressed* (New York: Continuum, 1970), 88.

54. From Emily Lawrence, "'We Will Rebuild:' Hebron Family Resists Unrelenting Settler Violence," Electronic Intifada, February 3, 2012, http://electronicintifada.net/content/we-will-rebuild-hebron-family-resists-unrelenting-settler-violence/10889.

55. Eleanor McKinney, ed., *The Exacting Ear: The Story of Listener-Sponsored Radio, and an Anthology of Programs from KPFA, KPFK, and WBAI,* (New York: Pantheon Books/Random House, 1966), 11–12.

56. KPFA circa 1949, Berkeley; KPFK circa 1959, Los Angeles; WBAI circa 1960, New York; KPFT circa 1970, Houston; WPFW circa 1977, Washington, DC. There are approximately 170 affiliates that take Pacifica programming, which is distributed over an Internet portal.

57. About 80 percent of support for Pacifica radio comes from listeners.

58. "Lynn Chadwick Joins CPB Staff," Radio World, March 7, 2005, http://www.radioworld.com/article/lynn-chadwick-joins-cpb-staff/11952.

59. There are almost two dozen members on the Pacifica National Board, representing local station boards.

60. Nicole Sawaya to Lew Hill, Departure Letter from Pacifica, September 24, 2008, http://pacificaradio.wordpress.com/2008/09/24/nicole-sawayas-departure-letter-from-pacifica-september-2008/.

TRUTH EMERGENCY

Deconstructing Narratives of Power to Reclaim the Common Good

Introduction by Mickey Huff and Dr. Paul W. Rea

> *Those engaged in the manufacturing of history often introduce distortions at the point of origin well before the history is written or even played out. This initial process of control is not usually left to chance but is regularly pursued by interested parties who are situated to manipulate the record.*

—Michael Parenti, *History as Mystery*[1]

> *We'll know our disinformation program is complete when everything the American public believes is false.*

—William Casey, director of the Central Intelligence Agency, 1981[2]

For several years now, Project Censored has been describing Americans' general lack of awareness about what is going on in the country, and in the world, as a literal and ongoing Truth Emergency.[3] It is a state of psychic numbing and information overload, one which results from the ubiquitous din of establishment propaganda and top-down managed news. Many Americans do not know what they do not know, and many cannot discern between what is real and what is manufactured. Still others show little interest outside their daily lives.[4]

Although our culture is awash in information, many citizens often lack an adequate understanding of what that information means because the institutions that disseminate this information—particularly, the news media—seldom connect the dots. This section of *Censored* is dedicated to connecting those dots among core issues about which so many are unaware, and to deconstructing official narratives of power to better understand the deep politics of the ruling elite's information control and propaganda. Since the birth of the Occupy movement, this plutocracy is now referred to as the 1 percent. And it may be through Occupy that the alternate narratives of the 99 percent will change the present course of history.[5]

If journalism is the rough draft of history, this section of *Censored 2013* occasions a rude awakening, for the rough drafts are not always accurate. Whether it be a journalist's deadlines, ignorance of an issue, or fear of offending a source, an advertiser, or an owner of a major media outlet, there are many possible reasons that these drafts are not always accurate, for they tend to become narratives in maintenance of the established order rather than factually inclusive reports about a complex and diverse world.

OBJECTIVITY AS A SOURCE OF BIAS

One ironic way these official narratives are reinforced in the corporate media is under the guise of objectivity. In their rush for a scoop, journalists may not seek a variety of testimonies about a given event, miss crucial details, or fail to fact check reports. But more problematic is that many journalists may be subject to prevailing biases that frame how they report events at their inception, even if purportedly operating under the principle of objectivity.[6]

Objectivity is an enticing standard for journalism to pursue, but it creates at least three basic types of problems. First, as Daniel C. Hallin has shown, journalists adhere selectively to the principle of "objectivity," doing so only for stories located within the domain of "legitimate controversy."[7] By contrast, stories deemed to fall outside the domain of legitimate controversy—including those held to be matters of common consensus or "beyond the pale"—do not require journalistic objectivity.

Second, as Robert Entman has documented, when mobilized in service of objectivity, journalists' commitment to "balance" produces its own characteristic form of news "slant."[8] To assume that all perspectives are equal for the sake of objectivity or "balance" is an impediment to accurate reportage—as can be seen in how corporate media pay great attention to a small minority of global warming deniers who are often funded by oil industry front groups. To assume that all perspectives are equal for the sake of objectivity is an impediment to accurate reporting.

This is not to suggest censorship of unpopular or minority viewpoints; rather, it is an appeal to the triumph of reason in a transparently sourced, fact-based world.

A third problem with objectivity as currently practiced involves establishment journalism's overwhelming reliance on official, bureaucratic sources. While the debate over whether professional journalists harbor liberal or conservative biases appears never ending, critical media scholars point out that journalists' nearly absolute reliance on official sources constitutes a clearer, deeper form of bias. As Mark Fishman has written, "the world is bureaucratically organized for journalists."[9] In reproducing official views of the world and public affairs in it, establishment journalism rarely treats vernacular views, including those of diverse publics, outside the halls of power and privilege. These seldom get a fair hearing in the corporate media, if they get one at all.[10]

Taken together, these three problems with objectivity contribute to a situation where establishment journalists accept official sources' claims and perspectives without questioning their underlying assumptions, much less placing them in a broader context of competing narratives. Thus a cherished convention of establishment journalism—objectivity—contributes to the maintenance of the public's unquestioning belief in historical myths that shape and support official narratives.

NARRATIVES FRAME PERCEPTION

In the United States, culturally conditioned assumptions like exceptionalism, or the belief in the country's unique moral mission, are powerful and pervasive. They further bolster establishment views, which in turn maintain order and reinforce hierarchies. They represent an underlying bias—e.g., this is what America is and is not, this is what America does and does not do. Thus historical, mythic narratives are a significant part of educational and media institutions in the United States, and they frame perception.[11]

Further, given the fact that corporate media reporters are paid by major private, for-profit companies with connections to powerful people, it is foolish to assume that all views will receive a fair hearing.[12] In this way, pretensions to objectivity can be a real problem when it comes to reporting narratives that challenge the status quo.

Much of the information we receive comes from mass media and institutions of education, all of which are subject to some degree of government oversight and control. The leading public institutions of our society—the government, the mass media, and educational institutions—are increasingly influenced or outright owned by extremely wealthy transnational corporations that have vested interests in returns on venture capital, not in democracy. These interests adhere to the bottom line first and foremost, not necessarily to promote sound public policy, journalism, or scholarship.

THE STACKED DECK OF HISTORY

Political scientist Michael Parenti has argued that "history is not just what the historians say it is, but what government agencies, corporate publishing conglomerates, chain store distributors, mass media pundits, editors, reviewers, and other ideological gatekeepers want to put into circulation. Not surprisingly, the deck is stacked to favor those who deal the cards."[13]

One must ask: how might those dealing the cards influence the reporting of news? One way is by framing—that is, controlling—what is considered legitimate information and what is not (i.e., what "makes the news" and what's "on the test"), solely on the basis of what the dealers say it is, period. Official accounts of the past not only impact perception in the present, but they also consistently crowd out vernacular views, often rendering them obscure, or even illegitimate. In a world based on a binary understanding of narratives and pretenses of objectivity, these alternative views are by definition unofficial. While they may go largely unheard, that does not mean they are untrue.

In his dystopian novel *1984*, George Orwell wrote, "Who controls the past controls the future: who controls the present controls the past." Today, corporate journalists shape societal trends, deciding whether stories will be heard or not. Corporate publishers, and their boards of directors, advertising sponsors, and lobbyists not only manage the content of news broadcasts and history texts, they also influence public officials in drafting policies that enable such revisionism, blocking alternative views that do not support official assumptions by concealing the fact that alternates even exist.

Parenti also observed that these are the "interested parties who are situated to manipulate the record." The initial reporting of how events take place—who is involved, who benefits, what the facts are—is a crucial stage in the construction of history. The veracity of these reports is also connected to the level of awareness a chronicler has of pertinent history.

Uncritical acceptance of official narratives, often as a result of conventional education and past reporting, can shade journalists' interpretations of the present. If a range of topics and views can be situated as outside the limits of thinkable thought, as scholar Noam Chomsky wrote in *Necessary Illusions*, this poses a serious problem for both a free press and a well-informed, self-governing electorate.[14]

The cumulative effect of these conceptual limitations is a society that believes it is engaged in the critical thought process when, in fact, it considers only a narrow spectrum of possibilities. These vernacular, or unofficial, views represent the "unhistory" of our times, as pointed out recently by Chomsky.[15] That is, these are the stories seldom told, expunged from historical record, regardless of their factual efficacy.

In manipulating the historical record as it unfolds, censorship occurs at the moment of inception and continues to shape and frame public perceptions in ways that distract attention from cause-and-effect analysis of events, often by concealing the power elite's motives and the role these play in political and economic matters. In the process, a false reality—or false consciousness as Nafeez Mosaddeq Ahmed refers to in the foreword—is promoted as propaganda in maintenance of the powerful.

OCCUPYING THE PAST IN THE PRESENT AND
RECLAIMING OUR FUTURE

In fall of 2011, the dealers of the stacked deck Parenti described were dealt an unfamiliar hand, one that may yet turn the tables. This past year, activists in the Occupy Wall Street movements captured the attention of millions around the world. At first, the corporate media took little notice. When there was significant coverage, the claims of Occupy activists were misrepresented. Corporate media sensationalized their coverage and framed Occupy as dangerous. They vilified and attacked Occupy in various ways, characterizing its participants as a ragtag collection of drug-addled, homeless miscreants and black-hooded anarchists, possibly funded by al-Qaeda. Many in the corporate media criticized Occupy for lacking clear leadership and a unified message.[16] Throughout the spring and early summer of 2012, establishment media discounted the movement as waning despite its ongoing actions.

But one message of Occupy was very clear from the start—the deck *is* stacked. We *are* in a new Gilded Age. We *do* live in an increasingly unequal world, with the economic and political elites controlling that outcome. The meme of the 1 percent vs. the 99 percent was born as a powerful vernacular counter narrative, one that has only grown in scope, helping to reshape and reframe discourse about the world in which we live and the one that we, the people, would like to create. Not surprisingly, a counter narrative critical of capitalism's gross economic inequalities faces a cold reception from both corporate media and their establishment pundits.

But a new, collective counter narrative is growing. From Occupy to teacher and student rallies, and from privacy activists to social justice seekers past and present, change is underway, counter narratives are gaining audience. By reintroducing, highlighting, and giving further voice to these alternative views, we attempt to show that more is required to understand not only the past but, more importantly, the present. We are *living* a people's history, as the late historian Howard Zinn might suggest. These oft-ignored and underreported perspectives not only represent the diversity of America's social fabric; they also challenge the dominant power structure, their official narrative propaganda, and what CIA head William Casey once called the "disinformation program." The following chapters present underreported, fact-based narratives and illustrate these narratives' significance in maintaining not only a truly free press but also a vibrant democratic culture. This section provides the tools with which to better understand the censorship of voices and movements that challenge ruling interests. Each of the following chapters deconstructs official narratives in an effort to reclaim the more democratic and egalitarian principles of the commons. Antoon De Baets presents a taxonomy of the censorship of history. He explains not only how forces act to manipulate the past (often in maintenance of propaganda in the present), but also how this very process can backfire once censorship is understood as an existing problem. Peter Phillips and Kimberly Soeiro expose the architects of global economic and political realms under the rubric of the 1 percent. Adam Bessie investigates the motives and framing methods of those behind the so-called education "reform" movement while calling out their pedagogy of Taylorism. Elliot D. Cohen takes a blunt look at the Big Brother stewards of the national security state and uncovers a most dangerous war, one waged against the public right to know and communicate about what the powerful are doing in society. Laurel Krause challenges the custodians of historical interpretation and gatekeepers of evidence in the 1970 shootings at Kent State University—to seek justice for victims and families, and to set the historical record straight. In doing so, she hopes to connect past to present and energize the public to protect the rights of dissent for those who speak out against contemporary injustices. Kenn Burrows and Michael Nagler conclude this section with nonviolent solutions to many challenges we currently face as humans in a fragile world. By showing realistic alternatives to current predicaments that seem intractable, Burrows and Nagler undermine the purveyors of fear who would marginalize, rather than empower, the 99 percent.

The official narratives and interests of the 1 percent are not an option for the rest of us: the fate of the planet may well depend on what we collectively choose to do in the next few years. These researchers remind us that we must inhabit the past in order to enlighten our understanding of the present and move mindfully toward the future. It behooves us to hear them out, as they deconstruct narratives of power in effort to reclaim the common good, creating a more just world.

PAUL W. REA, PHD, has taught humanities at the Ohio State University and St. Mary's College of California. His latest book is *Mounting Evidence: Why We Need a New Investigation Into 9/11.*

Notes

1. Michael Parenti, *History as Mystery* (San Francisco: City Lights, 1999), 129.
2. Quoted in Donald L. Bartlett and James B. Steele, "America's Two-Class Tax System," *Philadelphia Inquirer*, June 12, 2012, http://www.philly.com/philly/news/20110416_Lest_you_have_any_doubt_that_the_overtaxed_American_NO_HEAD_SPECIFIED.html, and originally posted by the Investigative Reporting Workshop at the American University School of Communication under the title "Tax Time: Are Corporations Paying Their Fair Share?," What Went Wrong: The Betrayal of the American Dream, April 16, 2011, http://americawhatwentwrong.org/story/taxes-and-corporations/. For more details on the Central Intelligence Agency's control of mass media in the US see Carl Bernstein, "The CIA and the Media," *Rolling Stone*, October 20, 1977, http://carlbernstein.com/magazine_cia_and_media.php.
3. For more on the Truth Emergency, see Peter Phillips et al., "Truth Emergency Meets Media Reform," in *Censored 2009: The Top 25 Censored Stories of 2007–08*, eds. Peter Phillips and Andrew Roth (New York: Seven Stories Press, 2008), 281–95; Peter Phillips and Mickey Huff, "Truth Emergency: Inside the Military Industrial Media Empire," in *Censored 2010: The Top 25 Censored Stories of 2008–09*, eds. Peter Phillips and Mickey Huff (New York: Seven Stories Press, 2009), 197–220; Mickey Huff and Peter Phillips, eds., *Censored 2011: The Top 25 Censored Stories of 2009–10*, sec. 2, "Truth Emergency" (New York: Seven Stories Press, 2010), 221–352; and the Truth Emergency conference website from 2008 at http://truthemergency.us. In past editions of *Censored*, we have used the concepts of knowinglessness and hyperreality to describe the Truth Emergency we face. In addition to the aforementioned sources, see Andrew Hobbs and Peter Phillips, "The Hyperreality of a Failing Corporate Media System," in *Censored 2010: The Top 25 Censored Stories of 2008–09*, eds. Peter Phillips and Mickey Huff, 251–59. For more detail on this concept, see Jean Baudrillard, "The Procession of Simulacra," in *The Norton Anthology of Theory and Criticism*, eds. Vincent B. Leitch et al. (New York: Norton, 2001), 1729–41; the excerpt from this book on which the theory of hyperreality is built is available online at http://www.stanford.edu/dept/HPS/Baudrillard/Baudrillard_Simulacra.html.
4. For more data on this phenomenon, see Rick Shenkman, *Just How Stupid Are We: Facing the Truth about the American Voter* (New York: Basic Books, 2008). See an interview with Shenkman on *The Alcove*, http://www.youtube.com/watch?v=ob1foOtEB9E. See chapter 3 for more on this topic.
5. On "deep politics," see Peter Dale Scott, "The Doomsday Project and Deep Events: JFK, Watergate, Iran-Contra, and 9/11," Global Research, November 22, 2011, http://www.globalresearch.ca/index.php?context=va&aid=27806. For more on government control of media, which the CIA claimed they played like "A Mighty Wurlitzer" as a result of programs like Operation Mockingbird, see Daniel Brandt, "Journalism and the CIA: The Mighty Wurlitzer," NameBase NewsLine, no. 17 (April–June 1997), http://www.namebase.org/news17.html, particularly the endnotes; and Bernstein, "The CIA and the Media."
6. See, for example, Ruben Luengas, "Away with Objectivity," *Truthdig*, November 7, 2011, http://www.truthdig.com/report/page2/away_with_objectivity_20111107.
7. Daniel C. Hallin, "The Media, the War in Vietnam, and Political Support: A Critique of the Thesis of an Oppositional Media," *Journal of Politics* 46, no. 1 (February 1984): 21–22.
8. Robert Entman, "Objectivity, Bias, and Slant in the News," *Democracy without Citizens: Media and the Decay of American Politics* (Oxford: Oxford University Press, 1989), 30–38.
9. Mark Fishman, *Manufacturing the News* (Austin: University of Texas, 1980), 51.
10. On conflicting official and vernacular interpretations in historical narratives, see John Bodnar, *Remaking America: Public Memory, Commemoration, and Patriotism in the Twentieth Century*

(Princeton: University of Princeton Press, 1992); and Jill A. Edy, *Troubled Pasts: News and the Collective Memory of Social Unrest* (Philadelphia: Temple University Press, 2006).

11. For more on historical mythic narratives in America, see the collection of essays in Andrew J. Bacevich, ed., *The Short American Century: A Postmortem* (Cambridge: Harvard University Press, 2012)—an introduction of which was published as "The Elusive American Century," *Harper's*, February 2012, 13–16, http://harpers.org/archive/2012/02/page/0015?redirect=1593184173. Also see Stephen M. Walt, "The Myth of American Exceptionalism," *Foreign Policy*, November 2011, http://www.foreignpolicy.com/articles/2011/10/11/the_myth_of_american_exceptionalism. States Walt, "Most statements of 'American exceptionalism' presume that America's values, political system, and history are unique and worthy of universal admiration. They also imply that the United States is both destined and entitled to play a distinct and positive role on the world stage. The only thing wrong with this self-congratulatory portrait of America's global role is that it is mostly a myth." Also see Lewis H. Lapham, "Ignorance of Things Past: Who Wins and Who Loses When We Forget American History," *Harper's*, May 2012, 26–33, http://harpers.org/archive/2012/05/0083894.

12. Since 2000, Fairness and Accuracy in Reporting (FAIR) has produced an annual "Fear and Favor" study, examining problems that contribute to censorship or manipulation in journalistic accounts. The most recent study: "12th Annual Fear & Favor Review: Power and Profit Continue to Twist the News," in *Extra!*, April 2012, http://www.fair.org/index.php?page=4523.

13. Parenti, *History as Mystery*, 198. For a recent example of institutional manipulation of the historical record, see Eric Foner, "Twisting History in Texas," *Nation*, April 5, 2010, http://www.thenation.com/article/twisting-history-texas.

14. Noam Chomsky, *Necessary Illusions: Thought Control in Democratic Societies* (Boston: South End Press, 1999), 33. See also Scott Burchill, "The Limits of Thinkable Thought," *Z Communications*, February 4, 2000, http://www.zcommunications.org/the-limits-of-thinkable-thought-by-scott-burchill. Burchill reminds us that "George Orwell offered a preliminary explanation of how thought control also operated in liberal democracies. . . . Orwell warned that in a democracy an orthodoxy was 'a body of ideas which it is assumed that all right-thinking people will accept without question. . . . Anyone who challenges the prevailing orthodoxy finds himself silenced with surprising effectiveness.'"

15. Noam Chomsky, "Anniversaries from 'Unhistory,'" *In These Times*, February 6, 2012, http://www.inthesetimes.com/article/12679/anniversaries_from_unhistory.

16. On corporate media coverage of Occupy, see John Knefel, "Bored With Occupy—and Inequality," *Extra!*, May 2012, http://www.fair.org/index.php?page=4533.

CHAPTER 5

Censorship Backfires
A Taxonomy of Concepts Related to Censorship[1]

by Dr. Antoon De Baets

INTRODUCTION: TRACING CENSORSHIP

The question of how we know when censorship occurred has several sides. Problems of evidence of censorship do not only arise from practical obstacles, but also from its very nature as a knowledge-related phenomenon. Three epistemological paradoxes are worth mentioning.

First, many forms of censorship are invisible and difficult to trace, since censorship normally takes place in an atmosphere of secrecy. Michael Scammell wrote that censorship hides itself: "One of the first words to be censored by the censors is the word 'censorship.'"[2] Clive Ponting made a similar remark: "In a secretive country, the extent of secrecy is itself a well-kept secret."[3] The less visible the censorship, the more effective it is.[4]

Second, in repressive societies there is less information about more censorship, whereas in a democratic society there is more information about less censorship. Under dictatorial regimes, insiders (or outsiders allowed to visit the country) who are aware of censorship mostly do not report it because they fear research or career troubles or backlash effects on themselves or their wider circle. The result is wide underreporting. Authors who do mention the subject typically do so in passing. Sometimes they treat it more extensively, as they write under the vivid impression of a recent famous case. If they systematically research and report it, and become whistleblow-

223

ers, they may encounter disbelief. Data from the censors themselves are generally lacking, at least until the moment when a post-conflict transition arrives. Several exceptional but most important moments of repression, and moments of large operations in particular, are ill-suited for recording. Active recording of repression of scholars typically requires stability and routine. In more democratic regimes, censorship is certainly not absent, but it is usually less unobserved and less uncriticized.

These twin paradoxes entail a third one that comes to light when censorship is seen as problematic: studying censorship is the beginning of its suspension. Censorship has a backfire effect and the study of censorship is itself one of the manifestations of that effect. In this chapter, we limit our attention to one particular field of censorship study: the censorship of history. Although the censorship of history is a well-known and obvious area of interest, it has also been, until recently, a relatively underestimated and neglected field of systematic historical research. Scarcity and abundance of information about the censorship of history may be determined not only by the extent of the censors' success (see paradoxes one and two), but also by very uneven research efforts (see paradox three). They make it often difficult to distinguish important and typical information about censorship from surrounding data and, hence, to identify patterns and trends in the relationships between history, power, and freedom.

The question of how we know when censorship occurred, therefore, presupposes transparent definitions of the set of concepts surrounding censorship and secrecy. The term censorship, the leading specialist in media law Eric Barendt wrote, is emptied of real meaning if it is applied to any social convention or practice that makes communication for some individuals more difficult.[5] Therefore, the emphasis here lies on the coercive and the tutelary practices of the state or other authorities. Even with this fundamental caveat, and whatever the regime, it is often difficult to distinguish the censorship of history from similar restrictions on the activities of historians and thus to demarcate it from surrounding concepts. Bearing that in mind, I have attempted to give interrelated definitions of some key concepts in the following mini-dictionary.[6]

Preliminary notes

Legal experts make a basic distinction between *facts* and *opinions*.[7] They use "information" as a synonym of facts, and "thoughts," "ideas," "beliefs," "comments," "views," or "value judgments" as synonyms of opinions. Historians prefer to call opinions "interpretations." *Silence, omission,* and *secrecy* are general terms. Silence covers all types of omission. Omission can be deliberate; when it is, it is the result of (responsible or irresponsible) selection. Secrecy covers all types of intentional concealment.[8]

CONCEPTS RELATED TO CENSORSHIP

CENSORSHIP OF HISTORY: the systematic control over historical facts or opinions and their exchange—often by suppression—imposed by or with the connivance of the government or other powers.[9]

Types. Pre-censorship (prior restraint) or post-censorship, direct or indirect, formal or informal, official or unofficial, public or private.

Often accompanied by self-censorship and propaganda. "Other powers" include superiors, institutions, sponsors, source providers, and pressure groups.

SELF-CENSORSHIP OF HISTORIANS: irresponsible omission by historians, often after pressure, of historical facts or opinions—or avoidance of investigating them in the first place—for fear of negative consequences.

Also called the *Schere im Kopf* (scissors in the head) in German-speaking countries. Most efficient, widest spread, least visible form of censorship. Often due to the chilling effect produced by censorship instilling a climate of threat and fear. It restricts the public's access to information.

HISTORICAL PROPAGANDA: systematic *manipulation* of historical facts or opinions by or with the connivance of the government or other powers.

Types. By commission (i.e., by falsification or lie), by omission, by denial.

Also called "positive censorship."[10] Second and third types close to censorship and self-censorship. Censorship is often part of propaganda campaigns, but propaganda, being broader, does not necessarily imply censorship.

CONCEPTS LARGER THAN CENSORSHIP

ABUSE OF HISTORY: the use of history with an intent to deceive.[11]
Part of irresponsible history. Censorship is the abuse of history committed under the control of others. Propaganda is often an abuse of history. The result of abuse can be termed "pseudoscientific history," "pseudo-history," or "bogus history."[12]

IRRESPONSIBLE HISTORY: the abusive or negligent use of history.
Part of the misconduct by historians.

MISCONDUCT BY HISTORIANS: violations of legal, professional, or moral norms, which are either general or specifically related to history (the latter being called irresponsible history).
General misconduct includes, for example, the use of offensive language in classrooms or the intimidating and discriminatory treatment of colleagues and students.

CONCEPTS DIFFERENT FROM CENSORSHIP

Diffuse Collective Agency

SOCIAL FORGETTING (AMNESIA, OBLIVION): situation in which specific historical facts or opinions are or seem generally forgotten.
One special type is traumatic social forgetting in post-conflict situations. Reasons for social forgetting vary with agents (victims of crime, survivors of crime, perpetrators, new regimes . . .). In its pure form, "social forgetting" is rare and it has a self-defeating quality (nobody remembers something that is generally forgotten). It is often an incorrect label: social forgetting can be an involuntary result, but it can also be the result of suppression, including self-censorship or censorship. "Social forgetting" is close to censorship when induced.

It is the same as censorship when enforced. Thus, "selective amnesia" or "taboo" is an often more correct label.

HISTORICAL TABOOS (BLANK SPOTS, BLACK HOLES, MEMORY HOLES, ZONES OF SILENCE): historical facts or opinions that cannot be mentioned, especially when they are embarrassing for reasons of privacy, reputation, or legitimation of power and status.[13]

Because taboo facts or opinions are embarrassing, they are either falsified, omitted, or denied. They may result in social forgetting, with which they are often confused. Taboos are related to irresponsible omission. They are often part of propaganda (when facts are falsified), censorship (when facts are omitted), or both (when facts or opinions are denied). Taboos are close to censorship when induced. They are the same as censorship when enforced. Frequently accompanied by self-censorship.

HISTORICAL MYTHS: uncorroborated historical facts or unsubstantiated historical opinions. All myths have authors, although the latter's identification is typically difficult.

Sometimes historical myths amount to lies. High risk of propaganda.[14]

DENIAL OF HISTORICAL FACTS: opinion that events underlying corroborated historical facts did not take place.

Synonym of negation (especially in French). Sometimes confusingly called "historical revisionism." If historical revisionism means replacing less accurate historical facts and less plausible opinions with more accurate and plausible ones, it is a normal feature of scholarly procedure. Denial is often negation with intent to deceive. It is censorship if the denialist view is imposed by authority. In the latter case, it is often accompanied by historical taboos and social forgetting. Minimization of the importance of corroborated historical facts is often a disguised form of denial. Denialism or negationism is frequent in debates about genocide, crimes against humanity, and war crimes. Denial of historical facts can be a form of hate speech, which is the advocacy of national, racial, or religious hatred that constitutes incitement to discrimination, hostility, or violence.[15]

Unofficial (Private or Nongovernmental) Agency

CHARGE OF (1) INVASION OF PRIVACY OR (2) DEFAMATION AND INSULT: charge (or threat of charge) that historian (1) invades the private life or correspondence or (2) harms the reputation, or insults the honor, of living or deceased historical subjects.

Privacy and reputation of the living are universal human rights.[16] Posthumous privacy and posthumous reputation are partially moral, partially legal concepts. Privacy invasion or defamation charges are frequently disguised censorship attempts. Their chilling effect often induces self-censorship.

COMMISSIONED HISTORY: historical genre produced when a person or institution gives a time-limited assignment, optionally including contracts and funding, to historians or others to write a specified historical work.

Called official history when the institution is official. High risk of censorship and propaganda by commissioning entities; high risk of self-censorship by historians.

Official Agency

LEGAL FORGETTING (INCLUDING PRESCRIPTION, PARDON, AND AMNESTY): annulment of prosecution, judgment, and/or sentence for a criminal act.

Legal forgetting transforms into censorship if the act that became statute-barred, pardoned, or amnestied cannot be mentioned in historical works.

OFFICIAL HISTORY: history commissioned and/or controlled by an official institution.

High risk of censorship and propaganda by official institutions; high risk of self-censorship by historians.[17]

OFFICIAL SECRECY OF CURRENT AND ARCHIVAL RECORDS: official restriction on access to current and archival records deemed necessary for one of six purposes: respect of the rights or reputations of others, for the protection of national security or of public order, or of public health or morals.[18]

Official secrecy of records is censorship if the restriction is unlawful (not provided by law), involving purposes not mentioned in the list, and/or unnecessary in a democratic society (e.g., if a restriction on archival access is disproportional). When it is illegitimate, secrecy conceals sensitive information, protects arbitrariness, evades control and criticism, impoverishes debate, and reduces accountability.

SELECTION OF ARCHIVES: selection (including destruction) of records by archivists.

Censorship if the selection is not part of a lawful and transparent procedure in which archivists assess content of records carefully.

Historians' Agency

REJECTION OF HISTORICAL WORK BY PEERS: rejection, after peer review, of historical manuscripts, books, research proposals, and historical courses.

Rejection of historical work can occur in different contexts: publication, employment, tenure, promotion, grants, congresses, and prizes. No censorship if part of a transparent quality control procedure in which peers assess content carefully. May be censorship if carried out by peers, anonymous or not, whose interests conflict, or appear to conflict, with the historians under review.

COPYRIGHT: part of intellectual property; consists of a moral right (of authors to be recognized as creators of their works and to object to any defamatory distortion or mutilation of these works) and an economic right—constituting an incentive for intellectual creation—until (in general) 50 years after the historian's death.

No censorship if fair practice clauses allow free use of excerpts in historical teaching and research (provided that the work and its author are acknowledged). The violation of the moral right may induce a chilling effect on authors.

PLAGIARISM: Deliberate presentation of historical facts or opinions expressed originally by others as own work (that is, without due acknowledgement of original authors).

Copyright violation. May induce chilling effect on original authors.

THEFT OF MANUSCRIPTS
Copyright violation. Form of censorship.

PIRACY OF MANUSCRIPTS: illegal reproduction or distribution of copyrighted work of others.

Copyright violation. Censorship if name of author is omitted.

OMISSION BY HISTORIANS OF OWN HISTORICAL OPINIONS: *absolute* right not to mention own historical opinions.

Part of the right to silence (the right not to speak), itself derived from the universal right of freedom of expression.[19] Applied principally in cases where historians refuse to make explicit their own moral evaluations about the past. Omission by historians of own historical opinions is no self-censorship.

OMISSION BY HISTORIANS OF HISTORICAL FACTS: *exceptional* right not to mention historical facts affecting the privacy and reputation of persons, either living or dead, in cases where informed consent by the latter or their authorized representatives cannot be obtained, *after* a fair balancing test in which the omission is weighed against the public interest.

Part of right to silence. No self-censorship if applied properly. Censorship or self-censorship if applied outside the narrow exceptional-right formula.

CONFIDENTIALITY OF HISTORICAL FACTS OR OPINIONS AFTER CONDITIONS IMPOSED BY ARCHIVE HOLDERS: duty of historians, under a legal embargo or after a confidentiality pledge, not to publish or publicly mention historical facts or opinions (nor their authors' names) accessed by them.

High censorship risk if legal embargo or confidentiality requirement is excessive.

NONDISCLOSURE OF INFORMATION SOURCES BY HISTORIANS: *exceptional* right of historians.[20]

Here "information sources" mean the names of those possessing the information; given that historians possess countervailing scholarly duties of transparency and accountability, nondisclosure should be balanced against disclosure with a presumption in favor of the latter. Censorship risk if the use of the right is not (sufficiently) justified.

CODE OF ETHICS FOR HISTORIANS: set of principles clarifying the legal, professional, and moral accountability and autonomy of historians.[21]

Codes of ethics do not restrict freedom of expression, but clarify its limits. They are more concerned with the *intention and conditions* accompanying the conduct of historians, rather than with its *content*.[22] Censorship risk if applied or enforced when not emanating from a recognized, democratically organized association of historians. Codes of ethics should conform to academic freedom, which, according to the UNESCO, is "[T]he right [of higher-education teaching personnel], without constriction by prescribed doctrine, to freedom of teaching and discussion, freedom in carrying out research and disseminating and publishing the results thereof, freedom to express freely their opinion about the institution or system in which they work, freedom from institutional censorship and freedom to participate in professional or representative academic bodies."[23]

EPILOGUE: THE BACKFIRE

Effect of Censorship

The results of censorship are often ambiguous. In 213 BCE, the Chinese emperor Qin Shi Huang ordered a large-scale book burning of historical works and had possibly hundreds of intellectuals executed in an attempt to eliminate tradition and its guardians. This major censorship operation hampered the development of historical writing, not only because much information was destroyed, but also because it provided an excuse to future scholars to falsify ancient texts. At the same time, however, it caused an immense arousal of historical consciousness: Han scholars tried to recover and edit whatever texts remained and a cult of books developed. Thus the aim of censorship defeated itself.

Censorship may have unintended positive effects. Alberto Manguel spoke of "the paradoxical ability of censorship that, in its efforts to suppress, it highlights that which it wishes to condemn."[24] Hermann Weber recognized this effect after the dictatorship had withered away: "For decades the exclusion of 'blank spots' had been ordered . . . only to provoke a stronger and almost obsessive interest in these issues nowadays."[25]

If it is not all-pervading, censorship provides an indirect incentive for creativity and criticism. Taboos always attract curiosity. Repression may discourage that curiosity for decades. But when history as a classical vehicle of the past is silenced and compromised, every utterance—graffiti, literature, theater, film—becomes its potential vehicle. Thus, the censorship of history generates the emergence of substitutes: whenever the silenced and silent historians are not able to refute the heralded truths of official historical propaganda, philosophers, poets, novelists, playwrights, filmmakers, journalists, storytellers, and singers take care of the historical truth and keep it alive. Paradoxically, the ostensible vulnerability of many of these substitutes is their power: writing, for example, is a solitary act requiring little institutional support. Sometimes, fictional genres are not taken seriously by the authorities and hence escape their attention. Thus, censorship may not suppress alternative views but rather generate them, and, by doing so, become counterproductive.[26] Censorship backfires.

ANTOON DE BAETS, PHD, is a historian working at the University of Groningen, the Netherlands. He has more than 125 publications to his name, most recently on the censorship of history and the ethics of historians. His work includes several books, such as *Censorship of Historical Thought: A World Guide, 1945–2000* (Westport, CT: Greenwood Press, 2002) and *Responsible History* (New York: Berghahn Books, 2009). Since 1995, he has coordinated the Network of Concerned Historians. He is currently writing his new book *History of the Censorship of History (1945–2010)*.

Notes

1. An earlier version of this article appeared under the title "Taxonomy of Concepts Related to the Censorship of History," in Susan Maret, ed., *Research in Social Problems and Public Policy* 19, Government Secrecy (Bingley, UK: Emerald Group Publishing Limited, 2011), 53–65, doi:10.1108/S0196-1152(2011)0000019007.

2. Michael Scammell, "Censorship and Its History: A Personal View" in *Information, Freedom and Censorship: World Report 1988*, article 19 (London: Times Books, 1988), 1–18.

3. Clive Ponting, *Secrecy in Britain* (Cambridge, MA: Blackwell, 1990). This characteristic of censorship is similar to that of falsification, see Pierre Vidal-Naquet, *Assassins of Memory: Essays on the Denial of the Holocaust* (1987; repr., New York: Columbia University Press, 1992), 51: "It is the distinguishing feature of a lie to want to pass itself off as the truth."

4. See also Peter Novick, *That Noble Dream: The "Objectivity Question" and the American Historical Profession* (Cambridge: Cambridge University Press, 1988), 331: "With respect to the consequences of repression, one confronts the paradox that the measure of its effectiveness is the scarcity of overt instances."

5. Eric Barendt, *Freedom of Speech* (Oxford: Oxford University Press, 2005).

6. The introduction and epilogue of this chapter owe much to Antoon De Baets, "Censorship and History (1945–Present)" in *The Oxford History of Historical Writing, Volume 5: 1945 to Present*, eds. Axel Schneider and Daniel Woolf (Oxford: Oxford University Press, 2010), 52–73.

7. Frederick Schauer, *Free Speech: A Philosophical Inquiry* (Cambridge: Cambridge University Press, 1982); and Barendt, *Freedom of Speech*. The nongovernmental organization Article 19 defines opinions as statements "which either do not contain a factual connotation which could be proved to be false, or cannot reasonably be interpreted as stating actual facts given all the circumstances, including the language used (such as rhetoric, hyperbole, satire, or jest)." See Article 19, *Defining Defamation: Principles on Freedom of Expression and Protection of Reputation* (London: Article 19, 2000), principle 10 ("expressions of opinion").

8. Sissela Bok, *Secrets: On the Ethics of Concealment and Revelation* (New York: Vintage Books, 1983).

9. Compare Stuart Hampshire and Louis Blom-Cooper, "Censorship?" *Index on Censorship* 6, no. 4 (1977): 55–63; and Scammell, "Censorship and Its History."

10. Stephen Spender, "Thoughts on Censorship in the World of 1984" in *Censorship: 500 Years of Conflict*, ed. Vartan Gregorian (Oxford: Oxford University Press, 1984), 116–127.

11. Antoon De Baets, *Responsible History* (New York: Berghahn Books, 2009).

12. For surveys of pseudohistorical theories, see Robert Carroll, *The Skeptic's Dictionary* (Hoboken, NJ: Wiley, 2003); Karl Corino, ed., *Gefälscht! Betrug in Politik, Literatur, Wissenschaft, Kunst und Musik* (Reinbek: Rowohlt, 1992); Kenneth L. Feder, *Frauds, Myths, and Mysteries: Science and Pseudoscience in Archaeology* (Mountain View, CA: Mayfield, 1999); Werner Fuld, *Das Lexikon der Fälschungen* (Frankfurt am Main: Eichborn, 1999); and William F. Williams, ed., *Encyclopedia of Pseudoscience* (Chicago: Fitzroy Dearborn, 2000).

13. For typologies of taboo topics that are potentially subject to censorship, see Hampshire and Blom-Cooper, "Censorship?"; and Marc Ferro, *L'Histoire sous surveillance: Science et conscience de l'histoire* (Paris: Calmann-Lévy, 1985), 52–60. A frequently used synonym for taboos is blank spots. According to Thomas S. Szayna, "Addressing 'Blank Spots' in Polish–Soviet Relations," *Problems of Communism* 37, no. 6 (1988): 37–38, the concept was apparently first used in Poland by Solidarity to indicate the topics too embarrassing to discuss openly and honestly. They were either ignored (such as the deportations of 1939) or falsified (such as the 1940 Katyn massacre), but they did not necessarily imply that the scholars or the public had no knowledge of them. Also see Vera Tolz, "'Blank Spots' in Soviet History," *Radio Liberty Research* (1988): 1–3. For the synonymous term black holes, see Milan Šimečka, "Black Holes," *Index on Censorship* 5 (1988): 52–54, who defines them as "segments of history cloaked in total darkness, devoid of life, of persons, of ideas." Another synonymous term, memory holes, was invented by George Orwell, *Nineteen Eighty-Four* (London: Secker & Warburg, 1949), 40.

14. Myths may provide meaning for those who hold them. As conjecture, they may anticipate or inspire future scientific theories. The power of myths to give meaning is clear from George

Schöpflin's taxonomy, which distinguishes eight motifs in myths: territory, redemption and suffering, unjust treatment, election and civilizing mission, military valor, rebirth and renewal, ethnogenesis and antiquity, and kinship and shared descent. See his "The Functions of Myth and a Taxonomy of Myths," in *Myths and Nationhood*, eds. Geoffrey Hosking and George Schöpflin (London: Hurst, 1997), 28–35. For reflections on the excusability of the use of historical myths, see Bernard Lewis and P. M. Holt, eds., *Historians of the Middle East* (London: Oxford University Press, 1962), 451–502; J. H. Plumb, *The Death of the Past* (London: Macmillan; Boston: Houghton Mifflin, 1969), 19–61; David C. Gordon, *Self-Determination and History in the Third World* (Princeton, NJ: Princeton University Press, 1971), 177–192; Jan Vansina, *Oral Tradition as History* (London: James Currey, 1985), 91–108; William Hardy McNeill, "Mythstory, or Truth, Myth, History, and Historians," *American Historical Review* 91, no. 1 (1986): 1–10, 6–9; and Bernard Lewis, *History Remembered, Recovered, Invented* (1975; repr., Princeton, NJ: Princeton University Press, 1987), passim.

15. UN General Assembly, Resolution 2200A, International Covenant on Civil and Political Rights, 1966, http://www2.ohchr.org/English/law/ccpr.htm.

16. UN General Assembly, Resolution 217A, "The Universal Declaration of Human Rights," December 10, 1948, http://www.un.org/en/documents/udhr. Privacy, honor, and reputation belong to the group of so-called "personality rights." They are enshrined in article 12 of the Universal Declaration of Human Rights. Privacy is the right to respect for one's private life, home, and correspondence. Honor is a person's self-esteem. Reputation is the appraisal of a person by others, a person's good name or fame. Defamation is usually defined as the act of damaging another's reputation ("fame"), in oral (slander) or written (libel) form. For the distinction between honor and reputation, and between defamation, insult, hate speech, blasphemy, and privacy invasion, see article 19, *Defamation ABC: A Simple Introduction to Key Concepts of Defamation Law*, November 2006, http://www.article19.org/data/files/pdfs/tools/defamation-abc.pdf, 1–3, 5, 9–10; and Barendt, *Freedom of Speech*, 170–92, 227–46, 295–302.

17. Herbert Butterfield, "Official History: Its Pitfalls and Criteria," in *History and Human Relations* (London: Collins, 1951), 182–224; and Susan L. Maret, *On Their Own Terms: A Lexicon with an Emphasis on Information-Related Terms Produced by the U.S. Federal Government*, Federation of American Scientists, 2009, accessed March 10, 2010, http://www.fas.org/sgp/library/maret.pdf.

18. UN General Assembly, International Covenant.

19. Ibid.

20. Council of Europe, Recommendation No. R, Of the Committee of Ministers to Member States on the Right of Journalists not to Disclose Their Sources of Information, March 8, 2000, http://www.coe.int/t/dghl/standardsetting/media/doc/cm/rec(2000)007&expmem_EN.asp. The European Court of Human Rights has confirmed the right to nondisclosure of sources, most notably in *Goodwin v. the United Kingdom* at Strasbourg in 1996.

21. For a worldwide catalog of codes of ethics for historians, archivists, and archaeologists, see Ethics section of the Network of Concerned Historians website (ConcernedHistorians.org).

22. De Baets, *Responsible History*.

23. UNESCO, Recommendation Concerning the Status of Higher-Education Teaching Personnel, November 11, 1997, http://portal.unesco.org/en/ev.php-URL_ID=13144&URL_DO=DO_TOPIC&URL_SECTION=201.html.

24. Alberto Manguel, "Daring to Speak One's Name," *Index on Censorship* 24, no. 1 (1995): 16–29.

25. Hermann Weber, "'Weisse Flecken' in der DDR-Geschichtsschreibung," in ed. Rainer Eckert et al., *Krise-Umbruch-Neubeginn: Eine kritische und selbstkritische Dokumentation der DDR-Geschichtswissenschaft 1989/90* (Stuttgart: Klett-Cotta, 1992), 369–91.

26. See Leszek Kolakowski, "Totalitarianism and the Virtue of the Lie," in ed. Irving Howe, *1984 Revisited: Totalitarianism in Our Century* (New York: Harper & Row, 1983), 135; and Yuri Afanasev, "Return History to the People," *Index on Censorship* 3 (1995): 56–60. Also see Marc Bloch's remarks on the wary reception of propaganda and censorship in the trenches of World War I, which resulted in a revival of oral tradition, Marc Bloch, *Apologie pour l'histoire ou métier d'historien* (written 1941; published 1949, repr., Paris: Colin, 1967), 50–51.

CHAPTER 6

The Global 1 Percent Ruling Class Exposed

by Dr. Peter Phillips and Kimberly Soeiro

The Occupy movement has developed a mantra that addresses the great inequality of wealth and power between the world's wealthiest 1 percent and the rest of us, the other 99 percent. While the 99 percent mantra undoubtedly serves as a motivational tool for open involvement, there is little understanding as to who comprises the 1 percent and how they maintain power in the world. Though a good deal of academic research has dealt with the power elite in the United States, only in the past decade and a half has research on the transnational corporate class begun to emerge.[1]

Foremost among the early works on the idea of an interconnected 1 percent within global capitalism was Leslie Sklair's 2001 book, *The Transnational Capitalist Class*.[2] Sklair believed that globalization was moving transnational corporations (TNC) into broader international roles, whereby corporations' states of origin became less important than international argreements developed through the World Trade Organization and other international institutions. Emerging from these multinational corporations was a transnational capitalist class, whose loyalities and interests, while still rooted in their corporations, was increasingly international in scope. Sklair writes:

> The transnational capitalist class can be analytically divided into four main fractions . . . (i) owners and controllers of TNCs and their local affiliates; (ii) globalizing bureaucrats and politicians; (iii) globalizing professionals; (iv) consumerist elites (merchants and media). . . . It is also important to

note, of course, that the TCC [transnational capitalist class] and each of its fractions are not always entirely united on every issue. Nevertheless, together, leading personnel in these groups constitute a global power elite, dominant class or inner circle in the sense that these terms have been used to characterize the dominant class structures of specific countries.[3]

Estimates are that the total world's wealth is close to $200 trillion, with the US and Europe holding approximately 63 percent. To be among the wealthiest half of the world, an adult needs only $4,000 in assets once debts have been subtracted. However, an adult requires more than $72,000 to belong to the top 10 percent of global wealth holders, and more than $588,000 to be a member of the top 1 percent. Meanwhile, the poorest half of the global population together possesses less than 2 percent of global wealth.[4] The World Bank reports that, in 2008, 1.29 billion people were living in extreme poverty, on less than $1.25 a day, and 1.18 billion more were living on less than $2.00 a day.[5] Starvation.net reports that 35,000 people, mostly young children, die every day from starvation in the world.[6] The numbers of unnecessary deaths have exceeded 300 million people over the past forty years. Farmers around the world grow more than enough food to feed the entire world adequately. Global grain production yielded a record 2.3 billion tons in 2007, up 4 percent from the year before—yet, billions of people go hungry every day. Grain.org describes the core reasons for ongoing hunger in a recent article, "Corporations Are Still Making a Killing from Hunger": while farmers grow enough food to feed the world, commodity speculators and huge grain traders like Cargill control global food prices and distribution.[7] Identifying the power of the global 1 percent—who they are and what their goals are—are clearly life and death questions.

It is also important to examine the questions of how wealth is created, and how it becomes concentrated. Historically, wealth has been captured and concentrated through conquest by various powerful entities. One need only look at Spain's appropriation of the wealth of the Aztec and Inca empires in the early sixteenth century for an historical example of this process. The histories of the Roman and British empires are also filled with examples of wealth captured.

Once acquired, wealth can then be used to establish means of production, such as the early British cotton mills, which exploit workers' labor power to produce goods whose exchange value is greater than the cost of the labor, a process analyzed by Karl Marx in *Capital*.[8] A human being is able to produce a product that has a certain value. Organized business hires workers who are paid below the value of their labor power. The result is the creation of what Marx called surplus value, over and above the cost of labor. The creation of surplus value allows those who own the means of production to concentrate capital even more. In addition, concentrated capital accelerates the exploition of natural resources by private entrepreneurs—even though these natural resources are actually the common heritage of all living beings.[9]

In this chapter, we ask: Who are the the world's 1 percent power elite? And to what extent do they operate in unison for their own private gains over benefits for the 99 percent? We will examine a sample of the 1 percent: the extractor sector, whose companies are on the ground extracting material from the global commons, and using low-cost labor to amass wealth. These companies include oil, gas, and various mineral extraction organizations, whereby the value of the material removed far exceeds the actual cost of removal.

We will also examine the investment sector of the global 1 percent: companies whose primary activity is the amassing and reinvesting of capital. This sector includes global central banks, major investment money management firms, and other companies whose primary efforts are the concentration and expansion of money, such as insurance companies.

Finally, we analyze how global networks of centralized power—the elite 1 percent, their companies, and various governments in their service—plan, manipulate, and enforce policies that benefit their continued concentration of wealth and power.

THE EXTRACTOR SECTOR: THE CASE OF FREEPORT-MCMORAN (FCX)

Freeport-McMoRan Copper & Gold, Inc. (FCX) is the world's largest extractor of copper and gold. The company controls huge deposits in Papua, Indonesia, and also operates in North and South America, and in Africa. In 2010, the company sold 3.9 billion pounds of copper, 1.9 million ounces of gold, and 67 million pounds of molybdenum. In 2010, Freeport-McMoRan reported revenues of $18.9 billion and a net income of $4.2 billion.[10]

The Grasberg mine in Papua, Indonesia, employs 23,000 workers at wages below three dollars an hour. In September 2011, workers went on strike for higher wages and better working conditions. Freeport had offered a 22 percent increase in wages, and strikers said it was not enough, demanding an increase to an international standard of seventeen to forty-three dollars an hour. The dispute over pay attracted local tribesmen, who had their own grievances over land rights and pollution; armed with spears and arrows, they joined Freeport workers blocking the mine's supply roads.[11] During the strikers' attempt to block busloads of replacement workers, security forces financed by Freeport killed or wounded several strikers.

Freeport has come under fire internationally for payments to authorities for security. Since 1991, Freeport has paid nearly thirteen billion dollars to the Indonesian government—one of Indonesia's

CENSORED 2013

largest sources of income—at a 1.5 percent royalty rate on extracted gold and copper, and, as a result, the Indonesian military and regional police are in their pockets. In October 2011, the *Jakarta Globe* reported that Indonesian security forces in West Papua, notably the police, receive extensive direct cash payments from Freeport-McMoRan. Indonesian National Police Chief Timur Pradopo admitted that officers received close to ten million dollars annually from Freeport, payments Pradopo described as "lunch money." Prominent Indonesian nongovernmental organization Imparsial puts the annual figure at fourteen million dollars.[12] These payments recall even larger ones made by Freeport to Indonesian military forces over the years which, once revealed, prompted a US Securities and Exchange Commission investigation of Freeport's liability under the United States' Foreign Corrupt Practices Act.[13]

In addition, the state's police and army have been criticized many times for human rights violations in the remote mountainous region, where a separatist movement has simmered for decades. Amnesty International has documented numerous cases in which Indonesian police have used unnecessary force against strikers and their supporters. For example, Indonesian security forces attacked a mass gathering in the Papua capital, Jayapura, and striking workers at the Freeport mine in the southern highlands. At least five people were killed and many more injured in the assaults, which shows a continuing pattern of overt violence against peaceful dissent. Another brutal and unjustified attack on October 19, 2011, on thousands of Papuans exercising their rights to assembly and freedom of speech, resulted in the death of at least three Papuan civilians, the beating of many, the detention of hundreds, and the arrest of six, reportedly on treason charges.[14]

On November 7, 2011, the *Jakarta Globe* reported that "striking workers employed by Freeport-McMoRan Copper & Gold's subsidiary in Papua have dropped their minimum wage increase demands from $7.50 to $4.00 an hour, the All Indonesia Workers Union (SPSI) said."[15] Virgo Solosa, an official from the union, told the *Jakarta Globe* that they considered the demands, up from the (then) minimum wage of $1.50 an hour, to be "the best solution for all."[16]

Workers at Freeport's Cerro Verde copper mine in Peru also went on strike around the same time, highlighting the global dimension of the Freeport confrontation. The Cerro Verde workers demanded pay raises of 11 percent, while the company offered just 3 percent.[17]

The Peruvian strike ended on November 28, 2011.[18] And on December 14, 2011, Freeport-McMoRan announced a settlement at the Indonesian mine, extending the union's contract by two years. Workers at the Indonesia operation are to see base wages, which currently start at as little as $2.00 an hour, rise 24 percent in the first year of the pact and 13 percent in the second year. The accord also includes improvements in benefits and a one-time signing bonus equivalent to three months of wages.[19]

In both Freeport strikes, the governments pressured strikers to settle. Not only was domestic military and police force evident, but also higher levels of international involvement. Throughout the Freeport-McMoRan strike, the Obama administration ignored the egregious violation of human rights and instead advanced US–Indonesian military ties. US Secretary of Defense Leon Panetta, who arrived in Indonesia in the immediate wake of the Jayapura attack, offered no criticism of the assault and reaffirmed US support for Indonesia's territorial integrity. Panetta also reportedly commended Indonesia's handling of a weeks-long strike at Freeport-McMoRan.[20]

US President Barack Obama visited Indonesia in November 2011 to strengthen relations with Jakarta as part of Washington's escalating efforts to combat Chinese influence in the Asia–Pacific region. Obama had just announced that the US and Australia would begin a rotating deployment of 2,500 US Marines to a base in Darwin, a move ostensibly to upgrade military presence in the region, and to allow participation in "joint training" with Australian military counterparts. But some speculate that the US has a hidden agenda in deploying marines to Australia. The Thai newspaper the *Nation* has suggested that one of the reasons why US Marines might be stationed in Darwin could be that they would provide remote security assurance to US-owned Freeport-McMoRan's gold and copper mine in West Papua, less than a two-hour flight away.[21]

Public opinion is strongly against Freeport in Indonesia. On August 8, 2011, Karishma Vaswani of the BBC reported that "the US mining firm Freeport-McMoRan has been accused of everything from polluting the environment to funding repression in its four decades working in the Indonesian province of Papau. . . . 'Ask any Papuan on the street what they think of Freeport, and they will tell you that the firm is a thief,' said Neles Tebay, a Papuan pastor and co-ordinator of the Papua Peace Network."[22]

Freeport strikers won support from the US Occupy movement. Occupy Phoenix and East Timor & Indonesia Action Network activists marched to Freeport headquarters in Phoenix on October 28, 2011, to demonstrate against the Indonesian police killings at Freeport-Mc-MoRan's Grasberg mine.[23]

Freeport-McMoRan chairman of the board James R. Moffett owns over four million shares with a value of close to $42.00 each. According to the FCX annual meeting report released in June 2011, Moffett's annual compensation from FCX in 2010 was $30.57 million. Richard C. Adkerson, president of the board of FCX, owns over 5.3 million shares. His total compensation was also $30.57 million in 2010.[24] Moffett's and Adkerson's incomes put them in the upper levels of the world's top 1 percent. Their interconnectness with the highest levels of power in the White House and the Pentagon, as indicated by the specific attention given to them by the US secretary of defense, and as suggested by the US president's awareness of their circumstances, leaves no doubt that Freeport-MacMoRan executives and board are firmly positioned at the highest levels of the transnational corporate class.

Freeport-McMoRan's Board of Directors

▸ James R. Moffett—Corporate and policy affiliations: cochairman, president, and CEO of McMoRan Exploration Co.; PT Freeport Indonesia; Madison Minerals Inc.; Horatio Alger Association of Distinguished Americans; Agrico, Inc.; Petro-Lewis Funds, Inc.; Bright Real Estate Services, LLC; PLC–ALPC, Inc.; FM Services Company.

▸ Richard C. Adkerson—Corporate and policy affiliations: Arthur Andersen Company; chairman of International Council on Mining and Metals; executive board of the International Copper Association, Ltd.; The Business Council; Business Roundtable;

Advisory Board of the Kissinger Institute on China and the United States; Madison Minerals, Inc.

‣ Robert J. Allison Jr.—Corporate affiliations: Anadarko Petroleum Corporation (2010 revenue: $11 billion); Amoco Corporation.

‣ Robert A. Day—Corporate affiliations: CEO of W. M. Keck Foundation (2010 assets: more than $1 billion); attorney in Costa Mesa, California.

‣ Gerald J. Ford—Corporate affiliations: Hilltop Holdings, Inc.; First Acceptance Corporation, Pacific Capital Bancorp (annual sales: $13 billion); Golden State Bancorp, FSB (federal savings bank that merged with Citigroup in 2002); Rio Hondo Land & Cattle Co. (annual sales: $1.6 million); Diamond A—Ford Corporation, Dallas (sales: $200 million); Scientific Games Corporation; SWS Group, Inc. (annual sales: $422 million); American Residential Communities LLC.

‣ H. Devon Graham Jr.—Corporate affiliations: R. E. Smith Interests (an asset management company; income: $670,000).

‣ Charles C. Krulak—Corporate and governmental affiliations: president of Birmingham-Southern College; commandant of the Marine Corp., 1995–1999; MBNA Corporation; Union Pacific Corporation (annual sales: $17 billion); Phelps Dodge Corporation (acquired by FCX in 2007).

‣ Bobby Lee Lackey—Corporate affiliations: CEO of McManus-Wyatt-Hidalgo Produce Marketing Co.

‣ Jon C. Madonna—Corporate affiliations: CEO of KPMG LLP (professional services auditors; annual sales: $22.7 billion); AT&T (2011 revenue: $122 billion); Tidewater, Inc. (2011 revenue: $1.4 billion).

‣ Dustan E. McCoy—Corporate affiliations: CEO of Brunswick Corporation (revenue: $4.6 billion); Louisiana-Pacific Corporation (2011 revenue: $1.7 billion).

‣ B. M. Rankin Jr.—Corporate affiliations: board vice chairman of FCX; cofounder of McMoRan Oil & Gas LLC in 1969.

‣ Stephen H. Siegele—Corporate affiliations: founder/CEO of Advanced Delivery & Chemical Systems, Inc.; Advanced Technology Solutions, Inc.; Fluorine On Call, Ltd.

The board of directors of Freeport-McMoRan represents a portion of the global 1 percent who not only control the largest gold and copper mining company in the world, but who are also interconnected by board membership with over two dozen major multinational corporations, banks, foundations, military, and policy groups. This twelve-member board is a tight network of individuals who are interlocked with—and influence the policies of—other major companies controlling approximately $200 billion in annual revenues.

Freeport-McMoRan exemplifies how the extractor sector acquires wealth from the common heritage of natural materials—which rightfully belongs to us all—by appropriating the surplus value of working people's labor in the theft of our commons. This process is protected by governments in various countries where Freeport maintains mining operations, with the ultimate protector being the military empire of the US and the North Atlantic Treaty Organization (NATO).

Further, Freeport-McMoRan is connected to one of the most elite transnational capitalist groups in the world: over 7 percent of Free-port's stock is held by BlackRock, Inc., a major investment manage-ment firm based in New York City.

THE INVESTMENT SECTOR: THE CASE OF BLACKROCK, INC.

Internationally, many firms operate primarily as investment organi-zations, managing capital and investing in other companies. These firms often do not actually make anything except money, and are keen to prevent interference with return on capital by taxation, regulations, and governmental interventions anywhere in the world.

BlackRock, based in Manhattan, is the largest assets management firm in the world, with over 10,000 employees and investment teams in twenty-seven countries. Their client base includes corporate, pub-lic, union, and industry pension plans; governments; insurance com-panies; third-party mutual funds; endowments; foundations; chari-ties; corporations; official institutions; sovereign wealth funds; banks; financial professionals; and individuals worldwide. BlackRock ac-quired Barclays Global Investors in December of 2009. As of March 2012, BlackRock manages assets worth $3.68 trillion in equity, fixed income, cash management, alternative investment, real estate, and advisory strategies.[25]

In addition to Freeport-McMoRan, BlackRock has major holdings in Chevron (49 million shares, 2.5 percent), Goldman Sachs Group (13 million shares, 2.7 percent), ExxonMobil (121 million shares, 2.5 percent), Bank of America (251 million shares, 2.4 percent), Monsan-to (12 million shares, 2.4 percent), Microsoft Corporation (185 million shares, 2.2 percent), and many more.[26]

BlackRock manages investments of both public and private funds, including California Public Employees' Retirement System, Califor-nia State Teachers' Retirement System, Freddie Mac, Boy Scouts of America, Boeing, Sears, Verizon, Raytheon, PG&E, New York City Employee Retirement System, Los Angeles County Employees Re-tirement Association, General Electric, Cisco, and numerous others.

According to BlackRock's April 2011 annual report to stockhold-ers, the board of directors consists of eighteen members. The board is classified into three groups—Class I, Class II, and Class III—with terms of office of the members of one class expiring each year in rotation. Members of one class are generally elected at each annual meeting and serve for full three-year terms, or until successors are elected and qualified. Each class consists of approximately one-third of the total number of directors constituting the entire board of directors.[27]

BlackRock has stockholder agreements with Merrill Lynch & Co., Inc., a wholly owned subsidiary of Bank of America Corporation; and Barclays Bank PLC and its subsidiaries. Two to four members of the board are from BlackRock management; one director is designated by Bank of America/Merrill Lynch; two directors, each in a different class, are designated by PNC Bank; two directors, each in a different class, are designated by Barclays; and the remaining directors are independent.[28]

BlackRock's Board of Directors

Class I Directors (terms expire in 2012):

- William S. Demchak—Corporate affiliations: senior vice chairman of The PNC Financial Services Group, Inc. (assets: $271 billion); JPMorgan Chase & Co. (2011 assets: $2.2 trillion).
- Kenneth B. Dunn, PhD—Corporate and institutional affiliations: professor of financial economics at the David A. Tepper School of Business at Carnegie Mellon University; former managing director of Morgan Stanley Investment (assets: $807 billion).
- Laurence D. Fink—Corporate and institutional affiliations: chairman/CEO of BlackRock; trustee of New York University; trustee of Boys Club of NY.
- Robert S. Kapito—Corporate and institutional affiliations: president of BlackRock; trustee of Wharton School, University of Pennsylvania.
- Thomas H. O'Brien—Corporate affiliations: former CEO of PNC; Verizon Communications, Inc. (2011 revenue: $110 billion).
- Ivan G. Seidenberg—Corporate and policy affiliations: board chairman of Verizon Communications; former CEO of Bell At-

lantic; Honeywell International Inc. (2010 revenue: $33.3 billion); Pfizer Inc. (2011 revenue: $64 billion); chairman of the Business Roundtable; National Security Telecommunications Advisory Committee; President's Council of the New York Academy of Sciences.[29]

Class II Directors (terms expire in 2013):

▸ Abdlatif Yousef Al-Hamad—Corporate and institutional affiliations: board chairman of Arab Fund for Economic and Social Development (assets: $2.7 trillion); former Minister of Finance and Minister of Planning of Kuwait, Kuwait Investment Authority. Multilateral Development Banks, International Advisory Boards of Morgan Stanley, Marsh & McLennan Companies, Inc., American International Group, Inc. and the National Bank of Kuwait.

▸ Mathis Cabiallavetta—Corporate affiliations: Swiss Reinsurance Company (2010 revenue: $28 billion); CEO of Marsh & McLennan Companies Inc. (2011 revenue: $11.5 billion); Union Bank of Switzerland-UBS A.G. (2012 assets: $620 billion); Philip Morris International Inc. (2010 revenue: $27 billion).

▸ Dennis D. Dammerman—Corporate affiliations: General Electric Company (2012 revenue: $147 billion); Capmark Financial Group Inc. (formally GMAC); American International Group (AIG) (2010 revenue: $77 billion); Genworth Financial (2010 assets: $100 billion); Swiss Reinsurance Company (2012 assets: $620 billion); Discover Financial Services (2011 revenue: $3.4 billion).

▸ Robert E. Diamond Jr.—Corporate and policy affiliations: CEO of Barclays (2011 revenue: $32 billion); International Advisory Board of the British-American Business Council.

▸ David H. Komansky—Corporate affiliations: CEO of Merrill Lynch (division of Bank of America 2009) (2011 assets management: $2.3 trillion); Burt's Bees, Inc. (owned by Clorox); WPP Group plc (2011 revenue: $15 billion).

▸ James E. Rohr—Corporate affiliations: CEO of PNC (2011 revenue: $14 billion).

Class III Directors (terms expire in 2014):

‣ Murry S. Gerber—Corporate affiliations: executive chairman of EQT (2010 revenue: $1.3 billion); Halliburton Company.

‣ James Grosfeld—Corporate affiliations: CEO of Pulte Homes, Inc. (2010 revenue: $4.5 billion); Lexington Realty Trust (2011 assets: $1.2 billion).

‣ Sir Deryck Maughan—Corporate and policy affiliations: Kohlberg Kravis Roberts (2011 assets: $8.6 billion); former CEO of Salomon Brothers; from 1992 to 1997 a Chairman of the US-Japan Business Council; GlaxoSmithKline plc (2011 revenue: $41 billion); Thomson Reuters Corporation (2011 revenue: $13.8 billion).

‣ Thomas K. Montag—Corporate affiliations: president of Global Banking & Markets for Bank of America (2011 revenue: $94 billion); Merrill Lynch (division of Bank of America, 2009; 2011 assets management: $2.3 trillion); Goldman Sachs (2011 revenue: $28.8 billion).

‣ Linda Gosden Robinson—Corporate affiliations: former CEO of Robinson Lerer & Montgomery; Young & Rubicam Inc.; WPP Group plc (2011 revenue: $15 billion); Revlon, Inc. (2011 revenue: $1.3 billion).

‣ John S. Varley—Corporate affiliations: CEO of Barclays (2011 revenue: $32 billion); AstraZeneca plc (2011 revenue: $33.5 billion).

BlackRock is one of the most concentrated power networks among the global 1 percent. The eighteen members of the board of directors are connected to a significant part of the world's core financial assests. Their decisions can change empires, destroy currencies, and impoverish millions. Some of the top financial giants of the capitalist world are connected by interlocking boards of directors at BlackRock, including Bank of America, Merrill Lynch, Goldman Sachs, PNC Bank, Barclays, Swiss Reinsurance Company, American International Group (AIG), UBS AG, Arab Fund for Economic & Social Development, JPMorgan Chase & Co., and Morgan Stanley.

A 2011 University of Zurich study, research completed by Stefania Vitali, James B. Glattfelder, and Stefano Battiston at the Swiss Federal Institute of Technology, reports that a small group of companies—mainly banks—wields huge power over the global economy.[30] Using data from ORBIS 2007, a database listing thirty-seven million companies and investors, the Swiss researchers applied mathematical models—usually used to model natural systems—to the world economy. The study is the first to look at all 43,060 transnational corporations and the web of ownership between them. The research created a "map" of 1,318 companies at the heart of the global economy. The study found that 147 companies formed a "super entity" within this map, controlling some 40 percent of its wealth. The top twenty-five of the 147 super-connected companies includes:

1. Barclays PLC*
2. Capital Group Companies, Inc.
3. FMR LLC
4. AXA
5. State Street Corporation
6. JPMorgan Chase & Co.*
7. Legal & General Group PLC
8. Vanguard Group, Inc.
9. UBS AG
10. Merrill Lynch & Co. Inc.*
11. Wellington Management Company, LLP
12. Deutsche Bank AG
13. Franklin Resources, Inc.
14. Credit Suisse Group*
15. Walton Enterprises LLC
16. Bank of New York Mellon Corporation
17. Natixis Global Asset Management, S. A.
18. Goldman Sachs Group, Inc.*
19. T Rowe Price Group, Inc.
20. Legg Mason, Inc.
21. Morgan Stanley*
22. Mitsubishi UFJ Financial Group, Inc.
23. Northern Trust Corporation
24. Société Générale CIB
25. Bank of America Corporation*

* BlackRock Directors

Notably, for our purposes, BlackRock board members have direct connections to at least seven of the top twenty-five corporations that Vitali et al. identify as an international "super entity." BlackRock's board has direct links to seven of the twenty-five most interconnected corporations in the world. BlackRock's eighteen board members control and influence tens of trillions of dollars of wealth in the world and represent a core of the super-connected financial sector corporations.

Below is a sample cross section of key figures and corporate assets among the global economic "super entity" identified by Vitali et al.

KEY FIGURES AND CORPORATE CONNECTIONS WITHIN THE GLOBAL ECONOMIC "SUPER ENTITY"

▸ Capital Group Companies—Privately held, based in Los Angeles, manages $1 trillion in assets.

▸ FMR—One of the world's largest mutual fund firms, managing $1.5 trillion in assets and serving more than twenty million individual and institutional clients; Edward C. (Ned) Johnson III, Chairman and CEO.

▸ AXA—Manages $1.5 trillion in assets, serving 101 million clients; Henri de Castries, chairman and CEO of AXA; director of Nestlé (Switzerland).

▸ State Street Corporation—Operates from Boston with assest management at $1.9 trillion; directors include Joseph (Jay) L. Hooley, chairman, president, and CEO of State Street Corporation; Kennett F. Burnes, retired chairman, president, and CEO of Cabot Corporation (2011 revenue: $3.1 billion).

▸ JP Morgan Chase & Co. (2011 assets: $2.3 trillion)—Directors include: James A. Bell, retired executive VP of The Boeing Company; Stephen B. Burke, CEO of NBCUniversal, LLC, and executive VP of Comcast Corporation; David M. Cote, chairman and CEO of Honeywell International, Inc.; Timothy P. Flynn, retired chairman of KPMG International; and Lee R. Raymond, retired chairman and CEO of ExxonMobil Corporation.

▸ Vanguard (2011 assets under management: $1.6 trillion)—Directors include: Emerson U. Fullwood, VP of Xerox Corporation; JoAnn Heffernan Heisen, former VP of Johnson & Johnson, among other companies; Mark Loughridge, senior VP and CFO of IBM (information technology services), senior VP and general manager of Global Financing; Alfred M. Rankin Jr., CEO of NACCO Industries, Inc., chairman, president, and director of National Association of Manufacturers, director of Goodrich Corp., and chairman of the Board of the Federal Reserve Bank of Cleveland.

▸ UBS AG (2012 assets: $620 billion)—Directors include: Michel Demaré, board member of Syngenta and the IMD Foundation (Lausanne); David Sidwell, former executive VP and CFO of Morgan Stanley.

▸ Merrill Lynch (Bank of America) (2011 assets management: $2.3 trillion)—Directors include: Brian T. Moynihan, CEO of Bank of America Corporation; Rosemary T. Berkery, general counsel for Bank of America/Merrill Lynch (formerly Merrill Lynch & Co., Inc), member of New York Stock Exchange's Legal Advisory Committee, director at Securities Industry and Financial Markets Association; Mark A. Ellman, managing director of Credit Suisse, First Boston; Dick J. Barrett, cofounder of Barrett Ellman Stoddard Capital Partners, MetLife, Citi Group, UBS, Carlyle Group, ImpreMedia, Verizon Communications, Commonewealth Scientific and Industrial Research Org, Fluor Corp, Wells Fargo, Goldman Sachs Group.

The directors of these super-connected companies represent a small portion of the global 1 percent. Most people with assets in excess of $588,000 are not major players in international finance. At best, they hire asset management firms to produce a return on their capital. Often their net worth is tied up in nonfinancial assets such as real estate and businesses.

ANALYSIS: TCC AND GLOBAL POWER

So how does the transnational capitalist class (TCC) maintain wealth concentration and power in the world? The wealthiest 1 percent of the world's population represents approximately forty million adults. These forty million people are the richest segment of what Willian

Robinson and Jerry Harris have described as "first tier populations" that reside in "core" countries and, to a lesser extent, in "peripheral" tier countries.[31] Most of this 1 percent have professional jobs with security and tenure working for or associated with established institutions. Approximately ten million of these individuals have assets in excess of one million dollars, and approximately 100,000 have financial assets worth over thirty million dollars. Immediately below the 1 percent in the first tier are working people with regular employment in major corporations, government, self-owned businesses, and various institutions of the world.

As seen in our analyses of Freeport-McMoRan and BlackRock, corporate elites are interconnected through direct board connections with some seventy major multinational corporations, policy groups, media organizations, and other academic or nonprofit institutions. The investment sector sample shows much more powerful financial links than the extractor sample; nonetheless, both represent vast networks of resources concentrated within each company's board of directors. Though this chapter outlines only two examples of the superconnected copmanies, research performed by the authors of eight of the other companies replicates this pattern of multiple board corporate connections, policy groups, media and government, controlling vast global resources. These interlocking relationships recur across the top interconnected companies among the transnational corporate class, resulting in a highly concentrated and powerful network of individuals who share a common interest in preserving their elite domination.

Sociological research shows that interlocking directorates have the potential to faciliate political cohesion. A sense of a collective "we" emerges within such power networks, whereby members think and act in unison, not just for themselves and their individual firms, but for a larger sense of purpose—the good of the order, so to speak.[32]

Transnational corporate boards meet on a regular basis to encourage the maximization of profit and the long-term viability of their firm's business plans. If they arrange for payments to government officials, conduct activities that undermine labor organizations, seek to manipulate the price of commodities (e.g. gold), or engage in insider trading in some capacity, they are in fact forming conspiratorial alliances inside those boards of directors. Our sample of thirty directors inside two connected companies have influence with some of the most powerful policy groups in the world, including British–American Business Council, US–Japan Business Council, Inc., Business Roundtable, Business Council, and the Kissinger Institute. They influence some ten trillion dollars in monetery resouces and control the working lives of many hundreds of thousands of people. All in all, they are a power elite unto themselves, operating in a world of power elite networks as the *de facto* ruling class of the capitalist world.

Moreover, this 1 percent global elite dominates and controls public relations firms and the corporate media. Global corporate media protect the interests of the 1 percent by serving as a propaganda machine for the superclass. The corporate media provide entertainment for the masses and distort the realities of inequality. Corporate news is managed by the 1 percent to maintain illusions of hope and to divert blame from the powerful for hard times.[33]

Four of the thirty directors in our two-firm sample are directly connected with public relations and media. Thomas H. O'Brien and Ivan G. Seidenberg were both on the board of Verizon Communications, Inc., where Seidenberg served as chairman. Verizon reported over $110 billion in operating revenues in 2011.[34] David H. Komansky and Linda Gosden Robinson are associated with the board of WPP Group, which describes itself as the world leader in marketing communications services, grossing over $65 billion in 2011. WPP is a conglomerate of many of the world's leading PR and marketing firms, in fields that include advertising, media investment management, consumer insight, branding and identity, health care communications, and direct, digital, promotion, and relationship marketing.[35]

Even deeper inside the 1 percent of wealthy elites is what David Rothkopf calls the superclass. David Rothkopf, former managing director of Kissinger Associates and deputy undersecretary of commerce for international trade policies, published his book *Superclass: The Global Power Elite and the World They Are Making*, in 2008.[36] According to Rothkopf, the superclass constitutes approximately 0.0001 percent of the world's population, comprised of 6,000 to 7,000 people—some say, specifically, 6,660. They are the Davos-attending, Gulfstream/private jet–flying, money-incrusted, megacorporationinterlocked, policy-building elites of the world, people at the absolute peak of the global power pyramid. They are 94 percent male, predominantly white, and mostly from North America and Europe. These are the people setting the agendas at the Trilateral Commission, Bilderberg Group, G-8, G-20, NATO, the World Bank, and the World Trade Organization. They are from the highest levels of finance capital, transnational corporations, the government, the military, the academy, nongovernmental organizations, spiritual leaders, and other shadow elites. Shadow elites include, for instance, national security organizations in connection with international drug cartels, who extract 8,000 tons of opium from US war zones annually, then launder $500 billion through transnational banks, half of which are US-based.[37]

Rothkopf's understanding of the superclass is one based on influence *and* power. Although there are over 1,000 billionaires in the world, not all are necessarily part of the superclass in terms of influencing global policies. Yet these 1,000 billionaires have twice as much wealth as the 2.5 billion least wealthy people, and they are fully aware of the vast inequalities in the world. The billionaires and the global 1 percent are similar to colonial plantation owners. They know they are a small minority with vast resources and power, yet they must continually worry about the unruly exploited masses rising in rebellion. As a result of these class insecurities, the superclass works hard to protect this structure of concentrated wealth. Protection of capital is the prime reason that NATO countries now account for 85 percent of the world's defense spending, with the US spending more on military than the rest of the world combined.[38] Fears of rebellions and other forms of unrest motivate NATO's global agenda in the war on terror.[39] The Chicago 2012 NATO Summit Declaration reads:

> As Alliance leaders, we are determined to ensure that NATO retains and develops the capabilities necessary to perform its essential core tasks—collective defence, crisis management and cooperative security—and thereby to play an essential role promoting security in the world. We must meet this responsibility while dealing with an acute financial crisis and responding to evolving geo-strategic challenges. NATO al-

lows us to achieve greater security than any one Ally could attain acting alone. We confirm the continued importance of a strong transatlantic link and Alliance solidarity as well as the significance of sharing responsibilities, roles, and risks to meet the challenges North-American and European Allies face together . . . we have confidently set ourselves the goal of NATO Forces 2020: modern, tightly connected forces equipped, trained, exercised and commanded so that they can operate together and with partners in *any* [emphasis added] environment.[40]

NATO is quickly becoming the police force for the transnational capitalist class. As the TCC more fully emerged in the 1980s, coinciding with the collapse of the Union of Soviet Socialist Republics (USSR), NATO began broader operations. NATO first ventured into the Balkans, where it remains, and then moved into Afghanistan. NATO started a training mission in Iraq in 2005, has recently conducted operations in Libya, and, as of June 2012, is considering military action in Syria.

It has become clear that the superclass uses NATO for its global security. This is part of an expanding strategy of US military domination around the world, wherby the US/NATO military-industrial-media empire operates in service to the transnational capitalist class for the protection of international capital anywhere in the world.[41]

Sociologists William Robinson and Jerry Harris anticipated this situation in 2000, when they described "a shift from the social welfare state to the social control (police) state replete with the dramatic expansion of public and private security forces, the mass incarceration of the excluded populations (disproportionately minorities), new forms of social apartheid . . . and anti-immigrant legislation."[42] Robinson and Harris's theory accurately predicts the agenda of today's global superclass, including

▸ President Obama's continuation of the police state agendas of his executive predecessors, George W. Bush, Bill Clinton, and George H. W. Bush;

- the long-range global dominance agenda of the superclass, which uses US/NATO military forces to discourage resisting states and maintain internal police repression, in service of the capitalist system's orderly maintenance;
- and the continued consolidation of capital around the world without interference from governments or egalitarian social movements.[43]

Furthermore, this agenda leads to the further pauperization of the poorest half of the world's population, and an unrelenting downward spiral of wages for everyone in the second tier, and even some within the first tier.[44] It is a world facing economic crisis, where the neoliberal solution is to spend less on human needs and more on security.[45] It is a world of financial institutions run amok, where the answer to bankruptcy is to print more money through quantitative easing with trillions of new inflation-producing dollars. It is a world of permanent war, whereby spending for destruction requires even more spending to rebuild, a cycle that profits the TCC and its global networks of economic power. It is a world of drone killings, extrajudicial assassinations, and death and destruction, at home and abroad.

As Andrew Kollin states in *State Power and Democracy*, "There is an Orwellian dimension to the Administration's (Bush and later Obama) perspective, it chose to disregard the law, instead creating decrees to legitimate illegal actions, giving itself permission to act without any semblances of power sharing as required by the Constitution or international law."[46]

And in *Globalization and the Demolition of Society*, Dennis Loo writes, "The bottom line, the fundamental division of our society, is between, on the one hand, those whose interests rest on the dominance and the drive for monopolizing the society and planet's resources and, on the other hand, those whose interests lie in the husbanding of those resources for the good of the whole rather than the part."[47]

The Occupy movement uses the 1 percent vs. 99 percent mantra as a master concept in its demonstrations, disruptions, and challenges to the practices of the transnational capitalist class, within which the global superclass is a key element in the implementation of a superelite agenda for permanent war and total social control. Occupy is exactly what the superclass fears the most—a global democratic movement that exposes the TCC agenda and the continuing theater of government elections, wherein the actors may change but the marquee remains the same. The more that Occupy refuses to cooperate with the TCC agenda and mobilizes activists, the more likely the whole TCC system of dominance will fall to its knees under the people power of democractic movements.

PETER PHILLIPS is a professor of sociology at Sonoma State University and president of the Media Freedom Foundation/Project Censored.

KIMBERLY SOEIRO is a sociology student at Sonoma State University, library researcher, and activist.

Special thanks to Mickey Huff, director of Project Censored, and Andy Roth, associate director of Project Censored, for editing and for important suggestions for this chapter.

Notes

1. For a more scholarly background on this subject, the following are required reading: C. Wright Mills, *The Power Elite* (New York: Oxford University Press, 1956); G. William Domhoff, *Who Rules America?: Challenges to Corporate and Class Dominance*, 6th ed. (Boston: McGraw Hill Higher Education, 2009); and William K. Carroll, *The Making of a Transnational Capitalist Class: Corporate Power in the 21st Century* (London: Zed Books, 2010).
2. Leslie Sklair, *The Transnational Capitalist Class* (Oxford: Blackwell, 2001).
3. Sklair, "The Transnational Capitalist Class and the Discourse of Globalization," *Cambridge Review of International Affairs* (2000), http://www.theglobalsite.ac.uk/press/012sklair.htm.
4. Tyler Durden, "A Detailed Look At Global Wealth Distribution," ZeroHedge.com, October 11, 2010, http://www.zerohedge.com/article/detailed-look-global-wealth-distribution.
5. The World Bank, "World Bank Sees Progress Against Extreme Poverty, But Flags Vulnerabilities," press release, February 29, 2012, http://web.worldbank.org/WBSITE/EXTERNAL/NEWS/0,,contentMDK:23130032~pagePK:64257043~piPK:437376~theSitePK:4607,00.html.
6. Mark R. Elsis, "The Three Top Sins of the Universe," Lovearth.net, February 9, 2002, quoted in Starvation.net, http://www.starvation.net.
7. GRAIN, "Corporations are Still Making a Killing from Hunger," *Seedling*, April 2009, http://www.grain.org/article/entries/716-corporations-are-still-making-a-killing-from-hunger.
8. On the extraction of surplus-value from labor, see Karl Marx, *Capital: A Critique of Political Economy*, vol. 3 (New York and London: Penguin, [1894] 1991).
9. See, for example, Paul Burkett, "Capital's 'Free Apporriation' of Natural and Social Conditions," in *Marx and Nature: A Red and Green Perspective* (New York: St. Martins, 1999); for additional information on the Fair Share of the Common Heritage, see http://www.fairsharecommonheritage.org/.
10. Freeport-McMoRan Copper & Gold, "Notice of Annual Meeting of Stockholders," June 15, 2011, document April 28, 2011, http://www.fcx.com/ir/downloads/FCXProx2011.pdf.
11. "Freeport Indonesia Miners, Tribesmen Defend Road Blockades," Reuters Africa, November 4, 2011, http://af.reuters.com/article/metalsNews/idAFL4E7M410020111104.

12. Farouk Arnaz, "Police Admit to Receiving Freeport 'Lunch Money,'" *Jakarta Globe*, October 28, 2011, http://www.thejakartaglobe.com/news/police-admit-to-receiving-freeport-lunch-money/474747.

13. Agence France-Presse, "US Mining Giant Still Paying Indonesia Military," Google News, March 22, 2009, http://www.google.com/hostednews/afp/article/ALeqM5jJMKtoD9LnT34URkkkJmTjaSf8EA.

14. "Indonesia Must Investigate Mine Strike Protest Killing," Amnesty International News, October 10, 2011, http://www.amnesty.org/en/news-and-updates/indonesia-must-investigate-mine-strike-protest-killing-2011-10-10; and "West Papua Report," November 2011, http://www.etan.org/issues/wpapua/2011/1111wpap.htm.

15. Camelia Pasandaran, "Striking Freeport Employees Lower Wage Increase Demands," *Jakarta Globe*, November 7, 2011, http://www.thejakartaglobe.com/business/striking-freeport-employees-lower-wage-increase-demands/476800.

16. Ibid.

17. Omar Mariluz, "Update: 1-Union Lifting Strike at Freeport's Peru Minem" Reuters Africa, November 28, 2011, http://af.reuters.com/article/metalsNews/idAFN1E7AR1K520111128.

18. Ibid.

19. Eric Bellman and Tess Stynes, "Freeport-McMoRan Says Pact Ends Indonesia Strike," *Wall Street Journal*, December 14, 2011, http://online.wsj.com/article/SB10001424052970203893404577098222935896112.html.

20. John Pakage, "When There Is No Guarantee of the Security of Life for the People of Papua," West Papua Media Alerts, March 1, 2012, http://westpapuamedia.info/tag/freeport-McMoRan.

21. Termporn C., "Reasons to Go to Darwin," *Nation* (Thailand), November 30, 2011, http://www.nationmultimedia.com/opinion/Reasons-to-go-to-Darwin-30170893.html

22. Karishma Vaswani, "US Firm Freeport Struggles to Escape Its Past in Papua," BBC News (Asia-Pacific), August 8, 2011, http://www.bbc.co.uk/news/world-asia-pacific-14417718.

23. WPACTION, "Occupy Phoenix & ETAN Freeport McMoRan Demonstration Oct. 28th 2011," YouTube, http://www.youtube.com/watch?v=CvJxy2GvOHE.

24. Freeport-McMoRan Copper & Gold, Notice of Annual Meeting of Stockholders, June 15, 2011, http://www.fcx.com/ir/downloads/FCXProx2011.pdf.

25. "Who is BlackRock?" BlackRock, About page, http://www2.blackrock.com/global/home/AboutUs/index.htm.

26. Data for this section is drawn from StreetInsider.com.

27. BlackRock, Notice of 2011 Annual Meeting of Stockholders, April 26, 2011, http://www.sec.gov/Archives/edgar/data/1364742/000119312511109713/ddef14a.htm.

28. Ibid., 5.

29. Data for the corporations listed in this section comes fron the annual report at each corporation's website. Biography information was gained from the FAX annual report to investors and online biographies for individuals wihen available.

30. Stefania Vitali, James B. Glattfelder, and Stefano Battiston, "The Network of Global Corporate Control," *PLoS ONE* 6.10 (October 26, 2011), http://www.plosone.org/article/info%3Adoi%2F10.1371%2Fjournal.pone.0025995.

31. Willian Robinson and Jerry Harris, "Towards a Global Ruling Class? Globalization and the Transnational Capitalist Class," *Science and Society* 64, no. 1 (Spring 2000):11–54. Robinson and Harris characterize today's global society in terms of a "three-tiered social structure." The first tier "hold 'tenured' employment in the global economy and are able to maintain, and even expand, their consumption." The second tier form a growing army of "casualized" workers who face chronic insecurity in the conditions of their employment. This leaves a third tier of destitute people who have been "structurally excluded from productive activity" and are "completely unprotected with the dismantling of welfare and developmentalist states." People in this lowest tier have extremely limited income opportunities and struggle to survive on a few dollars a day. These are the 2.5 billion people who live on less than two dollars a day, die by the tens of thousands every day from malnutrition and easily curible illnesses, and who have probably never even heard a dial tone.

32. Val Burris, "Interlocking Directorates and Political Cohesion Among Corporate Elites," *American Journal of Sociology* 111, no. 1 (July 2005): 249–83.

33. Peter Phillips and Mickey Huff, "Truth Emergency: Inside the Military Industrial Media Empire," in *Censored 2010: The Top Censored Stories of 2008–09* (New York: Seven Stories, 2009), 197–220.

34. Verizon, "2Q 2012 Quareterly Earnings Report," Investor Relations, http://www22.verizon.com/investor; Hoover's describes Verizon as "the #2 US telecom services provider overall after AT&T, but it holds the top spot in wireless services ahead of rival AT&T Mobility." Hoover's Inc., "Verizon Communications Inc.," http://www.hoovers.com/company/Verizon_Communications_Inc/rfrski-1.html.

35. "WPP at a Glance," WPP, About page, http://www.wpp.com/wpp/about/wppataglance.

36. David Rothkopf, *Superclass: The Global Power Elite and the World They Are Making* (New York: Farrar, Straus, and Giroux, 2008).

37. Peter Dale Scott, *American War Machine, Deep Politics, the CIA Global Drug Connection, and the Road to Afghanistan* (Lanham, MD: Rowman & Littlefield Publishers, 2010). See also Censored story #22, "Wachovia Bank Laundered Money for Latin American Drug Cartels," in chap. 1 of this volume.

38. Rothkopf, "Superclass," Carnegie Endowment for International Peace, public address, April 9, 2008.

39. "Defence Against Terrorism Programme," NATO, Topic: DAT Programme, http://www.nato.int/cps/en/SID-EBFFE857-6607109D/natolive/topics_50313.htm?selectedLocale=en.

40. "Summit Declaration on Defence Capabilities: Toward NATO Forces 2020," NATO, Official Texts, May 20, 2012, http://www.nato.int/cps/en/SID-1CE3D0B6-393C986D/natolive/official_texts_87594.htm.

41. For an expanded analysis of the history of US "global dominance," see Phillips, Bridget Thornton, and Celeste Vogler, "The Global Dominance Group: 9/11 Pre-Warnings & Election Irregularities in Context," Project Censored, May 2, 2010, http://www.projectcensored.org/top-stories/articles/the-global-dominance-group/; and Phillips, Thornton, and Lew Brown, "The Global Dominance Group and U.S. Corporate Media," in *Censored 2007: The Top 25 Censored Stories* (New York: Seven Stories, 2006), 307–33.

42. Robinson and Harris, "Towards a Global Ruling Class?"

43. John Pilger, *The New Rulers of the World* (New York: Verso, 2003).

44. Michel Chossudovsky and Andrew Gavin Marshall, eds., *The Global Economic Crisis: The Great Depression of the XXI Century* (Montreal: Global Research Publishers, 2010).

45. Dennis Loo, *Globalization and the Demolition of Society* (Glendale, CA: Larkmead Press, 2011).

46. Andrew Kolin, *State Power and Democracy: Before and During the Presidency of George W. Bush* (New York: Palgrave Macmillan, 2011), 141.

47. Loo, *Globalization*, 357.

CHAPTER 7

The Information War
How Government Is Seeking Total Information Awareness and What This Portends for Freedom and Democracy

by Dr. Elliot D. Cohen

There is a silent war afoot that corporate media do not cover, the most pervasive war that could ever be waged. It uses high-tech equipment and involves the largest, most powerful corporations on earth; it is more lucrative for these corporate allies than any other war that has been or ever will be fought. This war's battlefield has no barriers. It is being fought everywhere and anywhere, including in cyberspace, and involves anyone on the planet who has the power to think.

The war in question is the acquisition and control of the rich supply of information growing exponentially with the advances of science: a paranoid, vigilant campaign by government, across borders, to ensure that no one has the franchise of knowledge except the highest echelons of national command and control.

Not only is this an all-out war on anyone who has information, it is a war on the freedom to possess information, to keep it confidential, to communicate freely, and to publish. It is a war against the First Amendment rights to freedom of speech, press, and assembly. All these previously protected modes of communication are quietly under attack.

Like all wars, there is a pretext for invasion. The Iraq War was officially fought to free the Iraqis from Saddam Hussein's tyrannical rule—never mind the profits amassed by the military-industrial complex, and never mind the Downing Street Memos that summed up the reality but were censored then summarily dismissed by servile corporate media.

The war in Afghanistan, we were led to believe, was a war to quash al-Qaeda and the Taliban—never mind that giant oil companies, notably Chevron, sought to make billions through construction of the Trans-Afghanistan Pipeline for natural gas transport across the region, and the Taliban were sabotaging the project—or that the secretary of state during the Bush administration was the former chief executive officer of Chevron. And it may be just another coincidence that Obama is withdrawing (most of) the US troops by 2014, when that pipeline is slated for completion.

Most Americans have believed these pretexts, so have supported or helped to fight these wars. The war to acquire and control information is the same. Most Americans believe they need to surrender their privacy to be safe. They believe that mass, warrantless surveillance of all their e-mails, telephone calls, and Internet searches is intended to protect them from another 9/11 attack, or worse. They believe that they should willingly surrender their right to privacy and allow the National Security Agency (NSA) to access even their most intimate and personal electronic correspondence. They do not ask questions because it would be unpatriotic, and who would want to sell out the safety and security of a "free" nation?

The paradox of giving up one's freedom to defend one's freedom quietly perpetuates with no vigilant media to drive home the self-defeating nature of the expectation. "National security" has become the buzzword for trumping the right to control one's personal information. Yet hardly anyone asks whether there is a more balanced approach to national security. Is it really a matter of all or nothing—either we are safe, or we retain control over our personal information, but not both?

TOWARD "TOTAL INFORMATION AWARENESS"

In 2002, John Poindexter, the ex-felon who came up with the idea of Total Information Awareness, proposed the idea of a "privacy appliance" that could protect the masses of private information stored on NSA mega-computers. According to a 2003 congressional report, "this device cryptographically protected to prevent tampering ... would ensure that no one could abuse private information without an immutable digital record of their misdeeds."[1]

The appliance would work by hiding personal information behind a veil of encryption, and when emerging behavior patterns would suggest a terrorist plot, a Foreign Intelligence Surveillance (FIS) court warrant would be issued to un-encrypt the information relevant to the possible terrorist plot, leaving all other encrypted information in the massive database intact. Thereby, privacy would be protected without sacrificing the integrity of the search for terrorist operations.

This could have worked, but the budget to support development of the software was scrapped. Yet massive stores of private information data continue to grow exponentially, along with the probabilities of serious privacy violations.

If the government were truly interested in preserving citizens' rights to control their personal information, it would have made the investment in the research and development of such a "privacy appliance." A more consistent explanation for the failure to protect privacy is that the government prefers to maintain full control of *all* information in the database, whether or not it has anything to do with potential terrorist plots.

Under the USA PATRIOT Act, if the federal government, in the course of investigating a suspected terrorist plot, learns that you are growing marijuana plants, it can use this information to prosecute you for a federal violation of narcotics laws. Contrary to the Fourth Amendment, probable cause is not necessary to obtain the information. The pretext of having discovered your illegal activity while hunting for terrorists would be sufficient to render the evidence against you admissible.

So, the government interest is not merely in stopping terrorism, and it is certainly not about protecting privacy. The government seeks the acquisition and control of information—"Total Information Awareness"—and it is willing to give itself the legal authority to obtain it.

INTERNET FREEDOMS UNDER SIEGE

Freedom of speech is now quietly under attack in this war to acquire and control the vast sea of information. The most magnificent forum for the free exchange of ideas ever conceived is, of course, the Internet. But the Internet's free architecture is under attack and it appears that, on this front, the war is being won.

The first major legal victory that threatened the democratic potential of the Internet came in 2005 in the Brand X case, when the US Supreme Court changed the legal status of the Internet from a common carrier to a private one.[2] Prior to this decision, the Internet pipes were considered to be like a telephone line or a public roadway: public utilities open for use by anyone. The telecommunication and telephone companies who operated them could not restrict their use to select individuals or companies. But with the change in legal status, giant Internet gatekeepers like Comcast and AT&T overcame a major barrier in giving special priority to some voices over others. No longer was every bit necessarily equal. These companies could now restrict traffic on the Net, much as the owner of a private road could keep out trespassers.

Accordingly, in the 2010 case *Comcast v. FCC*, a federal appeals court gave Comcast and other telecoms the legal right to block and slow Internet traffic in order to "manage" their networks.[3] On the surface, the pretense was to prevent file-sharing websites from "hogging" bandwidth, but what it really meant was that these companies did not have to treat all information equally and could therefore determine what data (programming, electronic messages, applications, etc.) could be transmitted over their networks.

Now, the companies' next logical step is to use this legal authority to set up a system of Internet "toll booths" where content providers would have to "pay for priority."[4] This means that the amount of bandwidth a website operator would get would depend on how much the operator could afford to pay.

Bandwidth determines the speed at which data can be downloaded—the higher the bandwidth, the faster the download. Thus, for giant corporate media like News Corp. (Fox), Time Warner (CNN), and Comcast (NBC), which can afford the highest bandwidth, this would mean the power to dominate the Internet and to effectively preempt the messages of independent media and other content providers.

The kicker is that giant Internet service providers, such as Comcast, AT&T, and Verizon, work for the United States government. Pursuant to the 2008 Foreign Intelligence Surveillance Amendments

Act, these companies must assist the federal government in providing the facility for monitoring all electronic communications passing through their switches.[5] These companies also receive special government perks including tax breaks, favorable antitrust laws and decisions, and government contracts.

Moreover, pursuant to the 2012 National Defense Resources Preparedness Executive Order decreed by the Obama administration, the government now has the legal authority to install government equipment (which includes surveillance equipment) inside electronic communication service providers.[6] So, the giant telecom companies presently serve as conduits for government exercise of power and control over mass data transport.

For democracy, the marriage between giant electronic communication companies and government portends grave danger. These behemoth corporations have legal discretionary power to block or slow content providers; and they, in turn, work for the government. Unless clear limits on this discretionary power are established, the government now not only has the legal authority to police all online activities, it also has a segue into censoring them.

In fact, the 2011–12 session of Congress attempted to expand its power to block websites through passage of the Stop Online Piracy Act (SOPA). On the surface, SOPA sought to protect intellectual property rights, such as those of the motion picture and book publishing industries, by preventing foreign websites from posting pirated material. However, on closer inspection, this act would have given government—again going through Internet service providers—the power to shut down websites adverse to its own political interests.

The act would have deputized these companies with the discretionary power to block any website if they had "reasonable belief" that some of the website's content violated copyright law. Thus, the uploading of a single objectionable file could have led to the blocking of an entire website by the service provider, pursuant to the act.[7] Public outcry, along with protests from Google and Wikipedia, appear to have helped stop SOPA's passage, but this was only a temporary reprieve.

On the heels of SOPA, another bill has at the time of this writing passed the House of Representatives. The Cyber Intelligence and Sharing Protection Act (CISPA) would go further than SOPA in monitoring and controlling information. Although SOPA was restricted to information alleged to violate intellectual property rights, CISPA allows for the sharing of personal information between government and private industry for purposes of addressing possible "cyber threats."[8]

According to the act, "notwithstanding any other provision of law," Internet service providers such as Comcast, Verizon, and AT&T, and other private cybersecurity and data management companies, can with legal impunity share their customers' personal information with the federal government.[9] This means that CISPA, if passed, will trump all other civil rights protections, thereby making all of our personal information, from health care records to credit card information, fair game for the government.

According to an amendment added to the act prior to passing the House, data can be shared with government for purposes of "(1) cybersecurity, (2) investigation and prosecution of cybersecurity crimes, (3) protection of individuals from the danger of death or physical injury, (4) protection of minors from physical or psychological harm, and (5) protection of the national security of the United States."[10] Given this range of "harms," spanning both physical and psychological types, as well as vague terms such as "cybersecurity" and "national security," it is evident that CISPA, if it becomes law, would seriously increase the likelihood of government abuses of personal and confidential information.

From the perspective of giant cybersecurity companies, CISPA would be a gold mine. One such notable company is Sciences Applications International Corporation (SAIC).[11] This military contractor was at the front lines of helping the Bush administration to build the technologies for launching its warrantless, mass spying program. Now SAIC is lobbying for CISPA[12] because the bill would make it a major player in putting the final legal touches on the Total Information Awareness system of mass surveillance that SAIC helped build during the Bush administration.

Not surprisingly, SAIC is already assisting the NSA in building a giant, data-mining center in Utah.[13] As discussed in the "The Police and Civil Liberties" Censored News Cluster in chapter 1, this state-of-the-art surveillance center will provide the hub of electronic data monitoring for all electronic information including e-mail messages, Internet searches, and phone conversations. With CISPA in place, there will also be a direct legal route to integrate all other private information into this massive database. SAIC's role in this process will be to help create the software infrastructure that would seamlessly link and analyze masses of data.

In this attempt to monitor and control the world's information, the quid pro quo relationship between government and companies like SAIC and other cybersecurity and data-mining companies is crucial. It is a violation of the Fourth Amendment for the US government to access personal data such as health care records and credit card information directly—but this same constitutional restriction does not apply to private corporations like SAIC and the giant telecoms. Thus the government can obtain this information through corporate mediators and claim not to have violated the Fourth Amendment. Without our knowledge or consent, American citizens' constitutional rights are being bypassed.

The modus operandi here is a familiar one, of the government retroactively legalizing its own prior illegal activities or those of its corporate helpers. It was practiced frequently by the George W. Bush administration, such as when millions of Americans were illegally wiretapped without court warrants. By passing the Foreign Intelligence Surveillance Amendments Act (FISA) in 2008, the administration gave itself permission to continue the practice. More specifically, the 2008 act canceled the requirement of an earlier 1973 FISA Act that required an FIS court warrant for wiretapping; it also gave full retroactive and prospective legal immunity to electronic communications companies that helped the government spy on millions of Americans.[14] FISA rendered null and void class action lawsuits filed against these companies on behalf of Americans who had had their right to privacy abridged.

Now the Obama administration is doing the same thing. For the past decade, the government has installed surveillance equipment in private telecommunications and telephone companies. Pursuant to the 2008 FISA, it requires electronic communications companies to cooperate in mass, warrantless, surveillance dragnets. Following the

2012 National Defense Resources Preparedness Executive Order, the Obama administration has given itself permission to continue to install and operate such equipment in these private companies. And, with the possible passage of CISPA, or (eventually) a similar law, the Obama administration is in the process of giving itself permission to trump all privacy protections in acquiring everyone's personal information from these same companies.

THE LEGALIZATION OF DOMESTIC PROPAGANDA

Not only private, personal information is under attack. In May 2012, the Obama administration permitted itself to infect the reservoir of public information with government propaganda. The Smith-Mundt Modernization Act of 2012 trumps prior antigovernment propaganda legislation and gives the government legal authority to spread propaganda domestically as well as abroad. The act permits government to spread its propaganda "to foreign audiences through press publications, radio, motion pictures, the Internet, and other information media," and then to circulate this same propaganda within the United States.[15]

The Obama administration has already begun influencing social media: "sock puppet" software secretly manipulates social media sites such as Facebook, by using fake online personas to start Internet conversations in order to spread pro-American propaganda.[16]

Such information warfare was no stranger to the Bush administration, which, for a time, operated an Office of Strategic Influence: a high-level Pentagon program intended to manipulate the public by waging information warfare against the media.[17] The difference now is that the Obama administration has passed a law giving itself permission to pollute public information with government propaganda. It's all quite "legal" now.

Given this modus operandi, law has devolved into a network of permissions granted by government *to itself* to violate the laws that had previously been in place. Thus, government has eviscerated the rule of law—and is now poised to obtain unfettered access to all of our personal information, to control what flows down the information pipes, and to pollute the mainstream with government propaganda.

This most insidious war of them all, unannounced and unpublished, quietly steals off with our most valuable possession: the freedom and autonomy to make informed judgments and to maintain control over our personal information.

THE HORIZON OF INFORMATION WARFARE TECHNOLOGY

It can—and predictably will—get much worse, considering the information warfare technology on the horizon. Already in existence are private companies that crawl the Internet and collect information on employees, predicting their future behavior and determining whether or not they should be fired.[18] Imagine a state in which your DNA and other biometric data is on file and used to determine if you are a health risk and should be fired from your job—and know that the government is already developing a massive biometric database.[19] Imagine that your thoughts and emotions could be recorded and stored in a data file so that your subjective world would be visible to the government. Imagine that the government could remotely control your thoughts and emotions, and reprogram you if deemed necessary. Chillingly, Defense Advanced Research Projects Agency (DARPA) is currently experimenting with and attempting to develop such technologies.[20]

The next generation of Internet is slated to be an "Internet of Things" in which objects are chipped and tracked online. In subsequent generations of Internet we may look forward to an "Internet of People," whereby people are chipped and tracked online for the sake of "national security"—with the companies doing the tracking on the government payroll. This is already beginning to happen, with a growing trend toward placing computer chips into human beings in order to track them.[21]

Think about the endgame. Total information awareness and control, taken to its logical conclusion, would divest us of our individuality and our humanity, turning us into mere things, manipulated and used, leading to devastation potentially worse than a nuclear holocaust: the enslavement of the human mind itself, the utter demise of the human spirit.

Ironically, those who defend the government's information warfare—its intrusions into our private sphere of knowledge, and its attempt to control public knowledge—generally do so on the grounds of saving freedom. Beware these patriotic protractors of freedom, for they are supporting the end of freedom.

POPULAR RESISTANCE TO INFORMATION WARFARE

How can we fight back?

In addition to supporting the emergence of new, independent media outlets that keep the vital fluids of information circulating through the corpus of the free world, we must insist on privacy protections, to prevent these lifelines from being "tapped." The more information we acquire, the less vulnerable and easy to manipulate we will become. And the greater our range of privacy protections, the less ammunition government will have to use against us.

All Americans, as well as all citizens of the free world, must insist on their privacy. Organizations such as the Electronic Frontier Foundation (EFF), the Electronic Privacy Information Center (EPIC), and the American Civil Liberties Union (ACLU) are already actively attempting to defend the right to privacy through court systems. But these public interest organizations, and others like them, are only as good as the grassroots support they receive. Therefore, we should all be willing to join petitions and class action suits to stop steady government encroachments on our privacy.

At least for now, the Internet remains a magnificent platform for democratic resistance in the war being waged to acquire and control our information. Citizens of the world must use this forum while it lasts to denounce the trends and policies described here. This window of opportunity is diminishing day by day; unless we act now, it may close forever.

We can no longer depend on corporate media to keep us apprised of government activities. The people must emerge as the "Fifth Estate," to keep a watchful eye on our so-called "Fourth Estate," thereby keeping it honest. Accordingly, we must look forward to a worldwide movement and establish a league of citizen journalists who use the Internet to bond, train, and speak truth to power. In authentic democracy, the power to govern in an informed way never leaves the people, and where information is itself under attack by the politico-corporate media establishment, the people must be the purveyors of real news. We must therefore build a strong universal voice, and a public consciousness that speaks unequivocally of the urgency to protect our reservoir of information—both public and private. We must preserve human freedom and the constitutional rights that protect it. Passive acquiescence is not an option.

ELLIOT D. COHEN is a contributor to *Truthout* and *Truthdig*, editor in chief of *The International Journal of Applied Philosophy*, ethics editor for *Free Inquiry* magazine, and blogger for *Psychology Today*. One of his more recent books is *Mass Surveillance and State Control: The Total Information Awareness Project* (Palgrave Macmillan, 2010).

Notes

1. Shane Harris and Tim Naftali, "Tinker, Tailor, Minor, Spy: Why the NSA's Snooping is Unprecedented in Scale and Scope," *Slate*, January 3, 2006, http://www.slate.com/articles/news_and_politics/politics/2006/01/tinker_tailor_miner_spy.html.
2. Elliot D. Cohen, "Web of Deceit: How Internet Freedom Got the Federal Ax, And Why Corporate News Censored the Story," BuzzFlash, July 18, 2005, http://www.buzzflash.com/contributors/05/07/con05238.html.
3. "Key Issues: Comcast v. FCC," *Public Knowledge*, http://www.publicknowledge.org/issues/comcast-v-fcc.
4. Marguerite Reardon, "Verizon CTO Predicts 'Toll Free' Data," CNET, May 8, 2012, http://reviews.cnet.com/8301-12261_7-57430190-10356022/verizon-cto-predicts-toll-free-data.
5. FISA Amendments Act of 2008, HR 6304, 110th Cong. (2008), http://www.opencongress.org/bill/110-h6304/text.
6. White House, "Executive Order, National Defense Resources Preparedness," March 16, 2012, http://www.whitehouse.gov/the-press-office/2012/03/16/executive-order-national-defense-resources-preparedness.
7. Cohen, "Congress May Pass a Bill Similar to China's Internet Censorship, With Corporations in Charge," BuzzFlash, November 22, 2011, http://blog.buzzflash.com/node/13171.
8. T. C. Sottek, "The Cyber Intelligence Sharing and Protection Act: CISPA Explained," *Verge*, April 27, 2012, http://www.theverge.com/2012/4/27/2976718/cyber-intelligence-sharing-and-protection-act-cispa-hr-3523.
9. Cyber Intelligence Sharing and Protection Act of 2011, HR 3523, 112th Cong. (2011), http://www.gpo.gov/fdsys/pkg/BILLS-112hr3523ih/pdf/BILLS-112hr3523ih.pdf.
10. Amendments to HR 3523, 112th Cong. (2012), http://www.rules.house.gov/Media/file/PDF_112_2/Reports/HRPT-112-HR3523HR4628.pdf.
11. Lee Fang, "CISPA (aka SOPA 2.0) Pushed Forward by For-Profit Spying Lobby," *Truthout*, April 16, 2012, http://truth-out.org/news/item/8538-cispa-aka-sopa-20-pushed-forward-by-for-profit-spying-lobby.
12. "SAIC, Inc: Bill Lobbied," *Open Secrets*, http://www.opensecrets.org/lobby/clientbills.php?id=D000000369&year=2012.
13. Fang, "CISPA (aka SOPA 2.0)."
14. FISA Amendments Act of 2008, HR 6304, 110th Cong., § 702 h(1) (2008), http://www.govtrack.us/congress/bills/110/hr6304.

15. Smith-Mundt Modernization Act of 2012, HR 5736, 112th Cong. (2012), http://www.govtrack.us/congress/bills/112/hr5736.
16. Jeff Jarvis, "Revealed: US Spy Operation That Manipulates Social Media," *Guardian*, March 17, 2011, http://www.guardian.co.uk/technology/2011/mar/17/us-spy-operation-social-networks.
17. See, for example, Rachel Coen, "Behind the Pentagon's Propaganda Plan," *FAIR Extra!*, April 2002, http://www.fair.org/extra/0204/osi.html.
18. Mike Elgan, "'Pre-Crime' Comes to the HR Dept.," *Datamation*, September 29, 2010, http://www.datamation.com/entdev/article.php/3905931/Pre-crime-Comes-to-the-HR-Dept.htm.
19. Alissa Bohling, "First, Your Shoes; Next, Your DNA: Elliot Cohen on How Surveillance Is Erasing Freedom and Autonomy, Step by Incremental Step," *Truthout*, January 5, 2011, http://archive.truthout.org/first-your-shoes-next-your-dna-elliot-cohen-how-surveillance-erasing-freedom-and-autonomy-step-incre.
20. Cohen, *Mass Surveillance and State Control: The Total Information Awareness Project* (New York: Palgrave Macmillan, 2010), 142ff.
21. Ibid., 140.

CHAPTER 8

GERM Warfare
How to Reclaim the Education Debate from Corporate Occupation

by Adam Bessie

INTRODUCTION

"Do or Die" in DC

I could hear the exhaustion in Stacey's voice—perhaps she had the flu, one brought on by long hours teaching sixth-grade language arts classes in a "failing" public middle school, which serves a high-poverty, primarily African-American community under the shadow of the White House. Since the start of the fall semester, it's been a sprint for Stacey. On the first day of school, in the first of three classes, she was greeted by a crowd of fifty eleven-year-old children.[1] Many came from the local housing projects, and most of their parents were unemployed—which is consistent with the staggering 20 percent unemployment rate that afflicted the African-American community in Washington DC in 2011.[2] At the time, the nation's capital had a poverty rate of 20 percent, and in the areas where Stacy's students came from, poverty was even more concentrated and sometimes climbs as high as 40 percent.[3]

It's "do or die," Stacey's principal told the staff from day one—a phrase that carries particular gravity given there are about nine murders a month in the DC metro area.[4] In fact, the day we talked, there was a shooting near the school. However, the principal wasn't referring to the violence or poverty Stacey's students are exposed to, but rather a high-stakes standardized test, one that would decide the fate of the school. Six weeks after the start of the semester, Stacey's 150 students needed to be prepared to take a standardized test on basic reading skills, to fill in the right bubbles—or else.

Stacey, in her second year teaching at a school fighting for its life, needed to "hit the ground running," preparing her students for the first of a series of tests that would decide their collective fates. Her school needed to raise its Adequate Yearly Progress (AYP), an "accountability measure" implemented nationally in 2002 by the bipartisan education reform bill No Child Left Behind (NCLB), which holds schools responsible for the test scores of its students.[5] Over the previous few years, Stacey's school had consistently failed to make AYP, and if her school doesn't didn't gain higher standardized test scores by the end of the academic year, it would be shuttered.

As for the teachers, said Stacey, "Either we meet AYP or we find new jobs."

Yet, the first six weeks of the semester felt more like "crowd control" than anything resembling the actual teaching that she had been trained for in her credential program in South Carolina. And even when the crowd was controlled enough for instruction, Stacey neither had the time nor the academic freedom to actually teach. "Constant test prep is the expectation," Stacey told me, her voice weakening, as she described the required "scripted, prepackaged curriculum," consisting of practice tests and "constant skill and drill" handouts to ensure that the school wouldn't close.

"We're just supposed to read passages and answer multiple choice questions," Stacey reported, letting out a deep, frustrated sigh. "As someone who doesn't believe in any of that, work is a constant struggle. I feel like my students are already so trapped, and I feel like I'm trapping them even further when I do what [the administration] tells me is the correct thing to do."

But Stacey learned quickly that if she wanted to keep her job, she needed to play by the rules and teach to the script. "If I do what I know my students will benefit from (language experience, novel studies, word play, inquiry) I risk bad evaluations, and therefore I risk my job and my livelihood," Stacey explained, pointing out that much of her evaluation—and thus her job—is based on her IMPACT rating, which is, in essence, her students' test scores. So even if the school were to survive this fight, Stacey could still be let go should her students not demonstrate "adequate" improvement.[6]

"I'm not treated like a professional at all," she exclaimed, outraged. "I'm not trusted to make decisions about my children, yet I'm held accountable."

THE GLOBAL EDUCATION REFORM MOVEMENT: A THREAT TO OUR EDUCATIONAL COMMONS

Fighting for her professional life while fighting to save her students from poverty and violence, Stacey is left utterly exhausted and utterly demoralized—a trend reflected in the lowest teacher morale in the last twenty years.[7] Like many public school teachers who have committed themselves to helping children learn in America's poorest neighborhoods, Stacey is on the front lines of a battle—not just for her students, her job, or her school. Stacey is fighting for the very future of high-quality, open-access, equitable national public education against the powerful forces of GERM—the Global Education Reform Movement.

GERM has invaded her school, the nation, and many other Western nations. GERM—a term coined by Finnish educator Pasi Sahlberg, and more popularly known as "education reform"—models public education on corporate philosophies and practices, handing over public institutions to corporate-style management, and ultimately, corporations themselves.[8] Once a philosophy only discussed in elite neoconservative think tanks and by Republican politicians, GERM policies have been adopted by Democratic leaders and injected into the mainstream American consciousness not merely by an uncritical corporate media, but at times a complicit one. GERM poses a terminal threat to public education; it takes our educational commons and hands the system over to corporate America.[9]

While GERM is a particularly virulent and powerful strain of corporate infection in our American democracy, there is a movement fighting to keep public education alive and thriving. This truly grassroots movement—of educators, parents, community activists, and students themselves—is fighting to challenge GERM, and starting to win battles on a local and national level. To reclaim our public schools from corporate occupation, though, this grassroots movement must

reclaim the conversation, challenge the GERM narrative, and give Stacey and her students their voices back.

This is no test: it's "do or die."

EXPOSING THE GERM EPIDEMIC: THE CIVIL RIGHTS ISSUE OF OUR GENERATION

"Education is the civil rights issue of our generation," Republican presidential candidate and former Massachusetts governor Mitt Romney announced at a recent press conference, where he also claimed that our public schools are in a state of "national emergency." In the speech, the former Bain Capital chief executive officer Romney portrayed himself a civil rights hero, fighting against systemic racism and inequality that provides American children a "third world education."[10] And the cause of this educational emergency? It's not the foreclosure crisis, deep unemployment in minority communities, the increasing racially segregated schools, nor the 21 percent childhood poverty rate, which Romney, who made twenty-seven million dollars in 2010, never mentions.[11] Rather, this grave civil rights injustice has been inflicted by excessively powerful "special interests" and "union bosses" that put their needs in front of the poor, minority children. And Romney plans to be the 1 percent's very own Martin Luther King Jr., a "champion of real education reform in America," saving the underprivileged from the greed of the powerful.

Romney's speech on education—with the superrich as champions of social justice, and teachers like Stacey protecting a status quo of racism and poverty—would be hilarious . . . that is, if anyone seemed to get the joke. The Global Education Reform Movement fable that Romney tells—of Broken Schools held hostage by Bad Teachers and Evil Unions, only to be saved by the heroics of the Free Market—is cliché not only for conservative politicians, but is also championed by Democrats, most prominently, President Barack Obama. And today, GERM—once an extreme conservative economic theory—is the only education reform philosophy discussed in the halls of political power. How did this happen?

THE GENESIS OF GERM

While GERM has only gone viral in the last decade, it was designed nearly fifty years ago, by the "grandmaster of free-market economic theory," Milton Friedman.[12] Friedman, a Nobel Prize–winning economist, was the architect of the "small government" ethos that now dominates the Republican Party—in fact, he is said to have inspired former president Ronald Reagan's free-market economic philosophy, which involves cutting taxes and government regulation, and selling public industry to the private sector.[13] Hailed as a hero by economic conservatives, prominent progressives believe that the former Reagan advisor's policies have been central in creating the increasingly stratified and privatized economy, dominated by an oligarchic class—the wealthiest 1 percent. Naomi Klein authored the best-selling book *The Shock Doctrine*, devoted to the corrosive influence of Friedman's "free market" philosophy, which she argues dominates the world and exploits disaster to enrich the wealthy.[14] Further, after the economic disaster of 2008, Jeff Madrick, director of policy research at the Center for Economic Policy Analysis, concluded "There is a direct line from Milton Friedman's ascendancy in the 1970s to the debacle on Wall Street today."[15] Wall Street's disaster has also consumed the nation's public schools, whose budgets continue to be eaten away in the name of "responsible belt-tightening" of public services.

Whatever one thinks about the success of Friedman's economic philosophy, GERM clearly shares its "free-market" DNA. Friedman is considered the "Father of Modern School Reform,"[16] and articulated GERM's pro-corporate philosophy, policies, and even phrasing in his seminal 1955 essay "The Role of Government in Education," and later in his 1962 deregulation manifesto, *Capitalism and Freedom*—the same book in which he explained his economic theories most vividly. Friedman calls for the privatization of public education, and the creation of a "competitive education market." In doing so, he radically reconceived the nature of public education, reframing it as a service industry, rather than public service. He claimed that private, profit-based enterprise would provide better education than the government. Thus, Friedman argued the government should have a very limited role in education—by providing funding, and applying some regulation—and beyond that, there should be competition between schools for students and their parents, whom he referred to as "consumers." Friedman thought that if schools and teachers were subjected to such competition, "the development and improvement of all schools would thus be stimulated." To this end, he invented the "voucher," funding from the government that "education consumers" used to choose their schools from a variety of "service providers."[17] He also then advocated for "merit pay," for paying teachers based not on their years of service or education attained, but on their "performance."[18] According to Friedman, these corporate measures would, in turn, make schools more "efficient" and "productive," which would increase the quality of the "educational service."

Today, "education reform" is a friendly, benign-sounding euphemism for privatizing public education while reconceiving it as a competitive market following Friedman's theories. A disciple of Friedman, American Enterprise Institute (AEI) resident scholar Frederick Hess elaborated by stating explicitly that the current education reform movement is a "serious deregulatory project . . . to establish a genuine marketplace in education," not unlike the telecommunications, energy, or airline industries.[19] What Hess meant is that public education is a service like any other—like a phone company, an energy provider, or an airline—and that it should be "reformed" to act more like these service providers, so that "consumers" have a "choice." According to Hess, there should be "incentives and consequences for producers and consumers," so that schools behave more like your cell phone provider. "To get schools to respond more meaningfully to competitive pressure, incentives and rules must be changed in order to ensure that the competitive pressure is actually felt," Hess concluded. To translate, successful schools—like successful businesses—should be rewarded, while "failing schools," those that can't produce a competitive educational service, should be punished, not unlike Stacey's school discussed at the outset of this chapter.

But Friedman's greatest influence on GERM isn't his theories. Rather, it is the way in which he has successfully *framed* schools as businesses. Friedman did not just propose a set of education policies. He proposed a fundamentally different way of thinking about and discussing education. His use of industrial and corporate language— "efficiency," "productivity," and "consumer"—encourages the reader to imagine schools in terms of the private sector, of corporations, or "factories," as the University of California–Berkeley cognitive linguist George Lakoff observed. A business has a primary goal of pleasing the consumer, keeping costs low, raking in revenue, and ultimately making money. A business's primary goal is not to enrich the public good, but rather the private entity itself. However, as Lakoff argued, "Education is about more than making money. It is about coming to know the world, about learning to think critically, and about developing the capacity to create new knowledge, new social institutions, and new kinds of businesses."[20] Of course, education serves a critical economic function, but it is also serves to enrich culture, our morals, our quality of life, and our democracy—and to view education as a business, as a private service rather than a public good, is to strip it of these critical values.

Therein is the most potent symptom of Friedman's education philosophy: in framing education as a business, GERM reduces the incredibly complex, rich, vibrant, and human process of education into a mechanized production line, with goals of "efficiency" and "productivity" replacing learning, growth, creativity, community, and democracy. It is a pedagogy of Taylorism on a twentieth-century assembly line.[21]

A BIPARTISAN ILLNESS

After decades in the laboratory, Friedman's theories were released nationwide under No Child Left Behind (NCLB), establishing GERM as federal law. While it did not go nearly as far as Friedman or Hess would have liked (enacting vouchers), NCLB did accept their metaphor—that schools are businesses, and public education would serve students better if modeled as such. Even the name—No Child Left Behind—frames education as a competition, one with winners, and losers. NCLB made this metaphor a reality, providing real consequences for schools that could not "keep up" on standardized test scores, providing escalating corporate-style punitive measures for schools like Stacey's that do not meet Adequate Yearly Progress. NCLB assumes that real learning can be measured by multiple-choice standardized tests, and that these standardized tests reflect the performance of the school, but not the effects of society, community, or family—like socioeconomics, or access to health care—though there is overwhelming evidence that test scores are most strongly correlated with these out-of-school influences.[22]

Once a school is declared "failing," it is subject to corporate takeover, much like Romney would have taken over a "failing business" and imposed new management while at Bain. Because NCLB views schools as businesses, then "failure" rests solely on the shoulders of the employees—the teachers and the principal. The remedy, therefore, is in providing appropriate incentives and consequences ("carrots and sticks") to improve the "performance" of the school; the threat of school closure is such a consequence, which motivates the staff to focus exclusively on the test, as are mass firings. By focusing relentlessly on the test, the teachers no longer have control over how to teach, as they must focus on the content to be tested as a matter of career survival. In some cases, school districts actually buy "commercially packaged reading instruction programs, which tell teachers exactly which page to be on each day as well as every word and line they are allowed to say while teaching reading, all in preparation for the high-stakes testing," as former public school teacher and education professor Wayne Au reported.[23] The teachers—and students—must submit to the corporate testing regimen, in order to once again be considered on the "right path," away from "failure," and toward "success." The "winners" in this Race to the Top are determined then by corporate testing standards and outcomes, not honed critical thinking skills, creativity, expressive ability, empathy, nor increased cognitive development. Ultimately, NCLB is a race toward standardization and conformity—for schools, teachers, and children themselves.

If the school still does not meet AYP after conforming to the corporate testing regimen and being stripped of its academic freedom, it can be "turned around," a business euphemism for mass layoffs and new management. In the "turnaround model," the principal and no less than half of the staff is fired and replaced—often by nonprofit or for-profit corporations who specialize in this process. The school also can be "restarted," with all staff fired and replaced, "converted" into a nonprofit or for-profit charter school (which are not unionized), or closed, with the students moved to other higher performing schools, including charters.[24] In this fashion, schools in the poorest neighborhoods not only begin to look like businesses, but are actually handed over to private enterprise which receive public funding, thus fulfilling Friedman's philosophy that government should manage schooling as minimally as possible.

Though President Barack Obama has publicly distanced himself from NCLB, his signature program, Race to the Top (RttT) spreads Friedman's GERM even further. Much like NCLB, RttT adopts the metaphor that education is a competition—a race—and enacts policies that treat it as such, to make schools and teachers feel the "competitive pressure" that Hess describes. Though Obama claimed in the 2012 State of the Union that we should "stop teaching to the test," RttT still relies on these tests to identify "failing schools," which are subject to punitive measures and corporate takeover.[25] Obama promises to "turn around" the 5,000 lowest scoring schools, using GERM style corporate interventions. Further, RttT created a four-billion-dollar contest for grants for which states (and soon, districts) can "compete," though the state has to submit to tying standardized test scores not just to schools, but to teacher and principal evaluations, not unlike the IMPACT program that evaluates Stacey in Washington DC.[26] And to receive federal dollars, cash-strapped states and districts, must also open their doors to charter schools, which draw public funds, but can be run by private enterprise. And what's more, RttT looks to reach out more explicitly to private enterprise. Obama's Secretary of Education Arne Duncan has called on "education entrepreneurs" to help "reform America's lowest performing public schools."[27] By "reform," Duncan is referring to Friedman and Hess's definition—of transforming public education into a business, with business leaders, and not educators, leading the charge.

Ultimately, the Obama administration didn't laugh as multimillionaire businessman Mitt Romney framed himself as a civil rights hero, because they have done the same. In fact, Obama and Duncan used the exact same catchphrase—"Education is the civil rights issue of our generation"—to promote RttT. In 2009, Obama, Duncan, and Rev. Al Sharpton met with Republican stalwart Newt Gingrich to declare "Education is the civil rights issue of our generation," and that they "put aside their differences" to "reform" education. At the event, Gingrich—who wrote a book in 2011 titled *To Save America: Stopping Obama's Secular-Socialist Machine*—put aside his fear of Obama's impending socialist revolution to commend him for supporting corporate education policies, such as merit pay, and charter schools. Not surprisingly, George W. Bush is credited as the "architect of this school of thought," as he used the exact same phrase in 2002, the day before Martin Luther King Jr.'s birthday, in support of his recently enacted bill, NCLB. This led education writer Liz Dwyer to conclude "Let's Stop Comparing Education to the Civil Rights Movement."[28]

However, the real architect of GERM is Milton Friedman, who predicted that Democrats would come around to his perspective and see that the path to social justice is through the privatization of education. "The Democratic Party should be the natural supporter of vouchers," Friedman told libertarian magazine *Reason* in 2005, less than a year before his death. "In Ted Kennedy's words, the Democrats are supposed to be the 'voice of the voiceless.' The voiceless would benefit the most from full-scale universal vouchers. You know, if you ask the voiceless, they are all in favor of vouchers. So I think, sooner or later, the nearly religious support for the anti-voucher position will crumble."[29] And while RttT does not support vouchers (as Romney does),

Friedman's prediction has been borne out, as Obama and the Democratic Party are now the foremost carriers of Friedman's GERM.

TRANSMITTING GERM: THE GLOBAL EDUCATION REFORM MOVEMENT GOES VIRAL

The Corporate Media's Bully Pulpit

We're going to take on teachers next, we're going to go after teachers . . .

—Andrew Breitbart, Fox News[30]

In the days following Mitt Romney's education speech, the phrase "failing schools" appeared in nearly 5,000 news articles according to a search on Google News. Before 2008, the loaded term—which suggests schools, and not society, are to blame for educational problems—had very little traffic on Google.[31] Veteran reporter Paul Fahri, in his own search on LexisNexis in January 2012, found 544 news stories in that month; in contrast, in January of 1992, it appeared thirteen times. As a result of his extensive evaluation of education coverage, Fahri found that "the prevailing narrative is that the nation's educational system is in crisis, that schools are 'failing,' that teachers aren't up to the job and that America's economic competitiveness is threatened as a result." Further, he concluded that this narrative was not accurate: "If anything, America has been a largely successful experiment in universal, open access public education . . . by many important measures—high school completion rates, college graduation, overall performance on standardized tests—America's educational attainment has never been higher."[32]

But one is very unlikely to read about the successes of public education in the corporate media, which has spread the GERM narrative uncritically to the public. The Failing School, the Bad Teacher, and the Evil Union are the main characters in the GERM narrative, which has evolved into a powerful meme—or viral idea—so widely spread that it has become the commonplace way in which education is debated. Indeed, reporters have adopted this narrative, and its loaded terms like "failing schools," and "bad teachers" without rigorous investigation.[33]

Thus, Breitbart's mission—to "go after the teachers"—has been fulfilled by the corporate media, even after he passed away in early 2012.

CNN host Fareed Zakaria—considered a "liberal journalist" by Breitbart TV[34]—is a prime example of how this misleading narrative reveals what's "wrong with mainstream media coverage of education," according to Fahri. In a series of specials and an article in *Time*, Zakaria claimed that the poor quality of our nation's schools have put the American Dream at risk, especially for minorities and the underprivileged, much like Romney's claims. Zakaria lists a litany of facts—including dismal graduation rates, and low test scores—that show that our education is in a state of crisis, and further, we are being "outsmarted" by other nations and the world. Zakaria interviewed former IBM CEO Louis Gerstner, who pinned the blame on the teachers: "We need far better teachers . . . we have too many teachers that are not strong enough today." In all coverage, Zakaria has neither challenged nor questioned this sweeping generalization.[35]

In fact, Zakaria didn't challenge Gerstner because he agrees with him, that teachers have destroyed our schools, and are threating our economy. In the course of another of Zakaria's reports devoted to "Fixing Education," teachers bear the brunt of the blame for this crisis. The word "teacher" is mentioned forty-seven times, and "poverty" five times over the course of the episode.[36] When discussing Finland, whose students score at the top of the world in standardized tests, he observed that 4 percent of children live in poverty—compared to over 20 percent in the United States. Rather than discuss what socioeconomic conditions have lead to one in five children living in poverty—and how this might affect their education—Zakaria focused on teachers: "Can an education system overcome poverty? And can the US create an army of great teachers like in Finland?" Through these juxtaposed questions, Zakaria implied that teachers bear the brunt of responsibility for "overcoming poverty"—and what's more, that our teachers aren't up to the job. Zakaria concluded, "Part of the reason we're in this crisis is that we have slacked off and allowed our education system to get rigid and sclerotic." In other words, the schools, the teachers, and their "rigid" unions have failed due to lack of motivation—not society at large. As a result, our slacker schools—and not society—need to be reformed. By framing the issue in this fashion,

Zakaria is essentially promoting the GERM narrative, rather than questioning, challenging, or exploring it like a leading, influential journalist that is part of a major news organization should.

Taking Zakaria and Breitbart's lead, the corporate media has made a crusade of rooting out and exposing real-life "bad teachers," employing a statistical model taken from the business world. In both New York and Los Angeles, teachers "rankings" were released to the press, based on a "value-added" analysis of their students' standardized test scores, setting off teacher bashing headlines like *Business Insider*'s "These Are the Worst Teachers in New York City."[37] While the idea of ranking teachers makes for dramatic headlines, the reliability of the value-added system is still under intense debate. The National Research Council, for one, argued that "valued added . . . should not be used to make operational decisions because such estimates are far too unstable to be considered fair or reliable."[38] This debate, which is still unsettled in the academic world, has been either downplayed or ignored by the corporate media, swept up in the search to publicly flog these "bad teachers," as a sort of public service. Further, by ranking educators numerically, based on the standardized tests scores of their students, these corporate outlets reveal an astonishingly narrow definition of learning, and teaching—that education is a process that can be quantified, like the manufacture of no. 2 pencils.[39]

In 2010, after the *Los Angeles Times* released the rankings of LA public school teachers, fifth-grade teacher Rigberto Ruelas was publicly shamed from such a teacher witch hunt. Rigberto—who taught in a tough, impoverished city area like Stacey in DC—had "near perfect attendance for 14 years on the job," and "reached out to the toughest kids . . . tutor[ing] them on weekends and after school, visit[ing] their homes, encourag[ing] them to aim high and go to college." One such student, Andromeda Palma, a thirteen-year-old eighth grader, cried as she shared her memories of his impact: "He told me it is not about where you are from. . . . Now I am doing real good because of him." Still, he was rated "less effective" than his peers based on his "value-added score," and went missing shortly thereafter, then was found dead. Rigberto had committed suicide, and had left no note, but did leave behind considerable anger about how such a committed, passionate public servant could be publicly maligned, his work fourteen years of service reduced to a single number based on a standardized test.[40]

While public education has been maligned—even dubbed a "dragon" in the media—since at least the mid-1800s, the GERM attacks today are more vitriolic and personal, focused on individual teachers rather than just the system as a whole. "This historical badgering of schools has evolved recently into a more direct and personal attack on teachers," associate professor of education Paul Thomas observes, describing the treatment of teachers like Rigberto—by Breitbart, by the media, and by GERM policies like NCLB—as "bullying."[41] Rather than exploring the incredibly complex issue of education with comprehensive investigations into the efficacy and consequences of GERM policies, the corporate media transmits GERM to the public unfiltered, demonizing public education, while scapegoating public school teachers for America's socioeconomic ills.

GRASSROOTS GERM: STUDENTS FIRST, TEACHERS LAST

A bad usage can spread by tradition and imitation even among people who should and do know better.

—George Orwell, "Politics and the English Language"[42]

No wonder Stacey seemed exhausted when I talked to her on the phone in February of this year: not only was the pressure for her students to pass the standardized test in April reaching a fever pitch, but everywhere she looked, she saw that her school was "failing" because of her. Indeed, she was doing such a bad job that she put the entire American Dream—and economy—at risk, at least according to CNN's Zakaria. What's more, she feared that her IMPACT value-added score could be released to the public, where she could be embarrassed like Rigberto. Playing the scapegoat for a frightened and angry nation can be a tiring affair.

However, it appeared that the tide might be turning against the unremitting teacher bashing, as a viral e-mail honoring "great teachers" found its way into my college e-mail inbox. The contest asked entrants to write a "six-word essay" to describe what it means to be a "great teacher," as a means to honor hard-working, underappreciated, and much maligned educators like Rigberto and Stacey. And the entries read like liberal bumper stickers: "Encouraging the discouraged to defy obstacles," "Transforms barred windows into open doors," "Destroy chains. Shape wings. Inspire flight," "Open books, open minds, open doors." The contest felt like just the sort of corny self-esteem boost besieged teachers needed, an oasis of applause and liberal clichés to make up for an exhaustion borne of dried-up budgets and a year of scorching criticism.[43]

Upon a cursory inspection, the contest seemed to check out as an authentic pro-teacher event; it was authored by StudentsFirst, a progressive-sounding group that seemed a perfect antidote to GERM's corporate, privatizing assault on public education and teachers. StudentsFirst dubbed itself "a grassroots movement to reform America's public education and keep our best teachers in the classroom." The StudentsFirst website employed progressive-sounding language, claiming that the organization wanted to "empower" and work toward "social justice," arguing in its mission statement that "every child, regardless of their zip code, deserves to attend a great school; all families should have quality school options available." To add to the progressive credentials, the founder of the organization was a teacher, and called herself a "life-long Democrat," while the vice president of communications was a senior spokesperson on the Obama-Biden 2008 campaign, and also "a former teacher and union member," who knows "that when we treat teachers like the professionals they are, our students come out on top."[44]

StudentsFirst is actively involved in changing state and federal policy to ensure we have "great teachers." The organization authored the petition "Pay Effective Teachers What They Deserve" at Change.org, a popular website that allows anyone to start a "grassroots" campaign in three easy, hassle-free steps. "America's most qualified teachers are grossly underpaid. Those [teachers] who show they can move kids along academically should be compensated accordingly," read the petition, which was sandwiched between countless other petitions for progressive causes on Change.org—to reinstate a Boy Scout leader who was fired for being gay, to maintain a plastic bottle ban in the Grand Canyon, or to stop the needless slaughter of goats by the Department of Defense. In short, it looks like StudentsFirst has the progressive credentials and power to fight on behalf of teachers.[45]

Yet, StudentsFirst is anything but a grassroots movement committed to teachers. Rather, StudentsFirst is highly sophisticated Astroturf—or a movement intended to look populist, like a real, organic uprising of the public, when in fact it is funded by the elite, and forwards their agenda.[46] The lobbying group was founded by Michelle Rhee, the former Washington DC superintendent who was a major force in creating the IMPACT rating—a "value-added" analysis—that evaluates Stacey. Rhee, who taught for only three years—and never at a public school—became a celebrity for her attacks on the Bad Teacher. Most notably, she was featured on a *Time* cover holding a broom, signifying her policy sweeping "bad teachers" out of the classroom—which is what she did in DC. "I'm going to fire somebody in a little while," Rhee said to John Merrow's crew while shooting a segment for PBS *NewsHour* called the "The Influence of Teachers," inviting them to televise the teacher's career execution. "Do you want to see that?"[47] Rhee became famous for this cutthroat, autocratic managerial style, referring to herself as the "decider" (much like former president George W. Bush); as a result, she was widely applauded by education outsiders, business leaders in particular, as standardized test scores raised during this time. There are now three separate investigations into whether these raised scores are the result of cheating, due to exceptional statistical irregularities found in the test,[48] calling into question her extensive GERM reforms including "merit pay." Further, seventy-five teachers that were fired en masse in 2008 during Rhee's tenure were reinstated, as they were denied due process, not told why they were being fired, nor provided an opportunity to provide "their side of the story."[49]

For her efforts, though, Rhee—and StudentsFirst—earned applause from Breitbart's *Big Government* blog: "StudentsFirst is making headway in the education reform movement, and should be commended by students and taxpayers for their hard work."[50]

Rhee has become the face of GERM through StudentsFirst, and she hopes to replicate her DC work nationwide. StudentsFirst works against teacher tenure, teacher's unions, and collective bargaining, while it works for merit pay, increasing charter schools, and access to vouchers—in short, all of the key elements that Friedman envisioned that became the GERM. Rhee also has powerful friends from the corporate world. Though she keeps her donors somewhat hidden, "public records indicate that they include billionaire financiers and wealthy foundations," according to a report by Reuters. The organization has received millions from Wal-Mart heirs, the neoconservative Broad Foundation, and hedge fund managers that have donated "substantially" to a Political Action Committee supporting Mitt Romney, while still more have yet to be identified.[51] In her first year at StudentsFirst, Rhee acted as a political advisor to three Republican Governors—including Governor Scott Walker, who effectively stopped collective bargaining in the state of Wisconsin, resulting in the much-televised "Wisconsin Uprising," and a subsequent recall effort.[52] Rhee, the "life-long Democrat," will be speaking with former President George W. Bush at a for-profit college conference summer of 2012.[53] While she speaks with Bush and works on behalf of Republican governors, she was also invited to the White House by President Obama, and gave a speech with his Secretary of Education Arne Duncan.[54]

Yet, Rhee—who makes up to $50,000 a speech[55]—claims Students-First is a "grassroots" movement, as real people are making real donations to the cause. These individual members, she claims, have made a million dollars in small donations,[56] suggesting that there is an real populist movement supporting these GERM policies—even if the policies are also supported by hedge fund managers who have never been to a public school, nor will send their children to one. A professor at a New York University, Ric Brown, wonders how many of the signers actually know what StudentsFirst stands for, as they have gone to great lengths to cloak their message in progressive-sounding language and vague euphemisms. When he received the petition in his inbox, he quickly signed it, thinking it was supporting higher pay for teachers—he didn't realize, until closer inspection, that the petition was in support of "merit pay." "It was very deceptive," Brown concluded. "It would be very easy to collect a lot of members this way."[57] And indeed, they have—as StudentsFirst boasts that it is "one million members strong," and nearly 500,000 have signed their petition to "Pay Effective Teachers What They Deserve," in favor of GERM policies, fulfilling Breitbart's mission.[58]

MINORITY REPORT: HIJACKING CIVIL RIGHTS TO SPREAD GERM

Before Rhee and her multimillionaire supporters, before Obama and Bush, GERM existed in Milton Friedman's laboratory for decades, but had difficulty getting outside the walls of academia and into real schools—largely because the public did not share the conservative enthusiasm for privatizing education. "In roughly two dozen referenda across the country over the past few decades, voucher advocates have yet to record a single win," observed Frederick Hess.[59] In short, people weren't voting for Friedman's signature reform—vouchers. Conservative think tanks recognized they had a marketing problem; that they were not selling vouchers and they were not selling GERM effectively to the public. A new strategy needed to be developed: how could the reformers get the public to buy GERM?

In the late 1990s, Diane Ravitch, a distinguished professor of education history (and now reformed education "reformer" who eventually blew the whistle on the corporate takeover of public education in her best-selling book *The Death and Life of the Great American School System*) worked at the Manhattan Institute, a New York–based conservative think tank that was trying to solve this critical question. GERM advocates realized that their policies needed to be *reframed*, presented in a way that would appeal to the public. Vouchers didn't have popular support, so conservative think tanks decided to throw their weight behind charter schools, "because they achieved almost the same result as vouchers—a transfer of government dollars from government to private control." But exchanging vouchers for charters, by itself, wasn't enough. Charters were not popularly known, nor could the public personally relate to the Manhattan Institute's sterile economic theories and language that informed their corporate philosophies. Therein, a new strategy was born—co-opting progressive language to sell privatized education policies to the public.

"There was explicit discussion about the importance of presenting the charter idea as a way to save poor minority children. In a city and state that was consistently liberal, that was a smart strategy," Ravitch recalled in an e-mail to the author.[60] Hess noticed these strategies were being used throughout the country, and observed that "the case for school choice was thus not argued in terms of efficiency or deregulation, but instead presented as a moral imperative—an obligation to give poor, black inner-city parents the kinds of educational choices taken for granted by suburban home owners."[61] Indeed, the heart-wrenching propaganda documentary *Waiting for Superman*—which features Rhee—relies on this "social justice" narrative, while selling the audience on charters, and railing against unions. Today, co-opting liberal language, values, and morals—appealing to "social justice," "civil rights," and "equality"—has become standard in selling GERM, from Romney to Rhee. This marketing strategy has worked, as we see in Rhee's extensive mailing list, and in the fact that prominent "liberals" like Zakaria support it. Ravitch, herself a lifelong "liberal" who became such a reformer, lured in by similar promises, concluded: "In retrospect, it seems strange that so many liberals bought an idea that emanated from conservative think tanks and conservative thinkers."[62]

BUILDING A RESISTANCE TO GERM: RECOGNIZE, RESIST, REFRAME, AND RECLAIM

American education has a long history of infatuation with fads and ill-considered ideas. The current obsession with making our schools work like a business may be the worst of them, for it threatens to destroy public education. Who will stand up to the tycoons and politicians and tell them so?

—Diane Ravitch, *The Death and Life of the Great American School System*[63]

A central front in the battle for GERM is not in the schools, but in the public's mind. The "tycoons and politicians" to which Ravitch referred have taken this lesson to heart, and invest not just in policy, but in an extensive propaganda campaign to convince the public that our schools are failing, and that the free market is the only solution. Rather than expose these efforts, rather than investigate the GERM narrative and hold reformers accountable for their claims, the corporate media has been swept up in spreading it. And as a result, grassroots supporters of public education are losing this battle, as corporate reformers essentially control the conversation on education, from the White House to the television in your living room.

Yet, there is hope.

All these efforts to hide GERM from the public suggest that the grassroots activists have far more power than they may even recognize. Why must StudentsFirst go to such great lengths to hide who funds them? Why must they hide their policy agenda under misleading euphemisms? And why, overall, must the corporate reformers invest so much energy—and money—into misdirection? Because, ultimately, corporate reformers know that if the public could actually see the true intent and nature of policies, if they could look past the slick marketing, then Friedman's GERM would shrivel back into obscurity. If grassroots defenders of public education could recognize GERM, if they could resist its misleading narrative and pose a new frame—a new way of discussing and thinking about education—they can begin to reclaim the conversation from corporate occupation and actually improve public education, from the ground up.

CONCLUSION: A REAL GRASSROOTS MOVEMENT TO RE-CLAIM PUBLIC EDUCATION

We need to improve our public education system—of this there is no doubt. But it is not "failing schools," nor "bad teachers," nor their "self-interested unions" that harm our schools, but rather the Global Education Reform Movement—and Friedman's destructive economic philosophy from which it was born. The corporate education policies of NCLB and RttT place faith in business people and billionaires to educate our children, rather than in educators who work with the children themselves. By transferring public education to private management, our schools have become more unaccountable and less responsive to the individual needs of children, their parents, and the community at large, and more responsive to the needs of the company, the shareholder, the market—the need to make a profit. Ultimately, GERM narrows education in classrooms across America from a journey of discovery and into process of indoctrination: in doing so, GERM diminishes the essential joy and passion of learning from teachers and children, squelching the curiosity, creativity, critical thinking, and humanity needed for the twenty-first-century economy, democracy, and community.

GERM is not improving our schools but destroying them—as are the devastating austerity measures that target our poorest schools and our most vulnerable children, increasing class sizes while decreasing services inside of the schools. Outside of school, our poorest children face the same cuts, as the same austerity measures cut social services and other public services—such as police and fire—making their communities more difficult and dangerous places to live. As a result of the foreclosure crisis and persistent unemployment, more and more of our children live in poverty, with jobless parents, in jobless communities, forgotten by the "free market," as a result of economic policies that enrich the wealthy at the expense of the poor.

Stacey is right—it is not she who should be held accountable for her students' struggle. Stacey did not create the poverty her children live in; she did not destroy the economy her children's parents struggle in; she did not staff her class with fifty students; she did not even design the limited curriculum that she is required to teach.

This is the story grassroots defenders of public education tell: it is not teachers like Stacey who have failed; it is the politicians and tycoons of GERM who have failed our children. An answer will not come from these distant technocratic elite, but rather from children, educators, parents, and the communities working collaboratively to develop schools that enrich, rather than impoverish, our children, and our society at large.

We can reclaim our schools, and our fair share of the educational commons, Stacey concludes, "if more teachers would not allow themselves to be silenced anymore, if we speak up, if we write, if we present what we know to be true—loudly."

ADAM BESSIE is an assistant professor of English at Diablo Valley College, a community college in the San Francisco Bay Area. He has been a full-time public school educator, teaching courses on writing, reading, and literature, for the last decade, teaching also in high school and four-year colleges. Adam has contributed to the Project Censored series for the last two years, and has published essays on the *Daily Censored* blog, Common Dreams, the *Washington Post's* "Answer Sheet," *Truthout*, and many other sources. Most recently, Adam coauthored with Dan Archer the first work of graphic journalism on education reform: "The Disaster Capitalism Curriculum: The High Price of Education Reform," in which you can see many of the issues discussed here illustrated, online at *Truthout*.

Special Thanks: I had many discussions with scholars, activists, and journalists that helped in shaping this chapter, especially veteran Oakland educator and *Education Week* writer Anthony Cody, New York University education professor Diane Ravitch, University of California–Berkeley cognitive linguistics professor George Lakoff, *Dissent* magazine editor Joanne Barkan, and graphic journalist Dan Archer. A special thanks goes to "Stacey," who had the courage to speak up—and to do so eloquently. Also special thanks to my editor and friend Mickey Huff, for encouraging me to write the chapter, and for helping to polish it. Most of all, though, a very special thanks to my wife, Corin, a public high school social studies teacher, whose insights and editing help were invaluable. This chapter is dedicated to our son, Sol, born during its writing, who is my inspiration.

Notes

1. "Stacy" is a pseudonym for a real Washington DC–based teacher who wished to remain anonymous, out of fear for reprisals on her career. We communicated through a series of e-mails from February 19, 2012, through June 1, 2012. We also spoke February 29, 2012. You can see her story illustrated by Dan Archer and Adam Bessie, "The Disaster Capitalism Curriculum: The High Price of Education Reform (Episode I)," *Truthout*, May 31, 2012, http://truth-out.org/art/item/9391-the-disaster-capitalism-curriculum-the-high-price-of-education-reform-episode-i.
2. Algernon Austin, "No Relief in 2012 from High Unemployment for African Americans and Latinos," Economic Policy Institute Issue Brief #332, February 16, 2012, http://www.epi.org/publication/ib322-african-american-latino-unemployment.

3. Alemayehu Bishaw, "Areas With Concentrated Poverty: 2006–2010," United States Census Bureau, December 2011, http://www.census.gov/prod/2011pubs/acsbr10-17.pdf.

4. District of Columbia Metropolitan Police Department, "District Crime Data at a Glance," last updated June 1, 2012, http://mpdc.dc.gov/mpdc/cwp/view,a,1239,q,561242,mpdcNav_GID,1523,mpdcNav,%7C.asp.

5. For an easy-to-read overview of No Child Left Behind, see "No Child Left Behind," *Education Week*, last updated September 19, 2011, http://www.edweek.org/ew/issues/no-child-left-behind/. For an official summary of NCLB see Rod Paige, "Key Policy Letters Signed by the Education Secretary or Deputy Secretary," United States Department of Education, July 24, 2002, http://www2.ed.gov/policy/elsec/guid/secletter/020724.html.

6. "An Overview of IMPACT," District of Columbia Public Schools, http://www.dc.gov/DCPS/In+the+Classroom/Ensuring+Teacher+Success/IMPACT+(Performance+Assessment)/An+Overview+of+IMPACT#0.

7. Mary Ann Giordano, "Teachers' Morale Reaches 20-Year Low," *New York Times' SchoolBook*, March 8, 2012, http://www.nytimes.com/schoolbook/2012/03/08/teachers-morale-reaches-20-year-low. You can see the original series of surveys—started in 1984—on which Giordano's commentary is based in "MetLife Survey of the American Teacher," *MetLife*, http://www.metlife.com/about/corporate-profile/citizenship/metlife-foundation/metlife-survey-of-the-american-teacher.html?WT.mc_id=vu1101.

8. Pasi Sahlberg, "Global Educational Reform Movement is Here!" *Pasi Sahlberg Blog*, April 2, 2012, http://www.pasisahlberg.com/blog/?p=68. See also Pasi Sahlberg, *Finnish Lessons: What Can the World Learn from Educational Change in Finland?* (New York: Teachers College Press, 2011).

9. The theme of education and the commons, along with how corporate media owners overlapping with many involved in the so-called "education reform" movement was expanded upon in Oakland CA, January 22, 2012, at an all-day conference titled, "The Attack on Public Education and Privatization," where the author of this chapter spoke with Project Censored director Mickey Huff, Steve Zeltzer, Dr. Gray Brechin, Kathleen Carroll, Jack Gerson, and professors George Wright and Peter Matthews. See http://occupyeducationca.org/wordpress/?p=217 for more details.

10. Corey Dade, "Romney Pivots to Education Platform Seeking Latino Votes," *NPR Blogs*, May 23, 2012, http://www.npr.org/blogs/itsallpolitics/2012/05/23/153518350/romney-stresses-education-platform-in-seeking-latino-votes. See also "Romney: American Kids Get 'Third World Education,'" *CBS MoneyWatch*, May 23, 2012, http://www.cbsnews.com/8301-505245_162-57440299/romney-american-kids-get-third-world-education/.

11. "What Mr. Romney's returns illustrated, instead, was the array of perfectly ordinary ways in which the United States tax code confers advantages on the rich, allowing Mr. Romney to amass wealth under rules very different from those faced by most Americans who take home a paycheck," Nicholas Confessore and David Kocieniewski found in their investigation, "For Romneys, Friendly Code Reduces Taxes," *New York Times*, January 24, 2012, http://www.nytimes.com/2012/01/25/us/politics/romneys-tax-returns-show-21-6-million-income-in-10.html?_r=1&pagewanted=all.

12. Holcomb Noble, "Milton Friedman, Free Markets Theorist, Dies at 94," *New York Times*, November 16, 2006, http://www.nytimes.com/2006/11/16/business/17friedmancnd.html?pagewanted=all.

13. Peter Goodman, "A Fresh Look at the Apostle of Free Markets," *New York Times*, April 13, 2008, http://www.nytimes.com/2008/04/13/weekinreview/13goodman.html?pagewanted=all.

14. Naomi Klein, *The Shock Doctrine* (New York: Metropolitan Books, 2008). See a comprehensive critique of Klein by Johan Norberg in "Defaming Milton Friedman," *Reason*, October 2008, http://reason.com/archives/2008/09/26/defaming-milton-friedman/singlepage. Norberg claims Klein is "dead wrong about Friedman." For further reading on how the Shock Doctrine concept applies to education see "Shock Doctrine, Manufactured Education Crisis and Media's Distorted Portrayal of American Education," *New York City Eye* (blog), April 2, 2012, http://nycityeye.blogspot.com/2012/04/shock-doctrine-manufactured-education.html; David Sirota,

"The 'Shock Doctrine' Comes to Your Neighborhood Classroom," *Salon*, September 6, 2011, http://www.salon.com/2011/09/06/shockreform/; and Adam Sanchez, "Disaster Schooling: The Education 'Shock Doctrine,'" *International Socialist Review* 71 (May/June 2010), http://www.isreview.org/issues/71/feat-disasterschooling.shtml.

15. Jeff Madrick, "The End of the Age of Milton Friedman," *Huffington Post*, March 31, 2008, http://www.huffingtonpost.com/jeff-madrick/the-end-of-the-age-of-mil_b_94228.html.

16. Milton Friedman, interview by Nick Gillespie, "The Father of Modern School Reform," *Reason*, December 2005, in *Hoover Digest* 1 (2006), http://www.hoover.org/publications/hoover-digest/article/7122.

17. Anyone seriously interested in privatization of education—and public services in general— should read Milton Friedman's "The Role of Government in Education," in *Capitalism and Freedom* (Chicago: University of Chicago Press, 2002), 85–108.

18. Milton Friedman, "Busting the School Monopoly," *Newsweek*, December 5, 1983, *The Friedman Foundation for Educational Choice*, http://www.edchoice.org/The-Friedmans-on-School-Choice/Milton-Friedman-on-Busting-the-School-Monopoly.aspx.

19. Frederick Hess, "Does School Choice 'Work'?" *National Affairs* 5 (Fall 2010): 35–53, http://www.nationalaffairs.com/doclib/20100918_Hess_pdf[1].pdf.

20. George Lakoff, with whom I talked during the writing of this chapter, has published extensively on "framing," or on how metaphor and language in general guide the way we think, most often at an unconscious level, especially in *The Political Mind: A Cognitive Scientist's Guide to Your Brain and Its Politics* (New York: Penguin, 2009). This passage comes from an excerpt of a Lakoff speech at University of California–Berkeley, "Privatization is *the* Issue," Keep California's Promise, August 7, 2009, http://keepcaliforniaspromise.org/77/privatization-is-the-issue.

21. Taylorism was based on the theories of Frederick Taylor in the late nineteenth and early twentieth century. Its main goal was to apply scientific management techniques to maximize production in the workplace. For a brief overview of this concept, see Jonathan Rees, "Frederick Taylor In The Classroom: Standardized Testing And Scientific Management," *Radical Pedagogy* 3, no. 2 (Fall 2001), http://radicalpedagogy.icaap.org/content/issue3_2/rees.html. Taylorism applied to education is essentially what Friedman prescribed. But, Rees, an academic historian, concludes in contradiction, "If teachers cannot choose methods and topics that engage both them and their students, education will suffer. . . . The reason for this is that contrary to the assumptions of standardized test advocates, education is not an ordinary commodity. It cannot accurately be measured in discreet units. Thus, it defies numerical measurement. Furthermore, there is no one best way to teach anything. Different content and different methods will work for different teachers in different settings. Destroying teacher prerogatives by introducing evaluation methods akin to scientific management will inevitably hurt production rather than help it along."

22. Paul Thomas, *Ignoring Poverty in the U.S.: The Corporate Takeover of Public Education* (North Carolina: Information Age Press, 2012); and Helen Ladd and Edward Fiske, "Class Matters. Why Won't We Admit It?" *New York Times*, December 11, 2011, http://www.nytimes.com/2011/12/12/opinion/the-unaddressed-link-between-poverty-and-education.html?pagewanted=all.

23. Wayne Au, "Playing Smart: Resisting The Script," *Rethinking Schools* 26, no. 3 (Spring 2012), http://rethinkingschools.org/archive/26_03/26_03_au.shtml.

24. See a pamphlet intended to provide advice for "turnaround" non-profits and corporations: Jeff Kutash et al., *The School Turnaround Field Guide*, FSG Social Impact Advisors, September 2010, http://www.wallacefoundation.org/knowledge-center/school-leadership/district-policy-and-practice/Documents/the-school-turnaround-field-guide-executive-summary.pdf.

25. "Obama's State of the Union Address: Full Text," *CBS News Political Hotsheet*, January 24, 2012, http://www.cbsnews.com/8301-503544_162-57365343-503544/obamas-state-of-the-union-address-full-text.

26. Joy Removits, "Race to the Top 2012 Invites School Districts to Compete," *Huffington Post*, May 22, 2012, http://www.huffingtonpost.com/2012/05/22/race-to-the-top-2012-school-districts_n_1534517.html.

27. "We cannot let another generation of children be deprived of their civil right to a quality education," Secretary of Education Arne Duncan says, pushing for more charter schools to be opened in a press release: "States Open to Charters Start Fast in 'Race to Top,'" United States Department of Education, June 8, 2009, http://www2.ed.gov/news/pressreleases/2009/06/06082009a.html.

28. Liz Dwyer, "Let's Stop Comparing Education to the Civil Rights Movement," *GOOD*, May 25, 2012, http://www.good.is/post/let-s-stop-comparing-education-to-the-civil-rights-movement.

29. Friedman and Gillespie, "The Father of Modern School Reform."

30. "Breitbart Announces His Next Big Move: 'Go After the Teachers,'" Media Matters for America, April 18, 2011, http://mediamatters.org/mmtv/201104180045.

31. Google Trends is a free search function that allows users to see the traffic on a specific term, along with key articles that used that term. See http://www.google.com/trends.

32. Paul Fahri, "Flunking the Test," *American Journalism Review* (April/May 2012), http://www.ajr.org/Article.asp?id=5280.

33. Mickey Huff and Adam Bessie et al., "Framing the Messengers: Junk Food News and News Abuse for Dummies," *Censored 2012: The Top Censored Stories and Media Analysis 2010–11* (New York: Seven Stories Press, 2011), 183–228.

34. John Sexton, "Liberal Graduation Speakers Outnumber Conservatives 7 to 1," *Big Government* (blog), May 15, 2012, http://www.breitbart.com/Big-Government/2012/05/15/Examiner-Liberal-Graduation-Speakers-Outnumber-Conservatives-7-to-1.

35. Fahri, "Flunking the Test"; Louis Gerstner, interview by Fareed Zakaria, "Restoring the American Dream," *GPS with Fareed Zakaria*, CNN, October 30 and 31, 2010, http://www-cgi.cnn.com/video/#/video/podcasts/fareedzakaria/site/2010/10/31/gps.podcast.10.31.cnn, http://transcripts.cnn.com/TRANSCRIPTS/1010/30/fzgps.01.html. It is also worth noting the cross ownership of media outlets here as CNN and *Time* are owned by the same parent corporate company Time Warner, as one can see with NBC, MSNBC (owned by General Electric and Microsoft), and the Bill and Melinda Gates Foundation (a major contributor to the "education reform" movement which also has the popular show *Education Nation* on the NBC networks which promotes "reform" policies).

36. "Restoring the American Dream: Fixing Education," *GPS with Fareen Zakaria*, CNN, November 11, 2011, http://transcripts.cnn.com/TRANSCRIPTS/1111/12/fzgps.01.html.

37. Julie Zeveloff, "These Are the Worst Teachers in New York City," *Business Insider*, February 25, 2012, http://articles.businessinsider.com/2012-02-25/lifestyle/31098426_1_math-teachers-public-school-teachers-zero.

38. "Too Unreliable," Room for Debate, *New York Times*, May 24, 2011, http://www.nytimes.com/roomfordebate/2010/09/06/assessing-a-teachers-value/value-added-assessment-is-too-unreliable-to-be-useful. Here you can find a debate on "value-added analysis," at which prominent Stanford University Education professor Linda Darling-Hammond cites this study.

39. See note 21 in this chapter for more on this concept of the pedagogy of Taylorism.

40. Alexandra Zavis and Tony Barboza, "Teacher's Suicide Shocks School," *Los Angeles Times*, September 28, 2010, http://articles.latimes.com/2010/sep/28/local/la-me-south-gate-teacher-20100928.

41. Paul Thomas, "The Bully Politics of Education Reform," *The Daily Censored* (blog), http://www.dailycensored.com/2012/04/06/the-bully-politics-of-education-reform.

42. George Orwell, "Politics and the English Language," in *Shooting an Elephant and Other Essays* (London: Secker and Warburg, [1946] 1950), http://www.orwell.ru/library/essays/politics/english/e_polit.

43. "StudentsFirst Six-Word Essay Contest," StudentsFirst.org, http://www.studentsfirst.org/pages/official-rules.

44. StudentsFirst.org homepage and staff page, http://www.studentsfirst.org/ and http://www.studentsfirst.org/staff.

45. "Pay Effective Teachers What They Deserve," petition sponsored by StudentsFirst, http://www.change.org/petitions/pay-effective-teachers-what-they-deserve.

46. For a definition and thorough discussion of "Astroturf," see Anthony DiMaggio, "A Tea Party Among Us: Media Censorship, Manufactured Dissent, and the Right-Wing Rebellion," *Censored 2012: The Top Censored Stories and Media Analysis of 2010–11* (New York: Seven Stories Press, 2011), 351–66.

47. Adam Bessie, "Our Cutthroat Curriculum," Answer Sheet, *Washington Post*, May 6, 2011, http://www.washingtonpost.com/blogs/answer-sheet/post/our-cutthroat-curriculum/2011/05/05/AFuiFP3F_blog.html.

48. Jack Gillum and Marisol Bello, "When Standardized Test Scores Soared in D.C., Were the Gains Real?" *USA Today*, March 30, 2011, http://www.usatoday.com/news/education/2011-03-28-1Aschooltesting28_CV_N.htm; Michael Winerip, "Amid a Federal Education Inquiry, an Unsettling Sight," *New York Times*, February 26, 2012, http://www.nytimes.com/2012/02/27/education/duncan-and-rhee-on-panel-amid-dc-schools-inquiry.html?pagewanted=all; and M. Catharine Evans and Ann Kane, "D.C. Cheating Scandal: A Conspiracy of Silence," *American Thinker*, March 22, 2012, http://www.americanthinker.com/2012/03/dc_cheating_scandal_a_conspiracy_of_silence.html.

49. Sommer Mathis, Sarah Larimer, and Kevin Robillard, "D.C. Teachers Fired by Rhee to Be Reinstated," TBD/News Channel 8, February 8, 2011, http://www.tbd.com/articles/2011/02/d-c-teachers-fired-by-rhee-to-be-reinstated-51340.html.

50. Kyle Olson, "AFT's Anti-Michelle Rhee Website Illustrates Unions are Buckling Under Reform Pressure," *Big Government* (blog), September 7, 2011, http://www.breitbart.com/Big-Government/2011/09/07/AFT---s-Anti-Michelle-Rhee-Website-Illustrates-Unions-Are-Buckling-Under-Reform-Pressure.

51. Stephanie Simon (Reuters), "Activist Targeting U.S. Schools, Backed by Big Bucks," *Chicago Tribune*, May 15, 2012, http://articles.chicagotribune.com/2012-05-15/news/sns-rt-us-usa-education-rheebre84e10a-20120515_1_michelle-rhee-studentsfirst-grade-level.

52. Joanne Barkan, "Hired Guns on the Astroturf: How to Buy and Sell School Reform," *Dissent*, Spring 2012, http://dissentmagazine.org/article/?article=4240.

53. David Halperin, "Scams and Frauds (Plus George W. Bush and Michelle Rhee) at Upcoming Subprime College Conference," *Huffington Post*, April 20, 2012, http://www.huffingtonpost.com/davidhalperin/scams-and-frauds-plus-geo_b_1441368.html.

54. "White House Visitors Database," *Washington Post*, http://apps.washingtonpost.com/svc/politics/white-house-visitors-log/searchResults?query=Michelle+Rhee&ignoreTours=true. Rhee visited the White House on December 14, 2009.

55. Valerie Strauss, "Guess What Michelle Rhee Charged a School to Speak," Answer Sheet, *Washington Post*, October 26, 2011, http://www.washingtonpost.com/blogs/answer-sheet/post/guess-what-michelle-rhee-charged-a-school-to-speak/2011/10/24/gIQAen6GJM_blog.html.

56. Simon, "Activist Targeting U.S. Schools, Backed by Big Bucks."

57. Stephen Sawchuk, "Relationship Between Advocacy Groups, Unions Uneasy," *Education Week*, May 22, 2012, http://www.edweek.org/ew/articles/2012/05/23/32adv-union_ep.h31.html?r=366288102.

58. Sharra Weasler, "One Million Strong," StudentsFirst.org, January 6, 2012, http://www.studentsfirst.org/blog/entry/one-million-strong/. As of June 1, 2012, the petition "Pay Effective Teachers What They Deserve" had 492,771 signatures of the 500,000 goal.

59. Hess, "Does School Choice 'Work'?"

60. Diane Ravitch, e-mail message to Adam Bessie, December 27, 2011.

61. Hess, "Does School Choice 'Work'?"

62. Ravitch, e-mail to Bessie.

63. Ravitch, *The Death and Life of the Great American School System* (New York: Basic Books, 2010). See this excerpt—and more—at the National Education Association, http://www.nea.org/home/39774.htm.

CHAPTER 9

Kent State
Was It about Civil Rights or Murdering Student Protesters?

by Laurel Krause with Mickey Huff

When Ohio National Guardsmen fired sixty-seven gun shots in thirteen seconds at Kent State University (KSU) on May 4, 1970, they murdered four unarmed, protesting college students and wounded nine others. For forty-two years, the United States government has held the position that Kent State was a tragic and unfortunate incident occurring at a noontime antiwar rally on an American college campus. In 2010, compelling forensic evidence emerged showing that the Federal Bureau of Investigation (FBI) and the Counter Intelligence Program (COINTELPRO) were the lead agencies in managing Kent State government operations, including the cover-up. At Kent State, lawful protest was pushed into the realm of massacre as the US federal government, the state of Ohio, and the Ohio National Guard (ONG) executed their plans to silence antiwar protest in America.

The new evidence threatens much more than the accuracy of accounts of the Kent State massacre in history books. As a result of this successful, ongoing Kent State government cover-up, American protesters today are at much greater risk than they realize, with no real guarantees or protections offered by the US First Amendment rights to protest and assemble. This chapter intends to expose the lies of the state in order to uncensor the "unhistory" of the Kent State massacre, while also aiming toward justice and healing, as censoring the past impacts our perspectives in the present.

The killing of protesters at Kent State changed the minds of many Americans about the role of the US in the Vietnam War. Following this massacre, there was an unparalleled national response: hundreds of universities, colleges, and high schools closed across America in a student strike of more than four million. Young people across the nation had strong suspicions the Kent State massacre was planned to subvert any further protests arising from the announcement that the already controversial war in Vietnam had expanded into Cambodia.

Yet instead of attempting to learn the truth at Kent State, the US government took complete control of the narrative in the press and ensuing lawsuits. Over the next ten years, authorities claimed there had not been a command-to-fire at Kent State, that the ONG had been under attack, and that their gunfire had been prompted by the "sound of sniper fire." Instead of investigating Kent State, the American leadership obstructed justice, obscured accountability, tampered with evidence, and buried the truth. The result of these efforts has been a very complicated government cover-up that has remained intact for more than forty years.[1]

The hidden truth finally began to emerge at the fortieth anniversary of the Kent State massacre in May 2010, through the investigative journalism of John Mangels, science writer at the Cleveland *Plain Dealer*, whose findings supported the long-held suspicion that the four dead in Ohio were intentionally murdered at Kent State University by the US government.

Mangels commissioned forensic evidence expert Stuart Allen to professionally analyze a tape recording made from a Kent State student's dormitory window ledge on May 4, 1970, forever capturing the crowd and battle sounds from before, during, and after the fusillade.[2] For the first time since that fateful day, journalists and concerned Americans were finally able to hear the devastating soundtrack of the US government murdering Kent State students as they protested against the Vietnam War.

The cassette tape—provided to Mangels by the Yale University Library, Kent State Collection, and housed all these years in a box of evidence admitted into lawsuits led by attorney Joseph Kelner in his representation of the Kent State victims—was called the "Strubbe tape" after Terry Strubbe, the student who made the recording by placing a microphone attached to a personal recorder on his dormitory window ledge. This tape surfaced when Alan Canfora, a student protester wounded at Kent State, and researcher Bob Johnson dug through Yale library's collection and found a CD copy of the tape recording from the day of the shootings. Paying ten dollars for a duplicate, Canfora then listened to it and immediately knew he probably held the only recording that might provide proof of an order to shoot. Three years after the tape was found, the *Plain Dealer* commendably hired two qualified forensic audio scientists to examine the tape.

But it is really the two pieces of groundbreaking evidence Allen uncovered that illuminate and provide a completely new perspective into the Kent State massacre.

First, Allen heard and verified the Kent State command-to-fire spoken at noon on May 4, 1970. The command-to-fire has been a point of contention, with authorities stating under oath and to media for forty years that "no order to fire was given at Kent State," that "the Guard felt under attack from the students," and that "the Guard reacted to sniper fire."[3] Yet Allen's verified forensic evidence of the Kent State command-to-fire directly conflicts with guardsmen testimony that they acted in self-defense.

The government claim—that guardsmen were under attack at the time of the ONG barrage of bullets—has long been suspect, as there is nothing in photographic or video records to support the "under attack" excuse. Rather, from more than a football field away, the Kent State student protesters swore, raised their middle fingers, and threw pebbles and stones and empty tear gas canisters, mostly as a response to their campus being turned into a battlefield with over 2,000 troops and military equipment strewn across the Kent State University campus.

Then at 12:24 p.m., the ONG fired armor-piercing bullets at scattering students in a parking lot—again, from more than a football field away. Responding with armor-piercing bullets, as Kent State students held a peaceful rally and protested unarmed on their campus, was the US government's choice of action.

The identification of the "commander" responsible for the Kent State command-to-fire on unarmed students has not yet been ascertained. This key question will be answered when American leadership decides to share the truth of what happened, especially as the Kent State battle was under US government direction. Until then, the voice ordering the command-to-fire in the Kent State Strubbe tape will remain unknown.

The other major piece of Kent State evidence identified in Allen's analysis was the "sound of sniper fire" recorded on the tape. These sounds point to Terry Norman, FBI informant and provocateur, who was believed to have fired his low-caliber pistol four times, just seventy seconds before the command-to-fire.

Mangels wrote in the *Plain Dealer*, "Norman was photographing protestors that day for the FBI and carried a loaded .38-caliber Smith & Wesson Model . . . five-shot revolver in a holster under his coat for protection. Though he denied discharging his pistol, he previously has been accused of triggering the Guard shootings by firing to warn away angry demonstrators, which the soldiers mistook for sniper fire."[4]

Video footage and still photography have recorded the minutes following the "sound of sniper fire," showing Terry Norman sprinting across the Kent State commons, meeting up with Kent Police and the ONG. In this visual evidence, Norman immediately yet casually hands off his pistol to authorities and the recipients of the pistol show no surprise as Norman hands them his gun.[5]

The "sound of sniper fire" is a key element of the Kent State cover-up and is also referred to by authorities in the *Nation* editorial, "Kent State: The Politics of Manslaughter," from May 18, 1970:

> The murders occurred on May 4. Two days earlier, [Ohio National Guard Adjutant General] Del Corso had issued a statement that sniper fire would be met by gunfire from his men. After the massacre, Del Corso and his subordinates declared that sniper fire had triggered the fusillade.[6]

Yet the Kent State "sound of sniper fire" remains key, according to White House Chief of Staff Bob Haldeman, who noted President Richard Nixon's reaction to Kent State in the Oval Office on May 4, 1970:

> Chief of Staff Bob Haldeman told him [of the killings] late in the afternoon. But at two o'clock Haldeman jotted on his

ever-present legal pad "*keep* P. filled in on Kent State." In his daily journal Haldeman expanded on the President's reaction: "He very disturbed. Afraid his decision set it off . . . then kept after me *all day* for more facts. *Hoping rioters had provoked the shootings—but no real evidence that they did.*" Even after he had left for the day, Nixon called Haldeman back and among others issued one ringing command: "need to get out story of sniper."[7]

In a May 5, 1970, article in the *New York Times*, President Nixon commented on violence at Kent State:

> This should remind us all once again that when dissent turns to violence it invites tragedy. It is my hope that this tragic and unfortunate incident will strengthen the determination of all the nation's campuses, administrators, faculty and students alike to stand firmly for the right which exists in this country of peaceful dissent and just as strong against the resort to violence as a means of such expression.[8]

President Nixon's comment regarding dissent turning to violence obfuscated and laid full blame on student protesters for creating violence at Kent State. Yet at the rally occurring on May 4th, student protester violence amounted to swearing, throwing small rocks, and volleying back tear gas canisters, while the gun-toting soldiers of the ONG declared the peace rally illegal, brutally herded the students over large distances on campus, filled the air with tear gas, and even threw rocks at students. Twenty minutes into the protest demonstration, a troop of National Guard marched up a hill away from the students, turned to face the students in unison, and fired.

The violence at Kent State came from the National Guardsmen, not protesting students. On May 4, 1970, the US government delivered its deadly message to Kent State students and the world: if you protest in America against the wars of the Pentagon and the Department of Defense, the US government will stop at nothing to silence you.

Participating American militia colluded at Kent State to organize and fight this battle against American student protesters, most of them too young to vote but old enough to fight in the Vietnam War.[9] And from new evidence exposed forty years after the massacre, numerous elements point directly to the FBI and COINTELPRO (Counter Intelligence Program) as lead agencies managing the government operation of the Kent State massacre, including the cover-up, but also with a firm hand in some of the lead-up.

Prior to the announcement of the Cambodian incursion, the ONG arrived in the Kent area acting in a federalized role as the Cleveland-Akron labor wildcat strikes were winding down. The ONG continued in the federalized role at Kent State, ostensibly to protect the campus and as a reaction to the burning of a Reserve Officers' Training Corps (ROTC) building. Ohio Governor James "Jim" Rhodes claimed the burning of the ROTC building on the Kent State University campus was his reason for "calling in the guard," yet in this picture of the burning building, the ONG are clearly standing before the flames as the building burns.[10]

From eyewitness accounts, the burning of the ROTC building at Kent State was completed by undercover law enforcement determined to make sure it could become the symbol needed to support the Kent State war on student protest.[11]

According to Dr. Elaine Wellin, an eyewitness to the many events at Kent State leading up to and including May 4th, there were uniformed and plain-clothes officers potentially involved in managing the burning of the ROTC building. Wellin was in close proximity to the building just prior to the burning and saw a person with a walkie-talkie about three feet from her telling someone on the other end of the communication that they should not send down the fire truck as the ROTC building was not on fire *yet*.[12]

A memo to COINTELPRO director William C. Sullivan ordered a full investigation into the "fire bombing of the ROTC building." But only days after the Kent State massacre, every weapon that was fired was destroyed, and all other weapons used at Kent State were gathered by top ONG officers, placed with other weapons and shipped to Europe for use by North Atlantic Treaty Organization (NATO), so no weapons used at Kent could be traced.

From these pieces of evidence, it becomes clearer that the US government coordinated this battle against student protest on the Kent State campus. Using the playbook from the Huston Plan, which refers to protesting students as the "New Left," the US government employed provocateurs, staged incidents, and enlisted political leaders to attack and lay full blame on the students. On May 4, 1970, at Kent State University, the US government fully negated every student response as they criminalized the First Amendment rights to protest and assemble.[13]

The cover-up adds tremendous complexity to an already complicated event, making it nearly impossible to fairly try the Kent State massacre in the American justice system. This imposed "establishment" view that Kent State was about "civil rights"—and not about murder or attempted murder—led to a legal settlement on the basis of civil rights lost, with the US government consistently refusing to address the death of four students and the wounding of nine.[14]

Even more disheartening, efforts to maintain the US government cover-up at Kent State recently went into overdrive in April 2012, when President Barack Obama's Department of Justice (DOJ) formally announced a refusal to open a new probe into the wrongs of Kent State, continuing the tired 1970 tactic of referring to Kent State as a civil rights matter.[15]

The April 2012 DOJ letters of response also included a full admission that, in 1979, after reaching the Kent State civil rights settlement, the FBI Cleveland office destroyed what they considered a key piece of evidence: the original tape recording made by Terry Strubbe on his dormitory window ledge. In a case involving homicides, the FBI's illegal destruction of evidence exposes their belief to be "above the law," ignoring the obvious fact that four students were killed on May 4, 1970. As the statute of limitations never lapses for murder, the FBI's actions went against every law of evidence. The laws clearly state that evidence may not be destroyed in homicides, even when the murders are perpetrated by the US government.

The destruction of the original Strubbe tape also shows the FBI's intention to obstruct justice: the 2012 DOJ letters on Kent State claim that, because the original Strubbe tape was intentionally destroyed, the copy examined by Allen cannot be compared to the original or authenticated. However the original Strubbe tape, destroyed by the DOJ, was never admitted into evidence.

The tape examined by Stuart Allen, however, is a one-to-one copy of the Kent State Strubbe tape admitted into evidence in Kent State legal proceedings by Joseph Kelner, the lawyer representing the victims of Kent State. Once an article has been admitted into evidence, the article is considered authentic evidentiary material.

Worse than this new smokescreen on the provenance of the Kent State Strubbe tape and FBI efforts to destroy evidence is that the DOJ has wholly ignored or refuted the tremendous body of forensic evidence work accomplished by Allen, and verified by forensic expert Tom Owen.[16] If the US Department of Justice really wanted to learn the truth about what happened at Kent State and was open to understanding the new evidence, DOJ efforts would include organizing an impartial examination of Allen's analysis and contacting him to present his examination of the Kent State Strubbe tape. None of this has happened.

Instead, those seeking justice through a reexamination of the Kent

State historical record based on new evidence have been left out in the cold. Congressman Dennis Kucinich, involved in Kent State from the very beginning as a Cleveland city council person, asked important questions in a letter to the DOJ on April 24, 2012, titled, "Analysis of Audio Record of Kent State Shooting Leaves Discrepancies and Key Questions Unaddressed":

> While I appreciate the response from the Justice Department, ultimately, they fail to examine key questions and discrepancies. It is well known that an FBI informant, Terry Norman, was on the campus. That FBI informant was carrying a gun. Eyewitnesses testified that they saw Mr. Norman brandish that weapon. Two experts in forensic audio, who have previously testified in court regarding audio forensics, found gunshots in their analysis of the audio recording. Did an FBI informant discharge a firearm at Kent State? Did an FBI informant precipitate the shootings?
>
> Who and what events led to the violent encounter that resulted in four students dead and nine others injured? What do the FBI files show about their informant? Was he ever debriefed? Has he been questioned to compare his statement of events with new analysis? How, specifically, did the DOJ analyze the tape? How does this compare to previous analysis conducted by independent sources that reached a different conclusion? The DOJ suggested noises heard in the recording resulted from a door opening and closing. What tests were used to make that determination? Was an independent agency consulted in the process?
>
> For more than a year, I have pushed for an analysis of the Strubbe tape because Kent State represented a tragedy of immense proportions. The Kent State shooting challenged the sensibilities of an entire generation of Americans. This issue is too important to ignore. We must demand a full explanation of the events.[17]

Concerned Americans may join Congressman Kucinich in demanding answers to these questions and in insisting on an independent, impartial organization—in other words, *not* the FBI—to get to the bottom of this.

The FBI's cloudy involvement includes questions about Terry Norman's relationship to the FBI, addressed in Mangels's article, "Kent State Shootings: Does Former Informant Hold the Key to the May 4th Mystery?":

> Whether due to miscommunication, embarrassment or an attempted cover-up, the FBI initially denied any involvement with Norman as an informant.
>
> "Mr. Norman was not working for the FBI on May 4, 1970, nor has he ever been in any way connected with this Bureau," director J. Edgar Hoover declared to Ohio Congressman John Ashbrook in an August 1970 letter.
>
> Three years later, Hoover's successor, Clarence Kelley, was forced to correct the record. The director acknowledged that the FBI had paid Norman $125 for expenses incurred when, at the bureau's encouragement, Norman infiltrated a meeting of Nazi and white power sympathizers in Virginia a month before the Kent State shootings.[18]

Even more telling, Norman's pistol disappeared from a police evidence locker and was completely retooled to make sure that the weapon—used to create the "sound of sniper fire" on May 4—would not show signs of use. Indeed, every "investigation" into Kent State shows that the FBI tampered, withheld, and destroyed evidence, bringing into question government involvement in both the premeditated and post-massacre efforts at Kent State. In examining all inquiries into Kent State, an accurate investigation has never occurred, as the groups involved in the wrongs of Kent State have been investigating themselves.[19]

The Kent State students never had a chance against the armed will of the US government in its aim to fight wars in Vietnam, Cambodia, and Laos back in 1970. Further, the First Amendment rights to protest and assemble have shown to be only vacuous platitudes. Forty-two years later, the Obama administration echoes the original drone of the US government denying the murder of protesters, pointing only to civil rights lost. When bullets were fired on May 4th at Kent

State, US government military action against antiwar protesters on domestic soil changed from a civil rights breach to acts of murder and attempted murder.

Congressman Kucinich, in an interview with Pacifica Radio after his exchanges with DOJ by May of 2012, said,

> There are some lingering questions that could change the way that history looks at what happened at Kent State. And I think that we owe it to the present generation of Americans, the generation of Americans that came of age during Kent, the students on campus, we owe it to the Guardsmen, who it was said opened fire without any provocation what so ever . . . we have to get to the truth.[20]

As long as American leadership fails to consider killing protesters a homicidal action and not just about civil rights lost, there is little safety for American protesters today, leaving the door wide open for more needless and unnecessary bloodshed and possibly the killing of American protesters again. This forty-two-year refusal to acknowledge the death of four students relates to current US government practices toward protest and protesters in America, as witnessed at Occupy Wall Street over the past year. When will it ever become legal to protest and assemble in America again? Will American leadership cross the line to kill American protesters again?[21]

In a rare editorial addressing this issue, journalist Stephen Rosenfeld of *AlterNet* wrote,

> History never exactly repeats itself. But its currents are never far from the present. As today's protesters and police employ bolder tactics, the Kent State and Jackson State anniversaries should remind us that deadly mistakes can and do happen. It is the government's responsibility to wield proportionate force, not to over-arm police and place them in a position where they could panic with deadly results.[22]

Though forty-two years have passed, the lessons of Kent State have not yet been learned.

NO MORE KENT STATES[23]

In 2010, the United Kingdom acknowledged the wrongs of Bloody Sunday, also setting an example for the US government to learn the important lessons of protest and the First Amendment. In January 1972, during "Bloody Sunday," British paratroopers shot and killed fourteen protesters; most of the demonstrators were shot in the back as they ran to save themselves.[24]

Thirty-eight years after the Bloody Sunday protest, British Prime Minister David Cameron apologized before Parliament, formally acknowledging the wrongful murder of protesters and apologized for the government.[25] The healing in Britain has begun. Considering the striking similarity in events where protesters were murdered by the state, let's examine the wrongs of Kent State, begin to heal this core American wound, and make a very important, humane course correction for America. When will it become legal to protest in America?

President Obama, the Department of Justice, and the US government as a whole must take a fresh look at Stuart Allen's findings in the Kent State Strubbe tape. The new Kent State evidence is compelling, clearly showing how US covert intelligence took the lead in creating this massacre and in putting together the ensuing cover-up.

As the United States has refused to examine the new evidence or consider the plight of American protest in 2012, the Kent State Truth Tribunal formally requested the International Criminal Court (ICC) at the Hague consider justice at Kent State.[26]

Who benefited the most from the murder of student protesters at Kent State? Who was really behind the Kent State massacre? There is really only one US agency that clearly benefited from killing student antiwar protesters at Kent State: the Department of Defense.

Since 1970 through 2012, the military-industrial-cyber complex strongly associated with the Department of Defense and covert US government agencies have actively promoted never-ending wars with enormous unaccounted-for budgets as they increase restrictions on American protest. These aims of the Pentagon are evidenced today in the USA PATRIOT Act, the further civil rights–limiting National Defense Authorization Act (NDAA), and new war technologies like CIA drones.

Probing the dark and buried questions of the Kent State massacre is only a beginning step to shine much-needed light on the United States military and to illuminate how the Pentagon has subverted American trust and safety, as it endeavors to quell domestic protest against war at any cost since at least 1970.

LAUREL KRAUSE is a writer and truth seeker dedicated to raising awareness about ocean protection, safe renewable energy, and truth at Kent State. She publishes a blog on these topics at *Mendo Coast Current*. She is the cofounder and director of the Kent State Truth Tribunal. Before spearheading efforts for justice for her sister Allison Krause, who was killed at Kent State University on May 4, 1970, Laurel worked at technology start-ups in Silicon Valley.

MICKEY HUFF is the director of Project Censored and professor of social science and history at Diablo Valley College. He did his graduate work in history on historical interpretations of the Kent State shootings and has been actively researching the topic more since his testimony to the Kent State Truth Tribunal in New York City in 2010.

Notes

1. For more background on Kent State and the many conflicting interpretations, see Scott L. Bills, *Kent State/May 4: Echoes Through a Decade* (Kent OH: Kent State University Press, 1982). Of particular interest for background on this chapter, see Peter Davies, "The Burning Question: A Government Cover-up?," in *Kent State/May 4*, 150–60. For a full account of Davies's work, see *The Truth About Kent State: A Challenge to the American Conscience* (New York: Farrar, Straus & Giroux, 1973). For a listing of other works see Selected Bibliography on the Events of May 4, 1970, at Kent State University, http://dept.kent.edu/30yearmay4/source/bib.htm.

2. John Mangels, "New Analysis of 40-Year-Old Recording of Kent State Shootings Reveals that Ohio Guard was Given an Order to Prepare to Fire," *Plain Dealer* (Cleveland), May 9, 2010, updated April 23, 2012, http://blog.cleveland.com/metro/2010/05/new_analysis_of_40-year-old_re.html; Interview with Stuart Allen analyzing new evidence who said of the efforts, "It's about setting history right." See the footage "Kent State Shootings Case Remains Closed," CNN, added April 29, 2012, http://www.cnn.com/video/?/video/us/2012/04/29/justice-department-will-not-reopen-kent-state-shootings-case.cnn.

3. Submitted for the Congressional Record by Representative Dennis Kucinich, "Truth Emerging in Kent State Cold Case Homicide," by Laurel Krause, http://thomas.loc.gov/cgi-bin/query/z?r111%3AE14DE0-0019%3A. For a brief introduction on the history and emerging historiography of the Kent State shootings, see Mickey S. Huff, "Healing Old Wounds: Public Memory, Commemoration, and Conflicts Over Historical Interpretations of the Kent State Shootings, 1977–1990," master's thesis, Youngstown State University, December 1999, http://etd.ohiolink.edu/view.cgi?acc_num=ysu999620326.

   For the official government report, see *The Report of the President's Commission on Campus Unrest* (Washington: US Government Printing Office, 1970), also known as the Scranton Commission. It should be noted that the Scranton Commission stated in their conclusion between pages 287 and 290 that the shootings were "unnecessary, unwarranted and inexcusable" but criminal wrongdoing was never established through the courts and no one was ever held accountable for the shootings. Also, it should be noted, that the interpretation that the guard was ordered to fire conflicts with Davies's interpretation, in note 1 here, that even though he believes there was a series of cover-ups by the government, he has not attributed malice. For more on the Kent State cover-ups early on, see I. F. Stone, "Fabricated Evidence in the Kent State Killings," *New York Review of Books*, December 3, 1970, http://www.nybooks.com/articles/archives/1970/dec/03/fabricated-evidence-in-the-kent-state-killings.

4. Mangels, "Kent State Tape Indicates Altercation and Pistol Fire Preceded National Guard Shootings (audio)," *Plain Dealer* (Cleveland), October 8, 2010, http://www.cleveland.com/science/index.ssf/2010/10/analysis_of_kent_state_audio_t.html.

5. Kent State Shooting 1970 [BX4510], Google Video, at 8:20 min., http://video.google.com/videoplay?docid=-3727445416544720642.

6. Editorial, "Kent State: The Politics of Manslaughter," *Nation*, April 30, 2009 [May 18, 1970], http://www.thenation.com/article/kent-state-politics-manslaughter.

7. Charles A. Thomas, *Kenfour: Notes On An Investigation* (e-book), http://speccoll.library.kent.edu/4may70/kenfour3.

8. John Kifner, "4 Kent State Students Killed by Troops," *New York Times*, May 4, 1970, http://www.nytimes.com/learning/general/onthisday/big/0504.html#article.

9. Voting age was twenty-one at this time, until the passage of the Twenty-Sixth Amendment to the US Constitution in 1971, which lowered the voting age to eighteen, partially in response to Vietnam War protests as youth under twenty-one could be drafted without the right to vote.

10. It should also be noted, that Rhodes was running for election the Tuesday following the Kent shootings on a law and order ticket.

11. "My Personal Testimony ROTC Burning May 2 1970 Kent State," YouTube, April 28, 2010, http://www.youtube.com/watch?v=6ppBkB4caYo&feature=youtu.be; Freedom of Information Act, FBI, Kent State Shooting, File Number 98-46479, part 7 of 8 (1970), http://vault.fbi.gov/kent-state-shooting/kent-state-shooting-part-07-of-08/view.

12. *The Project Censored Show* on *The Morning Mix*, "May 4th and the Kent State Shootings in the 42nd Year," Pacifica Radio, KPFA, 94.1FM, May 4, 2012 live at 8:00 a.m., archived online at http://www.kpfa.org/archive/id/80293 and http://dl.dropbox.com/u/42635027/20120504-Fri0800.mp3. For Wellin on ROTC, see recording at 28:45.

Show description: The May 4th Kent State Shootings 42 Years Later: Justice Still Not Served with Congressman Dennis Kucinich commenting on the DOJ's recent refusal to reopen the case despite new evidence of a Kent State command-to-fire and the 'sound of sniper fire' leading to the National Guard firing live ammunition at unarmed college students May 4, 1970; Dr. Elaine Wellin, Kent State eyewitness shares seeing undercover agents at the ROTC fire in the days before, provocateurs in staging the rallies at Kent, and at Kent State on May 4th; we'll hear from investigator and forensic evidence expert Stuart Allen regarding his audio analysis of the Kent State Strubbe tape from May 4th revealing the command-to-fire and the 'sound of sniper fire' seventy seconds before; and we hear from Kent State Truth Tribunal director Laurel Krause, the sister of slain student Allison, about her efforts for justice at Kent State and recent letter to President Obama..

Also see Peter Davies' testimony about agents provocateurs and the ROTC fire cited in note 1, "The Burning Question: A Government Cover-up?," in *Kent State/May 4*, 150–60.

13. The Assassination Archives and Research Center (AARC), "Volume 2: Huston Plan," http://www.aarclibrary.org/publib/contents/church/contents_church_reports_vol2.htm.

14. Associated Press, "Kent State Settlement: Was Apology Included?," *Eugene Register-Guard*, January 5, 1979, http://news.google.com/newspapers?nid=1310&dat=19790105&id=xvJVAAAAIBAJ&sjid=BuIDAAAAIBAJ&pg=3696,963632.

15. Mangels, "Justice Department Won't Reopen Probe of 1970 Kent State Shootings," *Plain Dealer* (Cleveland), April 24, 2012, http://www.cleveland.com/science/index.ssf/2012/04/justice_department_wont_re-ope.html; and kainah, "Obama Justice Dept.: No Justice for Kent State," *Daily Kos*, May 2, 2012, http://www.dailykos.com/story/2012/05/02/1086726/-Justice-Dept-No-Justice-for-Kent-State.

16. Mangels, "New Analysis."

17. Letters between the Department of Justice and Representative Dennis Kucinich, archived at the Congressman's website, April 20 and April 24 of 2012, http://kucinich.house.gov/upload-

edfiles/kent_state_response_from_doj.pdf and http://kucinich.house.gov/news/documentsingle.aspx?DocumentID=292306.

18. Mangels, "Kent State Shootings: Does Former Informant Hold the Key to the May 4 Mystery?," *Plain Dealer* (Cleveland), December 19, 2010, http://www.cleveland.com/science/index.ssf/2010/12/kent_state_shootings_does_form.html.

19. Freedom of Information Act, FBI.

20. *The Project Censored Show* on *The Morning Mix*, "May 4th and the Kent State Shootings in the 42nd Year."

21. Steven Rosenfeld, "Will a Militarized Police Force Facing Occupy Wall Street Lead to Another Kent State?," *AlterNet*, May 3, 2012, http://www.alternet.org/rights/155270/will_a_militarized_police_force_facing_occupy_wall_street_lead_to_another_kent_state_massacre.

22. Ibid.

23. Laurel Krause, "No More Kent States," *Mendo Coast Current*, April 21, 2012, http://mendocoastcurrent.wordpress.com/2012/04/21/13-day-for-kent-state-peace.

24. Laurel Krause, "Unjustified, Indefensible, Wrong," *Mendo Coast Current*, September 13, 2010, http://mendocoastcurrent.wordpress.com/2010/09/13/unjustified-indefensible-wrong.

25. Associated Press, "Bloody Sunday Report Blames British Soldiers Fully," *USA Today*, June 15, 2010, http://www.usatoday.com/news/world/2010-06-15-Bloody-Sunday-Ireland_N.htm; and Cameron's direct quote from Henry McDonald, Owen Bowcott, and Hélène Mulholland, "Bloody Sunday Report: David Cameron Apologises for 'Unjustifiable' Shootings," *Guardian*, June 15, 2010, http://www.guardian.co.uk/uk/2010/jun/15/bloody-sunday-report-saville-inquiry.

26. Laurel Krause, "To the Hague: Justice for the May 4th Kent State Massacre?," *Mendo Coast Current*, May 7, 2012, http://mendocoastcurrent.wordpress.com/2012/05/07/may-4th-kent-state-massacre-a-call-for-truth-justice; for more on the Kent State Truth Tribunal, see www.TruthTribunal.org.

CHAPTER 10

The Creative Tension of the Emerging Future

Facing the Seven Challenges of Humanity

by Kenn Burrows and Dr. Michael Nagler

Every great and deep difficulty bears in itself its own solution.

—Niels Bohr, quantum physicist

A great deal of social pathology and human suffering can be traced to the demoralizing image of humanity that is upheld by popular culture, primarily through the mass media. The degradation of the human image and progressive loss in confidence about human society and destiny is one of humanity's greatest problems. Popular culture's default image of the human being remains that of a primarily physical object separated from all others and doomed to compete for increasingly scarce resources because of its dependency on consumption for happiness. This objectification and commercialization of every aspect of human life has led to the breakdown of relationships and communities, and the degradation of our environment. Consequently, a culture of fear shapes our collective attention, making the world appear mean and dangerous, and blinding us to prevalence of human goodness.

By contrast, the convergence of "new" science (including quantum theory, neuroscience, and cognitive psychology) with the ancient wisdom traditions underlying all world religions offers an uplifting image of humankind. Collectively, we all stand to benefit from this convergence, which promises to reduce violence and promote physical health and collective peace. Momentous discoveries in new physics, evolutionary biology, and positive psychology provide an image of human beings deeply connected with, in Albert Einstein's words, "the whole of nature in its beauty,"[1] including our fellow humans. The convergence of "new" science and ancient wisdom is a new and potentially powerful basis for rewriting our cultural narrative.

This chapter focuses on seven key challenges facing humanity in this time of global crisis and new possibility.

▶ Competing Worldviews and Polarity Management
▶ Violence and Nonviolent Activism
▶ The Human Footprint and the Environment
▶ Managing Information: Media, News, and Education
▶ Redefining Wealth and Economy
▶ Science, Technology, and Society
▶ Collaborative Leadership, Trust, and the Common Good

These interdependent challenges stem from a *single* crisis of perception. As mental creatures, we perceive the world in terms of our beliefs and assumptions. The outer world reflects our inner world and most "problems" we face originate with our limited perception. All the views we hold have blind spots.

Across and within societies, divisions and diversity separate people—by heritage, class, race, political affiliation, and more. We are a diverse people in need of common moral vision and purpose to draw us together. Mahatma Gandhi provided this for his people in his time. His vision of humanity's common welfare informs this chapter.

Today's challenges require us to think in holistic and systemic ways. In this view, many of these challenges are not problems to be fixed so much as polarities to be managed. We must let go of polarized thinking (*either/or*) in favor of integrating polarities by seeing them as complementary (*both/and*) aspects of larger systems: for example, mind *and* body, local *and* global, nature *and* culture, public *and* private, tradition *and* innovation, liberal *and* conservative.

Interdependent polarities balance each other. "Problems" arise only when an overemphasis on one pole causes a lack of integration in the system as a whole. Polarity management involves focusing on one polarity and then the other, valuing the best in both, so that each element tempers the excesses and overcomes the limitations of the other.[2] At a personal level, this means learning to hold the "creative tension" among divergent points of view.

That said, polarity management does not require being wishy-washy or overly inclusive; it means thinking critically and confidently about alternatives, most significantly perhaps in instances where real polar choices must be made—for example, between violence and nonviolence, which we discuss subsequently.

This chapter invites the reader into a deeper conversation about our collective dilemma—with the hope that, together, we can learn to hold the creative tension in each of these seven areas in order to support ongoing cultural change toward a more just, creative, and abundant life.

COMPETING WORLDVIEWS AND POLARITY MANAGEMENT

Every conflict is one between different angles of vision,
illuminating the same truth.

—Mahatma Gandhi

For over half a century, psychologists and others have studied the values and ideological commitments that differentiate the political left and right. This research consistently identifies two antithetical value systems with contrasting understandings of freedom, right and wrong, the individual, the state, and collective good. For example, in examining liberal and conservative values, Jonathan Haidt argues that people are fundamentally "groupish" (tribal) and tend to congregate in homogenous, partisan communities—each a separate moral enclave with its own understanding of the "facts."[3] Group members tend to reinforce each other's point of view in a process Haidt calls "consensual hallucinations."[4]

Partisan political confrontations are part of an adversarial frame of mind that Deborah Tannen calls "argument culture," which she finds increasingly prevalent in our major cultural institutions, including media, law, and education.[5] Within this adversarial culture, blaming the other is standard public discourse, and compromise is seen as weakness.

Polarized thinking is typical of the dynamics between competing sides in many conflicts: One side—the innovators—identifies a set of problems and promotes ideas or policies to address them. Standing in opposition, the traditionalists identify with the current system, and they feel allegiance to its strengths. Traditionalists see shortcomings in innovators' plans and seek to preserve the old ways.[6]

By contrast, the goal of polarity management is not to blame one side or even to seek solutions constructed from polarized positions. Instead, the aim is to identify and fully integrate the strengths and weaknesses of all sides. In this view, each side is partly right but also incomplete. Mediators and organizational consultants regularly help disputants engage in this process, encouraging disputants to examine their own positions' weaknesses and the others' strengths. A time-tested tool, mediation gives disputants the chance to devise solutions that address each party's needs, fears, and issues.[7]

VIOLENCE AND NONVIOLENT ACTIVISM

Peace researcher Johan Galtung identifies three levels on which violence disrupts human life: direct, structural, and cultural.[8] Direct violence is physical. Structural violence refers to structures in a society, usually economic or political, that inflict violence on a specific group or groups. Cultural violence is more subtle, but arguably more important because it legitimizes direct violence and structural violence. Violence has become a cultural norm in twenty-first-century United States, as evidenced by a perusal of the top stories in *Censored 2013*, including the militarization of domestic police departments, the nation's shameful incarceration rates, and sexual violence suffered by women who serve in the US military.

Gandhi believed that principled nonviolence was the only form of struggle that contains the seeds of renewal, because it presumes that the opponent, or a sleeping public, is a potential partner whose latent awareness can be awakened. Though the logic of nonviolence is compelling and experience validates its effectiveness, the prevailing culture leaves us poorly prepared to recognize this. How often do nonviolence advocates hear, "It never would have worked against the Nazis"? Yet it worked brilliantly at Rosenstrasse, the 1943 Berlin demonstration that forced the Gestapo to release several thousand Jews.[9]

The "meme" of nonviolence is catching on, thanks to the two waves of liberation struggles, first in Eastern Europe and, more recently, in the Middle East. But the word "nonviolence" only entered the English language in 1926 and there is still a good deal of confusion about its meaning and potential.

Nonviolence is powerful. Its power derives from resisting disruptive drives like anger or fear, which confrontations typical arouse. Violence takes a heavy toll on its perpetrators.[10] However, successfully withstood, the negative drive becomes a creative power. Activists must learn how to respond to physical force with spiritual strength. This requires the inner cultivation of what Gandhi called soul force. Martin Luther King Jr. explained, "We did not cause outbursts of anger. We harnessed anger under discipline for maximum effect."[11]

Principled nonviolence is proactive and constructive. Gandhi suggested a general guide for activism: 10 percent resistive and 90 percent constructive.[12] Most movements today either protest without constructive work or (more rarely) undertake constructive work without skillful means of handling conflict. When activists learn how to build the world they want, nonviolently, confronting the inevitable resistance to their constructive efforts with love, rather than rancor or bitterness, it's hard to imagine how anything could stop them.[13]

THE HUMAN FOOTPRINT AND THE ENVIRONMENT

Humans have left their mark on at least 83 percent of Earth's surface.[14] From peak oil to food security, from climate change to population growth, our negative impacts on the environment can make the future seem treacherous and uncertain. In this view, anyone considering our impacts might react with fear and hopelessness—or disbelief.

An alternative perspective emphasizes our collaborative and innovative capacities. If each of us has an ecological "footprint" that is a quantitative measure of our individual environmental impact on the planet, it is also true that we have an ecological "handprint."[15] Your ecological handprint is defined qualitatively in terms of community participation and community development—mobilizing for stronger communities with less impact on the environment.

Communities around the globe are doing just this. For example, Australia, India, and Canada are just three of the countries that participate in UNESCO's Education for Sustainable Development program to reach people and mobilize action on individual, community, national, and global levels.[16]

MANAGING MEDIA: INFORMATION, SOCIAL NETWORKS, AND NEWS

Media no longer just influence our culture. They are our culture.

—Center for Media Literacy[17]

The digital age has made an overwhelming amount of information accessible to many of us. Smartphones and tablets provide hyper-connectivity to social networks and cloud computing, radically changing the lives of those who are "always on" to the extent that information fatigue is common. Researchers recommend the following to manage the digital flood of information:

▸ Take *regular breaks*—get up often and move.
▸ Clarify your values and priorities, and *set limits* on time spent online.
▸ Create a *weekly technology sabbath* (no technology used for the day).
▸ Take a *seasonal technology fast* (going without for a week or longer).

Social networking sites such as Facebook, Twitter, and LinkedIn all enable users to create a profile within the website to represent themselves. These profiles allow users to interact through e-mail, instant messaging, and other integrated communication channels within the site.[18] The growing popularity of social networking sites over the past five years has been colossal. Facebook is expected to reach one billion members in August 2012.[19] But is this growing social network wholly positive for individuals and society?

Research shows that heavy use of social networks actually contributes to increased feelings of social isolation.[20] Researchers recommend the following to minimize social media's negative effects:

- Establish "sacred spaces" where there is no cell phone or Internet use, like the kitchen, living room, or car. This supports people communicating and connecting.
- Create events at home, work, or school that bring people together in conversation.
- Make an effort to connect to others in your environment. Say hello to people when you are out. Take a walk in nature.
- Remember that "friends" and "connections" on the Internet should not replace actual face-to-face interaction.[21]

Although personal loneliness is one real risk of overreliance on Internet social networks, it may not be the most dangerous. Social media speed the rate at which misinformation and rumors spread, enhancing the potential for manipulation. For example, as reported in *Censored 2012*, the US military has sought to manipulate social media sites by using fake online personas to influence Internet conversations and spread pro-American propaganda.[22] Social networks have the potential to ease the task of elite hegemony, a topic addressed in more detail by Elliot D. Cohen in chapter 7.

Journalism is undergoing its own integrative revolution. As editors seek innovations that will increase journalism's audience and inspire community involvement, a quiet revolution is underway to redefine the definition of "news." Peggy Holman of Journalism That Matters proposes adding a new question to the five (who, what, where, when, and why) that journalists conventionally pursue. Asking sources, "What's the best possible outcome you can see from this situation?" is central to this new journalism of possibility.[23] These possibility-oriented stories attract participation, inspire ideas, and activate individuals and community. When hard-hitting stories not only expose issues but also shed light on possible responses, something changes. Rather than leaving audience members informed but despairing or cynical about government, business, or their own community, such stories provide a hook for ordinary people to engage.

For additional examples of innovative journalism undertaken outside the constraints of corporate news, see chapter 4, "Media Democracy in Action."

INTEGRATIVE EDUCATION:
THE ART AND SCIENCE OF LIVING

What forms of education are appropriate for students facing the complexity of the twenty-first century? Scientific and technical education are often named, given the noteworthy successes of these fields over the last century. The sciences are best at describing physical realities—fostering a rational approach to education with a tendency to reduce life's complexities to abstract, intellectual understanding and objective descriptions.

Contrast this with engaged education focused on the social and creative arts—learning through direct (vs. abstract) experience. The arts teach students something that the sciences cannot—the primacy, uniqueness, and range of human experience. Studies show that mindfulness training and the multidimensional languages of art—sound, color, music, images, and narrative—can shift human consciousness in profound ways—awakening creative insight, and connecting us to more of who we are and what matters most. Art-based practices and mindful ritual have a great civilizing effect—helping to slow down, simplify, and transition to more sustainable, fulfilling lives—reminding us that we are surrounded by the luxuries of nature, art, and time—despite the hurry and excesses all around us.

True education is the return to the mind of the child.

—Mencius (Chinese philosopher, fourth century BCE)

Engaged learning also teaches us that baby mammals, including humans, learn best by playing and exploring. Instead of treating play as luxury, we can understand play as essential to creative living and complex problem solving—with play, not work, as the key to success.

Our global future is also calling us to develop greater social-emotional intelligence and to learn how to appreciate and relate to different cultures and worldviews. These pro-social skills and creative arts are associated with right-brained thought processes that support expanded, integrative thinking—making science, art and engaged learning natural partners in twenty-first-century education.

REDEFINING WEALTH AND ECONOMY

The human being can never be satisfied by wealth.

—from the Katha Upanishad

It is increasingly clear that under our current economic model, our societal problems run deeper than the financial page can explain, and that restoring economic growth will not solve them. The current debt crisis, resulting from a concentration of wealth and power in the hands of a few, presents a ripe opportunity for disillusioned and disenfranchised citizens to explore and transform our relationship to money.[24] In E. F. Schumacher's words, we need to develop a new economy that proceeds "as if people mattered."[25]

Until we disabuse ourselves of the fantasy that wealth—material possessions—fulfills our need for meaningful lives, nothing will prevent those who are good at accumulating it from doing so, inevitably at the expense of others. A 2010 study published in the *Proceedings of the National Academy of Sciences* found that once peoples' basic needs are met, additional income and other (external) rewards do not increase their happiness.[26] So what does support happiness? Is it possible to devise an economy where the standards that guides us are happiness and quality of life, instead of money and the gross national product?

Advocates for a new economy believe so. Guiding principles of this new economy include:

- ▶ collaboration and sharing;
- ▶ insuring access to necessary resources rather than ownership of them;
- ▶ stakeholder ownership;
- ▶ new indicators of economic success with a triple bottom line (social, environmental, and financial) as the standard for success;[27]

- local enterprise and community investment;
- and minimizing private rents for use of what should be public property or commons.[28]

In these ways, the new economy supports people's true needs, in contrast with one that artificially stimulates desires but leaves those true needs chronically starved.

Two fundamental principles from Gandhi's economic thinking are useful in understanding this new economy. First, the purpose of an economy is the satisfaction of material *needs*, not the satisfaction of human *wants*: "There is enough in the world for everyone's need; there isn't enough for everyone's greed." Our higher needs are not material and do not depend on finite resources. In a satisfying exchange, love and respect are resources that multiply with use. Second, our actual relationship to things—and to nonmaterial endowments like our talents and personal advantages—is that of *trustee*. Whatever the law may say, we are not their owners, and insofar as we use our endowments, our responsibility is to do so for the good of the whole.

In this view, three types of socioeconomic exchange redefine the meaning of wealth and help us to recover the natural relationship of cooperation.

1. A *gift economy* thrives among family and intimate friends: we help each other move, offer to babysit, or bring a sick neighbor a meal. The joy of giving without expecting anything in return promotes trust and solidarity. Occupy, Burning Man, and "free-cycling" networks exemplify the gift economy.

2. *Community exchange systems* include peer-to-peer production, crew funding, and worker-owned cooperatives.[29] *Peer-to-peer production* involves a free association of equals who pool resources to create products treated as commons rather than commodities.[30] The open-source, noncommercial design and distribution of some software is one example of this. Emphasizing collective intelligence and use value over market value, peer-to-peer exchange directly challenges the economic status quo of market allocation and corporate hierarchy. *Crew funding* brings together peoples' skills and resources to fund small businesses and other ventures.[31] According to the United Nations, nearly one billion people worldwide are member-owners of co-

operatives and co-ops are expected to be the world's fastest growing business model by 2025.[32] Worker-owned cooperatives provide for equitable distribution of wealth and genuine connection to the workplace, two key components of a sustainable economy.

3. *Community banking and state banks* provide an alternative to the multinational banks like the Bank of America, Wells Fargo, and Wachovia, whose financial misconduct has devastated so many people's lives.[33] Spurred by the Bank of North Dakota's success, fourteen states now have pending legislation to create or study the possibility of state-owned banks.[34] Bank of North Dakota has kept credit flowing throughout the financial crisis. It also keeps community banks thriving: North Dakota has more community banks per capita than any other state. Community banks serve local businesses, which in turn generate local jobs—a winning strategy in a job-starved market. Last year North Dakota had the lowest unemployment rate in the country.[35]

SCIENCE, TECHNOLOGY, AND SOCIETY

Science and the scientific method continue to bring humanity incredible knowledge and gifts; we stand in awe of, and in great debt to, the scientific community. Technology is a powerful force that has shaped and defined (to some degree) human life since the very beginning. Indeed, human history is directly related to the technologies of each era.[36]

Today, advances in science and technology have resulted in a computer-based age that offers many sectors of the population instant access to the world's information, as discussed above in the section on "Managing Media." However, technological developments often come at the expense of the environment and public health. For instance, as consumers replace outdated cellular phones and computers with the latest models, the disposal of the resulting toxic electronic waste impacts poor people and the environments in which they live, in places like China and Ghana.[37] And when market forces drive the development of technology, products that have undergone minimal testing or scientific oversight become available to consumers who do not fully know or understand the risks that they pose. In chapter 1, Elaine Wellin's "Environment and Health" news cluster reports on the risks posed by everyday household technologies including cell phones and microwave ovens, as well as carcinogenic ingredients in common bath products.

In Europe such concerns have led to regulatory policy premised on the *precautionary principle*: "Where the scientific data are insufficient, inconclusive or uncertain" or "where a preliminary scientific evaluation shows that potentially dangerous effects for the environment and human, animal or plant health can reasonably be feared . . . the risks are incompatible with the high level of protection sought by the European Union."[38] This legislation authorizes regulators to "stop distribution or order withdrawal from the market of products likely to be hazardous."[39]

There is active resistance to the precautionary principle in the US. American business interests describe it as unnecessary government regulation. Although laws authorize the Environmental Protection Agency and the Food and Drug Administration to intervene in cases of public health, compared with the EU, the US has limited centralized coordination of risk anticipation, risk assessment, risk reduction, and harm restitution.

COLLABORATIVE LEADERSHIP, TRUST, AND THE COMMON GOOD

There is no human institution [without] its dangers. The greater the institution the greater the chances of abuse. Democracy is a great institution and therefore it is liable to be greatly abused. The remedy, therefore, is not avoidance of democracy but reduction of possibility of abuse to a minimum.

—Gandhi

Commons movements—epitomized most recently by Occupy and its 99 percent—have the potential to produce fundamental changes in our economy and politics. But such movements require a new type of leadership to realize their potential for creating commons-based alternatives to private markets and polarized politics. Dan Pink suggests a set of integrative skills for twenty-first-century leaders and workers—skills such as storytelling, teamwork, empathy, play, and design that are associated with right-brained processes of intuition, creative thinking, and relationship. Activating these skills gets people thinking, feeling, and making associations across natural polarities.[40]

In particular, new leaders need to recognize the power of art (music, dance, story, poetry, image making) and ritual to galvanize communities in shared, meaningful experience. The arts bring us together and help lead the movement.

The collaborative leader needs to be process-oriented, developing skills and employing methods that facilitate meaningful dialogue and manage conflict.[41] Emphasizing process shifts leadership responsibility from a few central figures—the conventional paradigm for most movements—to collective participation. This way we discover how to build common trust and connection across our differences and support a culture of collaboration and sharing. Put another way, the challenge of collaborative leadership requires finding a balance between centralized and decentralized authority. In *The Starfish and the Spider*, Ori Brafman and Rod A. Beckstrom make the case for decentralization.[42] However, their subtitle, *The Unstoppable Power of Leaderless Movements*, is not entirely supported by their argument. What they actually show is that a harmonious combination of decentralization and localized authority is the hallmark of the most successful organizations. They call that harmonious balance the "sweet spot."

What is the "sweet spot" for a contemporary commons movement committed to principled nonviolence? We propose it would combine two things: an overall strategic plan and *appropriate* leadership. Lasting movements require some degree of leadership or they fall apart.

Gandhi exemplified the appropriate kind of leadership. Although he took final responsibility for all decisions in the midst of intense campaigns, openly calling himself a "general," the military analogy only went so far. The differences were clear, both in description and actual practice:

- ▸ He stepped back immediately when his authority ended.
- ▸ He carefully laid out a complete devolution of authority down to the individual level in case he and his "lieutenants" were arrested—as happened most famously during the Salt Satyagraha of 1930.
- ▸ He made the personal growth of his followers a primary concern.
- ▸ He kept nothing for himself. He left the world "worth" about five dollars in material possessions, having raised millions of rupees for various causes. His was truly "servant leadership."

Though Gandhi's presence is missing now, nothing prevents us from cultivating qualities like these in ourselves, or recognizing and supporting them in others. Thus, a kind of decentralized leadership could emerge that is not toxic and does not violate the spirit of the new social movements. The opposite of abusive authority isn't *no* authority; it's respected, selfless authority. Movement leaders should aim for an appropriate balance between setting direction and empowering others to take ownership.

Many in Occupy have begun to feel that the first wave of the movement—characterized by spontaneous protest coordinated through social media—has run its course, and it is time to dig in for a long, serious struggle. In this spirit, the Metta Center for Nonviolence offers its Roadmap, articulating the following principles:

▸ Person Power: the development of the individual's full capacity to contribute;
▸ Constructive Program: an emphasis on building community, supplying our own needs, and winning over the public, in order to create the world that we want; and
▸ Nonviolent Resistance: participants who are trained and prepared to resist in an appropriate way and intensity, at key leverage points.[43]

The steps of the Metta Center's road map help to resolve the dilemma pointed out by Paul Hawken:[44] Although Occupy may be a reflection of the largest social movement ever seen, it is not really a movement per se but a number of disconnected projects that lack developed leadership, a common ideology and a strategic overview.[45]

Conversation is at the heart of collaboration and a vital source of empowerment. Positive change begins with people discussing what they value. Meaningful conversation is an antidote to our increasing isolation from each other and a key to resolving important issues in our communities; it is perhaps the best remedy for the sense of alienation that underlies much of society's crime, vandalism, and terrorism. Authentic, nonpartisan conversation is the premier collaborative practice to empower ourselves and develop trusting relationships. In fact, the Latin and Indo-European roots of "con" and "vers" mean a "turning together." Talk is one-way. Conversation demands listening and talking in equal degrees. When we speak our truths and hear each other deeply, hearts and minds are opened, and we turn together.[46]

APPROPRIATE TRUST OR FEAR, OPPOSITION TO COLLABO-RATION AND TECHNOLOGIES OF SHARING

The most common way people give up their power is by thinking they don't have any.

—Alice Walker

At the heart of collaboration is our ability to create conditions that warrant appropriate trust. Knowing who and what are trustworthy is central to an equitable and secure future. Yet, we seem to have lost trust in one another and our collective institutions. An October 2011 poll found that fewer than one in seven Americans trust the government "to do what's right almost always or most of the time," an all-time low since pollsters began asking the question in 1958.[47] A similar percentage of those questioned in an earlier 2010 poll showed a lack of confidence in the government's "ability to stand up to vested interests."[48] If this is the dominant view of "The People," we need to do something about this. A people divided against itself cannot stand, and if there are issues of secrecy and corruption in government, we need to collectively organize and make the necessary reforms. Yet, without a sense of trust and common purpose, this is unlikely.

In our pain-avoiding culture, most people think that the mentally healthy life is the one characterized by the absence of crisis. Nothing could be farther from the truth. What characterizes mental (and social) health is how early we meet in crisis.

—M. Scott Peck

The information superstructure and global economic integration have led to more connections among people, markets, and ideas that ever before. And, there is great hope that peace between oppressors and the oppressed, and amongst warring factions, will be possible, using advances in information-sharing to build a platform for the generation and circulation of ideas and values. Cooperation on a global scale has the potential to increase economic performance, abolish war and famine, and achieve environmental sustainability.

Some may say collaboration is idealistic and unlikely. We would point at evolutionary history, which demonstrates the repeated organization of self-interested living processes into greater and greater unified cooperatives. The emergence of a cooperative society could well be the next step in a long trend in the evolution in which the nature of cooperative organization has progressively improved. We put our money on life and its evolutionary capacity—in other words, its greater diversity, complexity, capacity, and meaning. The cooperative future looks bright.

> *Make Connections*
> *Collaborate for Impact*
> *Learn and Innovate*
> *Dwell in Possibilities*
> *Incite Hope and the Love That Does Justice*
> —from the Interaction Institute for Social Change

KENN BURROWS has been an educator and consultant for over thirty years, teaching holistic health studies at San Francisco State University since 1991. He is founder of the Holistic Health Learning Center, a unique library and community action center staffed by student volunteers. He is also the producer of The Future of Health Care, a biennial conference. Prior to coming to SF State, he taught at Foothill Community College for twelve years and operated Stress-Care, a corporate training and consulting company. He also serves as faculty advisor to Project Censored as the SF State affiliate, and is a member of the executive board of the Media Freedom Foundation.

MICHAEL NAGLER is one of the most respected scholars and advocates of Gandhi and nonviolence in the world today. He is professor emeritus of classics and comparative literature at University of California–Berkeley, where he founded the Peace and Conflict Studies Program; founder and president of the Metta Center for Nonviolence (mettacenter.org); and author of, among other books and articles, *Our Spiritual Crisis* and *The Search for a Nonviolent Future*, which received a 2002 American Book Award and has been translated into Arabic, Italian, Korean, Croatian, and several other languages. Among other awards, he received the Jamnalal Bajaj International Award for Promoting Gandhian Values Outside India in 2007. Michael is a student of Sri Eknath Easwaran, founder of the Blue Mountain Center of Meditation (easwaran.org). He has lived at the center's ashram in Marin County since 1970 and is a presenter for their programs of passage meditation.

Notes

1. From a 1950 letter, quoted in Walter Sullivan, "The Einstein Papers: A Man of Many Parts," *New York Times*, March 29, 1972.
2. Barry Johnson, *Polarity Management: Indentifying and Managing Unsolvable Problems* (Amherst MA: HRD Press), 1996.
3. Jonathan Haidt, *The Righteous Mind: Why Good People Are Divided By Politics and Religion* (New York: Pantheon, 2012), 191ff.
4. Ibid., 107.
5. Larissa MacFarquhar, "Thank You for Not Fighting," *New York Times*, April 5, 1998, http://www.nytimes.com/books/98/04/05/reviews/980405.05macfart.html.
6. Johnson, *Polarity Management*.
7. Ibid.
8. Johan Galtung, "Cultural Violence," *Journal of Peace Research* 27 no. 3 (1990): 291–305.
9. See, for example, Peter Ackerman and Jack DuVall, *A Force More Powerful: A Century of Non-Violent Resistance* (New York: Palgrave, 2000), chap. 5.
10. For example, consider the high suicide rate among American soldiers returned from Iraq and Afghanistan, as reported in Peter Phillips and Craig Cekala, "Human Costs of War and Violence," in *Censored 2012: The Top Censored Stories and Media Analysis of 2010–11*, ed. Mickey Huff (New York: Seven Stories Press, 2011), 46–48. For an update on this story, see chap. 2 of this volume.
11. Martin Luther King Jr. quoted in Stephanie Van Hook, "How to Sustain a Revolution," *Truthout*, January 4, 2012, http://truth-out.org/opinion/item/5895-how-to-sustain-a-revolution.
12. As told to author Kenn Burrows by Arun Gandhi, grandson of Mahatma Gandhi.
13. See, for example, Michael Nagler, "Occupy 2.0: The Great Turning," *YES! Magazine*, April 5, 2012, http://www.yesmagazine.org/people-power/occupy-2.0-the-great-turning.
14. Hillary Mayell, "Human 'Footprint' Seen on 83 Percent of Earth's Land," *National Geographic News*, October 25, 2002, http://news.nationalgeographic.com/news/2002/10/1025_021025_HumanFootprint.html. The human "footprint" extends to the world's oceans as well; see, for example, "Oceans in Peril," Censored story #2 in chap. 1 of this volume.
15. Joel Smith, "It's Not About the Footprint: It's Also the Handprint," *Pacific Northwest Inlander*, April 18, 2012, http://www.inlander.com/spokane/article-17842-its-not-about-the-footprint.html. See also http://www.carbonhandprint.org.
16. United Nations Educational, Scientific and Cultural Organization, "Education for Sustainable Development (ESD)," http://www.unesco.org/new/en/education/themes/leading-the-international-agenda/education-for-sustainable-development.
17. Center for Media Literacy, "What Is Media Literacy? A Definition . . . And More," http://www.medialit.org/reading-room/what-media-literacy-definitionand-more.
18. Zizi Papacharissi, "The Virtual Geographies of Social Networks: A Comparative Analysis of Facebook, LinkedIn and A Small World," *New Media and Society* 11 (2009): 199–220.
19. Jon Russell, "Fueled by Emerging Markets, Facebook Set to Hit 1 Billion Users in August," *The Next Web*, January 12, 2012, http://thenextweb.com/facebook/2012/01/12/fuelled-by-emerging-markets-facebook-set-to-hit-1-billion-users-in-august.
20. RebeccaSweeney91, "Social Networking Sites; More Harm Than Good?," Online Conference on Networks and Communities, April 27, 2011, http://networkconference.netstudies.org/2011/04/social-networking-sites-more-harm-than-good.
21. Ibid.
22. Elliot D. Cohen, "Social Media and Internet Freedom," in *Censored 2012: The Top Censored Stories and Media Analysis of 2010–11*, ed. Mickey Huff (New York: Seven Stories Press, 2011), 58–60.
23. See, for example, Michelle Strutzenberger, "Create a Narrative of Possibility by Adding a New Question: Peggy Holman," Axiom News, October 21, 2011, http://axiomnews.ca/node/1798.
24. Rob Williams, "From Bankster Bailout to Blessed Unrest: News We Can Use to Create a US Economy for the 99%," in chap. 1 of this volume, develops this theme in more detail.

25. E. F. Schumacher, *Small Is Beautiful: Economics As If People Matter* (Point Roberts WA: Hartley & Marks, 1999[1973]).

26. Daniel Kahneman and Angus Deaton, "High Income Improves Evaluation of Life But Not Emotional Well-Being," *Proceedings of the National Academy of Sciences*, September 7, 2010, http://www.pnas.org/content/early/2010/08/27/1011492107.full.pdf+html. See also *David McRaney*, "The Fascinating Scientific Reason Why 'Money Doesn't Buy Happiness,'" *AlterNet*, *January 25, 2012*, http://www.alternet.org/health/153887/the_fascinating_scientific_reason_why_%22money_doesn't_buy_happiness%22.

27. The Kingdom of Bhutan has been a leader in this area. In 2011, sixty-eight countries joined Bhutan in cosponsoring a resolution titled "Happiness: Towards a Holistic Approach to Development," which the UN General Assembly adopted by consensus. In April 2012, Bhutan hosted an international meeting focused on the topic, "Wellbeing and Happiness: Defining a New Economic Paradigm." Held at the UN's New York headquarters, this meeting sought to launch a global movement toward measuring—and increasing—human happiness and quality of life as an alternative to the narrow, conventional measures of economic growth and development. See "Wellbeing & Happiness: Defining a New Economic Paradigm," Government of Bhutan, April 2, 2012, http://www.2apr.gov.bt.

28. See, for example, Gar Alperovitz, "The Rise of the New Economy Movement," *AlterNet*, May 20, 2012, http://www.alternet.org/economy/155452/the_rise_of_the_new_economy_movement.

29. In addition to the three forms detailed here, community exchange systems also includes the DIY (Do It Yourself) and DIWO (Do It With Others) movements, time banks, and community currency programs. See, for examples, http://makezine.com; the Bay Area Community Exchange Timebank, http://timebank.sfbace.org; and the Complementary Currency Resource Center, http://www.complementarycurrency.org.

30. Michael Bauwens, "Blueprint for P2P Society: The Partner State & Ethical Economy," *Shareable*, April 7, 2012, http://www.shareable.net/blog/a-blueprint-for-p2p-institutions-the-partner-state-and-the-ethical-economy-o.

31. See, for instance, http://crewfund.org.

32. Jessica Reeder, "The Year of the Cooperative," *Yes! Magazine*, February 1, 2012, http://www.yes-magazine.org/new-economy/2012-the-year-of-the-cooperative. See Censored story #7 in chap. 1 of this volume.

33. On the damage done by multinational banks, see Williams, "From Bankster Bailout to Blessed Unrest," in chap. 1 of this volume.

34. Kenn Burrows and Tom Atlee, "Collaboration and Common Good," in *Censored 2012: The Top Censored Stories and Media Analysis of 2010–11*, ed. Mickey Huff (New York: Seven Stories Press, 2011), 141–43.

35. Kelly McCartney, "Report: Public Banking Can Democratize the Economy," *Shareable*, May 31, 2011, http://www.shareable.net/blog/new-report-public-banking-can-democratize-the-economy.

36. For one perspective on technology's role in human evolution, see Kevin Kelly, "Technology's Epic Story," TEDxAmsterdam video, November 2009, http://www.ted.com/talks/lang/en/kevin_kelly_tells_technology_s_epic_story.html. Kelly defines technology as "anything useful invented by the (human) mind," including not only physical products, but also cultural inventions such as laws, libraries, and cities. He argues that technology helps us reinvent ourselves and our relationship with the natural and cultural world.

37. See, for example, "Guiyu: E-wasteland of the World," CNC, June 19, 2012, http://www.cnc-world.tv/news/v_show/25325_Guiyu:_E-wasteland_of_the_world.shtml; and Stephen Leahy, "Ghana: Toxic Electronic Waste Contaminates Surrounding Area," *All Africa*, November 1, 2011, http://allafrica.com/stories/201111020037.html.

38. Summaries of European Union Legislation, Glossary, http://europa.eu/legislation_summaries/glossary/precautionary_principle_en.htm.

39. "The Precautionary Principle," Europa: Summaries of European Union Legislation, February 2, 2000, http://europa.eu/legislation_summaries/consumers/consumer_safety/l32042_en.htm.

40. Daniel H. Pink, *A Whole New Mind: Why Right-Brainers Will Rule the Future* (New York: Berkeley Publishing Group, 2005).

41. The National Coalition for Dialogue and Deliberation offers rich materials to train and support community leaders, consultants, and citizens in developing collaborative leadership skills. See http://ncdd.org.

42. Ori Brafman and Rod A. Beckstrom, *The Starfish and the Spider: The Unstoppable Power of Leaderless Movements* (New York: Portfolio, 2006).

43. Metta Center for Nonviolence, "Roadmap: From Spontaneous Protest to Unstoppable Movement," http://vimeo.com/45555473.

44. Paul Hawken, *Blessed Unrest: How the Largest Movement in the World Came into Being and Why No One Saw It Coming* (New York: Viking, 2007).

45. For another perspective on Occupy, see Michael Levitin's contribution in chap. 4 of this volume.

46. Jack Ricchiuto, "The Power of Conversation," *Interaction Institute for Social Change Blog*, video, posted August 10, 2010, http://interactioninstitute.org/blog/2010/08/10/the-power-of-conversation-2. On the Interaction Institute for Social Change Blog, Jack Ricchiuto discusses four types of generative questions and related conversations that can help people shift their sense of alienation, distrust, and fragmentation so that they can experience greater connection and civic engagement.

47. Eric Alterman, "Think Again: The Era of the '1 Percent,'" *Center for American Progress*, October 6, 2011, http://www.americanprogress.org/issues/2011/10/ta100611.html.

48. Ibid.

PROJECT CENSORED INTERNATIONAL

Case Studies of "Unhistory" in the Making

Introduction by Dr. Andy Lee Roth

Fishery biologists and oceanographers in the mid-1990s developed the concept of "shifting baselines" to describe changes over time in expectations about what constituted a healthy ecosystem. The five chapters that comprise this section of *Censored 2013* exemplify how we might broaden the "shifting baselines" concept, first developed by biologists, to analyze the health—or degradation—of *sociopolitical* systems.

One original example of "shifting baselines" involved the number of salmon in the Pacific Northwest's Columbia River. In the 1990s, biologists determined that the Columbia's salmon population was twice as great as in the 1930s. That sounds excellent until you consider that the 1990s population amounted to only 10 percent of the salmon found there in the 1800s. Any determination of an ecosystem's health, or degradation, depends on what baseline we use. When we lose track of earlier conditions—such as the 1800s salmon population—we are subject to a shifting baseline.[1]

Sociologically, the phenomenon of shifting baselines exacerbates the challenges we face in resisting the oppressive consequences of hierarchical power in at least three institutional domains that are elementary for every contemporary society: (1) the increasing regulation of individual behavior in political and legal spheres; (2) the consolidation of wealth and the externalization of its consequences, which constitute economic power; and (3) the conglomeration of media and the consequent loss of diversity in news content.

Max Weber's *Protestant Ethic and the Spirit of Capitalism* can be understood as a case study in shifting baselines, documenting how the systematic accumulation of wealth, which the Christian church at best tolerated, shifted to the point that it became a desirable, even obligatory end under Calvinism. George Orwell's *1984* displayed insight into the utility of shifting baselines for consolidating and maintaining political order. In the Newspeak of this dystopian future, an "unperson" is someone erased from existence by the government for breaking the law. Just to mention an unperson's name is considered "thoughtcrime." More recently, Noam Chomsky has written about "unhistory," observing our failure to remember, much less commemorate, solemn anniversaries in our shared history.[2] When we lose track of earlier conditions, our baselines shift and we more readily accept, often without awareness of having done so, degradations that in the past we would have deemed unacceptable.

The five chapters that follow can be thought of as case studies of "unhistory" in the making. Though not explicit in any of them, the concept of shifting baselines can be seen at work in all. In chapter 11, Almerindo Ojeda analyzes how official language both vilifies the men and boys imprisoned by the United States in Guantánamo and diminishes our understanding of the violence they suffer there. Language abuse, Ojeda writes, enables prisoner abuse. His analysis explicates the fundamental role that official language plays in contributing to the US public's increasingly callous attitudes toward those detained indefinitely without trial at Guantánamo[3]—even though indefinite detention and torture violate national and international law.

When indefinite detention and torture become acceptable, then the baseline for other controversial practices may shift more easily as well. "Targeted killing," a euphemism for extrajudicial assassination, is one such case. In chapter 12, Andy Lee Roth documents how corporate news coverage contributes to a false sense of consensus about the legitimacy of US drone strikes as a means of targeted killing. In covering the United States' killing of Anwar al-Awlaki, an American citizen, corporate journalists essentially adapted government officials' descriptions of al-Awlaki as a true threat to the US and therefore a valid target. When the government's murder of one of its own citizens, without trial or verdict, is allowed to pass without protest, it becomes hard to imagine how American citizens, much less their political leaders, will feel much in the way of responsibility for Iraqi refugees devastated by the US invasions of Iraq.

As Angel Ryono shows in chapter 13, "media silence around the plight of the Iraqi refugees has political roots." Government officials have worked to disconnect the American public from the realities of the war, while corporate media have done little to inform the public about relevant distinctions among refugees, migrant workers, and "illegal" immigrants. Without any trustworthy baseline for what life in Iraq was like—not only before the US invasions, but also prior to Saddam Hussein's rule—Americans have no basis for fully appreciating the devastation of Iraqi society, much less the plight of Iraq's diasporic refugee population.

Of course, the United States' government and media do not possess a monopoly on shifting political baselines or unhistory. In chapter 14, Brian Covert examines the historical background for the March 2011 Fukushima Daiichi nuclear disaster. He tracks the vested interests linking Japan's corporate media and its atomic energy industry. "The media in Japan, like the government regulators, have been intimate with the nation's atomic energy club from the very start." Covert extracts from Japan's atomic unhistory the crucial role of media mogul Matsutaro Shoriki and analyzes how Japan's *kisha* (reporters') clubs contribute to press self-censorship.

Finally, in chapter 15, Tara Dorabji provides an on-the-ground report from Indian-occupied Kashmir, where from 1989 to 2011 the Indian government killed more than 70,000 Kashmiris and disappeared another 8,000. Dorabji reports two quite different responses: on one hand, "there is global silence"—unhistory in the making, the baselines shifting yet again to favor the powerful at the expense of ordinary people; on the other hand, a "strong current of popular, nonviolent uprising for freedom has been growing" in Kashmir.

Collectively these five chapters show how failure to notice change contributes to oppressive institutions. Though government and corporate institutions feature centrally in the analyses of Guantánamo, the US "covert" drone war, the plight of Iraqi refugees, the road to

Fukushima, and the ongoing Kashmir genocide, news media play a pivotal role too. When news media fail to inform the public, shifting baselines syndrome becomes more likely, producing "another chapter in the overflowing annals of unhistory."[4] By contrast, when journalism functions at its best, the news contributes to the maintenance of firm baselines by alerting the public when powerful interests transgress the boundaries that protect healthy, democratic societies.

Notes

1. See, for example, Randy Olson, "Slow Motion Disaster Beneath the Waves," *Los Angeles Times*, November 17, 2002, http://www.shiftingbaselines.org/op_ed/index.html.
2. Noam Chomsky, "Anniversaries from 'Unhistory,'" *In These Times*, February 6, 2012, http://www.inthesetimes.com/article/12679/anniversaries_from_unhistory.
3. For example, a February 2012 *Washington Post*–ABC News poll found that 70 percent of those polled supported keeping open the prison at Guantánamo for terrorist suspects, while just 13 percent strongly disapproved. See more at http://www.washingtonpost.com/wp-srv/politics/polls/postabcpoll_020412.html.
4. Chomsky, "Anniversaries."

CHAPTER 11

Guantánamospeak and the Manufacture of Consent

by Almerindo E. Ojeda

For those who stubbornly seek freedom around the world, there can be no more urgent task than to come to understand the mechanisms and practices of indoctrination. . . . Propaganda is to democracy what violence is to totalitarianism.

—Noam Chomsky

This *Occupy UC Davis—Dissent Lecture* was delivered December 1, 2011, at the Paulo Freire Open University (ex-Dutton Hall), University of California–Davis.

Much has been made about prisoner abuse at Guantánamo. And rightly so: Guantánamo is an ongoing crime against humanity. If you don't believe me, take a look at The Guantánamo Testimonials Project we have been carrying out at this campus. But even though a lot has been said, there and elsewhere, about *prisoner* abuse at Guantánamo, relatively little has been said about *language* abuse at the Cuban base. Yet, there has been a lot of it. And we need to talk about it. If only because prisoner abuse is *enabled* by language abuse.

Abusing a human being is not easy to do; consenting to do it is not something that comes naturally. As a matter of fact, the consent to abuse a fellow human being is something that needs to be *manufactured.*[1] It needs to be built. Like a house. Brick by brick and room by room.

How was this *consent to abuse* manufactured at Guantánamo? First you instill fear. You say that Guantánamo holds vicious criminals that would not hesitate to chew on hydraulic tubes to bring an airplane down. Then you cultivate hatred. You say that each and every one of the individuals detained at the base was personally responsible for 9/11. Then you abuse language; you engage in what Orwell would call *Guantánamospeak*. It is this third step that I want to focus on today.

The abuse of language at Guantánamo began by coining the term *war on terror*. A war is something that threatens the very survival of a nation. Consequently, no citizen of that nation can be against it. Except for the traitors who seek the destruction of their own nation. But is terrorism something that threatens the survival of our nation? It can lead to massive loss of life, as 9/11 did. And it can be a crime against humanity, as 9/11 was. But *threaten the survival of a nation*? Wars are events that have only two natural outcomes: victory or defeat. Consequently, if you do not root for victory, you are rooting for defeat. Only a traitor can root for defeat.

But casting our response to 9/11 in terms of a war creates a linguistic problem. What would you call someone you capture in that war? *Prisoner of war*? This would be extremely problematic, as prisoners of war have rights under the Geneva Conventions, one of them being the right to be free from coercive interrogation. But interrogate coercively is something our government very much wanted to do with these captives. So we called them *detainees* instead of *prisoners*. This has an added rhetorical advantage: it makes imprisonment at Guantánamo sound like a minor inconvenience—like being detained by traffic. *So we should consent to that.*

By the way, the verb *capture* is already loaded. Being captured is what happens to fugitives, possibly of justice, and hence to criminals. Never mind that some of the individuals held at Guantánamo were *captured* in their homes with their families. Or fleeing carpet bombing. Or coming out of a courthouse that had just cleared them from charges of terrorism. Or were handed to us by local militias in exchange for bounties—a practice that might be called *human trafficking* in legal circles.

Alternatively, Guantánamo prisoners may be called *enemy combatants*. This reinforces the context of war, and hence the survival of the nation. But mention of *war* again brings about the term of *prisoner of war.* So we should clarify the term enemy combatant and speak of *unprivileged* enemy combatants. Adding the adjective *unprivileged* manages to turn the *rights* of the Geneva Conventions into *privileges.* Privileges are things that are granted by the grace of a legitimate authority. Rights are something you have regardless of the generosity of the powers that be. Rights are something powers can no more grant than they can withhold.

And just for the record: Guantánamo prisoners *have* rights under the Geneva Conventions. Everyone held in an armed conflict is protected by these conventions. The fact that some captives did not wear uniforms only means that they do not have the rights Geneva grants to combatants. They would still have the rights granted to civilians. For civilians *are* protected by the Geneva Conventions as well as combatants. I should add that thinking that the Guantánamo prisoners are in fact protected by the Geneva Conventions is not my interpretation; it is the interpretation of the International Committee of the Red Cross, which is the accepted arbiter for the implementation of the Geneva Conventions. It is the organization the signatories of the Conventions, the United States included, have agreed to abide by.

But we digress. Let's return to *Guantánamospeak.*

Guantánamo prisoners are being coercively interrogated. This, of course, is not what it is called. That may enable dissent. In Guantánamo, when you are taken from your cell in order to be interrogated, you are said to be making good on *a reservation.* Or to be going for *an interview.* So being interrogated is like going to a restaurant. Or applying for a job. Nothing to dissent about there.

Interestingly, language does not always take the abuse lying down; sometimes, it fights back. Guantánamo personnel may say, for example, that so-and-so is *going to reservation,* a phrase that we would never use for making good on a reservation made at a restaurant (and betrays the attempt to veil the reference to interrogations, which are something one *would* "go to").

As has been thoroughly reported, interrogations at Guantánamo can be brutal. They may involve beatings, sleep deprivation, solitary confinement, exposure to temperature extremes, blaring noise, painful binding, and threats of death or harm to self or to others. Such practices are what independent observers call *torture.* But they cannot be called that in Guantánamo. That would sow the seeds of dissent. There, these practices are collectively referred to as procedures of *enhanced interrogation* instead. Interrogation is acceptable in a criminal setting, i.e. given legal protections. So what is wrong with enhancing an acceptable procedure? We should consent to it.

Each one of the aforementioned forms of torture has its own special entry in the dictionary of *Guantánamospeak*. Food deprivation is called *dietary manipulation*—a lapse, perhaps, as manipulation often refers to less-than-legitimate doings (language fights back again). Sleep deprivation is called *sleep management* (nothing wrong with managing sleep, is there? After all, you do not want to be a slouch). Under one of the modalities of sleep management, a prisoner can be moved, almost continuously from one cell to another for weeks. This involves full bodily searches, gatherings of belongings, three-chain shackling, marching from one cell to another, and unshackling. This is done around the clock for weeks, and as a consequence the prisoner is unable to sleep for more than one hour at a time. This form of sleep deprivation is referred to as the *frequent flyer program*—so the movement from cell to cell is to be thought of as the benefits program one gets from an airline by traveling a lot with it. This is supposed to be funny. The program is also called *Operation Sandman*, thus making a perverse reference to the nursery rhyme used to put children to sleep—and acknowledging, via sarcasm, the real purpose of the exercise.

The most common form of beating in Guantánamo comes in the context of forced cell removals. Suppose a noncompliant prisoner refuses to go to interrogation (or to make good on a reservation he never made). An Immediate Reaction Force is called in. An Immediate Reaction Force is a team of six guards in full riot gear that march into a cell, pepper spray the prisoner (some of you may know about this first-hand). . . . In any event, they pepper spray the prisoner, charge on him, slam him onto the ground, beat him up badly, hog-tie him, and take him wherever he needs to be—which, at that point, is usually the infirmary.

Interestingly, these events are called *irfs* (based on the acronym for Immediate Reaction Force), and the action itself is called an *irfing*. *Irf* is a new word of American English. But we didn't need it. We already had a term for that. It would be *aggravated battery*. But that phrase, of course, would sow dissent, and cannot be used.

Beyond aggravated battery, three-chain shackling (on wrists, ankles, and waist) is referred to as *wearing a three-piece suit*, thus making light of excessive binding by reference to an elegant suit of clothes. To *soften up* a *hardened terrorist* in reservation, the prisoner is made to squat on the floor over a metal eye-ring, to which he is painfully chained from his wrists and ankles. This is called a *stress position*, stress being an unavoidable feature of modern life. Independent observers might call that *binding torture* instead. Then, if all else fails, a prisoner is threatened with being taken to a country where he can be physically abused (beaten, electroshocked, cut, suffocated, or burned). This is a practice of *torture by proxy* from which we can remove ourselves linguistically by appealing to the aseptic term *extraordinary rendition*. Language is used here to conceal reality rather than to reveal it.

But the most common form of torture associated with the war on terror is waterboarding. Being a widespread form of torture, waterboarding goes under myriad names the world over. It is not certain that waterboarding actually happened at Guantánamo. But other forms of controlled suffocation (*dryboarding*) have been proposed as explanations for the first three deaths in custody at the base. The one pertinent testimony we have about actual waterboarding has reached us anonymously, allegedly from a guard, who said the practice happened *all the time* at Guantánamo, where it was not called *waterboarding* but *drown-proofing*. As if prisoners were being protected from drowning—which I guess is true. Except that it is we who are causing the drowning. And the protection is only from the natural outcome of drowning: death. And only to prolong the agony of the victim.

Incidentally, waterboarding is sometimes described as *simulated drowning*. Or as a procedure that induces the *misperception of drowning*. This is inaccurate and misleading. It is inaccurate because waterboarding is not simulated drowning; it is actual drowning. Only that it is controlled so as to prevent death and thus prolong the agony. *Controlled drowning* would therefore be closer to the mark. Describing waterboarding as *simulated drowning* is also misleading, as it suggests that the problem with waterboarding is *deception*—which would be no problem at all; deception is a perfectly legal interrogation tactic.

In 2004, the Supreme Court dealt the first of three blows to Guantánamo. It ruled that prisoners had to be given a semblance of their day in court. What they got was significantly less than a semblance. They got a farce. They were subjected to so-called Combatant Status Review Tribunals (CSRTs). They were called *tribunals* in order to say that the ruling of the Supreme Court was followed. But they were nothing like a real American tribunal. First, the prisoners were not allowed a lawyer, only a *personal representative*. And that representative was a member of the military. Consequently, the representative had the same employer as the prosecution. The tribunal took place before a panel of three judges. They too were members of the military, as was the "court of appeals" that could overturn the decisions of these tribunals.

As if this were not enough, the prisoner could be tried on secret evidence, so there was no way he could defend himself properly. Hearsay was admitted into the record as well. And the evidence brought about by the prosecution could not be questioned. It had to be taken as fact. This asymmetry between the claims of the prosecution and those of the defense can be traced linguistically in the transcripts of the CSRTs. The allegations of the prisoner are described as such by appealing to verbs of saying (what are known in the trade as *verba dicendi*). *Verba dicendi* are verbs like *says, alleges, claims*. Crucially, however, the charges of the prosecution are mentioned straight up without such verbs. The impression you therefore get is not one of a conflict between charges and refutations, but one of a clash between facts and counterclaims. The former breeds dissent; the latter, consent.

The outcomes of the CSRTs were also interesting specimens of *Guantánamospeak*. The verdicts of these tribunals were not, as one may expect, innocence or guilt. No; they were "*still* an enemy combatant" or "*no longer* an enemy combatant." For, finding that a prisoner was *not* an enemy combatant would question the original evidence supporting his capture. It would also raise the possibility that he was imprisoned without cause in the first place. But that would detract from the consent being manufactured.

Amazingly, in remarkably few cases, and in spite of having the cards stacked squarely against him, a prisoner could be ruled to be no longer an enemy combatant. At which point, the "court of appeals," which, as we said, was also employed by the military, convened a new tribunal to review the results. Such revised tribunals invariably reversed the ruling of the first tribunals, and found the prisoners to be correctly designated as enemy combatants after all. Interestingly, these new tribunals were called *reconvened tribunals*. As if the original tribunal had just taken a break for lunch and "reconvened" afterwards. Never mind that the new tribunal had an entirely different panel of judges, was allegedly handed new evidence, and reached the opposite verdict than the old one.

One of the constant fears in Guantánamo is that the prisoners would commit suicide (prison suicides reflect poorly on prisoner treatment). So suicides are linguistically impossible in Guantánamo. According to the prison manuals that have been made public, what we have there can only be described as *self-harm gestures*—like slapping your forehead or biting your fingernails, I suppose.

Hunger strikes are linguistically impossible in Guantánamo as well. Like prison suicides, prison hunger strikes are signs of poor conditions at the prison. Thus, what the Guantánamo manuals prescribe is the use, not of hunger strikes, but only of *total voluntary fasts*. This contorted Orwellian idiom removes hunger strikes from the realm of protest and transfers them into the realm of religious beliefs (the prisoners are religious fanatics anyway). And into the realm of free, voluntary activity, the existence of which would actually reflect well on the prison.

Incidentally, I mentioned that some Guantánamo manuals have been made public, thanks to the transparency organization WikiLeaks. This is no small matter, given the amount of censorship that clouds the base. Once again, censorship (which is unbecoming to a democracy) is called *secrecy*—an admissible practice in wartime. It is also called *redaction* when it is applied to a document. But to *redact* a document means to *write it* (or used to mean as much before the war on terror). By co-opting the term *redaction*, censorship vanishes into the very creation of the document; it becomes inevitable, and, hence, acceptable.

More than 600 of the 779 individuals who have been imprisoned at Guantánamo at one time or another have been released. A few of them went on to engage in hostilities against the United States or their interests (exactly how few is in dispute). This has been described as *recidivism*. Or as *returning to the battlefield*. Even if their captors never claimed that the so-called battlefield returnees had ever been in a battlefield in the first place. The possibility that these individuals were actually retaliating for the torture they endured at Guantánamo is seldom raised. For that would suggest that some of the violence we endure is the result of the violence we inflict.

Consenting to abuse a fellow human being is not something that happens naturally; it is something that needs to be *manufactured*.

ALMERINDO E. OJEDA, PHD, is professor of linguistics at the University of California–Davis, where he serves as founding director of the Center for the Study of Human Rights in the Americas and the principal investigator for its flagship Guantánamo Testimonials Project.

Note

1. Walter Lippmann coined the term *the manufacture of consent* in his 1921 book *Public Opinion* (see Chapter XV). According to Lippmann, the manufacture of consent was a form of propaganda that the *élite* had to unleash on the unenlightened masses of a modern democracy. Subsequently, Noam Chomsky and Edward Herman used the term in the title to a book they published in 1988. In *Manufacturing Consent*, they revealed the way in which the profit motive corrupts the mainstream media into manufacturing consent. The term *Guantánamospeak* is based on the term *Newspeak* that George Orwell coined in his book *1984*. The epigraph to this paper was taken from "Propaganda, American-style," an article that is available online at zpub.com/un/chomsky.

CHAPTER 12

Framing Al-Awlaki
How Government Officials and Corporate Media Legitimized a Targeted Killing

by Andy Lee Roth

A state is a human community that (successfully) claims the monopoly of the legitimate use of physical force within a given territory.

—Max Weber[1]

The US government has the right to order the killing of American citizens overseas if they are senior al-Qaeda leaders who pose an imminent terrorist threat and cannot reasonably be captured, Attorney General Eric H. Holder Jr. said Monday.

"Any decision to use lethal force against a United States citizen—even one intent on murdering Americans and who has become an operational leader of al-Qaeda in a foreign land—is among the gravest that government leaders can face," Holder said in a speech at Northwestern University's law school in Chicago. "The American people can be—and deserve to be—assured that actions taken in their defense are consistent with their values and laws."

—*The Washington Post*[2]

INTRODUCTION

As the United States pursues a global program of targeted killings unprecedented in the nation's history, thus flaunting "a capacity for violence [that] undermines its own standards of justice and individual rights," corporate media profoundly fail to inform the US public about targeted killings, contributing to an unaware populace who overwhelmingly support the Obama administration's international assassination program.[3]

According to a February 2012 opinion poll conducted by the *Washington Post* and ABC News, 83 percent of Americans approve of Obama's use of drone strikes against terrorist suspects overseas.[4] Moreover, 65 percent of Americans (including 58 percent of Democrats) approve of drone strikes "if those suspected terrorists are American citizens living in other countries." As suggested by this poll and others like it, the Obama administration does not have to worry about public opinion when it comes to drone strikes and even the targeted killing of American citizens suspected of terrorism.[5] Progressives, who have been highly critical of both Presidents George W. Bush and Barack Obama for extraordinary rendition, detainee mistreatment, and the suspension of habeas corpus, have not been equally vocal in their criticisms of targeted killings.[6]

Popular support for targeted killing begs the question of whether US citizens actually understand President Obama's counterinsurgency program, since, in the words of one critic, "The scale of our state-sponsored murder is masked from public view."[7] This chapter examines how corporate media, in consort with government officials, mask the use of drones in targeted killing from public attention. I argue that corporate media coverage of drones contributes to the public understanding of targeted killings as within the state's claim to a monopoly on the legitimate use of force.[8]

Claiming a monopoly on legitimate use of force only becomes necessary when there are competitors to challenge it. Since 9/11, the United States and other national governments have identified terrorists as the most significant challenge to such claims, most obviously and consequentially in President Bush's (unratified) declaration of a "global war on terror."

Based on Barack Obama's campaign rhetoric, many expected (and hoped) that he might break with the Bush administration's approach to counterterrorism. Indeed, in February 2009, shortly after Obama took office, a panel of sixty eminent judges and lawyers from around the world, convened by the International Commission of Jurists, called on President Obama to "immediately and publicly renounce" the "immense damage" done to international law by the Bush administration's war on terror.[9] Despite this and other appeals, Obama has, as president, in fact intensified and expanded Bush's global war on terror.[10] In Weberian terms, Obama's use of drones to target suspected terrorists far from any battlefield constitutes a significant expansion of the state's claim to a monopoly on the legitimate use of force "within a given territory": Where Weber theorized geographic limits to such claims, President Obama has defined the "given territory" claimed by the United States to include all of the world. Consequently, some critics now postulate an "Obama doctrine," premised on killing, rather than detaining, the nation's perceived enemies.[11]

The Bureau of Investigative Journalism (TBIJ) reports that, as of June 2012, the Obama administration has overseen 281 of the 333 drone strikes in the US's secret bombing campaign in Pakistan. The US does not officially acknowledge this campaign, although TBIJ reports that it has resulted in a death toll of somewhere between 2,490 and 3,194 people, including 482 to 832 civilians and 175 children.[12] In Somalia, TBIJ reports as many as 21 US military strikes since 2007 with a toll of up to 169 people, including 11 to 57 reported civilians.[13] Covert US strikes by the US military and the Central Intelligence Agency (CIA) in Yemen have killed between 326 to 931 people, including 58 to 146 civilians since 2003. At least 35 strikes have taken place since May 2011, leading TBIJ researchers to conclude that the US campaign of covert strikes in Yemen is "currently at the same level as the CIA's controversial drone campaign in Pakistan."[14]

These sobering figures expose a fundamental tension in the Obama administration, which has simultaneously sought to (1) distance itself from the Bush–Cheney administration, by denouncing government secrecy and excesses of executive power, while (2) refusing to inform the American public about its covert, global program of targeted killings. The tension between the two aims is aptly described as a "mind-bending philosophical conundrum."[15]

Given both the scope of Obama's targeted killing program and the US public's apparent support of it, this chapter undertakes a content analysis of corporate news coverage of targeted killings, and in particular the assassination of Anwar al-Awlaki. The aim of this content analysis is to assess the extent to which corporate news coverage contributes to the legitimation of targeted killing, or whether this coverage might call into question the US government's authority to execute suspected terrorists without due process. To do so, this chapter addresses three specific questions:

1. Whom do corporate journalists treat as authorized sources of information and opinion about targeted killings?

I examine direct quotations as an index of the range of perspectives offered by corporate media. This analysis provides one basis for understanding how corporate news coverage contributes to a false sense of consensus about the legitimacy of drone strikes as a means of targeted killing.

2. How do corporate media describe al-Awlaki?

Descriptions of al-Awlaki in corporate news coverage contribute to the framing of him as a true threat to the US and therefore a valid target.

3. What relevant aspects of the story do corporate media omit?

This is an "elephant outside the frame" issue. By considering sources of information and opinion outside the narrow range favored by corporate journalists, I show that corporate news coverage ignores the powerful economic interests driving the boom of drone use, domestically and worldwide.

Underlying these three specific questions is a fourth, broader issue that this chapter also addresses, even though the issue goes beyond the scope of the present analysis: *What does it mean to identify an action as "terrorism" or a person as a "terrorist"?* Is terrorism a crime, an act of war, or some new category of action?[16] In analyzing the lessons from a decade of counterterrorism legislation and its relation to national and international human rights law, Dr. Alex Conte of the International Commission of Jurists reports that "the lack of a universally agreed-upon definition of terrorism has resulted in the use of broad, over-reaching definitions of the term."[17]

For the most part, our leaders in Congress and the White House do not address these questions—and the corporate media follow their lead. So, I intend this study to contribute to a larger project, collectively undertaken by independent journalists, organizations such as Project Censored, and patriotic citizens across the US—to ask fundamental questions about our government's response to terrorism, and to hold our leaders accountable for those responses when they ignore due process, the rule of law, and international human rights.

METHODOLOGY

The database includes news stories published or broadcast between July 2010 and March 2012. The data include print stories from newspapers, including the *Christian Science Monitor*, the *International Herald Tribune*, the *Los Angeles Times*, the *New York Times*, *USA Today*, and the *Washington Post*; from weekly newsmagazines, including *Newsweek* and *US News and World Report*; and from three wire services: the Associated Press, the State News Service, and Reuters. Broadcast data includes televised stories by ABC, CNN, CBS, Fox, and NBC; and radio by NPR. The date range spans the time from when the US Department of the Treasury placed Anwar al-Awlaki on its list of Specially Designated Global Terrorists (July 16, 2010) to Attorney General Eric Holder's highly anticipated speech defending the Obama administration's claim that it can lawfully target American citizens (March 5, 2012).

Using the LexisNexis Academic database, I searched for references to the term "targeted killing" and its variants in the headlines and leads of print, broadcast, and wire stories during this time period. I conducted similar searches for "Anwar al-Awlaki" and the variant spellings of his name (e.g. al-Aulaqi). These searches generated eighty-six records. I excluded four of these from analysis because they were not news stories (e.g. editorials, opinion pieces, letters to the editor) or because they mentioned targeted killing or al-Awlaki only in passing. This left a data collection of eighty-two relevant news stories. Roughly estimated, this database encompasses just over 71,000 words of reporting, or approximately 2,000 to 2,400 column inches of newspaper text.[18]

For each relevant story, I coded (1) people whom journalists quoted directly, in print or through "sound bite," and (2) descriptions of al-Awlaki. I identified 288 instances of direct quotations and sound bites. I coded these by source type (e.g. executive branch, civil liberties advocates, etc.) and, when relevant, by their position on (a) the specific killing of al-Awlaki and/or on (b) the Obama administration's more general claims about the legitimacy of targeted killing. Because determining a quote's position on these two matters sometimes involved subjective interpretation, I sought to minimize ambiguity by only coding "pro" or "con" positions when the quotation under analysis clearly took one position or another; I coded ambiguous positions as "neutral" (See Tables 2 and 3, below).

In addition to analyzing quoted sources, I also tracked descriptions of al-Awlaki, whether these were produced by quoted sources or by reporters themselves. Following the sociological method of grounded theory, I identified every description of al-Awlaki and then began to cluster these descriptions into categories that emerged and developed as I read and re-read the collection of descriptions.[19] I explicate the resulting categories—including, for example, "American," "Superlatives," and "Target"—in more detail, below.

THE PREDOMINANCE OF GOVERNMENT OFFICIALS AS QUOTED SOURCES

Prior research by sociologists on news production demonstrates that elites, and especially government officials, are both "the sources and subjects of most political stories" because, for news workers, "'news' is about what those in power say and do."[20] Moreover, in periods of political crisis, "establishment journalism" focuses even more "firmly on official views of American policy."[21]

The range of sources quoted in stories on targeted killings is—with one important exception—typical of establishment journalism: it reflects the strong journalistic bias for government officials as authorized sources. Table 1 summarizes these findings:

TABLE 1. DISTRIBUTION OF QUOTATIONS BY SOURCE TYPE

Source Type	Quotes*	Percent
Executive	119	41
Civil Lib./Human Rights	42	15
Academic	24	8
Former Executive	17	6
Judicial	15	5
Former CIA	15	5
Congress	12	4
Think Tank	12	4
Other**	32	11
TOTAL	**288**	**100**

*"Quotes" include direct quotations from print news and sound bites from broadcast news.
**"Other," a residual category, includes legal counsel for the New York Times, presidential candidates not currently holding office, sources identified as "experts" but without an institutional affiliation, as well as foreign government officials, members of a Virginia mosque where al-Awlaki once preached, and sound bites of al-Awlaki himself.

Sources representing the executive branch (which includes not only the White House, but also the justice, defense, treasury, and state departments) are most frequently quoted. Within this broad category, justice department officials predominate (N=39, or 14 percent of the total quotes), followed by anonymous administration officials (N=33, 11 percent) and the president (N=16, 6 percent). Treasury and state department officials were each quoted four times.

Including sources from the judicial (N=15, 5 percent) and legislative (i.e. Congress, N=12, 4 percent) branches, current government officials account for the majority of quoted sources (N=146, 51 percent). Former executive officials, including members of prior presidential administrations (N=17, 6 percent) and retired CIA members (N=15, 5 percent) constitute a significant number of quoted sources. Reporters often quote former government officials as newsworthy sources that offer relevant insights on current events, based on their own past experience.[22] Journalists rely more heavily on former officials as news sources when current officials are reluctant to speak on record. When former government officials are included, the total for government

JUDGE, JURY, EXECUTIONER

U.S. DRONE WARS

Dr. STRANGEDRONE

officials quoted (N=178) reaches nearly 62 percent. Officials representing civil liberties organizations, such as the American Civil Liberties Union (ACLU) and the Center for Constitutional Rights (CCR), and human rights groups, such as Human Rights First, constitute the next largest group of sources (N=42, 15 percent). Overall, nongovernmental sources constitute approximately 38 percent of quoted sources.

Three conclusions can be drawn from the patterns depicted in Table 1. First, insofar as the majority of quoted sources are government officials, this shapes the range of perspectives on the validity of al-Awlaki's killing, and more broadly on the legitimacy of targeted killings. Of course, not all within the US government share a single position on these issues, but as media scholars who examine news coverage of military conflict recurrently demonstrate, in dealing with news about the United States' enemies, actual or perceived, the corporate media tend to reproduce the views of the White House and Pentagon.[23]

Second, insofar as government officials might differ on policy, Congress has historically been an important source of dissent with executive policy. For example, in studying news coverage of Vietnam, Daniel Hallin has shown how the US news media did not take an oppositional stance toward American policy in Vietnam until members of Congress began to question White House policy publicly.[24] The media's shift to an oppositional stance is best explained as "a reflection of and a response to a collapse of consensus—especially of elite consensus—on foreign policy."[25] Hallin's finding is especially relevant in the current context.

Members of Congress almost never appear as quoted sources in the current data. Quoted just twelve times, Congress accounts for a scant 4 percent of the 288 quotes analyzed. By comparison, congressional leaders were quoted only slightly more often (N=12) than members of the Virginia mosque where al-Awlaki once preached (N=8).

When quoted, members of Congress typically offered statements that betrayed the restrictions imposed on them by White House claims of national security, as can be seen in the following example: Sen. Dianne Feinstein (D-CA) believed al-Awlaki was "a lawful target" but called on the administration to provide details about its legal rationale in order "to maintain public support of secret operations."[26] This is the most critical quotation by a member of Congress in the data collected for this chapter—and in this quote Feinstein calls the administration to account only in order "to maintain public support of secret operations."

The low profile of congressional sources among those quoted is not only striking, but also consequential for the legitimation of targeted killing. As Hallin's research on news coverage of Vietnam shows, establishment news organizations did not adequately cover opposition to war in Vietnam until congressional elites publicly expressed opposition to administration policy. In the case of the Obama administration's policy of targeted killings, a paralyzed Congress yields to the administration, allowing corporate media to portray government consensus on that policy.

Why are members of Congress not more vocal on the issues of al-Awlaki's assassination and targeted killings? Whether they are supportive or actually opposed, Congress members have been muzzled by executive claims of secrecy to protect national security and/or co-opted by lobbyists representing drone manufacturers.[27] Greg Miller of the *Washington Post* reported how "divided oversight" of congressional committees "has failed to keep pace with the way military and intelligence operations have converged," with the result that disclosure of drone operations is generally limited to relevant committees in the House and Senate and sometimes only to their leaders. Those briefed must abide by restrictions that prevent them from discussing what they have learned with those who lack the requisite security clearances. The vast majority of lawmakers receive scant information about the administration's drone program.[28]

Miller details a bureaucratically organized distribution of knowledge in which divided oversight and limited knowledge effectively preclude most congress members from acting as checks on executive power or from informing the public. His report is exceptional: no other news story in the data examined for this chapter addressed these issues.

The third conclusion to be drawn from Table 1, and from the pattern of quoted sources it summarizes, is that civil liberties and human rights organizations constitute the primary alternative to official governmental perspectives on targeted killings. This is not inherently problematic, of course, since the ACLU, CCR, and similar organizations position themselves publicly as watchdogs against government abuses of power. However, a closer examination of *when* corporate media grant standing to representatives of the ACLU, CCR, and other organizations as authorized news sources gives cause for concern.

During the time period covered by the data, the ACLU and CCR joined together to bring a series of lawsuits against the US government, challenging it to release basic, accurate information about its targeted killing program, contesting its position that individuals who have been designated as terrorists cannot obtain legal representation, and ultimately arguing that the government cannot execute its own citizens, far from any battlefield, without due process.[29]

The lawsuits made ACLU and CCR officials newsworthy: each time one of the cases entered a new phase (e.g. filing, motions, testimony, decision), ACLU and CCR representatives became newsworthy because journalists orient to the distinct, bureaucratic phases of court cases as one basic way of reporting a developing news story.[30] Across the thirty-three times that news coverage directly quoted CCR or ACLU sources, I found just two that were not specifically associated with some phase of the ACLU and CCR lawsuits against the US government. It seems reasonable to conclude that, in the absence of those lawsuits, ACLU and CCR sources would have been quoted much less frequently—despite the reality that these organizations were consistently speaking out against the government's targeted killing program through their own publications and events, and in independent media outlets.[31] This finding underscores Herman and Chomsky's analysis that "non-routine" sources (like the ACLU and CCR) struggle for access. The lawsuits forced corporate news "gatekeepers" to include the oppositional perspectives of the ACLU and CCR. Without these sources, corporate news coverage seldom included perspectives critical of the government for al-Awlaki's death and other targeted killings.

I also analyzed quotations that took an explicit position on the killing of al-Awlaki. Table 2 summarizes these findings and suggests two conclusions.

TABLE 2. DISTRIBUTION OF QUOTES BY POSITION ON LEGITIMACY OF KILLING AL-AWLAKI

Position	Quotes	Percentage
Legitimate	12	50
Illegitimate	10	42
Neutral	2	8
TOTAL	**24**	**100**

First, there is a rough balance between quotes treating al-Awlaki's killing as legitimate (N=12) and those treating it as illegitimate (N=10). With such a small sample size, not too much can be inferred from these figures. At the very least, they reflect professional journalism's commitment to objectivity, especially as it is achieved through "balance," the practice of presenting "the views of legitimate spokespersons of the conflicting sides in any significant dispute" and providing "both sides with roughly equivalent attention."[32] Quoted sources that questioned the legitimacy of al-Awlaki's killing included representatives of the ACLU, CCR, academics, and a statement from the family of Samir Khan, an American citizen who was killed alongside al-Awlaki; by contrast, I found no direct quotations by current or former government officials that questioned the legitimacy of al-Awlaki's killing.

Second, it is noteworthy how few of the direct quotes specifically address the killing of al-Awlaki—just over 8 percent of the 288 direct quotes, in fact—even though the government's intent to kill him, or its having done so, were the central focus of many news stories. The significance of this finding is best understood in comparison with the distribution of quotes by position on the legitimacy of targeted killings in general, as summarized in Table 3:

TABLE 3. DISTRIBUTION OF QUOTES BY POSITION ON LEGITIMACY OF TARGETED KILLINGS

Position	Quotes	Percentage
Legitimate	58	46
Illegitimate	51	40
Neutral	17	14
TOTAL	**126**	**100**

A similar pattern of balance between "pro" and "con" positions is evident here, reinforcing the argument that journalistic commitments to balance and objectivity drive the selection of quoted sources.

Notably, many more quotations address the legitimacy of targeted killings in terms of the relatively abstract issue of executive privilege (Table 3, N=126), compared to the number of quotes focused on the legitimacy of the targeted killing of a specific person, Anwar al-Awlaki (Table 2, N=24).

The significance of this contrast is highlighted by a closer assessment of these direct quotes, in which two important patterns of argument become clear. Advocates for the legitimacy of targeted killing tend to express their support in abstract terms, as matters of counter-terrorism policy or executive privilege. They do not identify al-Awlaki by name or address the targeting of him specifically. The following quotations exemplify this pattern:

"It's a counterterrorism success for the United States and Yemeni and global counterterrorism forces." —Rick "Ozzie" Nelson, director of the Homeland Security and Counterterrorism Program at the Center for Strategic and International Studies[33]

"[The Awlaki hit] was a good strike." —Dick Cheney[34]

"It's something we had to do. . . . The president is showing leadership. The president is showing guts." —Rep. Peter King (R-NY), chairman of the House Committee on Homeland Security

"It's legal. . . .It's legitimate and we're taking out someone who has attempted to attack us on numerous occasions. And he was on that list." —Maryland Rep. C. A. Dutch Ruppersberger, the ranking Democrat on the House Committee on Intelligence[35]

In quotes by Nelson, Cheney, and King, the human victims disappear, even as their demise is evaluated in positive terms ("a success," "a good strike," "something we had to do"). In the fourth quotation, Ruppersberger acknowledges that a human being was targeted ("we're taking out someone") but quickly justifies it (". . . has attempted to attack us. . . . He was on that list").

President Obama's initial statement on al-Awlaki's death is one significant exception to the pattern of advocates for al-Awlaki's death not mentioning him by name. "The death of Awlaki is a major blow to al-Qaeda's most active operational affiliate," Obama said hours after the September 30 strike.[36]

Notably, insofar as Obama identified al-Awlaki by name, he avoided claiming US responsibility for the killing, even as he praised the result.

By contrast, opponents of targeted killing were more likely to refer to al-Awlaki's death specifically, and to identify him by name overtly, as exemplified in the following pair of quotations:

"The executive is claiming the power to go ahead and target al-Awlaki for assassination without going through anything that resembles traditional legal process." —New York University law professor Sam Rascoff, on National Public Radio[37]

"Upon information and belief. . . . Anwar al-Awlaki is now subject to a standing order that permits the CIA and JSOC to kill him." —ACLU and CCR's lawsuit[38]

Whether quoted sources mention al-Awlaki by name or not might seem too fine a distinction when the subject's life hangs in balance. But a handful of news stories treated precisely this point as newsworthy in its own right when reporting on Attorney General Eric Holder's March 2012 speech, which sought to justify the Obama administration's policy of targeted killings. Just twice in the text of his speech did Holder mention al-Awlaki by name, and neither time did he make reference to al-Awlaki's killing.[39] *The Washington Post* and the *Los Angeles Times*, respectively, reported:

Holder's discussion of lethal force against US citizens did not mention any individual by name, but his address was clearly animated by the killing of Anwar al-Awlaki.[40]

Holder did not mention the September slayings of Awlaki or Kahn, or the reported slaying of Awlaki's 16-year old son, Abdulrahman.[41]

In justifying the government's program of targeted killing, Attorney General Holder and other quoted government officials consistently avoid identifying al-Awlaki by name. This evasion is part of a broader pattern in which quoted sources legitimating US drone strikes speak in ways that make the strikes' human victims effectively disappear.[42]

A "TERRORIST" AND A "TARGET": DESCRIPTIONS OF AL-AWLAKI

Although government officials seldom identified al-Awlaki by name in direct quotations, they and others frequently formulated descriptions of him. Person-description is a rich sociological topic because description is *selective*, involving choices about what to describe and how to describe it.[43] This is especially true in institutional settings such as courts, where descriptions of identity, biography, and character feature prominently in determinations of innocence or guilt.[44]

This section analyzes how corporate journalists, and the sources that they select, describe Anwar al-Awlaki. The absence of public legal ruling for the September 30, 2011, extrajudicial execution of al-Awlaki makes print and broadcast news descriptions of him all the more significant. For want of official, legal justification, news reports become the primary, if not the sole, means available to the American public for understanding al-Awlaki's identity and judging the validity of the government's decision to kill him without formal charge or trial. This section analyzes four recurrent ways that corporate media described al-Awlaki, and argues that in aggregate these descriptions of al-Awlaki frame him as a true threat to the US and therefore a valid target.

1) "Yearbook" Descriptions

A number of the descriptions of al-Awlaki initially appear flattering and therefore harmless, the kinds of person-description one might more readily associate with high school yearbooks, rather than with a terrorist whose existence threatens the United States. Thus, al-Awlaki is repeatedly described as "charismatic,"[45] "inspirational,"[46] and "articulate."[47] He was "popular," a "rising star" who "used social media."[48] On the surface, these descriptions appear positive.

However, when combined with other frequently employed descriptions of al-Awlaki, especially those identifying him as a "militant" or "radical cleric,"[49] otherwise positive characteristics like charisma, popularity, and articulateness become sinister: the recurrent use of the term "cleric" is telling. By definition, "cleric" can refer to priests or leaders in any religious tradition, but in combining the term with "militant" or "radical," descriptions of al-Awlaki index his Muslim faith in ways that can invoke and perpetuate popular conceptions of terror carried out by Muslim zealots, including especially the 9/11 attacks. This specification of al-Awlaki's identity exemplifies a basic finding from Solomon Asch's classic study of how we form impressions of personality.[50] In Asch's terms, descriptions such as "militant" or "radical cleric" transform the overall impression of the person. Moreover, in al-Awlaki's case, a radical or militant Muslim cleric who is also charismatic, popular, and articulate poses a greater threat, because these otherwise positive attributes can be put to evil purposes, especially in deceiving the innocent and recruiting the gullible. Thus, Fox correspondent Catherine Herridge, describing al-Awlaki's use of the Internet, referred to him as "the Facebook friend from hell. He really leveraged social networking to spread this ideology of hate."[51]

2) American-born/American citizen

Much of the controversy surrounding the government's targeted killing of al-Awlaki derives from his status as a US citizen. Among the news reports examined for this research, every story that mentioned al-Awlaki by name also identified him as an American citizen or as having been born in the United States. Variations in how these reports formulate that important aspect of al-Awlaki's identity are subtle yet significant.

A number of reports identify al-Awlaki as American- or US-*born*. For example, in July 2011, after several US attempts to kill al-Awlaki had failed, ABC's Diane Sawyer introduced a segment titled "Fighting Terror" by saying: "US officials tell ABC News that top al-Qaeda leader Ayman al-Zawahiri and American-born terror leader Anwar al-Awlaki will soon announce what amounts to a terrorist merger . . ."[52] Describing al-Awlaki as an "American-born terror leader" may evoke pervasive government propaganda and policy regarding "individuals radicalized at home" and "homegrown terrorism."[53] The formulation "American-born" may also position him as expatriate who has forsaken his country of birth.

Thus, news reports frequently portrayed this aspect of al-Awlaki's identity as a basis for vilifying him. If citizenship protected al-Awlaki from targeted killing, one *Washington Post* editorial argued, then "in order for the kill order to stand, Awlaki should be stripped of his citizenship."[54] Others argued that, through words if not deeds, al-Awlaki had effectively renounced his citizenship, as exemplified in this exchange between CNN anchor Joe Johns and Rep. Mike Rogers (R-MI):

> JOHNS: . . . Is it wrong or right to target an American citizen in this way who has not been given the due process and protections of the US Constitution?
>
> ROGERS: Well, I think I'm going to argue with the premise of your question. Here is an individual who renounced his citizenship, who declared war on the United States, and openly joined an organization that had declared war on the United States . . .[55]

In point of fact, and contrary to a literal interpretation of Rogers's claim, there is no evidence that al-Awlaki ever formally renounced his US citizenship.[56] But the real point of Rogers's assertion seems to be that one cannot say what al-Awlaki repeatedly said and remain a US citizen. Regardless, in targeting al-Awlaki for death, the Obama administration has never denied his citizenship. Instead, they have shifted attention from al-Awlaki's nationality to the beliefs he made public through his Internet speeches, in order to cast him as an imminent threat to the United States.

3) Superlatives/Extreme Case Formulations

By describing al-Awlaki in superlative terms, such as "most wanted" or the "most serious terrorist threat to America," government officials and corporate media contribute to the identification of him as a legitimate target. For example:

> "A senior US government official described him simply as 'one of al-Qaeda's most dangerous terrorists.'" —*The Washington Post*[57]

> "It is here on these dangerous streets where, over the years, we have watched al-Qaeda flourish. And leading

them? Anwar al-Awlaki, the terrorist officials say is most likely to launch the next successful attack against Americans." —*World News with Diane Sawyer*[58]

"SAVANNAH GUTHRIE, anchor: And tonight one of America's most wanted terrorists is dead. His name may not have been as well known as Osama bin Laden's, but officials say Anwar al-Awlaki was just as dangerous . . .

JIM MIKLASZEWSKI: Savannah, al-Awlaki was considered so dangerous, President Obama put him on the US "kill or capture" list, the only American to be specifically targeted by American forces in the war against al-Qaeda. US intelligence officers considered al-Awlaki, the American-born cleric, the most serious terrorist threat to America." —*NBC Nightly News*[59]

In sociolinguistic terms, superlatives like "most dangerous," "most likely to launch the next successful attack," "most wanted," and "the only American" are "extreme case formulations." Anita Pomerantz and others have analyzed how extreme case formulations serve to "legitimize claims," especially by defending against or countering challenges to the "legitimacy of complaints, accusations, justifications, and defenses."[60] In al-Awlaki's case, by adopting government officials' extreme case formulations of him, corporate media contribute to the portrayal of al-Awlaki as an imminent threat to the United States, thus legitimizing the government's justifications for killing him.

In context, comparisons of al-Awlaki to Osama bin Laden—the embodiment of al-Qaeda and the leader behind the 9/11 attacks—constituted another sort of extreme case formulation. For example:

"Obama's counterterrorism chief, Michael Leiter, has said al-Awlaki posed a bigger threat to the US homeland than bin Laden did." —CNN[61]

"In some respects US officials consider Awlaki a more insidious threat than Osama bin Laden himself." —*NBC Nightly News*[62]

Just as hyperbolic descriptions of bin Laden as a "terrorist mastermind" oversimplified the complexity of Islamist terrorist networks such as al-Qaeda,[63] so comparisons of al-Awlaki to bin Laden simultaneously oversimplify the real threats posed by those networks while exaggerating the importance of al-Awlaki to them.

Although government officials frequently used extreme case formulations to describe al-Awlaki, these descriptions do not provide any specific evidence of his having an active, operational role in al-Qaeda. A tension between the superlative descriptions of al-Awlaki (e.g. "most dangerous") and the lack of conclusive evidence in support of those claims is clear in news reports describing al-Awlaki as a "suspected al-Qaeda operative,"[64] "an alleged member of al-Qaeda,"[65] or as someone "suspected of assisting in the attempted Christmas Day bombing of a commercial jetliner near Detroit."[66] These descriptions, and others like them, express a lack of certainty regarding al-Awlaki's links to al-Qaeda or his role in the Christmas Day bombing. Of course, use of terms such as "alleged" and "suspected" is conventional in news coverage of criminal cases, where the presumption of innocence holds unless and until guilt is proven in a court of law. By contrast, however, in al-Awlaki's case, government officials recurrently used extreme case formulations to condemn him, without providing specific evidence that might prove their claims. The claims regarding al-Awlaki's danger to the US may have been valid. But, as critics of his targeted killing argued, regardless of his guilt or innocence, the US Constitution required that he be charged and tried, as a matter of due process, before the state could legitimately execute him.

4) A Terrorist and a Target

Al-Awlaki's status as a terrorist became official on July 16, 2010, when the US Department of the Treasury placed him on its list of Specially Designated Global Terrorists.[67] At the time, the corporate media paid little or no attention to this crucial change in al-Awlaki's status: Eileen Sullivan and Matthew Lee of the Associated Press filed a story that day, but otherwise the nation's major news organizations did not report it until the ACLU and CCR brought a lawsuit against the treasury department's Office of Foreign Assets Control (OFAC) in order to obtain a special license to provide legal counsel for al-Awlaki, as an American designated for targeted killing without due process.[68]

Regardless of the legal contests over al-Awlaki's status, once government officials formally identified al-Awlaki as a terrorist, this shaped journalistic descriptions of him as a *target*. Al-Awlaki was an "elusive," but "high-value" and "prime" target.[69] Even more so, news reports reproduced official government descriptions of him as a "legitimate" and "lawful" target, as can be seen in the following examples:

> "Juan Zarate, a former deputy national security advisor in the Bush administration, says Awlaki's links to episodes like [the Christmas Day bombing] have made him a legitimate target." —National Public Radio[70]

> "[T]he Justice Department concluded that Mr. Awlaki was covered by the authorization to use military force against Al Qaeda that Congress enacted shortly after the terrorist attacks of Sept. 11, 2001—meaning that he was a lawful target in the armed conflict unless some other legal prohibition trumped that authority." —*The New York Times*[71]

Through practices of person-description, government officials and corporate media collaborated in framing al-Awlaki as a dangerous terrorist and, consequently, a legitimate and lawful target for killing.

THE TWO-BILLION-DOLLAR ELEPHANT OUTSIDE THE FRAME: TARGETED KILLING AS PROFITABLE

A close examination of news stories about al-Awlaki's killing demonstrates how corporate news coverage often functions as propaganda on behalf of the Obama administration's program of targeted killings, but this critique is not complete without examining aspects of the program that corporate news coverage omits. This is, to borrow imagery from filmmaker Errol Morris, "the elephant lurking just at the edge of the frame."[72] In the case of the corporate media's coverage of the US government's killing of al-Awlaki, there are multiple elephants lurking outside the frame, including wishful thinking that drones allow the US to wage "clean" or "costless" war,[73] recent and current administrations' preference for military over political solutions to foreign policy dilemmas,[74] and the corporate media's apparent amnesia regarding national and international law that predates (and invalidates) the congressional Authorization for Use of Military Force (AUMF) on September 18, 2001.[75] A full analysis of these recurrent shortcomings in corporate media coverage of targeted killings awaits future study.

The remaining section of the present study examines another elephant lurking outside the frame of the corporate media's coverage: the economic interests that indirectly influence the government's program of targeted killing. Corporate media ignore the "blurring of lines between the highly profitable business of killing people and the legitimate defense of US security."[76] Drones, including unmanned aerial vehicles (UAVs) such as General Atomics MQ-1 Predator, which launches Lockheed Martin's HELLFIRE missiles, are big business, and a strong growth area in a sagging US economy. How big? US government drone purchases—which do not include contracts for an array of related UAV services and payloads—rose from $588 million to $2.1 billion over the past five years.[77]

Where does this money go? Consider four examples of private contractors who reap enormous profits based on federal expenditures for drone technology:

▸ Boeing, which produces the A-160 and Scan Eagle, is the third-largest government contractor on Washington Technology's annual ranking of the top 100 government contractors. Boeing reported revenues of $68.7 billion in 2011, up 7 percent from 2010.[78]

▸ Northrop Grumman, which produces the Fire Scout, Global Hawk, and Hunter drones, and is developing prototypes of the EuroHawk and X-47B, reported revenues of $26.4 billion in 2011, a decrease compared to its 2010 revenue, but still leaving it as second in government contracts on Washington Technology's list, with $8.2 billion in military contracts for 2011.

▸ General Atomics, which produces the well-known Predator drone, is only #45 on Washington Technology's top 100 list of government contractors; however, its revenues have increased by 259 percent since 2008, reaching $634.5 million in 2011.

▸ AAI/Aerosonde, a subsidiary of Textron, Inc., produces the gasoline-powered Micro Air Vehicle (gMAV) and Shadow series drones. In 2011, Textron reported revenues of $11.2 billion, a 7 percent growth in revenue compared with 2010.[79]

One might think that these financial giants would not need extra backing, but that would be wrong. In 2002, these four corporations and others in the UAV industry formed UNITE, the UAS (Unmanned Aircraft Systems) National Industry Team, a 501(c)(6) nonprofit corporation to:

1. promote and preserve the unique business case for unmanned aircraft (UA);
2. regain and retain US leadership and competitiveness in the unmanned aircraft systems (UAS) international marketplace; and
3. foster early adoption of UA and UAS for safe commercial, public, and private use.[80]

According to the UNITE website, the alliance "has been actively (but 'behind the scenes') collaborating on and coordinating support of" the deployment of unmanned aircraft systems (UAS) in the national airspace (NAS):

> Recently the UNITE Board of Directors instructed the UNITE Management Council to increase collaborative activity and to no longer work "behind the scenes." This has resulted in what has been "perceived" as a re-emergence of UNITE when, in reality, it is just that UNITE has made a conscious decision to become more visible and more active.[81]

Recent reports on the domestic deployment of drones indicate that UNITE, and the corporations for which it serves as a front, are succeeding in their aims.[82]

Lobbyists such as UNITE and the Association for Unmanned Vehicle Systems International (AUVSI) meet willing sponsors in Congress: the House of Representatives has its own bipartisan drone caucus, with more than fifty members.[83] Formed in 2009 by Rep. Howard "Buck" McKeon (R-CA), the Unmanned Systems Caucus (formerly called the UAV Caucus), aims to "educate members of Congress and the public on the strategic, tactical, and scientific value of unmanned systems; actively support further development and acquisition of more systems, and to more effectively engage the civilian aviation community on unmanned system use and safety."[84]

In an era when our leaders exhort us about the necessity of "austerity" regarding education, health care, and other social services, the enormity of the government's contracts with defense industry giants including Boeing, Northrop Grumman, and General Atomics, not to mention the profits that these contractors reap, can be understood as obscene. In corporate news coverage of targeted killings, these profitable contracts, and the processes through which they get made, are just another elephant lurking outside the frame. Without the independent journalists who treat these latest developments in the military-industrial complex as an important beat, the American public would know little or nothing about this economic aspect of the United States' "drone war." As one astute critic summarizes, "Only corporations—the organizational mirror image of drones—profit from war."[85]

CONCLUSION

Force is as pitiless to the man who possesses it, or thinks he does, as it is to its victims; the second it crushes, the first it intoxicates.

—Simone Weil[86]

An informed public debate over when, where—and indeed whether—the US government can engage in targeted killing has yet to take place. Instead, in the news coverage examined for this study, corporate media present a narrow range of fact and opinion, drawn primarily from official government sources. The paralysis of Congress, due to divided oversight and economic conflicts of interest, aggravates the limitations of corporate media's heavy reliance on government officials.

Consequently, establishment news coverage conveys to the American public a false, intoxicating impression of consensus around the government's global campaign of drone strikes and targeted killings. More specifically, such coverage appears to have convinced the American public that Anwar al-Awlaki, a US citizen, was so dangerous that the government could not afford to charge and try him in a court of law, as required by the US Constitution. The legitimacy of this claim, for which our rulers have given no adequate or convincing legal justification, has been accepted and represented by the corporate media to the American public, with nearly nothing in the way of critical assessment.[87]

This is not for lack of informed experts with diverse perspectives whose inclusion would make public debate on targeted killing more meaningful and robust than it has been—figures such as Philip Alston, law professor at New York University, and former UN Special Rapporteur on extrajudicial, summary, or arbitrary executions (2004–2010), who reminds the American public and our leaders that "the serious challenges posed by terrorism are undeniable, but the fact that enemies do not play by the rules does not mean that the US government can unilaterally re-interpret them or cast them aside."[88]

We can be grateful for public figures like Professor Alston, nongovernmental organizations such as the American Civil Liberties Union and the Center for Constitutional Rights, as well as independent journalists, all of whom continue to raise uncomfortable but necessary questions about the legitimacy of targeting killing by a nation that purports to distinguish itself by adherence to due process and the rule of law. We must join them in the urgent tasks of challenging the legitimacy of the government's targeted killing program and the inadequacy of the corporate media's coverage of it.

I am grateful to Liz Boyd, Steve Clayman and Nick Wolfinger for insightful suggestions on earlier versions of this chapter

---

ANDY LEE ROTH, PHD, is the associate director of Project Censored.

Notes

1. Max Weber, "Politics as Vocation," in *From Max Weber: Essays in Sociology*, ed. H. H. Gerth and C. Wright Mills (New York: Routledge, [1919] 1998), 78.

2. Peter Finn and Sari Horwitz, "Holder: US Can Lawfully Target American Citizens," *Washington Post*, March 5, 2012, http://www.washingtonpost.com/world/national-security/holder-us-can-lawfully-target-american-citizens/2012/03/05/gIQANknFtR_story.html.

3. Quotation from Elizabeth Gould and Paul Fitzgerald, *Crossing Zero: The AfPak War at the Turning Point of American Empire* (San Francisco: City Lights Books, 2011), 212. Project Censored highlighted President Obama's "international assassination campaign" as story #3 in *Censored 2012: The Top Censored Stories and Media Analysis of 2010–11*, ed. Mickey Huff and Project Censored (New York: Seven Stories Press, 2011), 48–50. See also "Déja Vu: What Happened to Last Year's Top *Censored* Stories," chap. 2 in this volume.

4. *Washington Post*–ABC News Poll, February 1–4, 2012, http://www.washingtonpost.com/wp-srv/politics/polls/postabcpoll_020412.html. See, in particular, questions 13c and 14. The poll questioned a random, national sample of 1,000 adults and had a margin of sampling error of plus or minus four percentage points.

5. See, for example, Greg Sargent, "Liberals, Dems Approve of Drone Strikes on American Citizens Abroad," The Plum Line, *Washington Post*, February 8, 2012, http://www.washingtonpost.com/blogs/plum-line/post/liberals-dems-approve-of-drone-strikes-on-american-citizens-abroad/2012/02/08/gIQAIqCzyQ_blog.html.

6. On the disconnect between criticisms of Obama for failing to close Guantánamo and relative silence on his policy of targeted killings, see, for example, Stuart Gottlieb, "US Drones Have Executed Dozens of Alleged al Qaeda Members Along the Pakistan-Afghanistan Border," *Foreign Policy*, April 7, 2009.

7. Chris Hedges, "Murder Is Not an Anomaly in War," *Truthdig*, March 19, 2012, http://www.truthdig.com/report/item/murder_is_not_an_anomoly_in_war_20120319.

8. For sociologist Max Weber, all states depend on some form of legitimacy for their stability; legitimacy matters because it provides the basis for rule by consent rather than by coercion. See Max Weber, *The Theory of Social and Economic Organization*, edited by Talcott Parsons (New York: The Free Press, [1947] 1997).

9. Kevin Sullivan, "Jurists Decry Loss of Rights," *Washington Post*, February 18, 2009, http://www.washingtonpost.com/wp-dyn/content/article/2009/02/17/AR2009021703013.html; quoted in Gould and Fitzgerald, *Crossing Zero*, 206.

10. In August 2009, John Brennan, President Obama's chief counterterrorism advisor, publicly declared the "war on terrorism" over, but under Obama's leadership the US has continued to pursue, in ever more extreme fashion, what Brennan termed a "war with al-Qaeda" and "its violent extremist allies." See Jon Ward and Eli Lake, "White House: 'War on Terrorism' Is Over," *Washington Times*, August 6, 2009, http://www.washingtontimes.com/news/2009/aug/06/white-house-war-terrorism-over.

11. See, for example, Jonathan Turley, "Obama's Kill Doctrine," *Foreign Policy*, March 6, 2012, http://www.foreignpolicy.com/articles/2012/03/06/obama_s_kill_doctrine; and Asim Qureshi, "The 'Obama Doctrine': Kill, Don't Detain," *Guardian* (Manchester), April 11, 2010, http://www.guardian.co.uk/commentisfree/cifamerica/2010/apr/11/obama-national-security-drone-guantanamo.

12. Bureau of Investigative Journalism, "Covert Drone War—The Data," www.thebureauinvestigates.com/category/projects/drone-data. See also the New America Foundation's "Year of the Drone," http://counterterrorism.newamerica.net/drones.

13. Chris Woods, "Militants and Civilians Killed in Multiple US Somalia Strikes," Bureau of Investigative Journalism, February 22, 2012, http://www.thebureauinvestigates.com/2012/02/22/militants-and-civilians-killed-in-up-to-20-us-somalia-strikes-new-study-shows.

14. Chris Woods and Emma Slater, "Arab Spring Brings Steep Rise in US Attacks in Yemen," Bureau of Investigative Journalism, March 29, 2012, http://www.thebureauinvestigates.com/2012/03/29/arab-spring-saw-steep-rise-in-us-attacks-on-yemen-militants.

15. Gould and Fitzgerald, *Crossing Zero*, 209. In February 2012, the Associated Press reported that, "Nobel Peace Prize officials were facing a formal inquiry over accusations that they have drifted away from the prize's original selection criteria by choosing such winners as Barack Obama." Karl Ritter, "Nobel Peace Prize Jury Under Investigation," Associated Press, February 1, 2012.

16. See, for example, David K. Shipler, "Crime or War: Execution or Assassination?," *Shipler Report* (blog), October 1, 2011, http://shiplerreport.blogspot.com/2011/10/crime-or-war-execution-or-assassination.html.

17. Alex Conte, "A Decade Since UN Security Council Resolution 1373 (2001): Ten lessons learnt on counter-terrorism and human rights," September 29, 2011, http://www.icj.org/dwn/database/ICJ%20statement%20-%20OSCE%20HDIM%202011.pdf.

18. Of course, some of the stories were broadcast on television or radio. Characterizing the database in terms of newspaper column inches is just a handy metric for conveying its volume.

19. On grounded theory, see Kathy Charmaz, *Constructing Grounded Theory: A Practical Guide through Qualitative Analysis* (Thousand Oaks, CA: Sage, 2006).

20. Robert Entman and David Paletz, "Media and the Conservative Myth," *Journal of Communication* 30, no. 4 (1980), 164; and David Croteau and William Hoynes, *By Invitation Only: How the Media Limit Political Debate* (Monroe, ME: Common Courage, 1994), 177.

21. Daniel C. Hallin, *"The Uncensored War": The Media and Vietnam* (New York: Oxford University Press, 1986), 187.

22. See, for example, Andrew L. Roth, "Who Makes the News? Descriptions of Television News Interviewees' Public Personae," *Media, Culture & Society* 20 (1998), 92–93.

23. Edward S. Herman and Noam Chomsky, *Manufacturing Consent* (New York: Random House, [1988] 2002), 18–22. For clear and rigorous assessments of the propaganda model as it applies to recent US military interventions, see W. Lance Bennett, Regina G. Lawrence, and Steven Livingston, *When the Press Fails: Political Power and the News Media from Iraq to Katrina* (Chicago: University of Chicago Press, 2007), and Anthony R. DiMaggio, *Mass Media, Mass Propaganda: Examining American News in the "War on Terror"* (Lanham MD: Rowman & Littlefield, 2008).

24. Daniel C. Hallin, "The Media, the War in Vietnam, and Political Support: A Critique of the Thesis of an Oppositional Media," *Journal of Politics* 46, no. 1 (1984), 2–24.

25. Ibid., 20.

26. Pam Benson, "Administration Defends Killing US Terrorists, Targeted Attacks," CNN Wire, February 23, 2012, http://security.blogs.cnn.com/2012/02/23/obama-admin-defends-killing-american-terrorists.

27. The role of economic interests in muzzling Congress is considered, below, in the section titled "The Two-Billion-Dollar Elephant."

28. Greg Miller, "Under Obama, a Drone Network," *Washington Post*, December 28, 2011:A1.

29. See, for example, American Civil Liberties Union, "Al-Aulaqi v. Obama: Lawsuit Challenging Targeted Killings," http://www.aclu.org/national-security/al-aulaqi-v-obama and Center for Constitutional Rights, "CCR and the ACLU v. OFAC & Al-Aulaqi v. Obama," http://ccrjustice.org/Al-Aulaqi-v-Obama+.

30. This is one way that establishment journalism reproduces official bureaucratic definitions and understandings of newsworthy events. See Mark Fishman, *Manufacturing the News* (Austin: University of Texas, 1980).

31. See, for example, the CCR's archive of press releases, http://ccrjustice.org/press-releases and the ACLU's online pressroom, http://www.aclu.org/pressroom.

32. For analysis of how news professionals employ "balance" in an attempt to realize the ideal of objectivity, see Robert Entman, "Objectivity, Bias, and Slant in the News," in Entman, *Democracy without Citizens* (New York: Oxford University Press, 1989), 30–38, quote at 30.

33. Jessica Rettig, "Death of Anwar Al Awlaki Doesn't Solve Yemen's Problems," *US News & World Report*, September 30, 2011.

34. Joby Warrick, "Cheney Says Obama Owes Bush an Apology After Awlaki Killing," *Washington Post*, October 3, 2011:A6.

35. Matt Apuzzo, "Obama's OK on Killings Charts New Course for US," *San Francisco Chronicle*, October 1, 2011:A3.

36. Obama's statement on al-Awlaki's death was widely quoted in news coverage, not only in the immediate aftermath of the strike but also in the months following it. See, for example, Craig Whitlock, "After Yemen Attack, Little Comment," *Washington Post*, October 23, 2011:A3.

37. Sam Rascoff, professor at NYU Law School, *Morning Edition*, National Public Radio, August 4, 2010.

38. Warren Richey, "ACLU Wants Militant Cleric Taken Off US 'Kill List,'" *Christian Science Monitor*, August 31, 2010.

39. US Department of Justice, "Attorney General Eric Holder Speaks at Northwestern University School of Law," March 5, 2012.

40. Finn and Horwitz, "Holder."

41. Richard A. Serrano and Andrew R. Grimm, "Eric Holder: US Can Target Citizens Overseas in Terror Fight," *Los Angeles Times*, March 5, 2012, http://articles.latimes.com/2012/mar/05/news/la-pn-eric-holder-terrorism-awlaki-20120305.

42. On injuring as "the central activity of war" and how it is made to disappear, see Elaine Scarry, "The Structure of War," in *The Body in Pain* (New York: Oxford University Press, 1985), 60–157.

43. Roth, "Who Makes the News?," 83–88.

44. See, for example, Douglas W. Maynard, "Person-Descriptions in Plea Bargaining," *Semiotica* 42, no. 2/4 (January 1982), 195–213.

45. See, for example, "Al-Awlaki Targeted by US Military Drone in Yemen," CNN, May 6, 2011, http://articles.cnn.com/2011-05-06/world/yemen.drone.strike_1_awlaki-al-awlaki-al-qaeda-members?_s=PM:WORLD; "America Voice of Al- Qaeda Killed," *The Situation Room with Wolf Blitzer*, CNN, September 30, 2011; and *CBS Evening News*, September 30, 2011.

46. See, for example, *Today Show*, NBC, September 30, 2011; *All Things Considered*, NPR, September 30, 2011; and *The Situation Room*, CNN, September 30, 2011.

47. See, for example, "Ties to Mosque Haunt Congregation," *Washington Post*, October 1, 2011:A10; and *The Situation Room*, CNN, September 30, 2011.

48. *The Situation Room*, CNN, September 30, 2011; Bruce Riedel, "Al Qaeda's Not Dead Yet," *Newsweek*, October 17, 2011:28; and *Good Morning America*, ABC, October 1, 2011.

49. I identified at least thirty-seven instances where al-Awlaki was described as a "militant" or "radical cleric." See, for example, Ken Dilanian, "Family of Awlaki Decries Son's Killing," *Los Angeles Times*, October 20, 2011:A2; Warren Richey, "Judge Dismisses Bid to Remove Anwar Al-Awlaki from US 'Kill List,'" *Christian Science Monitor*, December 7, 2010; "Yemeni Court Sentences al-Awlaki," CNN, January 17, 2011; Charlie Savage, "Secret US Memo Made Legal Case to Kill a Citizen," *New York Times*, October 9, 2011:A1; and *Morning Edition*, NPR, August 4, 2010.

50. S. E. Asch, "Forming Impressions of Personality," *Journal of Abnormal and Social Psychology* 41, no. 3 (July 1946), 258–90.

51. *On the Record with Greta Van Susteren*, Fox News, September 30, 2011.

52. *World News with Diane Sawyer*, ABC News, July 19, 2011.

53. See, for example, "Empowering Local Partners to Prevent Violent Extremism in the United States," signed by President Obama on August 1, 2011.

54. "Obama's Assassination List; American Jihadists Should be Stripped of Citizenship, Then Killed," *Washington Post*, November 22, 2010:B2. In April 2010, Rep. Charles Dent (R-PA) introduced a bill, HR1288, which would have stripped al-Awlaki of his citizenship on the basis that his calls for attacks against the United States constituted a voluntary relinquishment, though the bill never made it out of subcommittee.

55. *The Situation Room*, CNN, September 30, 2011.

56. Joshua Keating, "Was Anwar al-Awlaki Still a US Citizen?," *Foreign Policy*, September 30, 2011.

57. Joby Warrick, "Abrupt Turn Made Cleric Leading Voice for Attacks on US," *Washington Post*, October 1, 2011:A10.

58. *World News with Diane Sawyer*, ABC, July 19, 2011.

59. *NBC Nightly News*, NBC, September 30, 2011.

60. Anita Pomerantz, "Extreme Case Formulations: A Way of Legitimizing Claims," *Human Studies* 9 (1986): 219–29.

61. "Al-Awlaki Targeted by US Military Drone in Yemen," CNN, May 6, 2011.

62. *NBC Nightly News*, NBC, September 30, 2011.

63. See, for example, DiMaggio, *Mass Media*, 263ff.

64. Miller, "Under Obama."

65. "After Bin Laden, Time for Clear US Policy on Targeted Killing," State News Service, May 10, 2011.

66. Richey, "ACLU."

67. US Department of the Treasury, "Treasury Designates Anwar Al-Aulaqi, Key Leader of Al-Qa'ida in the Arabian Peninsula," July 16, 2010.

68. Eileen Sullivan and Matthew Lee, "US-born Radical Cleric Added to Terror Blacklist," Associated Press, July 16, 2010. On the ACLU/CCR lawsuit against OFAC, see "ACLU and CCR v. Geithner," December 17, 2010, http://www.aclu.org/national-security/aclu-and-ccr-v-geithner.

69. "elusive": Peter Finn and Sudarsan Raghavan, "Yemeni al-Qaeda Remains a Threat," *Washington Post*, October 2, 2011:A1; "high-value": Joe Johns, anchor, *The Situation Room*, CNN, September 30, 2011; "prime": Sullivan and Lee, "US-born Radical cleric Added."

70. *Morning Edition*, NPR, August 4, 2010.

71. Savage, "Secret US Memo," A1.

72. Errol Morris, *Believing is Seeing: Observations on the Mysteries of Photography* (New York: Penguin, 2011).

73. "The lack of attention paid to the legal issues and civilian casualties surrounding the CIA's drone program underlies the general apathy of the American public towards drone warfare. . . . The 'costless war' erodes the political checks and accountability that are characteristic of waging war in a democratic society." Andrew Callam, "Drone Wars: Armed Unmanned Aerial Vehicles," *International Affairs Review* XVIII, no. 3 (Winter 2010). See also, DiMaggio, *Mass Media*, 272–73.

74. Gould and Fitzgerald, *Crossing Zero*, 201–02.

75. On the historical context for AUMF see, for example, the contributions to *US National Security, Intelligence and Democracy: From the Church Committee to the War on Terror*, edited by Russell A. Miller (New York: Routledge, 2008).

76. Gould and Fitzgerald, *Crossing Zero*, 176.

77. "Prime Award Spending Data," USAspending.gov, http://www.usaspending.gov/explore?fromfiscal=yes&fiscal_year=2011&productorservicecode=1550&fiscal_year=2006&tab=By+Agency&fromfiscal=yes&carryfilters=on&Submit=Go (accessed March 22, 2012).

78. "2011 Washington Technology Top 100: 18th Annual Rankings Track the Largest Government Contractors," Washington Technology, http://washingtontechnology.com/toplists/top-100-lists/2011.aspx.

79. Textron Annual Report, 2011, http://thomson.mobular.net/thomson/7/3264/4568.

80. UAS National Industry Team (UNITE), "Mission," http://www.uniteaero.com/Archives/UNITE%20v2/html/Mission.html.

81. UAS National Industry Team (UNITE), "About," http://www.uniteaero.com/Archives/UNITE%20v2/html/About_UNITE.html.

82. For example, US Customs and Border Protection begin using drones for aerial surveillance of the US–Mexico border in September 2010. "Predator Drones Set to Watch US-Mexico Border," Reuters, August 30, 2010.

83. Tom Barry, "How the Drone Warfare Industry Took Over Our Congress," AlterNet, November 30, 2011, http://www.alternet.org/story/153278/how_the_drone_warfare_industry_took_over_our_congress?page=2.

84. Unmanned Systems Caucus, "Mission & Main Goals," http://unmannedsystemscaucus.mckeon.house.gov/about/purpose-mission-goals.shtml.

85. Ed Kinane, "Drones and Dishonor in Central New York," Syracuse Peace Council, *Peace Newsletter*, October 2009, http://www.peacecouncil.net/pnl/09/788/788drones.htm.

86. Simone Weil, *The Iliad or Poem of Force* (Wallingford, PA: Pendle Hill, 1956), 11.

87. Critical reporting by Karen DeYoung and Greg Miller of the *Washington Post* constitutes rare but welcome exceptions. See, for example, Karen DeYoung, "US Sticks to Secrecy as Drone

Strikes Surge," *Washington Post*, December 20, 2011:A1, where she writes: "At home, the drone program has escaped serious public questioning because it is widely perceived as successful in eliminating insurgent leaders, has not put US personnel at risk and has taken place largely out of sight. Abroad, no other government has offered public support for the program." As previously noted, Miller has described how divided oversight of congressional committees has silenced members of Congress; see, Miller, "Under Obama."

88. American Civil Liberties Union, "Statement of U.N. Special Rapporteur on US Targeted Killings Without Due Process," August 3, 2010, http://www.aclu.org/national-security/statement-un-special-rapporteur-us-targeted-killings-without-due-process.

CHAPTER 13

A Morally Disengaged America
Sacrificing Iraqi Refugees to Terrorism Fears and Anti-Immigration

by Angel Ryono

*Americans are rightly happy to put the war in Iraq be-
hind them, but our moral and strategic obligations [do]
not end when the last boots [leave] the ground.*

—The List Project to Resettle Iraqi Refugees[1]

Is the United States suffering from a "media induced attention deficit
disorder?"[2] Or, are we afflicted with an advanced stage of the clas-
sically termed "American Amnesia?"[3] Whatever ails us, Americans
are increasingly disengaged from the moral responsibilities that result from our collective actions and, more importantly, inactions. By
looking at the history of global migration policies and international
refugee laws, it is clear that our government, too, encourages this amnesia with a dismal record of refugee care and protection.[4] Our disengagement is especially relevant when discussing the Iraqi refugee
crisis. Between 2005 and 2006, the US invasion triggered sectarian
violence, and Iraqi borders began to "hemorrhage" refugees. Some
Iraqis patiently wait with the desperate hope that our government will
grant them settlement in the US. However, these applicants are displaced internally, or to neighboring countries, because of the threats
of violence they receive or anticipate because of having assisted US
military and defense contractors. While millions of displaced Iraqis

currently live in limbo, the US corporate media have virtually stopped reporting on their status since 2007. The responsibility of adequate and accurate reporting now falls to independent journalists, some alternative media organizations, and humanitarian organizations.[5] Many of the humanitarian organizations doing the reporting are also working directly with Iraqi refugees, thus strained by scale of the crisis. Between 2005 and 2006, the US invasion triggered sectarian violence, and Iraqi borders began to "hemorrhage" refugees. By 2008, as news about Iraqi refugees nearly disappeared from mainstream media, the American public was encouraged to forget.[6] Does it not trouble the American conscience that our government feels no moral obligation to the Iraqi people after playing a direct role in displacing them?

American disengagement is not confined to Iraq; alongside the deportation of Cambodian refugees, as reported in a January 2012 Project Censored article, the Iraqi case brings to the foreground an uncomfortable reality. Our fear of terrorism and our anti-immigration culture establishes our political ignorance with regards to the duty to protect refugees as well as aid and abet our government in mistreating those who struggle to survive the consequences of mass violence. Are we willing to sacrifice innocent Iraqi refugees' lives because so many of us fear new immigrants? This article hopes to reawaken our conscience so that we may take legislative action or make personal contributions to assist Iraqi refugees.

In March 2003, George W. Bush declared war on Iraq, making Operation Iraqi Freedom the third US military attack on Iraq in fewer than twelve years.[7] The Bush administration insisted that Saddam Hussein's regime stockpiled nuclear and chemical weapons, and aimed to threaten the security of the American people. Bush claimed that initiating war with Iraq bore no other motive "except to remove a threat and restore control of [Iraq] to its own people."[8] The pretense for war has since been exposed by Central Intelligence Agency (CIA) agents who risked their anonymity to report how the executive branch misused intelligence. The United Nations, and both liberal and conservative think tanks, have agreed that there was no conclusive evidence of viable nuclear or chemical weapons technology in Iraq.[9] Americans might have already forgotten that, between 1990 and 1991, George H. W. Bush ordered an invasion of Iraq. The short but intense Operation Desert Storm displaced over 1.5 million Iraqis to Iran and Turkey. It is no wonder that antiwar protesters and human rights organizations decried G. W. Bush's decision as a humanitarian disaster—it was warned that at least two million refugees would result from the first two years of the invasion.[10]

The G. W. Bush administration claimed that US forces completed their mission in May 2003. Yet troops remained active in Iraq for nearly a decade, and what little infrastructure Iraqis had restored after previous US invasions was steadily destroyed.[11] Iraqi civilians felt increasingly insecure; they began to question or resent US presence.[12] Soon after Saddam Hussein was removed from leadership, armed groups used violence to vie for power, and some aimed to oust the occupying force. As sectarian violence and regional terrorism broke out in 2005 and 2006, G. W. Bush neglected the signs of a failed mission; he continued to pour US tax dollars into keeping troops in Iraq, and he allowed defense contractors to capitalize on "reconstruction" efforts. In 2006, the bombing of al-Askari Mosque in Samarra "sparked massive waves of displaced people beyond Iraq's borders. . . . This exodus constitutes the largest movement of refugees in the Middle East since the founding of the State of Israel."[13]

Finally, in December 2011, Defense Secretary Leon Panetta visited Baghdad to announce the end of the US military presence in Iraq. Panetta told US service men and women, "You will leave with great pride—lasting pride . . . secure in knowing that your sacrifice has helped the Iraqi people to begin a new chapter in history."[14] What does it really mean for Iraqis to "begin a new chapter in history" after a decade of military occupation? Let us examine what Iraqi people will need to consider in their transition out of conflict by reviewing the occupation's results:[15]

▸ The trial of Saddam Hussein was fraught with political interference and ultimately did not contribute to "reconciliation" in Iraq.
▸ No weapons of mass destruction were found.
▸ Some Iraqi militia members have been brought into what is considered by citizens of Iraq as questionable coalition gov-

ernment while insurgents in general have grown in numbers, complexity, and violence.[16]

- 4,500 US service members have been killed.
- 30,000 US service members have been wounded.
- Estimates of Iraqi civilian violent deaths range from 105,718 at the low end to 1.3 million at the upper end.[17]
- The total cost of the Iraq war has been more than three trillion dollars.[18]
- Up to five million Iraqis have fled the country since 2003, only a few thousand have returned, and most are not receiving formal assistance.

The last item in the list above begs the question: how can a country begin a new chapter when five million of its citizens live in exile? In addition to the engineers, physicians, and administrators (especially those associated with the Ba'ath Party or who worked for Saddam's regime) who fled early in the conflict, the United Nations High Commissioner for Refugees (UNHCR) estimates that about 40 percent of the refugees belong to Iraq's middle class. This means that Iraq has lost a significant percentage of its educated, likely politically moderate, and engaged citizens. A free and sovereign Iraq will be difficult to achieve without them.

To where have the millions of Iraqis fled? About two million refugees live in tenuous conditions in neighboring countries such as Syria, Jordan, Lebanon, Turkey, Egypt, the Islamic Republic of Iran and the Gulf Cooperation Council (GCC). There are no formal agreements for resettlement in Middle Eastern host countries. Some refugees, including families, have been on the move for three to five years—they are either searching for new, stable homes, or they live and work in the informal economy to avoid being deported to Iraq. Many stay in temporary shelters or refugee camps. Tens of thousands—a majority of whom are women and children—have become victims of human trafficking.

The UNHCR's 2012 report identified Iraq's refugee population as the group in greatest need of critical medical assistance in the Middle East. In Syria, over 25,000 Iraqis suffer critical medical conditions; moreover, an estimated 10 percent of the refugee population in Syria has suffered torture. Furthermore, countries such as Syria are undergoing domestic strife and internal instability. Compounding these challenges, the few existing assistance programs lack the capacity and resources to care adequately for all of Iraq's refugees. For example, UNHCR does not give direct support to refugees; it helps coordinate local assistance efforts and constantly negotiates with host governments for cooperation. With the crisis at the scale of millions of people, UNHCR must also play the role of alms person to the wealthier nations, to secure adequate funding for crucial work.

> Although most [Middle Eastern countries] are not state parties to the 1951 Convention relating to the Status of Refugees, they have abided by broad humanitarian principles, generally allowing refugees into their territory and granting them access to some basic services. In many aspects the approach taken by regional states such as Syria, Jordan and Lebanon are examples of providing protection despite domestic challenges.[19]

Over one hundred thousand Iraqi refugees strain Syria's capital, while only a few hundred thousand Iraqi refugees have been admitted for resettlement in Europe, Australia, and North America combined.[20] According to UNHCR, "Sweden has been the most welcoming, granting asylum to almost 9,000 Iraqis in 2006, almost 20 times more than the United States and about half the total for all of Europe that year."[21] The Irish have also extended support by increasing their annual contribution to UNHCR's work as well as legislating for resettled refugees to vote in Ireland. These efforts have historical roots, since the Iraqi refugee crisis evokes memories of displacement that occurred all over Europe during Hitler's invasion. Some countries acknowledge that adequate care for refugees will always require the effort and cooperation of the whole international community.

However, the bottom line for many US politicians is to *avoid* publicizing information that would implicate their involvement in unjust or illegal conduct in war. Therefore, the media silence around the plight of the Iraqi refugees has political roots. Government officials such as those in G. W. Bush's administration worked to disconnect the voting public from the reality of war. This is because the defense industry, and the political leaders who it courts, all stand to profit by obfuscating the real costs of war.[22]

What is the US government's record on caring for refugees? A review of refugee law and human migration policy history challenges some favored assumptions about US goodwill. After World War II, the vision for a globally integrated system to care for refugees and to appropriately manage human migration quickly faded as hegemonic US interests took center stage. According to author Rieko Karatani, "The current international framework for protecting migrants and refugees is often criticized as being fragmentary . . . [this] resulted from the battle between the United States and the international institutions."[23] A mixture of American exceptionalism,[24] the desire to maintain the position of global superpower, and a preoccupation with Cold War politics all contributed to the US government adopting policy to "calculate their needs, both economically and politically, and decide who and how many they wished to let in."[25] This policy has become such standard practice that little or no exceptions are made for refugees directly harmed by US foreign policies or armed forces. The US went further to erode the foundations of a "multilaterally organized migration scheme" by disregarding the authority and knowledge of long-standing institutions such as the International Labor Organization (ILO), instead creating agencies to care for refugees that "became inactive as soon as [they were] founded,"[26] and funding organizations that would work solely for the interests of the US.

All this amounts to a major sidestepping of responsibility to care for Iraqi refugees. Even today, the US government continues to stall or reject the immigration of refugees: "The United States took several thousand Iraqis a year after the [1991] Gulf War, but the numbers it accepted fell precipitously after the attacks of Sept. 11 and the [2003] invasion of Iraq."[27] By 2006, the US government "admitted a mere 202 refugees," and in 2007, admissions increased slightly to 466.[28]

The US government made vague promises to the UN to resettle Iraqi refugees who worked as full-time employees for US armed forces and intelligence. In 2007, some US legislators initiated public discussions about "the special dangers faced by Iraqis working for Americans and acknowledge the need to grant them safety in the United

States."[29] Rachel Schneller, who worked as a US diplomat in Iraq, tells the *New York Times* that the reputation of "working with Americans . . . has more or less become a death sentence in [the southern part] of Iraq. I must get desperate e-mails every other day from one of them."[30] However, testimony in 2001 by the Federal Bureau of Investigation (FBI) to Congress, about the potential risks that some Iraqi refugees pose to national security, quickly extinguished interest in the resettlement of select refugees. In fact, the FBI is currently investigating the files of more than 57,000 Iraqi refugees living in the US, most of whom were granted settlement after the First Gulf War. They now face the threat of deportation on the grounds that they pose risks to national security.[31] The FBI's actions tread uncomfortably into a violation of *Non-Refoulement* principle (protection against returning refugees to places where their lives and freedom will be threatened) and a circumvention of principles laid out in the Bill of Rights as well as the Universal Declaration of Human Rights. All refugees, without prior knowledge and due process, are targeted in FBI investigations. US officials estimated that the government would only accept a small fraction of the 9,000+ applications for resettlement filed by the UN on behalf of Iraq refugees. But, the government has delayed processing even those applications.[32]

The New York Times, perhaps the leading source among corporate media that is committed to reporting on the status of Iraqi refugees, estimates that at least 69,000 Iraqis worked for American contractors, as cleaners, construction workers, and drivers.[33] As of 2012, Iraqi refugees seeking asylum or resettlement in the US face difficult restrictions:[34]

▸ Refugees cannot apply to immigrate to the US from within Iraq; they must travel to Syria or Jordan to do so.
▸ If the applicant worked for a US contractor, it is likely their application would be rejected, regardless of evidence that working for the Americans has endangered them.
▸ Because of the popular uprising against President Bashar al-Assad and al-Assad's violent response, US officials refuse to send additional staff or diplomats to Syria in order to expedite the interviews required to resettle qualified Iraqi refugees.[35]

▶ In 2012, UNHCR decided to freeze the program to assist refugees in applying to resettle in the US because of multiple types of delays and the uncooperative nature of the US departments responsible for the refugee program.[36]

▶ Iraqis who worked to support American intelligence are not provided protection while they wait, in Iraq, for approval to immigrate to the US.

The UNHCR laments that there is "very little understanding of the difference between refugees and migrant workers."[37] This statement certainly applies to Americans and is reflected in our government's disorganized, disingenuous, and poor treatment of refugees, including non-Iraqis. Indeed, the US government has instituted harsh, broad anti-immigration policies that have impacted refugees from around the world.[38] As long as voting citizens do not question what the US government does abroad and are not able to distinguish among refugees, migrant workers, and "illegal" immigrants, we enable our government to impulsively spend public funds on military violence as a strategy for foreign relations. Though the current American bias and antipathy toward immigrants are cultivated separately, increasingly removed from the negative consequences of US actions abroad, a culture of fear and hate provides fertile grounds for public consent toward irresponsible and illiberal government actions with repercussions felt well beyond Iraq. For instance, thirty years after Congress passed special legislation to resettle those displaced as a result of US involvement in the Second Indochinese War, about 2,000 Cambodian refugees have either been deported or face deportation. The deportation of Cambodian refugees and the plight of Iraqi refugees who wait indefinitely for resettlement in the US make clear that our government is unconcerned with moral obligations to innocent lives that are lost or harmed as a consequence of its wars.

> The needs of Iraqi refugees remain substantial . . . Iraqis still continue to seek asylum in neighboring countries. Those who remain in countries of asylum have become more vulnerable as their displacement has lengthened and their coping mechanisms have become depleted. Despite their in-

creased vulnerability, the majority of Iraqi refugees have indicated little interest in returning to their country of origin.[39]

Will we continue to shut our minds and hearts to people who need our help, who risked their lives to support our troops and our fellow Americans who worked in Iraq, and who require our government to take responsibility for their safety? It is up to us to remind our elected officials that their neglect of Iraqi refugees means the disintegration of our society's moral fabric. At minimum, US citizens can pressure congress and the senate to conduct hearings in order to resume resettling the list of Iraqi refugees who have worked for US security forces.[40] Beyond the minimum, citizens can push for government officials to continue to fund, generously, the work of UNHCR and other regional assistance programs that support the welfare of Iraqi refugees.[41]

ANGEL RYONO is a graduate of Saybrook University. Her MA research discusses local and grassroots capacities for reconciliation and peacebuilding in Cambodia. In general, her writings investigate the realities of post-conflict transitions—what happens after we declare a war, or after genocide has ended? She is a contributor to the anthology *Peace Movements Worldwide* (ABC-CLIO) and to *Peacebuilding and Subjectivities of Peace: History, Memory, and Politics* (Routledge). She has served as the development manager for the Virtual Tribunal Project (now formally adopted as a UN archive project) for the Khmer Rouge Tribunal.

Notes

1. The List Project to Resettle Iraqi Refugees, 2012, http://thelistproject.org/history/europe-1933-1945.
2. Arthur Bruzzone, "Obama's Plummeting Numbers Reveal Larger Trends," *Huffington Post*, March 13, 2012, http://www.huffingtonpost.com/arthur-bruzzone/obamas-plummeting-poll-nu_b_1341892.html.
3. Rudy Perkins, "Obama's Worrisome Amnesia on Iraq War," *Daily Hampshire Gazette*, December 23, 2011, http://www.gazettenet.com/2011/12/23/obama039s-worrisome-amnesia-on-iraq-war?SESSd2014118de53aa565f89dc7cfa9e2706=gnews.
4. The US record with regard to refugee care and protection is part of a constellation of reasons that challenge the grounds on which US government officials have justified war. What we believe with regard to how innocent civilians should be treated during and after war disagrees with how US government actually prioritizes the protection of vulnerable civilians, funds organizations to care for displaced people, and treats asylum seekers and refugees settled in the US.
5. The competition of truths, or the "war of information," is another regretful feature of the recent US occupation in Iraq. Nearly a thousand embedded journalists signed contractual agreements with the US military in order to travel through the terrains of conflict with military protection, ultimately abandoning journalistic objectivity and impartiality. Independent and unembedded

journalists, like Dahr Jamail, are rare and few. Jamail's work involves unprotected travels in Iraq and a commitment to capture the experiences of civilians who are rendered invisible by the fog of war. Those who are committed to accurate and adequate reporting of the Iraq refugee crisis do not only struggle with resources to do so, but their work often does not have the same reach as corporate media.

6. S. Harris & Nir Rosen, "Between Iraq and a Hard Place," *New York Times Magazine*, May 13, 2007, http://video.nytimes.com/video/2007/05/11/magazine/1194817106017/the-flight-from-iraq.html.

7. Operation Desert Storm (1991), Desert Fox Air-Strike (1998), and Operation Iraqi Freedom (2003).

8. "Bush Declares War," CNN, March 19, 2003, http://articles.cnn.com/2003-03-19/us/sprj.irq.int.bush.transcript_1_coalition-forces-equipment-in-civilian-areas-iraqi-troops-and-equipment/2?_s=PM:US.

9. "Bush Legacy on Iraq: Misinformation on False Pretense, Center for American Progress, January 12, 2004, http://www.americanprogress.org/issues/2004/01/b19351.html.

10. "Oxfam's Iraq Refugee Plea," BBC News, March 18, 2003, http://news.bbc.co.uk/2/hi/uk_news/2861069.stm.

11. T. J. Nagy, "The Secret Behind the Sanctions: How the US Intentionally Destroyed Iraq's Water Supply," *USA Today*, September 2001, http://www.progressive.org/mag/nagy0901.html.

12. Cesar G. Soriano and Steven Komarow, "Poll: Iraqis Out of Patience," *USA Today*, April 28, 2004, http://www.usatoday.com/news/world/iraq/2004-04-28-poll-cover_x.htm.

13. The List Project to Resettle Iraqi Refugees, 2012, http://thelistproject.org.

14. Michael S. Schmidt, Robert F. Worth, and Thom Shanker, "In Baghdad, Panetta Leads Uneasy Moment of Closure," *New York Times*, December 15, 2011, Middle East edition, http://www.nytimes.com/2011/12/16/world/middleeast/panetta-in-baghdad-for-iraq-military-handover-ceremony.html?pagewanted=all.

15. The Costs of War, Watson Institute for International Studies, Eisenhower Study Group 2011, http://costsofwar.org.

16. Dahr Jamail, "Refugees Speak of Escape from Hell," Inter Press Service, April 7, 2007, http://dahrjamail.net/refugees-speak-of-escape-from-hell.

17. Iraq Body Count (http://www.iraqbodycount.org) estimates between 105,718 and 115,471 Iraqi civilians have died violent deaths. *Censored 2009* reported "Over One Million Iraqi Deaths Caused by US Occupation," as Censored story #1 for that year, based on the study conducted by the prestigious British polling group, Opinion Research Business (ORB). See Peter Phillips and Andrew Roth, eds., "Over One Million Iraqi Deaths Caused by US Occupation," *Censored 2009: The Top Censored Stories of 2007–08* (New York: Seven Stories Press, 2008), 20–25; Johnny Heald and Munqeth Daghir, "More than 1,000,000 Iraqis Murdered Since 2003 Invasion," *ZNet*, September 16, 2007, http://www.zcommunications.org/more-than-1-000-000-iraqis-murdered-since-2003-invasion-by-orb.

18. Linda J. Bilmes and Joseph E. Stiglitz, "The True Cost of the Iraq War: $3 Trillion and Beyond," *Washington Post*, September 5, 2010, http://www.washingtonpost.com/wp-dyn/content/article/2010/09/03/AR2010090302200.html.

19. *2012 Regional Response Plan: Iraqi Refugees*, United Nations High Commissioner for Refugees (UNHCR), 2011, 2–3, http://reliefweb.int/sites/reliefweb.int/files/resources/Full%20Report_604.pdf.

20. Ibid.

21. Markus Sperl, "Iraqi Refugees," *New York Times*, http://topics.nytimes.com/top/news/international/countriesandterritories/iraq/iraqi_refugees/index.html; and Sperl, "Fortress Europe and the Iraqi 'Intruders': Iraqi Asylum-Seekers and the EU, 2003–2007," UNHCR, October 2007, http://www.unhcr.org/470c9be92.html.

22. It is well known, perhaps considered common sense, that armed conflict, war, is a leading cause of human displacement. The International Committee of the Red Cross (ICRC) argues that if there is will on the part of political leaders and awareness on the part of the citizens, then most armed conflicts are preventable. To really understand the breadth of the effects of

CENSORED 2013

war, please visit: The Eisenhower Study Group, "The Costs of War," September 2011, Brown University, http://costsofwar.org.

23. Rieko Karatani, "How History Separated Refugee and Migrant Regimes: In Search of their Institutional Origins," *International Journal of Refugee Law* 17, no. 3 (2005), doi:10.1093/ijrl/eei019.

24. Here, "exceptionalism" means that while some Americans believe the mission of the country is to spread liberty, justice, and democracy around the world, Americans can be exempt from the obligation to participate in global efforts addressing such concerns.

25. Karatani, "How History Separated Refugee and Migrant Regimes."

26. Ibid.

27. "Iraqi Refugees," *New York Times*, http://topics.nytimes.com/top/news/international/countriesandterritories/iraq/iraqi_refugees/index.html.

28. Rachel L. Swarns and Katherine Zoepf, "More Iraqis Are Headed to US," *New York Times*, February 14, 2007, http://www.nytimes.com/2007/02/14/washington/14refugees.html.

29. David Rohde and Sabrina Tavernise, "Few Iraqis Reach Safe US Haven Despite Program," *New York Times*, August 29, 2007, http://www.nytimes.com/2007/08/29/world/middleeast/29refugees.html?pagewanted=1&adxnnl=1&ref=iraqirefugees&adxnnlx=133029028_2-nG6Dvf4pYubpIN4o/csDTA.

30. Ibid.

31. Aamer Madhani, "Terror Threat Slows Iraqi Refugee Flow to US," *USA Today*, February 6, 2012, http://www.navytimes.com/news/2012/02/gannett-terror-threat-slows-iraqi-refugee-flow-to-us-020612.

32. Rohde and Tavernise, *New York Times*, 2007.

33. Ibid.

34. Tim Arango, "Unrest and American Safety Concerns Strands Iraqis in Syria Awaiting Visas for US," January 23, 2012, *New York Times*, http://www.nytimes.com/2012/01/24/world/middleeast/unrest-strands-iraqis-in-syria-awaiting-american-visas.html.

35. Ibid.

36. *2012 Regional Response Plan: Iraqi Refugees*, 7.

37. Ibid., 78.

38. Angel Ryono, "The Quiet Campaign to Break Up Cambodian Refugee Families," Project Censored, January 3, 2012, http://www.projectcensored.org/top-stories/articles/the-quiet-campaign-to-break-up-cambodian-refugee-families.

39. *2012 Regional Response Plan: Iraqi Refugees*, 77.

40. Editorial, "Take Iraqi Refugees In," *Milford Daily News*, January 28, 2007, http://www.milforddailynews.com/opinion/8998973966395637759.

41. Refugee International, "Iraq," http://www.refugeesinternational.org/where-we-work/middleeast/iraq.

CHAPTER 14

On the Road to Fukushima
The Unreported Story behind Japan's Nuclear-Media-Industrial Complex

by Brian Covert

PROLOGUE

The most powerful earthquake to ever hit the islands of Japan struck on the afternoon of March 11, 2011. The magnitude 9 quake, centered about 70 kilometers (43 miles) off the Pacific coast, sent oceanic shock waves racing toward Japan's northeastern Tohoku region. Located squarely on the tsunami's course were coastal areas that are also home to several nuclear power plants, such as in Fukushima Prefecture, which is situated about 240 kilometers (150 miles) from Tokyo, the most populated metropolis on the planet. As it became clear that something had gone seriously wrong and, due to the tsunami, Japan now had a nuclear catastrophe on its hands at Fukushima, all eyes turned to the Japanese press.

But the Japanese press was nowhere to be found. In the immediate aftermath of reactor meltdowns and the release of radioactivity at the Fukushima Nuclear Power Plant, when evacuations and press restrictions had not yet been set by Japan's government, the major Japanese news companies did not have a single reporter on the ground in the area.[1] Such media companies in Japan usually spare no expense in having their reporters or photographers camp for days at a time outside the homes of suspects in sensationalized crime cases or when stalking scandal-tainted celebrities. But when it comes to pursuing real news stories of public concern, investigating the nation's political or corporate centers of power, and exercising the freedom of press as enshrined in the Japanese constitution, the news media of Japan can be strangely submissive or even silent. Nowhere has that been more on display than in the reporting of the Fukushima nuclear crisis.

How is it that one of the most technologically advanced, democratic societies in the world finds itself with a press that serves more as a lapdog to the powerful than as a watchdog for the public? How does Japan's nuclear power industry in particular fare in the news media? And more importantly, how is censorship fostered in such an environment and how did it get this way?

The answers to such questions can be found by taking a look back on the road to Fukushima that Japan has traveled since the Second World War. It is the story that most of the mainstream media in Japan are failing to report or to piece together in the wake of Fukushima, perhaps because, in many ways, the media itself *is* the story.

It is the story of how of the Japanese press has risen to become a global media power unto itself,[2] and how Japan's corporate-dominated news industry grew hand-in-glove with the nation's development of atomic energy and other major industries following the war. It is the story of a Japanese war crimes suspect imprisoned by US occupation forces, of Japan's preeminent media tycoon, of the godfather of Japanese nuclear power development, and of the father of Japanese professional baseball—all of whom happen to be the same man, the powerful Japanese predecessor of today's Rupert Murdoch.

It is the story of the power wielded by right-wing forces in Japan and, at the fringes, of the Japanese mafia. It is a story that also closely involves the United States of America as benefactor: the Central Intelligence Agency, the US Congress, and the US media establishment. It is the story of America's Cold War geopolitical priorities over the long-term security and environmental safety of the planet.

It is the story, in the end, of Japan's rise as a modern nuclear-media-industrial power from the ashes of Hiroshima and Nagasaki in 1945 up to Fukushima more than sixty-five years later. This report attempts to connect the dots of Japan's atomic past and present, providing the much bigger picture behind the individual acts of censorship surrounding Fukushima and, in doing so, will hopefully offer lessons for the future of a democratic, responsible press in Japan.

THE SHORIKI FACTOR

If there is one person who has stood at the nexus of nuclear power, media conglomeration, politics, and industrial development in post-war Japan, it would be Matsutaro Shoriki.

Shoriki, in the early 1920s, was a high-ranking official of the Tokyo Metropolitan Police Department, and in previous years had reportedly been involved in every major incident of police repression of social unrest.[3] That included the Great Kanto Earthquake of September 1923, Japan's deadliest natural disaster up to then, in which more than 100,000 people died and tens of thousands of others went missing.[4]

After the earthquake's ensuing panic and confusion and the Japanese government's declaration of martial law, the police took the opportunity to round up ethnic Koreans living in Japan, along with leading Japanese socialists, anarchists, labor activists, and other leftist dissidents of the day—some of whom were later reported killed.[5] This all happened on Shoriki's watch, and a month after the quake he was promoted to a department head position within the Tokyo police hierarchy.[6] Shoriki's law enforcement career came to a halt a couple months later, however, when a young Communist Party supporter attempted to shoot Hirohito, the emperor-to-be, in public. Shoriki was among those dismissed from their police posts for the lapse in security surrounding the assassination attempt.

It was the end of Shoriki's days as a hard-line police official, but just the beginning of his career as a central figure in the Japanese media world.

One month after his firing from the Tokyo metropolitan police, Shoriki—with no past media experience whatsoever—found himself serving as president of the *Yomiuri Shimbun* newspaper, then a fledgling 50,000-circulation Japanese metropolitan daily paper in Tokyo.[7] He had bought out a controlling stake in the newspaper through a huge personal loan from a cabinet minister then serving in the Japanese government. A rebellion immediately arose among the editorial staff of the paper, but the new owner had no regrets. "Instead of committing *hara-kiri*" (ritual disembowelment) over the police firing, "I bought a newspaper," Shoriki would boast.[8]

The openly pro-capitalistic, anticommunistic Shoriki quickly showed himself as having a finger on the public pulse, understanding well the links between three key areas: mass entertainment, mass mobilization, and massive profits.[9]

His *Yomiuri Shimbun* newspaper company sponsored tours in Japan of major league baseball players from the US—first in 1931, then again in 1934, when the *Yomiuri* paid for US baseball legends Babe Ruth, Lou Gehrig, and others to come and play in Japan. The next year, the *Yomiuri Shimbun* newspaper created its own baseball team, the Yomiuri Giants, in the exact image of the famed Giants baseball team of New York (later of San Francisco). In 1936, Japan's first professional baseball league was started, with Shoriki going on to serve as owner of the Yomiuri Giants pro team and as the first commissioner of the Nippon Professional Baseball league years later.

By the late 1930s and early 1940s, the winds of war were blowing in Japan. All of the Japanese press was expected by the military-dominated government to support Japan's war of aggression throughout East Asia and the Pacific, and the major news publications—from liberal to conservative—toed the line, either under government pressure or out of a sense of patriotism. Two days after the Japanese military attack on the US-occupied Pacific island of Hawaii in December 1941, the major newspapers in Japan sponsored a public rally in Tokyo denouncing the US and Britain. Shoriki, representing the *Yomiuri Shimbun* newspaper, was reportedly one of the main speakers.[10]

In the fifteen years since Shoriki had taken over the paper, the *Yomiuri* had gone from being a fairly liberal Tokyo metro daily paper to being an unashamedly conservative national daily newspaper—the third-largest daily paper in Japan, in fact—with a circulation of 1.2 million.[11] *The Yomiuri* became the most nationalistic of Japan's mainstream news media during World War II. For his efforts, Shoriki, like other press executives in Japan, was appointed to several key government propaganda organizations during the war, including as cabinet-level advisor in the government.[12]

BEHIND PRISON WALLS

Following the US atomic bombings of Hiroshima and Nagasaki, which killed more than 200,000 people in August 1945, and Japan's formal surrender a month later, the occupation forces under General Douglas MacArthur wasted no time in sniffing out suspected war criminals as part of victor's justice, Yankee-style.

The top ranking of war criminals, "Class A," applied to persons in the highest decision-making bodies in Japan who were believed to have taken part in the starting and/or waging of war against the Allied powers. Among those who were openly demanding that the Americans include Shoriki, the *Yomiuri* newspaper president, in that Class-A category were Shoriki's longtime enemies on the Japanese political left and, incredibly, some of the newspaper magnate's own editorial staff at the *Yomiuri Shimbun.*[13] Long considered to be something of a "dictator" within his paper,[14] Shoriki was now facing a serious mutiny by his crew at a very sensitive time in Japanese history. In December 1945, he was ordered by the US occupation forces to report to Japan's notorious Sugamo Prison in central Tokyo as an inmate.

The dozens of initial suspects of Class-A war crimes at the prison made up a virtual "who's who" of the most elite of Japanese political, military, and business circles. Shoriki was placed in cellblock 2-B of the prison, directly across from a prominent industrialist who had once been head of the mighty Nissan group of corporations.[15] As a media baron, Shoriki commanded respect even behind bars. The Buddhist priest in charge of counseling the accused war criminals at the prison recalled: "Mr. Shoriki, former president of the 'Yomiuri Newspaper,' I had met two or three times at banquets given by the Chief Priest, whose advisors in various matters we both had been. He [Shoriki] was still as vigorous as ever. . . ."[16]

George Herman Ruth, one of the US baseball idols invited by Shoriki to play for Japanese audiences back in the 1930s, had little sympathy for his former patron. "That bum [Shoriki] seemed like a pretty nice fellow," Babe Ruth, now retired from baseball, said on hearing the news of Shoriki's imprisonment in Tokyo. "I guess he was too nice, come to think of it. All any of them guys did was bow to us, and even then they must have had a knife in their kimona [sic]."[17]

Ruth even complained that the American ballplayers had been cheated during their tour of Japan a decade before: "Shoriki didn't pay us what he promised to pay. Most of us spent more money in Japan than we made."[18]

As Shoriki and the others languished in prison not knowing their fate, the US, at least in the early stages, proceeded with its plan of "reforming" Japan, putting a high priority on strengthening democratic institutions and the rights of the individual.

But a funny thing happened on the way to democracy: on a parallel track, the government of the United States, under the umbrella of the Truman Doctrine of President Harry Truman, was also proceeding on a "reverse course" in Japan. From 1947–48 onward, the US priority began shifting away from promoting democracy to fighting communism. General MacArthur's occupation forces in Tokyo now sought to "strengthen, not punish" right-wing Japanese leaders so as to secure Japan as a key ally especially against the regional influence of Communist China.[19]

The Cold War was starting and, almost overnight, the US had gone from purging its sworn wartime enemies on the political right in Japan to purging those on the left. Japanese ultra-rightist organizations and even the *yakuza*, Japan's mafia syndicates, were becoming useful tools for the US occupation authorities in suppressing the growing social movement of organized labor and liberal political dissent, including in the Japanese news media.[20]

And so it was that right-wing media mogul Matsutaro Shoriki walked out of the Tokyo prison gates on September 1, 1947—twenty-one months of prison time served and no war-crime charges filed against him.[21] Shoriki and many of his fellow Japanese war-criminal suspects were looking much more useful to the United States beyond—rather than behind—prison walls.

TELEVISION AND "ATOMS FOR PEACE"

In summer 1951, with the official end of the American occupation of Japan just around the corner, Shoriki and other released Japanese war criminal suspects were finally removed from General MacArthur's war-criminal "purge list" and were now free to resume their former public lives. Shoriki received his pardon on August 6, the sixth anniversary of the Hiroshima atomic bombing. The very next day, he went to work on his next big project: establishing Japan's first commercial television network.[22]

In this venture, Shoriki had warm support from conservative members of the US Congress, who, like their right-wing counterparts in Japan, apparently saw the mass media not as a way to inform or educate the poverty-stricken Japanese masses but rather as a means to essentially feed the Japanese public a steady stream of pro-American messages of progress and development in the postwar period.

Shoriki's key ally in the US Congress for this was Karl Mundt, a Republican senator from South Dakota. Through the mid-1940s, Mundt had served as an active member of the House Un-American Activities Committee (HUAC) that was investigating suspected Communist infiltration throughout US society. During that same period, Mundt pushed a bill through Congress in 1948 that became law, creating the *Voice of America* short-wave radio propaganda program.[23] But Mundt had an even bigger dream: using the rising medium of television to carry *VOA* broadcasts throughout the world, including in Japan, as a way to counter the growing global "red" menace. Mundt called his grand plan "Vision of America."[24]

It was Hidetoshi Shibata, then a popular conservative, America-friendly radio commentator on Nippon Hoso Kyokai (NHK, Japan's public broadcaster) and a former *Yomiuri* newspaper reporter under Shoriki, who eventually hooked up Mundt and Shoriki.[25] On August 14, only a week after Shoriki's pardon as a US-branded war crimes suspect, Mundt, at a press conference in Washington DC accompanied by a member of Japan's parliament, announced plans for a team of three American "experts" to fly to Japan the following week to firm up the plans for this new Japanese TV broadcasting network.[26] Another week later, the Japanese and American sides met in Tokyo and worked out the details: it was agreed that instead of making this new TV station a part of Mundt's worldwide "Vision of America" scheme, it would be a wholly Japanese-owned and Japanese-run network financed in part by airing *Voice of America* radio broadcasts within Japan.[27]

Shoriki had meanwhile regained his old position as the largest shareholder of the *Yomiuri* paper, and now persuaded the heads of his archrival daily newspapers, the liberal *Asahi* and *Mainichi*, to join the conservative *Yomiuri* in putting up joint capital of about ¥2 billion ($25 million) for the TV station. Shoriki also used his highly placed connections in Japanese government and financial institutions to further strengthen support for the new station, promoting the TV network as potentially attracting three million Japanese viewers within five years.[28]

In July 1952, just three months after the US occupation bureaucracy had packed its bags and gone home, the new Nippon Television Network (NTV) was granted its broadcasting license by Japanese media regulators. Shoriki became the first president of NTV in October 1952, and in August 1953, the station went on the air with black-and-white television programs. Now it was just a matter of getting the message out to the masses.

"Kilowatts, not killing"

At the United Nations in December 1953, US President Dwight Eisenhower announced the start of his "Atoms for Peace" program. Several months later in September 1954, US atomic energy commissioner Thomas Murray stood before a convention of American steelworkers at Atlantic City, New Jersey, and called for a nuclear power plant to be built in Japan with US know-how and manpower as "a dramatic and Christian gesture which would lift all of us far above the recollection of the carnage" of Hiroshima and Nagasaki nine years before.[29] An editorial in the *Washington Post* immediately and enthusiastically supported this "brilliant idea," stating: "How better, indeed, to dispel the impression in Asia that the United States regards Orientals merely as nuclear cannon fodder!"[30]

A few months after that in early 1955, Representative Sidney Yates, a Democrat from Illinois, took it even further when he stood on the floor of the US Congress and called for that proposed first nuclear power plant in Japan to be constructed, of all places, in the atomic-bombed city of Hiroshima. He was then sponsoring a bill in Congress for a 60,000-kilowatt nuclear power generating plant to be built in Hiroshima as part of Eisenhower's "Atoms for Peace"—a power plant, Yates said, that would "make the atom an instrument for kilowatts rather than killing."[31] (Plans for the Hiroshima nuclear plant eventually fizzled out.)

Back in Japan around that same time, Matsutaro Shoriki, while still president of NTV, campaigned in February 1955 for a seat in his own country's House of Representatives and won. He was appointed to the cabinet-level position of minister of state. Everything now seemed to be in place. For the better part of 1955, Eisenhower's newly established United States Information Service (USIS), with its mission of overseas "public diplomacy" (read: propaganda) and Shoriki's *Yomiuri Shimbun* newspaper, which now had a colossal circulation of more than two million readers,[32] worked closely together on plans to bring America's atomic-age vision to the Japanese people.[33]

The Atom Returns to Japan

On November 1, 1955, the USIS and Shoriki's *Yomiuri Shimbun* newspaper kicked off the opening of a futuristic, traveling "Atoms for Peace" exhibition at an event hall in downtown Tokyo, not far from the Imperial Palace.

The fifteen sections of the exhibition, touted as the first of its kind in Far East Asia, explained "how the boundless wealth of the atom has been unlocked, and now it is already being used in many ways for man's benefit in medicine and industry." The exhibition was to be shown in Tokyo for a month and a half, then rotated on to seven other major Japanese cities.[34] The exhibition included profiles of ten pioneering nuclear scientists; a small demonstration nuclear reactor; a movie about the peaceful uses of nuclear energy; panel displays; and an introduction to the medical, agricultural, and industrial uses of atomic isotopes.[35] On New Year's Day of 1956, while the exhibition was still touring Japan, state minister Shoriki was appointed the first chairman of the Japan Atomic Energy Commission, a move praised by US atomic energy commissioner Lewis Strauss as "an important contribution to international peace."[36]

The "Atoms for Peace" exhibition finally arrived in Hiroshima in May 1956 and was shown for three weeks at the recently opened Hiroshima Peace Memorial Museum, located within the city's Peace Memorial Park commemorating the victims of the 1945 US atomic bombing. An estimated 110,000 Japanese visitors came to see the "Atoms for Peace" exhibition in Hiroshima, and a reported 2.5 million people had seen the exhibition nationwide.[37] At the end of it all, notwithstanding some public and press criticism that arose, the "Atoms for Peace" exhibition in Japan was considered a resounding success, primarily due to the positive spin given to it by the Japanese media, especially the *Yomiuri* newspaper and NTV network headed by Shoriki.[38]

CODE NAME: PODAM

Tetsuo Arima, a professor of media studies at the elite Waseda University in Tokyo, goes where the Japanese mainstream press fears to tread in researching and making public the CIA's past connections to the media and nuclear power in Japan, having published several books on the subject in recent years. He has visited the US National Security Archive in Washington DC and obtained almost 500 pages of once-secret documents detailing the introduction of atomic energy technology to Japan.[39]

"Relations with PODAM have now progressed to the stage where outright cooperation can be initiated," Arima quotes one of those CIA documents as reading, concerning political maneuvering against the Japan Communist Party back in the 1950s.[40] Another document approves "PODAM" as being used to gain information about political developments and trends in Japan, along with information on persons working in Japanese newspapers and media. PODAM, the code name of a CIA asset, was none other than Japanese media tycoon Matsutaro Shoriki.[41]

Indeed, a cursory check of the National Security Archive website (gwu.edu/~nsarchiv) reveals Matsutaro Shoriki as being listed under the cryptonym PODAM as well as "POJACKPOT-1."[42] Equally revealing is Shoriki's TV station, Nippon Television, being listed in the archive's CIA file index as part of a project called "KMCASHIER."[43] Project KMCASHIER, as Arima notes, was a failed 1953 US plan to construct a massive microwave communications network covering four Asian countries (Japan, South Korea, Taiwan, and the Philippines) as part of a larger international microwave communications network. Japan's role in KMCASHIER was listed under the CIA code name of "POHIKE."[44] "POBULK" is listed in the archive index as the CIA code name for the *Yomiuri*, Shoriki's newspaper.

Arima found also that Shibata, the popular NHK radio newscaster who initially put Shoriki in touch with US senator Mundt of *VOA* fame, had contacted and met in Tokyo with persons connected with the CIA (presumably on Shoriki's behalf), both before and after Shoriki obtained the broadcast license for NTV.[45] The professor also came across a document dated May 5, 1955—placing it around the time of joint preparations by the USIS and Shoriki's *Yomiuri* newspaper for the "Atoms for Peace" exhibition—in which a "provisional" security clearance was sought for Shoriki as an "unwitting cutout."[46] This indicates that Shoriki would have been considered a trusted intermediary for passing along highly sensitive information, yet not necessarily aware of the details of that information or exactly how he was being used for such intelligence purposes.

According to one CIA document that Arima uncovered, Shoriki as atomic energy commissioner was so impatient to get nuclear power online in Japan following the 1955–56 "Atoms For Peace" exhibition that he seriously considered buying a small reactor to power his own home as a public show of atomic energy's benefits.[47] And what was PODAM's urgent motivation? To help reach his political aspiration of becoming the prime minister of Japan.

THE DEEP TIES THAT BIND

Japanese nuclear power, industrial production (especially in electronics), and the news media grew side by side in the critical Cold War years that would see Japan elevated to the status of "economic miracle." Without doubt, from the end of the Second World War onward, the media industry has been a crucial part of that whole corporate synergy in Japan—not an objective, neutral force standing outside it.[48]

That is still the situation today for the most part. The electric power companies in Japan advertise widely in the major print and broadcast media companies. Tokyo Electric Power Company (TEPCO)—operator of the Fukushima nuclear plant and two others—alone spent about ¥27 billion ($330 million) on public relations and other events promoting nuclear energy in 2010, ranking tenth highest among all Japanese corporations in the amount of money spent on such expenses that year.[49] Of that amount, TEPCO spent ¥9 billion ($110 million) directly on advertisements placed in the media.[50]

So what effect does this kind of relationship between nuclear energy and media in Japan have on news coverage? According to author and independent journalist Osamu Aoki, a former reporter for Japan's Kyodo News wire service, "Newspapers, TV, magazines—it makes no difference: because they receive these huge advertising monies, it's hard for them to criticize the power companies, especially with nuclear power. It's a taboo that's been going on for some time."[51]

Where Japan differs from the US and other developed countries is in the sheer breadth and depth of external press controls and media self-censorship in the form of the "*kisha* club" (reporters' club) system.[52]

The kisha clubs are press clubs attached to various Japanese government agencies (from the highest levels of government down to local government agencies), political parties, major corporations, consumer organizations . . . and electric power companies. At last count there were an estimated 800 to 1,000 kisha clubs nationwide. Membership in such clubs is mostly restricted to the big Japanese newspaper and broadcasting companies, with smaller Japanese media and the foreign press normally not allowed in. One important rule: kisha club reporters are not usually allowed to "scoop" fellow club members on any given story, even if they are reporters for rival Japanese news companies. In most cases a kisha club is based on the premises of the institution that the reporters are covering, with the operating expenses of the club paid by that institution. The kisha club rooms generally are off-limits to the average Japanese citizen, even when located inside of public buildings.

TEPCO, like other power companies around Japan, has its own in-house kisha club. And what was the chairman of TEPCO doing at the time of the March 11 quake/tsunami and subsequent Fukushima nuclear plant disaster? He was hosting Japanese journalists on a press junket in China, courtesy of the power company.[53]

According to an independent journalist attending a press conference hosted by TEPCO soon after the accident on March 11, 2011, not one of the power company's kisha club reporters got around to asking the TEPCO chairman at press conferences about the possibility of plutonium leaks from the Fukushima plant until the independent journalist himself raised the critical question two weeks after the accident. Another independent Japanese reporter working for Internet media was shouted down by the TEPCO kisha club reporters when he tried to ask the TEPCO chairman a question at the same press conference. These are not uncommon occurrences at kisha clubs in Japan.[54]

How did all of this translate in terms of Japanese versus overseas reporting on Fukushima soon after the accident? There were often major gaps between the two. On the morning of March 12, the day after the accident, for example, Japan's public broadcaster, NHK television, was telling evacuees from Fukushima to calmly "walk instead of drive to an evacuation area" while also repeating Japanese government assurances that there was "no immediate danger."[55] That same morning, the tone of reports carried on BBC News, as just one foreign news media source, was one of skepticism of such Japanese government assurances rather than blind acceptance.[56] That kind of gap between Japanese and overseas coverage would widen considerably as the Fukushima crisis went on, with the Japanese public increasingly voicing distrust of their government and suspicious that Japan's media were not reporting the whole story.

That is certainly true for one related issue that has been underreported in Japan for years: the so-called "nuclear gypsies"—the thousands of day laborers, many unskilled and homeless, that make up a large part of the workforce at Japan's fifty-four nuclear power plants nationwide—and the *yakuza* (organized crime) syndicates as suppliers of such temporary workers to the industry.[57] The underside of Japan's economic miracle in the postwar era was the existence of pools of cheap, "disposable" labor from the slums of the big cities, such as the Sanya district in Tokyo and Kamagasaki district in Osaka, working in the vast construction industry with which the *yakuza* have long been aligned. But the electric power companies today also use such day laborers, doing highly dangerous work with little or no job security, and many of these nuclear workers are financially exploited by the *yakuza* and other labor agents as well.

It has been left mainly to independent journalists in Japan to uncover and expose these facts. One of them, photographer Kenji Higuchi, had worked for decades before Fukushima, trying to tell an indifferent Japanese media and public the stories of these exploited, intimidated nuclear power plant workers and the illnesses that afflicted them after they had worked at the plants. Higuchi's efforts to get at the truth are the focus of a short documentary film, *Nuclear Ginza*, broadcasted in 1995 on Britain's Channel 4 television.[58] More recently, another Japanese independent journalist, Tomohiko Suzuki, went undercover as a day laborer at the Fukushima nuclear power plant after the March 2011 accident and found that the *yakuza* were still recruiting day laborers to work there, with top management at the Fukushima plant—like most construction companies in Japan—not necessarily knowing (or caring) how these workers got hired there in the first place.[59]

THE SELLING OF A "MIRACLE MAN"

To be fair, the Japanese people are not the only ones who have been sold a bill of goods about nuclear power and been shielded from seeing its dark side by the media. Americans have too, and the US media role over the years is one that has to be acknowledged in this post-Fukushima age. This is most clearly seen in the US media treatment of Matsutaro Shoriki and the vital role he played in bringing US-sponsored atomic energy to Japan during the Cold War years.

In 1946, six months after the American occupation of Japan had begun, the US progressive magazine the *Nation* correctly noted how "Shoriki's yellow journalism, combined with the scandalously low wages he paid his newsmen and printers, brought him rich profits, and his fervent support of aggression [in the Pacific War] won him a seat in the House of Peers and a position as Cabinet adviser."[60]

Compare that with the glowing coverage a few years later by US mainstream media: Shoriki as "bitterly anti-Communist" ally to the US and Japan's "most successful publisher," known "among Western newsmen as the [William Randolph] 'Hearst of Japan'" (*Time* magazine, 1954);[61] Shoriki as "father of professional baseball in Japan" who nobly sent then–US president Eisenhower an ancient suit of Japanese armor as a show of goodwill (*Washington Post*, 1954);[62] Shoriki as "Japan's Mr. Atom," a man who "has made a brilliant success of nearly everything he has tried" and who, "'if he lives long enough . . . will make Japan one of the leading atomic powers of the world'" (*New York Times Magazine*, 1957);[63] and Shoriki as pioneering TV network president aiming to make Japan the first country in the world to have color television (*Time*, 1959).[64]

Then there was the 1963 *Time* tribute to Shoriki as art connoisseur, head of his *Yomiuri Shimbun* newspaper's own symphony orchestra, architect of the "Yomuiri Land" amusement park in Tokyo named for his newspaper, and all-around Man for the Millennium. The article quoted Bob Considine, a well-known columnist for the Hearst media empire in the US, who sounded almost shocked with awe: "[W]henever editors speak of the great press lords of our age, they often mention Hearst and sometimes [Canadian-British tycoon Lord] Beaverbrook. But they *always* mention Shoriki."[65]

Just a few years earlier, this same Hearst underling and ghostwriter, Considine, had written the foreword to the American publishing industry's own nod to Japan's premier media baron in a 200-page book titled *Shoriki: Miracle Man of Japan—A Biography*. The book was published in 1957 by Exposition Press, back then a leading publisher of so-called "vanity books" that are essentially paid for by the person who is the subject of the biography—which, in this case, would have been Shoriki himself. The book was coauthored by the publishing company's president, Edward Uhlan. A *New York Times* obituary would later list *Shoriki: Miracle Man of Japan* as one of the late Uhlan's most noteworthy accomplishments.[66]

All in all, *Shoriki: Miracle Man of Japan* stands out as a cleverly crafted work of disinformation. It covers up Shoriki's infamous reputation as a police bureaucrat before the Second World War, plays down his wartime role in anti-US propaganda and war-criminal imprisonment by the US after the war, and plays up his subsequent achievements in baseball, news media, and atomic energy in Japan—with a strong line of anticommunist sentiment running throughout. Newspaper, magazine, and book publishing media in the US had now weighed in with Shoriki and his crusade for a pro-America, pro-nuclear Japan, and on the whole found him to be on the right side of the cause.

EPILOGUE: THE ROAD FROM FUKUSHIMA

When Matsutaro Shoriki died in 1969 at age eighty-four while in office as a representative of Japan's parliament (and while still NTV network president), his obituary in the *Washington Post* was surprisingly sparse. Nowhere did the *Post* mention that Shoriki, as Japan's first atomic energy commissioner, had been Washington's point man on nuclear energy development after the war—indeed, he had led Japan to embrace atomic power as a prime energy resource ten years after Hiroshima and Nagasaki. Also missing was Shoriki's tainted past as a former police official and as a prisoner during the US occupation of Japan. And of course, there was no mention at all of the CIA's interest in Shoriki as an asset of the agency.[67]

Just a few years later in 1976, however, the late Shoriki's name surfaced in connection with the "Lockheed scandal," a major political scandal in Japan involving bribe money paid by the US aerospace corporation Lockheed to a former Japanese prime minister. The conservative *Yomiuri* newspaper denied allegations of Shoriki, its ex-president, having been a past "recipient of CIA favors" and spoke of suing for libel the American publications that carried the stories.[68]

If most Japanese people know or remember anything at all about the late press lord today, it is probably the "Matsutaro Shoriki Award" bestowed in Shoriki's name every year with great fanfare to some outstanding Japanese baseball figure by NTV network and *Yomiuri Shimbun* newspaper—whose circulation of thirteen million readers today makes it reputedly the largest daily newspaper in the world.[69] The majority of Americans know even less about Shoriki, including the fact that the prestigious Museum of Fine Arts in Boston today has a respectable chair position named after him.[70] And for their part, few if any Japanese mainstream media companies in their news reporting are linking Shoriki to nuclear energy and the Fukushima accident of March 11, 2011—even though it was his influence and vision of a fully atomic-powered Japan, with firm support by the US, that had led Japan as a nation to that place.

Demands have arisen in the wake of Fukushima for Japanese government nuclear regulators and politicians to be more independent of the nuclear power industry that they are supposed to be keeping an eye on.[71] But looking to the future, there is one more party that equally needs to be separated from Japan's nuclear power establishment (or "nuclear power village," as it's called), and that is the Japanese press. The media in Japan, like the government regulators, have been intimate with the nation's atomic energy club from the very start. Until the day when the Japanese news media are finally weaned off the nation's nuclear power village, the whole truth about nuclear energy—and the corruption and great public dangers surrounding it—will continue to be mostly unseen and unknown in this country. Disengaging the Japanese press from the nuclear powers-that-be will not be easy, but it must be done.

One place to start would be to begin dismantling the Japanese kisha club system. This too will be no easy task, given the deep historical and institutional roots of the system. But if the toothless Japanese lapdog press of today is to regain the public credibility at home and abroad that it lost in the wake of the Fukushima nuclear power plant disaster—and if it is to earn the respect that it would deserve as a true watchdog of the people over Japan's centers of power in the future—then it is the Japanese news media that must now take the first steps in that direction on this long and uncertain road away from Fukushima.

BRIAN COVERT is an independent journalist and author based in Kawanishi, western Japan. He has worked for United Press International news service in Japan, as staff reporter for three of Japan's English-language daily newspapers, and as contributor to Japanese and overseas newspapers and magazines. He is currently a lecturer in the Department of Media, Journalism, and Communications at Doshisha University in Kyoto.

Notes

1. David McNeill, "Fukushima Lays Bare Japanese Media's Ties to Top," *Japan Times*, January 8, 2012, http://www.japantimes.co.jp/text/fl20120108x3.html.
2. Five of the world's top ten daily newspapers with the highest circulations are based in Japan. See Jochen Legewie, *Japan's Media: Inside and Outside Powerbrokers*, Communications & Network Consulting Japan K.K. (Tokyo, March 2010), 3, http://www.cnc-communications.com/fileadmin/user_upload/Publications/2010_03_Japans_Media_Booklet_2nd_Ed_JL.pdf.
3. Simon Partner, *Assembled in Japan: Electrical Goods and the Making of the Japanese Consumer* (Berkeley: University of California Press, 1999), 74.
4. August Kengelbacher, "Great Kanto Earthquake 1923," http://www.japan-guide.com/a/earthquake.
5. Sonia Ryang, "The Tongue That Divided Life and Death: The 1923 Tokyo Earthquake and the Massacre of Koreans," Japan Focus, September 3, 2007, http://www.japanfocus.org/-Sonia-Ryang/2513. For similar accounts, see also Mikiso Hane, *Reflections on the Way to the Gallows: Rebel Women in*

Prewar Japan (Berkeley: University of California Press, 1988), esp. 171, 176, 191–92; and *Asahi Shimbun* newspaper, "Murder of an Anarchist Recalled: Suppression of News in the Wake of the 1923 Tokyo Earthquake," Japan Focus, November 5, 2007, http://www.japanfocus.org/-The_Asahi_Shimbun_Cultural_Research_Center-/2569.

6. Shinichi Sano, *Kyokaiden: Shoriki Matsutaro to Kagemusha-tachi no Isseiki (ge)* [Biography of Matsutaro Shoriki, vol. 2] (Tokyo: Bungeishunju, 2011), 442.

7. Sano, *Kyokaiden: Shoriki Matsutaro to Kagemusha-tachi no Isseiki (jo)* [Biography of Matsutaro Shoriki, vol. 1] (Tokyo: Bungeishunju, 2011), 217.

8. "The Press: Lord High Publisher," *Time*, August 16, 1954, 74.

9. Partner, *Assembled in Japan*, 172.

10. Ben-Ami Shillony, *Politics and Culture in Wartime Japan* (New York: Oxford University Press, 1981), 99.

11. Sano, *Kyokaiden* [vol. 2], 446.

12. Partner, *Assembled in Japan*, 76; see also Shillony, *Politics and Culture*, 105.

13. "1,000 Ask Trial for Publisher," *New York Times*, October 30, 1945; see also Sano, *Kyokaiden* [vol. 1], 438–44.

14. "Yomiuri Chairman Defends Actions in Internal Feud," *Asahi Shimbun*, November 29, 2011, http://ajw.asahi.com/article/behind_news/AJ201111290056b.

15. Shinsho Hanayama, *The Way of Deliverance: Three Years with the Condemned Japanese War Criminals* (New York: Charles Scribner's Sons, 1950), 4; see also Partner, *Assembled in Japan*, 73–74.

16. Hanayama, *The Way of Deliverance*, 5.

17. "Ruth's Ex-Pal Held as Jap [sic] War Criminal," *Washington Post*, December 6, 1945, 15.

18. Ibid.

19. United States Department of State, "Milestones 1945–1952: Korean War and Japan's Recovery," http://history.state.gov/milestones/1945-1952/KoreanWar.

20. David E. Kaplan and Alec Dubro, *Yakuza—The Explosive Account of Japan's Criminal Underworld* (London: Futura Publications, 1987), esp. 69–71, 75–78.

21. Edward Uhlan and Dana L. Thomas, *Shoriki: Miracle Man of Japan—A Biography* (New York: Exposition Press, 1957), 181–82.

22. Partner, *Assembled in Japan*, 83.

23. Ibid., 78–79.

24. Ibid., 84.

25. Ibid., 78.

26. Ibid., 83–84.

27. Sano, *Kyokaiden* [vol. 2], 449; see also Partner, *Assembled in Japan*, 84.

28. Partner, *Assembled in Japan*, 84–86.

29. Edward F. Ryan, untitled article from *Washington Post* archives, September 22, 1954, 2.

30. "A Reactor for Japan," *Washington Post*, September 23, 1954, 18.

31. "Belgium and Japan Seek 1st 'A-for-Peace' Power," *Washington Post*, February 15, 1955, 5.

32. Sano, *Kyokaiden* [vol. 2], 450.

33. Ran Zwigenberg, "'The Coming of a Second Sun': The 1956 Atoms for Peace Exhibit in Hiroshima and Japan's Embrace of Nuclear Power," Japan Focus, February 6, 2012, http://japanfocus.org/-Ran-Zwigenberg/3685.

34. Robert Trumbull, "Japan Welcomes Peace Atom Show," *New York Times*, November 1, 1955, 14.

35. Tetsuo Arima, *Genpatsu—Shoriki—CIA* [Nuclear power—Shoriki—The CIA] (Tokyo: Shinchosha, 2011), 119.

36. Japan Atomic Energy Commission, text of letter from US ambassador in Japan John M. Allison to Matsutaro Shoriki, January 13, 1956, http://www.aec.go.jp/jicst/NC/about/ugoki/geppou/V01/N01/195605010V01N01.HTML.

37. Yuki Tanaka and Peter Kuznick, "Japan, the Atomic Bomb, and the 'Peaceful Uses of Nuclear Power,'" Japan Focus, May 2, 2011, http://www.japanfocus.org/-Yuki-TANAKA/3521. See also Zwigenberg, "'The Coming of a Second Sun,'" Japan Focus.

38. Ran Zwigenberg, "'The Coming of a Second Sun.'" 39. Tetsuo Arima, *Nippon Terebi to CIA—Hakkutsu-sareta "Shoriki Fairu"* [NTV and the CIA—The uncovered "Shoriki files"] (Tokyo: Takarajima-sha, 2011), 30.

40. Arima, *Genpatsu—Shoriki—CIA*, 113; see also "From Hiroshima to Fukushima: The Political Background to the Nuclear Disaster in Japan," World Socialist Web Site, June 23, 2011, http://wsws.org/articles/2011/jun2011/fuku-j23.shtml. Quotation is retranslated into English from the Japanese original.

41. Arima, *Genpatsu—Shoriki—CIA*, 112.

42. National Security Archive, "Cryptonyms and Terms in Declassified CIA Files—Nazi War Crimes and Japanese Imperial Government Records Disclosure Acts," dated June 2007, http://www.archives.gov/iwg/declassified-records/rg-263-cia-records/second-release-lexicon.pdf. Accessed on March 13, 2012.

43. Ibid.

44. Arima, *Nippon Terebi to CIA*, 63; see also Partner, *Assembled in Japan*, 86–87.

45. Arima, *Genpatsu—Shoriki—CIA*, 58.

46. Arima, *Nippon Terebi to CIA*. A copy of the document is partially displayed on the book's front cover.

47. Arima, *Genpatsu—Shoriki—CIA*, 110; see also "Tsunami: Japan's Post-Fukushima Future," *Foreign Policy*, 2011, 198, http://www.foreignpolicy.com/files/tutEkfeUr4fOa3v/06282011_Tsunami.pdf.

48. Partner, *Assembled in Japan*, 228.

49. "Advertising Expenditure of Leading Corporations (FY 2010)," Nikkei Advertising Research Institute, http://nikkei-koken.com/surveys/survey14.html.

50. "Toden Kokoku-hi 90-oku en no Hamon" [Ripple effect of Tokyo Electric's nine billion yen advertising expenses], *Tokyo Shimbun*, May 17, 2011, 26–27. The figure of nine billion yen is for 2009.

51. Translated commentary by Osamu Aoki on Asahi Newstar cable TV program *Nyusu no Me* [Eyes of the news], April 7, 2011, http://www.youtube.com/watch?v=-2Ma4eWhX_U&feature=related.

52. For an overview of how the "kisha club" system works and other related issues, see Tomoomi Mori, "Japan's News Media," in *Censored 2007: The Top 25 Censored Stories*, eds. Peter Phillips and Project Censored (New York: Seven Stories Press, 2006), 367–82.

53. Kanako Takahara, "Tight-lipped Tepco Lays Bare Exclusivity of Press Clubs," *Japan Times*, May 3, 2011, http://www.japantimes.co.jp/text/nn20110503f1.html.

54. Ibid.

55. *Days Japan* magazine, "Genpatsu Jiko Hodo no Kensho Shiryo" [Verified documentation of nuclear accident reporting], February 2012, 41.

56. Kenichi Asano, "BBC ni yoru Jiko Hodo" [Accident reporting by the BBC], *Days Japan*, February 2012, 60–61; see also "Japan Earthquake: Concerns over Nuclear Power Stations," BBC News, March 11, 2011, http://www.bbc.co.uk/news/world-asia-pacific-12719707.

57. "Japan's Desperate Nuclear Gypsies," Al Jazeera English, June 30, 2011, http://www.aljazeera.com/video/asia/2011/06/201163017301s833205.html.

58. *Nuclear Ginza*, Small World Productions, Cardiff, England, 1995, http://www.smallworldtv.co.uk/public/main.cfm?m1=c_75&m2=c_2&m3=c_56&m4=e_0. A Japanese subtitled version of the film can be viewed at http://www.youtube.com/watch?v=CNqoqyQJ5xs.

59. Tomohiko Suzuki, press conference at the Foreign Correspondents' Club of Japan, Tokyo, December 15, 2011, http://www.youtube.com/watch?v=6_lYwNyTyiU. Suzuki goes into more detail in his book *Yakuza to Genpatsu* [The yakuza and nuclear power] (Tokyo: Bungeishunju, 2011).

60. Andrew Roth, "Japan's Press Revolution," *Nation*, March 16, 1946, 315.

61. "The Press: Lord High Publisher," *Time*, 1954, 76.

62. Herb Heft, "Baseball Men Cite Good-Will Created on Trip by Giants," *Washington Post*, February 7, 1954:C2.

63. Foster Hailey, "Japan's Mr. Atom," *New York Times Magazine*, November 17, 1957, SM50.

64. "Show Business: Television Abroad—Come-On in Color," *Time*, August 3, 1959, 57.

65. "The Press: Publishers—Bigger & Better than Anyone," *Time*, May 24, 1963, 57–58. Emphasis in the original.

66. Edwin McDowell, "Obituaries: Edward Uhlan, 76, Founder and Leader Of Vanity Publisher," *New York Times*, October 26, 1988, http://www.nytimes.com/1988/10/26/obituaries/edward-uhlan-76-founder-and-leader-of-vanity-publisher.html.

67. "Matsutaro Shoriki, 84, Dies; Publisher of Japanese Daily," *Washington Post*, October 9, 1969, M10.

68. Richard Halloran, "Premier Miki Vows Lockheed Inquiry," *New York Times*, April 4, 1976, 2.

69. Legewie, *Japan's Media: Inside and Outside Powerbrokers*, 3.

70. ArtDaily.org, "Museum of Fine Arts, Boston, Announces New Chair of Art of Asia, Oceania, and Africa," September 20, 2008, http://www.artdaily.com/index.asp?int_new=26246&int_sec=2.

71. Norimitsu Onishi and Ken Belson, "Culture of Complicity Tied to Stricken Nuclear Plant," *New York Times*, April 26, 2011, http://www.nytimes.com/2011/04/27/world/asia/27collusion.html?pagewanted=all.

CHAPTER 15

An Occupation of Truth
Indian–Administered Kashmir

by Tara Dorabji

A few days before I left for India, American journalist David Barsamian was deported from New Delhi for his coverage of Kashmir. Barsamian reports for AlterNet, one of the few national free speech outlets in the United States. News reports quoted officials saying that his deportation resulted from his prior reporting on Kashmir. In 2009–10, he traveled to India on a tourist visa and later produced some reports from the trip.[1] If reporting the truth in Kashmir can get one deported, I was in danger.

On my first day in Srinagar, the local head of surveillance let me know he was fully aware of my arrival. It was a discreet enough interaction, but it served its purpose: I was being watched. Was I a threat? I wielded a pen and paper to record the stories of Kashmiris.

The silence surrounding India's occupation blankets the Kashmir Valley, like the morning smog obscures the Himalayan Mountains. Despite the Indian government's own estimate of only 500 to 700 armed militants in the area, Kashmir remains the most densely militarized land on earth. There are approximately 700,000 Indian military and paramilitary in Kashmir, policing a population of ten million.[2]

But there is a new face to the hundred-year-old struggle for Kashmiri sovereignty and independence. A strong current of popular, nonviolent uprising for freedom has been growing. It is evident in citizens like Sahil Tariq, age twelve, who lit up when I asked what his hope for Kashmir was. "I have a hope that there is . . . freedom in Kashmir." Sahil's father disappeared in 2002. For nine years he and his mother have searched for his father. Every day after school Sahil comes home to help his mother work—embroidering cloth to earn a few rupees.[3]

The recent, nonviolent uprising distinguishes itself from the armed rebellion of the early 1990s, yet the demand is the same: liberation from occupation—the independence of Kashmir.

Arguably, the Kashmiri independence movement goes back to 1846 when Kashmir came under the oppressive rule of the Dogra. Under the British partitioning of India in 1947, the matter of Kashmir was unresolved; it was not clear if Kashmir would go to India or Pakistan. In 1947, the first Indo-Pakistani War took place, with India taking Kashmir. In 1948, India brought the case of Kashmir to the United Nations, and Kashmir was officially recognized as a disputed territory. From the time that India claimed Kashmir until the early 1950s, Kashmiris experienced a high degree of self-rule, self-determination, and indigenous leadership.[4] Kashmir led the world in revolutionary land reform, implementing a broad redistribution of resources that created a population relatively equal in wealth. Under land-to-the-tiller legislation, 188,775 acres of land were transferred to 153,399 peasants. No individual could legally keep over twenty acres of land. And to keep land, the landowner had to get out there and work the land.[5] Today, after decades of occupation, many Kashmiris live in poverty: approximately 65 percent of the population does not have access to safe drinking water, and half the population lives without access to toilets.[6] Did the Indian ruling elite fear that an independent Kashmir would serve as a model for India? If left to self-rule, could Kashmir have led the way for a broad redistribution of resources in the subcontinent?

There are many interpretations of how and why the trust and relationship between Delhi and Srinagar eroded. The result was a deliberate stripping of Kashmiri independence. When the Indian constitution came into effect in 1950, Kashmiri sovereignty was protected by Article 370. Kashmir was autonomous, and Indian jurisdiction was limited to defense, foreign affairs, and communications. In 1952, Sheikh Abdullah, the leader of Kashmir, signed the Delhi Agreement, giving Kashmir autonomy. This was overturned in 1954, when Order 1954 was added to the Indian constitution, giving India jurisdiction over Kashmir.[7] While most of the rights under Article 370 have diminished, land protection in the valley is still observed. To this day, only Kashmiris can own land in the region. It is this provision that has prevented a complete repopulation of the area. But with the erosion of Kashmir's autonomy has come military repression and, arguably, attempted genocide.

Buried Evidence, the groundbreaking 2009 report released by International People's Tribunal on Human Rights and Justice in Indian-Administered Kashmir (IPTK), documented thousands of mass graves in Kashmir. The report captured the haunting words of Atta Mohammed, a Kashmiri gravedigger from Bimyar: "My nights are tormented and I cannot sleep; the bodies and graves appear and reappear in my dreams . . . the sound of the earth as I covered the graves . . . bodies and faces that were mutilated . . . mothers who would never find their sons. My memory is an obligation." From 2002 to 2006, Atta Mohammed buried 203 unidentified bodies.[8]

The torture and death in the valley of Kashmir can be buried no longer. Between 1989 and 2011, there were 8,000 documented disappearances and 70,000 deaths of Kashmiris resulting from the Indian occupation.[9] The conflict has left as many as 100,000 children orphaned.[10] According to a survey by Médecins Sans Frontières, 99 percent of Kashmiris surveyed reported experiencing crackdowns. Eighty-six percent experienced roundups or raids in villages. Forty-four percent reported psychological and physical mistreatment.[11] Yet, there is a global silence. Kashmir has many similarities with other global independence struggles that garner significant international support. In comparison, the Israeli occupation of Palestine caused 10,271 deaths from 1987 to January 2012. In Ireland, there were 3,710 deaths from 1969 to 2010. In Tibet, 1.2 million people died from 1949 to 1979.[12]

It is the dead who are breaking the silence that surrounds Kashmir. In July 2011, the State Human Rights Commission (SHRC) of Jammu and Kashmir released a report documenting 2,730 unidentified bodies in thirty-eight graveyards; 574 of the exhumed bodies were then identified.[13] The state report verified the findings of IPTK's report *Buried Evidence*. Khurram Parvez, liaison for IPTK and program coordinator for the Jammu and Kashmir Coalition of Civil Society, explained in an interview how the findings were initially swept under the rug: "The government said that these unmarked graves are all of foreign militants and people need not worry about it." There have been limited DNA tests. Parvez cited that DNA tests of fifty-three bodies identified that forty-nine were Kashmiri civilians, one was a Kashmiri combatant, and three were unidentified.[14]

When I spoke with Tahira Begum, whose husband disappeared in 2002, she said that she's known about the mass graves for over five years. Begum explained, "I went to the mass graves and saw the bones, the bones that add up to the absence of 10,000 men. I hug these bones. I hug them for their life."[15] For nine years, she has been searching for her husband. Begum said that each day she dies ten times, not knowing if her husband is dead or alive. Without her husband it is a struggle to make ends meet. Two of her sons live with her and help her to embroider after school. Her third son was placed in an orphanage.

The families of the disappeared continue their monthly protests and demand that the government take action to identify the bodies, as more and more bodies are uncovered. Begum joins with other families to protest every month, carrying the faces of the disappeared, pushing the state to run DNA tests on the thousands of unidentified bodies. "We are protesting every month in the square. I am not afraid. I must protest not just for my husband, or for my sons, but for all the families and the men who are disappeared."[16] In Kashmir, there is a special term for women whose husbands disappear: "half widows." By conservative estimates, there are 1,500 half widows in Kashmir. Half widows are not eligible for pensions or other government relief. They often suffer severe hardships as Begum does.[17]

One might wonder why the bodies of so many Kashmiris disappear. According to IPTK's Parvez, "It is the right of the family to have the body. The government does not want to give these bodies to the families because there is something to hide. They are hiding the marks of torture."[18] Torture is rampant. There are over 60,000 cases of documented torture in the valley of Kashmir. The torture includes the most heinous acts of water boarding, injecting petrol into anuses, rapes, psychological torture, and mutilation.[19] Internal correspondence released by WikiLeaks showed that the International Committee of the Red Cross (ICRC) sent evidence of torture in 2005 to

TENTATIVE INDO-PAK DIPLOMATIC THAW
INDIA FINALLY CRACKS A SMILE:

KASHMIR

diplomats in the United States. Between 2002 and 2004, The ICRC met with 1,491 detainees and torture was reported in 852 cases. The torture ranged from electric shock, suspension, sexual abuse, and water torture. Torture victims were rarely militants.[20]

"The most underreported phenomenon in Jammu and Kashmir is torture. If you go to any village hundreds of people in every village have been tortured, not just men, but women, children and old people as well," explained Parvez.[21] Sexual assaults are perhaps the most taboo to report. A Médecins Sans Frontières report found that about two-thirds of people surveyed had heard of a rape case, and one in seven Kashmiris reported actually witnessing rape.[22] In 1991, in the village of Poshpora, Kupwara, more than forty women were allegedly raped by the Indian army.[23]

Parvez was involved in documenting the torture of over 1,500 people who became impotent because their genitals were electrocuted. In our interview, he revealed that hundreds of boys have been raped by soldiers. In one case the abuse by the army was caught on video, yet still there were no convictions. Describing yet another case of torture, he said, "I have documented very horrible cases, but this is the most horrible." The army kept a sixty-year-old man in solitary confinement for one month. During that time, he wasn't given anything to eat but his own flesh. Soldiers cut the flesh from his body and served it to him. This was all he was given to eat for a month. Recounting the story, Parvez said, "This was something that shook me. We have hundreds of Guantánamo Bays here. Why is nobody talking about it?"[24]

LAWS, UPRISING, AND VIOLENCE

Violence permeates the everyday reality of life in Kashmir. The militarized insurgency of the 1990s has given way to popular, nonviolent uprisings. This unarmed people's movement is met by brutal force. In 2010, between June 11 and September 22, Indian paramilitary and military killed 109 Kashmiri—youth, women, and men alike. During these summer rebellions, massive popular protests flooded from the villages to the cities. The valley was on lockdown with seventy-three days of imposed curfews and seventy-five days of strikes.[25]

There are special laws that allow for the killings and torture of Kashmiri civilians to continue. The Public Safety Act (PSA) of 1978 allows for incarceration of civilians for up to two years on grounds of unconfirmed suspicion. In March 2011, Amnesty International reported that between 8,000 and 20,000 people have been held under the PSA over the past twenty years.[26]

The Armed Forces (Special Powers) Act allows security forces to preemptively shoot people to prevent future terrorist attempts.[27] In addition, it allows soldiers to detain residents without cause, search buildings without warrants, and destroy houses.[28]

It is perhaps this environment—where the army has the right to detain, shoot, and kill people at will—that spawned the large civil uprisings. For three consecutive summers in the valley, from 2008 to 2010, there were massive protests and general strikes that shut the city down for months. The strikes were met with enforced curfews. Grenades of tear gas exploded. New weapons were introduced like the "pressure pump" gun, which fires bullets that enter the body and can destroy organs, but leave hardly any external marks.[29] It was not only protesters who were killed. On June 12, 2010, Muhammad Rafiq Bangroo was severely beaten by police forces while watching a protest by his house. He died days later from the wounds. Yasmeen Jan was shot and killed when a bullet landed in her chest. She was standing near a window in her house. At times police fired into the funeral processions of the just dead, killing more. On August 2, 2010, nine-year-old Sameer Ahmad Rah was beaten to death by police forces. He was playing near a protest.[30] The names of the innocent dead go on and on.

During the summer of 2010, the city was shuttered. The local papers were not delivered. Some mornings, people could slip out at 5:00 a.m. to a local shop and get some food before the 6:00 a.m. curfew was enforced.[31] For days on end, people were trapped in their homes.

Like many of the modern-day people's movements, social media allowed people to communicate across empty streets. The local news stopped reporting the death toll, so citizens found information on the Internet. Kashmiris logged into Facebook to see ashes and death, and to read the news of who was shot dead and what was burned. Local reporters tallied the dead bodies on excel documents and e-mailed them around. Everyone waited. It took until the body count reached forty in the summer of 2010 before the BBC covered it.[32]

ARTISTS BANNED IN KASHMIR

Dark humor becomes a cathartic release for many living under occupation. It follows as no surprise that the cartoonist and artist Malik Sajad was targeted for his work. In 2008, he was invited to display his installation *Terrorism of Peace* at the India Habitat Center. During this time, there was a bombing in Delhi. Malik Sajad was taken by the police and interrogated. As the police began to bring evidence against him, they eventually referenced his installation to justify their actions because his art was "anti-India."[33]

In Kashmir, poetry and music are rooted in resistance. In traditional Kashmiri folk music, *ladi shah,* singers go from village to village singing songs of resistance. Today, music continues to be a tool to organize, with a new generation embracing hip-hop. Artist MC Kash recorded "I Protest," which went viral during the 2010 massive summer uprising. The song's lyrics speak to the new generation of protesters with words such as: "No more injustice / We won't go down / When we bleed / Alive in the struggle / Even the graves will speak!"[34] In an interview with the Associated Press, MC Kash said that watching a film on the occupation of Palestine inspired his work—he realized that the same thing was happening in Kashmir and that he had a responsibility to speak about it. When MC Kash became a hit, the police raided the recording studio where he recorded the song, and the staff was questioned. The studio closed its doors on MC Kash. He cannot record there anymore. When asked if he feared retaliation, MC Kash said, "[R]evolutionaries don't fear persecution or execution. If they throw me in the prison . . . I'll write on the walls." Yet the fear of retaliation is so great that another young hip-hop artist, Renegade, removed his songs from the Internet for fear that his family would be targeted.[35] Even so, the beats of resistance have found a new home on the Internet.

THE "K WORD"

Whatever you do, just don't mention the "K word." When British Prime Minister David Cameron visited India in July 2010, he was asked not to use the "K word." A few months later, US President Barack Obama went to Delhi and was warned to steer clear of Kashmir.[36] Just don't mention it. Mum is the word.

Some don't heed the warnings. When they speak truth about Kashmir, retaliation is the name of the game. Writing on Kashmir can get you banned from the world's largest democracy. Indian-born scholar and anthropologist Dr. Angana Chatterji resides in San Francisco, California, and is the cofounder of the IPTK. She is also the lead author of Buried Evidence. When she visits Kashmir, she is under constant surveillance: an armored jeep tails her everywhere she goes, and she has been detained. Even her mother, who lives in Delhi, has been interrogated by authorities.

In November 2010, Chatterji and her husband, academic Richard Shapiro, were en route to India. Shapiro was refused entry to India. Chatterji continued to Kashmir while her husband was forced to go back to the United States. There was no formal reason for Shapiro to be banned from India, though it seemed to be a punishment for Chatterji's work with the Tribunal on Human Rights.[37]

POLITICS OF MAPPING

The borders of Kashmir have been under dispute since 1947. For over fifty years, students in India have grown up seeing a false map of Kashmir, one that does not match the rest of the world. On the world map, Kashmir is carved up into Indian-occupied Kashmir and Pakistan-occupied Kashmir. There is also Aksai Chin and Shaksam Valley, under Chinese control.[38] In fact, when you look at Indian maps you find a disclaimer, such as this one on Maps of India's website: "All efforts have been made to make this image accurate. However Compare Infobase Limited and its directors do not own any responsibility for the correctness or authenticity of the same."[39] Since map distortion is an old and new art, you find this disclaimer across all the company's maps. Many of us in the United States are familiar with the distorted maps that show Greenland to be larger than all of South America. This map, of course, also has America in the center. This was the map I grew up with.

In India, printing a different (arguably more accurate) map of Kashmir can get you banned. In 2010, India censored the *Economist* after it released an issue with a map showing the disputed boundaries of Kashmir. Domestic maps of India show false borders, claiming land currently administered by both Pakistan and China as India. Subsequently, thirty-one issues of the weekly British magazine were banned. Indian authorities stamped "illegal" across the magazine. What was illegal about this map? Perhaps the accuracy of the Pakistan- and China-controlled portions of Jammu and Kashmir portrayed on the map. The map shows India controlling most of Kashmir with approximately 87,823 square miles. The Pakistan-controlled portion is depicted showing about 53,342 square miles, with the Chinese-controlled area covering 23,336 square miles.[40]

PATH TO FREEDOM

Looking at the high alpine lakes and valley surrounded by mountains, one cannot help but think of Switzerland. With a population of 7.6

million people, Switzerland's population is nearly half the size of Kashmir's. Despite its small size, Switzerland spends about 1 percent of its gross domestic product (GDP) on military. If Switzerland can be independent, why not Kashmir?

Could the future independence of Kashmir be a headwaters in creating a new type of democracy? In *A Letter to Fellow Kashmiris*, Mohamad Junaid delved into the possibility of freedom: "What it means is that the future free and independent Kashmir, to continue to remain free and independent, and to continuously live the moment of freedom, should not replicate any socio-economic blueprints (especially the ones handed out by institutions of the hegemonic global economic order), nor should it accept the kind of modular democracy a tragicomic version of which Indian government makes us Kashmiris suffer every few years."[41]

If the nonviolent, popular movement of Kashmir is allowed self-determination, perhaps a new brand of democracy will be born: a democracy that is not founded on control through military domination—one that does not wave the flag of democracy to cover up genocide.

TARA DORABJI has been a producer and host on KPFA radio since 2006 with a focus on South Asia, nuclear weapons, and environmental justice. She hosts and produces "Kashmir Speaks," a monthly segment on Kashmir, which is archived at dorabji.com. She is the author of poems, short stories, and numerous articles. Tara is currently working on her first novel.

Notes

1. Arundhati Roy, "The Dead Begin to Speak Up in India," *Guardian*, September 30, 2011, http://www.guardian.co.uk/commentisfree/libertycentral/2011/sep/30/kashmir-india-unmarked-graves.
2. Parvaiz Bukhari, "Summer of Unrest Challenging India," in *Until My Freedom Has Come: the New Intifada in Kashmir*, ed. Sanjay Kak (London: Penguin Books, 2011), 4–5.
3. Sahil Tariq, interview by Tara Dorabji, *The Morning Mix*, KPFA, December 26, 2011, http://www.kpfa.org/archive/id/76361.
4. Bukhari, "Summer of Unrest," 5.
5. Tariq Ali, "The Story of Kashmir," in *Kashmir: the Case For Freedom* (London: Verso 2011), 35.
6. Bureau Report, "34% People Have Access to Safe Drinking Water in Kashmir: Census Survey," Agence India Press, March 28, 2012, http://www.agenceindiapress.com/2012/03/34-people-have-access-to-safe-drinking-water-in-kashmir-census-survey.
7. "Chronology 1947–2010," in *Kashmir: the Case For Freedom* (see note 5), vii–ix.
8. Angana P. Chatterji et al., *Buried Evidence: Unknown, Unmarked, and Mass Graves in Indian-Administered Kashmir, A Preliminary Report* (Srinagar: International People's Tribunal on Human Rights and Justice in Indian-administered Kashmir, 2009), 18, http://www.kashmirprocess.org/reports/graves/toc.html.

9. Angana Chatterji, "The Militarized Zone," in *Kashmir: the Case For Freedom* (see note 5), 121.
10. Save the Children, *Orphaned in Kashmir*, February 2012.
11. Kaz de Jong et al., *Kashmir: Violence and Health* (Amsterdam: Médecins Sans Frontières, 2006), 2, http://www.artsenzondergrenzen.nl/pdf/KASHMIRFINALVERSION221106.pdf.
12. Chatterji, "The Militarized Zone," 121.
13. Investigation team of J&K SHRC, *Enquiry Report of Unmarked Graves in north Kashmir*, report (Srinagar: Office of the Sr. Superintendent of Police and J&K SHRC, 2011), 13, http://www.kashmirlife.net/index.php?option=com_content&view=article&id=1894:full-text-of-the-enquiry-report-of-the-investigation-team-of-jak-shrc-on-unmarked-graves-in-north-kashmir&catid=71:shrc-report&Itemid=213.
14. Khurram Parvez, interview by Tara Dorabji, *Morning Mix*, KPFA, December 26, 2011, http://www.kpfa.org/archive/id/76361.
15. Tahira Begum, interview by Tara Dorabji, Srinagar, October 2011.
16. Ibid.
17. Association of the Parents of Disappeared Persons, *Half Widow, Half Wife?: Responding to Gendered Violence in Kashmir*, (Jammu and Kashmir Coalition of Civil Society, 2011), 1, http://www.hks.harvard.edu/cchrp/sbhrap/projects/kashmir/Half_Widow_Half_Wife.pdf.
18. Parvez interview, December 26, 2011.
19. Chatterji, "The Militarized Zone," 109.
20. Jason Burke, "WikiLeaks Cables: India Accused of Systematic Use of Torture in Kashmir," *Guardian*, December 16, 2010, http://www.guardian.co.uk/world/2010/dec/16/wikileaks-cables-indian-torture-kashmir.
21. Khurram Parvez, interview by Tara Dorabji, Srinagar, October 2011.
22. Kaz de Jong et al., *Kashmir: Violence and Health*, 3.
23. APDP, *Half Widow, Half Wife?*, 3.
24. Parvez interview, October 2011.
25. Chatterji, "The Militarized Zone," 100.
26. Amnesty International, *A "Lawless Law": Detentions under the Jammu and Kashmir Public Safety Act*, (London: Amnesty International Limited, 2011), 4.
27. Gowhar Fazili, "Kashmiri Marginalities: Construction, Nature and Response," in *Until My Freedom Has Come* (see note 2), 218.
28. Bukhari, "Summer of Unrest," 4.
29. Sanjay Kak, "What Are Kashmir's Stone-Pelters Saying to Us?," in *Until My Freedom Has Come* (see note 2), 35.
30. Chatterji, "The Militarized Zone," 101–02.
31. Suvir Kaul, "Diary of a Summer," in *Until My Freedom Has Come* (see note 2), 22.
32. Aaliya Anjun and Saiba Varma, "Curfewed in Kashmir: Voices from the Valley," *Economic and Political Weekly* 45, no. 35 (2010), http://xa.yimg.com/kq/groups/2076232/1732282761/name/EPW+article.pdf.
33. Malik Sajad, "Terrorism of Peace," Kashmir Solidarity Network, August 26, 2010, http://kashmirsolidarity.wordpress.com/2010/08/26/malik-sajad.
34. MC Kash, "I Protest (Remembrance)," http://www.reverbnation.com/artist/artist_songs/828468.
35. Aijaz Hussain, "Kashmir Rapper Uses Rhymes to Protest Indian Rule," *Washington Times*, November 26, 2010.
36. Chatterji, "The Militarized Zone," 122.
37. Roy, "The Dead Begin to Speak Up."
38. Nitasha Kaul, "Kashmir: A Place of Blood and Memory," *openDemocracy*, August 31, 2010, http://www.opendemocracy.net/nitasha-kaul/kashmir-from-contact-zone-to-conflict-zone.
39. "Physical Map of India," MapsofIndia.com, http://www.mapsofindia.com/maps/india/physical-map.html.
40. Umar Ahmad, "The Great Indian Fiction on Kashmir," *Daily Rising Kashmir*, October 28, 2010.
41. Mohamad Junaid, "A Letter to Fellow Kashmiris," in *Until My Freedom Has Come* (see note 2), 281.

Acknowledgments

by Mickey Huff and Dr. Andy Lee Roth

We would like to thank everyone that has contributed to Project Censored over the past thirty-six years.

For those who contributed directly to this year's volume, we offer thanks and pay our respects:

To the courageous independent journalists who continue to file real news, without which the Project would be impossible. Your work inspires us.

To the faculty evaluators and student researchers at our college and university affiliates around the world, as the eyes and ears of Project Censored, you help us keep up with the cutting edge of independent journalism.

To the authors in Censored 2013, your research and writing connects the dots among the Top 25 stories, and your contributions are truly dispatches from the media revolution.

To our national and international judges, your dedication and expertise assures that our Top 25 list includes only the best, most significant independent news stories each year.

To our stalwart publishers at Seven Stories Press in New York, including the intrepid Dan Simon at the helm; Veronica Liu, our eagle-eyed editor; Jon Gilbert for his impeccable design layout; Crystal Yakacki for publicizing our print efforts; and Stewart Cauley for the cover design. You, and the entire Seven Stories crew—including Liz DeLong, Phoebe Hwang, Ruth Weiner, Anne Rumberger, Gabe Espinal, and Silvia Stramenga, as well as interns Sophia Archibald, Sophia Bamert, Eleanor Blair, Jesse Heuer, Jillian Kaplan, and Indre Telksnyte—have our deepest respect and appreciation for making the commitment to publish the Project's research, and for doing so in record time each year.

To Dr. Carl Jensen, founder of Project Censored in 1976, whose original vision and defiance of the status quo continue to inspire this Project.

To Dr. Peter Phillips, who has dedicated so much of his life to extending Project Censored's influence through his teaching, writing, and speaking. Peter is an exemplar of the educator as public intellec-

419

tual, engaging people in discussions about media, democracy, and human liberation wherever he goes.

To the Board of Directors at the Media Freedom Foundation, the nonprofit parent of Project Censored, who provide organizational structure, and invaluable counsel. You keep us on course in pursuing Project Censored's mission.

To our friends and supporters at Pacifica and KPFA 94.1 FM, Free Speech Radio in Berkeley CA, which hosts *The Project Censored Show* on *The Morning Mix* each week. Arlene Engelhardt, Tracy Rosenberg, Andrew Phillips, Anthony Fest, Steve Zeltzer, Dennis Bernstein, Miguel Molina, Bonnie Faulkner, and Kirsten Thomas have all contributed to making *The Project Censored Show* a strong presence on the air.

To Adam Armstrong, who helps Project Censored reach its global Internet audience.

To the inimitable Khalil Bendib, whose cartoons again add luster and edge to our annual volume.

To Abby Martin of Media Roots, colleague and ally in media freedom.

To Dr. Michel Chossudovsky and the Centre for Research on Globalization, who maintain the website GlobalResearch.ca.

To Allan Rees and No Lies Radio, who broadcast our events and lectures online.

To Dr. Paul Rea, for additional proofreading, editing, and manuscript suggestions.

To the Jodi Solomon Speaker's Bureau in Boston, for their assistance in arranging our many national speaking engagements; proceeds from these appearances provide crucial financial support for Project Censored.

To colleagues and staff at Diablo Valley College for their support and informed conversation, including Hedy Wong, Greg Tilles, Dr. Matthew Powell, Melissa Jacobson, Dr. Manual Gonzales, Nolan Higdon, Dr. Jacob Van Vleet, Adam Bessie, David Vela, Ellen Kruse, Obed Vazquez, Dr. Lyn Krause, Dr. Steve Johnson, Dr. Jeremy Cloward, Dr. Amer Araim, and Dr. Mark Akiyama.

To T. M. Skruggs and Elizabeth Shariff for their generous support.

To Dorothy Andersen, and the late Alfred F. Andersen, of the Fair Share of the Common Heritage, for helping us to reestablish the commons as a crucial element of public life.

On a personal note, to Meg, Liz, and our families and close friends, who have supported and encouraged us.

And to you, our readers, supporters, and global citizen-agitators: you share our goal of creating a truly free press, one that champions the voice of the People, in service of democratic self-government.

MEDIA FREEDOM FOUNDATION/PROJECT CENSORED BOARD OF DIRECTORS

AFFILIATED FACULTY AND STUDENTS CONTRIBUTING TO THE TOP 25 CENSORED STORIES IN CENSORED 2013

College of Marin
Students: Eric Humphrey, Annie Keating
Faculty Evaluator: Susan Rahman

DePauw University
Students: Mayra Garces, Natalie Hill
Faculty Evaluators: Kevin Howley, Glen David Kuecker

Florida Atlantic University
Students: Alyssa Barbieri, Alysha Klein, Lamise Mansur, Todd Roller
Faculty Evaluators: James F. Tracy

San Francisco State University
Students: Peter Duke, Shahin Karimbeik, Elizabeth Marinovich, Aaron Peacock, Robert Usher
Faculty Evaluator: Kenn Burrows

Santa Rosa Junior College
Students: Temple Chemotti, Josh Fowler, Eileen Harlin, Annika Jaeger, Liliana Valdez-Madera
Faculty Evaluator: Susan Rahman

Sonoma State University
Students: Beatriz Alcazar, Robert Block, Lyndsey Casey, Josh Crockett, Cary Escovedo, Taylor Falbisaner, Leta Frolli, Samantha George, Ellis Huber, Sean Lawrence, Rachel Miller-Hee, Joshua Nervis, Andrea Perez, Lisa Pollack, Harmen Sidhu, Dane Steffy, Nicole Trupiano, Kaitlyn Vargas, Morgan Womack, Taylor Wright
Faculty Evaluators: Gregg Adams, Noel Byrne, Heather Flynn, Diana Grant, Sheila Katz, Patrick Jackson, David McCuan, Peter Phillips, Robert Switky, Glenn Wallace, Crystal White

Universidad Complutense de Madrid
Student: Paloma Tur
Faculty Evaluators: Miguel Álvarez-Peralta, Luis Luján, Alfredo V. Moran, Bryan Polkey

Across the nation and around the world, a number of college and university classes that focus on media literacy incorporate Project Censored's work as a central part of their curricula. For a full sense of how many faculty and students contribute annually to the Project, see the Validated Independent News entries at Media Freedom International website (mediafreedominternational.org/category/validated-independent-news).

The following list represents faculty who were able to submit course rosters of participating classes in time for publication:

College of Marin (Susan Rahman, faculty): Lia Barth, Noel Bartholomew, Emily Bransford, Justin Burkhalter, Adam Gans, Janina Garcia, Corey Gill, Julia Hamaker, Rebecca Haverlah, Eric Humphrey, John Hurley, Theodore Johnson Slaveev, Emily Josef, Anne Keating, Delia Keller, Chanelle Manning, Lakesha McNaulty, Sherry Peden, Sydney Silver, Jordan Thomas

DePauw University (Dr. Kevin Howley, faculty): Nana Aduba-Amoah, Michael Appelgate, Thomas Balcom, Ben Brandstatter, Mallory Buth, Kendall Cochran, Kelsey Floyd, Chris Forbringer, Kate Hendrickson, Allison Kirby, Kelly Kohlndorfer, Kylee Lehrman, Mike Letten, Michael Rizzo, Sam Spahn, Tammy Taylor, Taylor Wagner, Stacey Way, Kacy Wendling, Elaine Wiley

Diablo Valley College (Mickey Huff, faculty): Clifton Damiens, Aaron Hudson, Michael Kolbe, Andy Liebig, Mike Lucacher, Kira McDonough, Andrew O'Connor-Watts, Juli Tambellini, and the fall 2011 and spring 2012 Money, Power, and Politics classes as well as the Critical Reasoning in History classes

Florida Atlantic University (Dr. James F. Tracy, faculty): Vanessa F. Ardila, Alyssa A. Barbieri, Amanda M. Borrero, Valerie M. Cacciaguida, Carey A. Campbell, Eva M. Cantillo, Paul D. Cohen, Mercedes B. Coppin, Stephen F. Cutolo, Philicia I. Douglas, Lauren A. Galiszewski, Monica G. Hernandez, Dana L. Hornor, Alysha A. Klein, Jasmine Lang, Brittany A. Lockley, Lamise Z. Mansur, Joanne C. Marszal, Sarah M. Moeller, Kirk J. Moncol, Camila S. Rocha Lima, Todd A. Roller, Monica Ruiz, Rachel A. Sieker

Indian River State College (Dr. Elliot D. Cohen, faculty): Rhett Lyman, Maria Ferreira, John Glanville, Christopher Reall, Breana Aspinwall, Gregory McNesky, Marisa Beasley, De'Raven R. Clemon, Joanna Julien, Kayleigh Nanny, William Mitchem, Haleigh Williams, Sergio Tierrablanca, Devin Moore, Grady Sams, Landy Wade, Wyatt Richard, Humira Belim, Vasthie St. Juste, Claudia G. Alvarez, Jeffrey Reiman, Amber Bodishbaugh, Joshua Hackett, Lyndsey Peters, T. J. Merone, Sarah Shonty, Brandon S. Daby, Julie Meikle, Ashley Smith, Allen (Alex) Wynne, Jason Hunt, Valerie Louis, Claudia G. Alvarez, Ashley Raynak

San Francisco State University (Kenn Burrows, faculty): Peter Duke, Shahin Karimbeik, Elizabeth Marinovich, Aaron Peacock, Robert Usher, Jani Sevilla, Tim Wilkins, Devery Sheffer, Val Eydelman, Andy Babkes, Nick Mahl, Ivan Sidorenko, Jeremy Kuhn, Katelyn Michelson, Laura Kelly, Jennifer Fong, Miri Sunkel

Santa Rosa Junior College (Susan Rahman, faculty): Albert Armanini, Ashley Brundidge, Austin Cahill, Elizabeth Campos, Tayler Chesnut, Jeffrey Covell, Aislinn Duguid, Mayra Echeverria, James Foster, Katie Given, Omar Gomez, David Gonzalez, Mariana Guevara, Erika Hernandez, Shelley Hickman, Annika Jaeger, Brandi Johnson, Nicholas Joyner, Laura Leone, Adam Magnusson, Elizabeth Maina, Adriana Martinez, Mauricio Martinez, Emily McCarthy, Taylor Millard, Lorena Miranda Rivas, Raechel Morgan, Mallory Nelson, Kevin Otterstetter, Rosa Pedone, Sivan Peleg, Norma Requenes, Corrina Rivera, Eric Roa, Cassandra Sanchez, Brittany Stewart, Liliana Valdez-Madera, Landon Vandergriend, Bonika Vega, Joseph Wiecks, Jimmy Wood, Carolina Avila, Isabel Avina, Emily Barkin, Cesar Bogarin, Michael Bordessa, Edward Buenrostro, Isabel Butler, Rebecca Calleja, Angel Castillo, Ashleigh Christie, Kyle Colby, Chelsea Cone, Bianka Dombroff, Lexi Eidsen, Victor Farfan, Joshua Fowler, Dukgi Goh, Maria Gutierrez, Eileen Harlin, Berenice Hernandez, Sandro Jean-Baptiste, Brycson King, Rahel Legesse, Kaytlyn Lohse, Natalie Mar, Angie McClure, Trevor McLaughlin, Danielle McLean, Samuel Minnifield, Brandan Moroni, Jessica Muthoni, Peter Njoroge, Elizabeth Nunes, Juan Perez, Tyler Post, Natalee Pughe, Alaina Ross, Kena Ruiz, Ernesto Sanchez, Karen Sanchez Munoz, Alborz Shakouri Partovi, Trey Smith, Megan Wandel, Randy Zaldana, Nanzieli Altamirano, Laura Arellano, Maranda Asbell, Torey Berncich, Ria Brigmann, Mitchell Cappa, Temple Chemotti, Soran Cover, Sara Ellis, Michael Flores, Andrea Garfia, Melanie Gutierrez, Jordan Hernandez, Melissa Hernandez, Ashley Herron, Imran Karim, Michaela Kolodin, Ryan Kunzman, Shelby Lawson, Zachary Lemas, Macayla Martin, Taylor McKinnie, Taylor Mitchell, Alberto Montes, Ashton Morales, Kevin Nahodyl, Anthony O'Campo Becker, Jon Odgers, Adam Panyasith, Jesse Parish, Adriana Pena Caldera, Jordan Ranft, Jessica Rodrigues, Jose Soriano, Zackary Templeton, Michael Uyeno, Mackenzie Vanderbur, Steven Vargas, Sharon Whealy

Sonoma State University (Peter Phillips, faculty): Beatriz Alcazar, Joshua C. Banuelos, Devin A. Bowen, Matthew Steven Burns, Lyndsey Mae Casey, Taylor A. Colacion, Olivia D. Comber, Holly B. Crimmins, David W. Dippe, Corinna Amber Espino, Bahareh Farhid, Christian J. Garcia, Michael Guglielmo, Zachary Herron Hallowell, Brandon Glen Karns,

Steven M. Lackey, Lindsay Marie Lytle, Carmen M. McCarthy, Maurisa D. McElhinny, Yessenia Mendez, Rachel Hannah Miller-Hee, Brenda Cristal Montanez, Brittany Nicole Morgan, Monica K. Mosley, Maira S. Nava-Alvarez, Colin Ross O'Kane, Laura Lynn O'Rourke, Nicholas P. Paine, Andrea M. Perez, James Louis Pomerantz, Thomas Robert Porter, Julio Manuel Rico, Corey Brennan Savio, Kyle B. Shaw-Powell, Lauren A. Shepard, Harmen S. Sidhu, Rebecca Vazquez, Glenn M. Wallace, Brian Wedderburn, Melissa L. Willis, Glenn M. Wallace, Shahalam Baig, Chelane Beavers, Jessica Belluomini, Ashley Berryhill, Matthew Burns, Bianca Calderon, Jacob Donnan, Cary Escovedo, Cheryl Fonseca, Leta Frolli, Jonathan George, Samantha George, Michael Guglielmo, Alyssa Hara, Tran Hoang, Ellis Huber, Sara Iadavaia, Max Ivey, Mollie Kavrell, Taylor Krenwinkel, Claire Lueders, Brenda Montanez, Joshua Nervis, Cameron Orsi, James Pomerantz, Alexis Pomush, Thomas Porter, Cory Samuelson, Brianna Santo, Corey Savio, Garrett Scafani, Gina Sevieri, Kimberly Soeiro, Dane Steffy, Marie Sweet, Nicole Trupiano, Ronald Tureck, Morgan Womack

Syracuse University (Jeff Simmons, faculty) Erika Cowan

PROJECT CENSORED 2011–12 NATIONAL AND INTERNATIONAL JUDGES

JULIE ANDRZEJEWSKI. Professor of Social Responsibility, Saint Cloud State University. Publications: five editions of an anthology entitled, *Oppression and Social Justice: Critical Frameworks.*

ROBIN ANDERSEN. Associate Professor and Chair, Department of Communication and Media Studies, Fordham University. Director of Peace and Justice Studies. Publications: *Critical Studies in Media Commercialism.*

OLIVER BOYD-BARRETT. Director of School, Professor of Journalism and Telecommunications, Bowling Green State University. Publications: *The International New Agencies: the Globalization of News, Media in Global Context.*

KENN BURROWS. Faculty member for The Institute for Holistic Health Studies, San Francisco State University. Producer and Director of the annual conference, Future of Health Care.

ERNESTO CARMONA. Chilean journalist and writer. Director of the Chilean Council of Journalists. Executive Secretary of the Investigation Commission on attacks against journalists, Latin American Federation of Journalists (CIAP-FELAP).

LIANE CLORFENE-CASTEN. Cofounder and President of Chicago Media Watch. Award-winning journalist with credits in national periodicals including *E Magazine*, the *Nation, Mother Jones, Ms., Environmental Health Perspectives, In These Times,* and *Business Ethics.* Author of *Breast Cancer: Poisons, Profits, and Prevention.*

ELLIOT D. COHEN. Professor, Indian River State College. Contributor to *Truthout* and *Truthdig;* editor in chief of *International Journal of Applied Philosophy. Ethics;* editor for *Free Inquiry Magazine.* Blogger for *Psychology Today.* Publications include *Mass Surveillance and State Control: The Total Information Awareness Project.*

JOSÉ MANUEL DE PABLOS. Professor, University of La Laguna (Tenerife, Canary Islands, Spain). Founder of Revista Latina de Comunicación Social, RLCS, a scientific journal / Laboratory of Information Technologies and New Analysis of Communication.

GEOFF DAVIDIAN. Milwaukee investigative journalist. Editor of the Putman Pit, an online newspaper.

LENORE FOERSTEL. Women for Mutual Security. Facilitator of the Progressive International Media Exchange (PRIME).

ROBERT HACKETT. Professor, School of Communication, Simon Fraser University. Codirector of News Watch Canada since 1993. Most recent publications include *Democratizing Global Media: One World, Many Struggles* (coedited with Yuezhi Zhao, 2005) and *Remaking Media: The Struggle To Democratize Public Communication* (with William K. Carroll, 2006).

KEVIN HOWLEY. Associate Professor of Communication, DePauw University. Editor of Understand Community Media. Author of *Community Media: People, Places, and Communication Technologies.*

CARL JENSEN. Professor Emeritus, Communication Studies, Sonoma State University. Founder and former director of Project Censored. Author of *Censored: The News That Didn't Make the News and Why* (1990–1996) and *20 Years of Censored News* (1997).

NICHOLAS JOHNSON.* Professor, College of Law, University of Iowa. Former FCC Commissioner (1966–1973). Author of *How to Talk Back to Your Television Set*.

CHARLES L. KLOTZER. Editor and publisher emeritus, *St. Louis Journalism Review*.

NANCY KRANICH. Past president of the American Library Association (ALA). Senior Research Fellow, Free Expression Policy Project.

DEEPA KUMAR. Associate Professor of Media Studies and Middle East Studies, Rutgers University. Author of *Outside the Box: Corporate Media, Globalization and the UPS Strike* (2007) and *Islamophobia and the Politics of Empire* (2012).

MARTIN LEE. Investigative journalist, media critic, and author. Founder of Fairness and Accuracy in Reporting in New York and former editor of *Extra!* magazine. Author of *Acid Dreams: The Complete Social History of LSD: The CIA, the Sixties and Beyond*.

DENNIS LOO. Associate Professor of Sociology, California State University Polytechnic University, Pomona. Coeditor of *Impeach the President: The Case Against Bush and Cheney* (Seven Stories Press, 2006).

PETER LUDES. Professor of Mass Communication, Jacobs University Bremen. Founder in 1997 of German initiative on news enlightenment, publishing the most neglected German news (Project Censored Germany).

WILLIAM LUTZ. Professor of English, Rutgers University. Former editor of *The Quarterly Review of Doublespeak*. Author of *The New Doublespeak: Why No One Knows What Anyone's Saying Anymore* (1966).

SILVIA LAGO MARTINEZ. Professor of Sociology, Universidad de Buenos Aires. Codirector of the Gino Germani Research Institute Program for Research on Information Society.

CONCHA MATEOS. Faculty member at Universidad Rey Juan Carlos (Madrid). Journalist for radio, television, and political organizations in Spain and Latin America. Coordinator for Project Censored Research in Europe and Latin America.

MARK CRISPIN MILLER. Professor of Media Ecology, New York University. Author and activist.

BRIAN MURPHY. Associate Professor of Communications Studies, Niagara University, specializing in Media Programming and Management, Investigation and Reporting, Media History and Theory, and International Communication.

JACK L. NELSON.* Professor Emeritus, Graduate School of Education, Rutgers University. Author of sixteen books, including *Critical Issues in Education* (1996), and more than 150 articles.

PETER PHILLIPS Professor of Sociology, Sonoma State University. Director of Project Censored (1996–2009). President of Media Freedom Foundation. Editor/coeditor of fourteen editions of *Censored*. Coeditor of *Impeach the President: The Case Against Bush and Cheney* (Seven Stories Press, 2006).

ANA I. SEGOVIA. Associate Professor, Department of Journalism, Complutense University of Madrid (Spain).

NANCY SNOW. Professor of Communications, California State University–Fullerton. Adjunct Professor of Communications and Public Diplomacy, University of Southern California's Annenberg School for Communication and Journalism. Author or editor of seven books, including *Information War* and *Propaganda, Inc.*

SHEILA RABB WEIDENFELD.* President of DC Productions, Ltd. Former press secretary to Betty Ford.

ROB WILLIAMS. Faculty member at Champlain College in Burlington, Vermont. Former board copresident with the Action Coalition for Media Education (ACME).

*Indicates having been a Project Censored judge since our founding in 1976

Report from Media Freedom Foundation

by Dr. Peter Phillips, president of Media Freedom Foundation

Media Freedom Foundation (MFF) is a nonprofit 501(c)(3) corporation that sponsors Project Censored and all its various programs.

The Media Freedom Foundation and Project Censored's mission is to educate the public about the importance of a free press for democratic self-government. In that capacity, training students in critical thinking and media literacy is a hallmark of Project Censored that distinguishes it from other media "watchdog" organizations. We are currently affiliated with nearly two-dozen colleges and universities, across the country and around the world. Faculty and students from these affiliate campuses research and nominate Validated Independent News stories that we post year-round on our Media Freedom International website. These stories become the candidates for the Top 25 Censored Stories each year. Teaching students about the importance of independent journalism is a vital part of our efforts to create a media-literate, and ultimately better, society. The acknowledgments identify faculty and students at some of the campuses contributing directly to *Censored 2013: Dispatches from the Media Revolution*.

In addition to classroom education, we regularly bring Project Censored's message of media freedom to the public by speaking at independent bookstores, community halls, and conferences. To arrange for one of our speaking team to visit your community or campus, see projectcensored.org/speakers.

The MFF and Project Censored websites provide original investigative research and video content, and daily news feeds from two-dozen independent sources that we trust for quality news, in addition to the Validated Independent News stories. We also maintain a Spanish-language site (proyectocensurado.org) and the *Daily Censored* blog (dailycensored.com), which features over fifty regular contributors posting news stories and opinion. MFF board member Abby Martin produces top-quality video content for our websites.

Weekly, we broadcast the one-hour *The Project Censored Show* on KPFA (Pacifica Radio, 94.1 FM, Berkeley, California) every Friday at 8:00 a.m. PST and online at KPFA.org. Our affiliate stations include Progressive Radio Network, No Lies Radio, and Pacifica stations across the country. Please ask your local public/nonprofit radio station to air our weekly shows. See the link to "The Project Censored Radio Show" on projectcensored.org for the archive of past broadcasts, which make excellent listening for high school and college classes.

Over the past two years, MFF/Project Censored has actively promoted the fair share of the common heritage. With special funding from Dorothy Andersen in honor of her late husband Alfred Andersen's work, MFF has held public events, organized essay contests, produced radio shows, and maintained a website (fairsharecommonheritage.org)—all to advance understanding of the world's material and cultural wealth as the common heritage of all living beings. MFF board member Mary Lia has coordinated this effort, with board member Kenn Burrows of San Francisco State University working in support.

We do all this on less than $80,000 a year. In addition to revenue from book sales and royalties, our primary support is from individual donors. A new option for donors this year is to pledge five dollars or more per month, and in return receive a copy of our annual yearbook. Please consider making a monthly pledge at projectcensored.org. All donations are tax-deductible. If you are affiliated with a nonprofit foundation, or can make a larger gift in support of our activities, we would appreciate hearing from you.

How to Support Project Censored

NOMINATE A STORY

To nominate a Censored story, send us a copy of the article and include the name of the source publication, the date that the article appeared, and page number. For news stories published on the Internet, forward the URL to mickey@projectcensored.org; andy@projectcensored.org; and/or peter@projectcensored.org. The deadline for nominating *Censored* stories is April 1 of each year.

Criteria for Project Censored news story nominations:

1. A censored news story reports information that the public has a right and need to know, but to which the public has had limited access.
2. The news story is recent, having been first reported no later than one year ago. For *Censored 2013*, the Top 25 list includes stories reported between April 2011 and March 2012. Thus, stories submitted for *Censored 2014* should be no older than April 2012.
3. The story has clearly defined concepts and solid, verifiable documentation. The story's claims should be supported by evidence—the more controversial the claims, the stronger the evidence necessary.
4. The news story has been published, either electronically or in print, in a publicly circulated newspaper, journal, magazine, newsletter, or similar publication from either a domestic or foreign source.

MAKE A TAX–DEDUCTIBLE DONATION

Project Censored is supported by the Media Freedom Foundation, a 501(c)(3) nonprofit organization. We depend on tax-deductible donations and foundation grants to continue our work. To support our efforts on behalf of independent journalism and freedom of information, send checks to the address below or call (707) 874-2695.

Donations can also be made online at http://www.projectcensored.org.

Please consider helping us fight news censorship.

Media Freedom Foundation
P.O. Box 571
Cotati, CA 94931
e-mail: mickey@projectcensored.org and peter@projectcensored.org
Phone: (707) 874-2695

About the Editors

MICKEY HUFF is the director of Project Censored and on the board of directors for the Media Freedom Foundation. He is a professor of social science and history at Diablo Valley College in the San Francisco Bay Area, where he is co-chair of the history department. Huff is cohost with former Project Censored director Dr. Peter Phillips of *The Project Censored Show*. The program airs weekly as part of *The Morning Mix* on Pacifica's KPFA Free Speech Radio in Berkeley CA, and rebroadcasts on several stations including No Lies Radio and the Progressive Radio Network out of New York City. He is also on the steering committee of Banned Books Week, working with members of the American Library Association and the American Booksellers Foundation for Free Expression, among others, as Project Censored is a cosponsor of the events this year.

Huff has been a lecturer at numerous colleges in the Bay Area, including in sociology at Sonoma State University. Huff speaks regularly at venues in northern California and across the US on issues of censorship, propaganda, media literacy, and recent historiography. He has been interviewed by members and/or affiliates of NPR, PBS, Pacifica, the New York Times Co., ABC, Russia Today, Progressive Radio Network, Republic Broadcasting, and many other commercial and independent news media outlets. Huff has been invited as a speaker to political activist events, art openings, and cultural happenings, and popular variety programs like Live Wire Radio out of Portland, Oregon.

Huff's work has appeared in academic journals and books published by Praeger, Palgrave Macmillan, Emerald, among others, and on many online news and commentary sites from the far left to the libertarian right including Global Research, *Truthout*, BuzzFlash, *Dissident Voice*, Information Clearing House, LewRockwell.com, the Daily Bell, among others. He testified as an expert at the Kent State Truth Tribunal in New York City in 2010 and has been an outspoken advocate for addressing historical inaccuracies in the Kent State shootings of 1970 as well as many other events in the recent past involving state crimes against democracy. Before becoming the current director of

Project Censored, Huff was the associate director, during which time the Project was honored with a PEN Literary Censorship Award. He was also previously codirector of the alternative public opinion polling group Retropoll.

As an educator, Huff teaches courses in the social sciences and US history with an emphasis on the recent past. He teaches classes on "Money, Power, and Politics," as well as critical thinking and contemporary historiography. This past year, his critical thinking courses focused on "History in the Making: Contemporary Historiography, Mass Media, and the Rough Draft of History," with the research subtopic, "America, 9/11, and the War on Terror: Case Studies in Media Myth-Making and the Propaganda of Historical Construction."

Huff is a member of numerous academic, professional, and community-based organizations. He is also a musician and composer of over twenty-five years. He lives with his family in northern California.

DR. ANDY LEE ROTH is associate director of Project Censored and a sociologist. He serves on the Media Freedom Foundation board of directors. His research appears in the 2008–11 editions of *Censored* and a number of social science journals, including the *Harvard International Journal of Press/Politics; Social Studies of Science; Media, Culture & Society;* and *Sociological Theory*. He lives in northern California with his sweetheart, Liz, and two extraordinary cats, Sasha and Ed.

Index

Freedom of Information Act, 37, 143,
162, 174, 310, 311
Fukushima Daiichi, 36, 87, 91, 335

Gaddafi, Mu'ammer Muhammad al, 109
Gandhi, Mahatma, 314, 315, 329
Gas, 12, 14, 18, 86, 89, 91, 100, 169, 183,
237, 242, 260, 299, 301, 412
Wells, 14, 73, 90, 250, 323
shale gas, 12, 14, 91
Germany, 66, 191, 427
Gestapo, 317
GI Bill, 40, 73, 74
Giangrande, Naresh, 81
Gilded Age, 218
Glass, Ira, 146, 147, 168
Glattfelder, James B., 62, 69, 247, 257
Global Education Reform Movement
(GERM), 25, 273, 275, 281, 291
global economy, 17, 37, 62, 69, 185, 247,
248, 257
global financial crisis, 36
Global Research, 103, 109, 110, 119, 120,
140, 220, 258, 433
global warming 16, 19, 162, 215
globalization, 65, 235, 255, 256, 257, 258,
420, 425, 427
Goldman, Adam, 32
Goldman Sachs 69, 83, 244, 247, 248,
250
Google, 24, 57, 138, 142, 143, 144, 156,
257, 263, 281, 295, 310
Gmail 142
Google Maps 142
YouTube, 142, 144, 220, 257, 310, 405
Google+, 143
Gramsci, Antonio 78, 84
Grand Old Party (GOP – Republican
Party) 153, 275
grassroots movement 15, 273, 285, 286,
288, 291
Great Depression 80, 258
Great Pacific Garbage Patch 24, 138,
144, 145
Greece 89
Guantánamo 25, 43, 104, 116, 117, 118,
159, 173, 199, 334, 335, 336, 337, 338,
339, 340, 341, 342, 343, 344, 369, 412
(Guantánamo Naval Base?) 117

"GuantánamoSpeak" 337, 338, 339, 340,
342, 344
Guardian 12, 18, 19, 60, 163, 174, 185,
197, 211, 231, 270, 311, 369, 416, 417
Gulag Archipelago 73
Guggenheim, Davis 71

Hairston, Monique 62, 79
Hague, the 308, 311
Hakim, Yalda 115, 120
Hallin, Daniel C. 214, 220, 370
Hamas 39
Hanauer, Nick 61
Harvard Business Review 12
Harvard University 13, 221
Belfer Center for Science and Inter-
national Affairs 13
Geopolitics of Energy Project 13
Hawken, Paul 78, 84, 326, 331
Hawley, Chris 32
HB56 43
health care 64, 96, 154, 167, 180, 184,
199, 210, 211, 252, 264–5, 278, 328,
367, 425
Hersh, Seymour 108, 113
Hezbollah 108
Higdon, Nolan 5, 24, 134, 137, 150–1,
171, 420
HigherMind Mediaworks 83
Hispanic 49, 72, 131
historical myth 215–6, 227, 234
historical revisionism 119, 227
Hoch, David 148–9
Hollywood 106, 157, 163, 211
home equity 68
Hoover, J. Edgar 306
Hopkins, Rob 81
House of Representatives (US) 38, 42, 68,
134, 283–4, 354, 357, 367, 393, 395
HR 347 38, 46, 55, 149
Hudson, Aaron 5, 24, 137–8, 144, 150,
423
Huff, Mickey 3–6, 21, 24–5, 27, 29, 31,
137, 149, 151, 171, 174–5, 177, 213, 220,
256, 258, 292–3, 295, 297, 309, 329–
30, 369, 419, 421, 423, 433
Human Costs of War and Violence 5, 33,
37, 39, 42–3, 103, 329
Human Rights Watch 110, 124, 135, 140